CHAOS THEORY

Edited by **Kais A. Mohamedamen Al Naimee**

Chaos Theory
http://dx.doi.org/10.5772/intechopen.68716
Edited by Kais A. Mohamedamen Al Naimee

Contributors

Carsten Syvertsen, Alexander Shimkevich, Nizar Albassam, Amer Zayegh, Yan-Guang Chen, Valeri Kontorovich, Zinaida Lovtchikova, Fernando Ramos-Alarcon, Victor Ayala, Heriberto Román-Flores, Wieslaw Leonski, Joanna K. Kalaga, Radoslaw Szczesniak, Marcin W. Jarosik, Hussein B. Al-Husseini, Kais A. M. Al Naimee, Ban Al Bayati, Sudad Ahmed, Ahmad Ahmad, Simon Fong, Rui Tang, Nilanjan Dey, Nikolai A. Alexandrovich Magnitskii, Eugen Anitas, Azat Mukhiddinuly Slyamov, Valerio Annovazzi-Lodi, Giuseppe Aromataris, Mauro Benedetti

Published by InTech
Janeza Trdine 9, 51000 Rijeka, Croatia

Publishing Process Manager Edi Lipovic
Technical Editor SPi Global
Cover InTech Design team

First published March, 2018
Printed in Croatia
Legal deposit, Croatia: National and University Library in Zagreb

Additional hard copies can be obtained from orders@intechopen.com

Chaos Theory, Edited by Kais A. Mohamedamen Al Naimee
p. cm.
Print ISBN 978-953-51-3945-4
Online ISBN 978-953-51-3946-1

For EU product safety concerns:
IN TECH d.o.o., Prolaz Marije Krucifikse Kozulić 3, 51000 Rijeka, Croatia,
info@intechopen.com or visit our website at intechopen.com.

Meet the editor

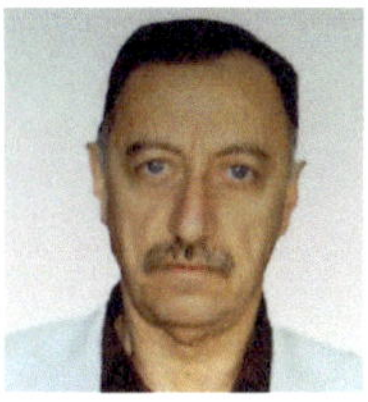

Kais A. Mohamedamen Al Naimee is a professor of quantum optics at the College of Science, University of Baghdad; he received his PhD degree from the University of Baghdad (1997) where he still teaches. He is an author and coauthor of more than 100 papers and a speaker in many conferences and meetings. His research interests are nonlinear dynamics in optics particularly in chaos, noise, chaotic communications, and control.
With a good background in nonlinear dynamics, chaos theory, and applications, the author of this leading book gives a systematic treatment of the basic principle of nonlinear dynamics in different fields.
The contributions from leading international scientists active in the field provide a comprehensive overview of our current level of background on chaos theory and applications in different sciences. In addition, they show overlap with the traditional field of control theory in scientific community.

Contents

Preface

Based on the positive feedback received from my group and members on our contributions in works of chaos and nonlinear dynamics, I have to focus more on concepts and applications.

During the last decades, nonlinear dynamics and complexity have evolved as one of the central issues in applied nonlinear sciences. Thousands of papers published in this field have been steadily growing since the first pioneering papers. I hope that this book will stimulate further development in this still thrilling area, which is centered on the overlap of the basic research and far-reaching applications.

This book covers several topics in nonlinear dynamics and chaos, particularly secure communications and synchronization in quantum dot devices. I sense that this book has been edited for all scientists. I invite readers to send suggestions and remarks.

I would like to thank all chapter authors who have contributed to this volume as well as the publishers for their excellent cooperation. Special thanks are due to Renata Sliva for her technical assistance.

Kais A. Mohamedamen Al Naimee
College of Science
University of Baghdad, Iraq

Chapter 1

Reinterpreting the Origin of Bifurcation and Chaos by Urbanization Dynamics

Yanguang Chen

Additional information is available at the end of the chapter

http://dx.doi.org/10.5772/intechopen.71035

Abstract

Chaos associated with bifurcation makes a new science, but the origin and essence of chaos are not yet clear. Based on the well-known logistic map, chaos used to be regarded as intrinsic randomicity of determinate dynamics systems. However, urbanization dynamics indicates new explanation about it. Using mathematical derivation, numerical computation, and empirical analysis, we can explore chaotic dynamics of urbanization. The key is the formula of urbanization level. The urbanization curve can be described with the logistic function, which can be transformed into one-dimensional map and thus produce bifurcation and chaos. On the other hand, the logistic model of urbanization curve can be derived from the rural–urban population interaction model, which can be discretized to a two-dimensional map. An interesting finding is that the two-dimensional rural–urban coupling map can create the same bifurcation and chaos patterns as those from the one-dimensional logistic map. This suggests that the urban bifurcation and chaos come from spatial interaction between rural and urban populations rather than pure intrinsic randomicity of determinate models. This discovery provides a new way of looking at origin and essence of bifurcation and chaos in physical and social sciences.

Keywords: period-doubling bifurcation, chaos, complexity, scaling, interaction, urbanization

1. Introduction

Chaos is one of the important subjects of science in the twentieth century. However, the problems of origin and essence of chaos were not really solved in last century, and they are passed on to the new century. The simplest model for understanding chaos is the well-known logistic map. The complicated behavior of the logistic growth brought to light by May [1] led to a profound insight into complex dynamics. Thus, chaos is always regarded as intrinsic randomicity of determinate dynamical systems. A pending question is how and why determinate systems have complicated behavior. Many studies are devoted to this problem, and many interesting conjectures are proposed. But the essence of bifurcation and chaos is still puzzling. In fact, a revealing research can be made from the viewpoint of urban dynamics. Urbanization provides a new way of understanding the origin and essence of chaos. Urban systems are complex systems, and the process of urbanization and urban evolution are nonlinear process associated with chaos and fractals [2–7]. Using mathematical derivation, numerical computation, and empirical analysis, we can reveal new knowledge about bifurcation and chaos based on the nonlinear dynamics of urban evolution.

New progress may be made by a simple formula of urbanization ratio. A basic and important measurement of urbanization is the proportion of urban population to the total population, which is termed "level of urbanization" in urban geography. The curve of urbanization level is termed "urbanization curve" and can be described with sigmoid functions such as logistic function, which can be discretized to a one-dimensional map. Using the formula of urbanization level, we can derive the logistic equation from the rural–urban population interaction model, which can be discretized to a two-dimensional map. Thus the one-dimensional logistic map can be associated with the two-dimensional rural–urban interaction map. As will be shown below, the two-dimensional rural–urban map can create the bifurcation and chaos that are identical in patterns to those produced by the one-dimensional logistic map. This suggests that the origin of bifurcation and chaos is two-population coupling and interaction rather than intrinsic randomicity of determinate models [8].

The study of chaos associated with bifurcation can help us understand natural and social systems deeply. This paper is a development based on a series of previous studies [8–14]. The rest of this work is organized as follows. In Section 2, the bifurcation and chaos from rural–urban population interaction dynamics are illustrated by using a two-dimensional map, and a phase portrait analysis of rural–urban interaction is performed. In Section 3, an empirical analysis is made by means of American census data to verify the rural–urban interaction model. The case study lays the foundation of experiments for the urbanization model. In Section 4, several related questions are discussed. First, the two-population interaction model is generalized to explain the ecological phenomena including logistic growth and oscillations of population. Second, the scaling laws of period-doubling cascade are compared with those of hierarchy of cities. Third, the nonlinear dynamics of urbanization curve is further generalized to the fractal dimension curve of urban growth. Fourth, the nonlinear replacement dynamics is outlined. Finally, the discussion is concluded with a brief summary.

2. Mathematical models

2.1. The two-population interaction model

A rural–urban population interaction model can lead to a new understanding of chaos. The theoretical model has been verified by the observational and statistical data from the real world [4]. Based on several assumptions, the spatial interaction model for rural–urban migration can be expressed as below [8]:

$$\begin{cases} \dfrac{\mathrm{d}r(t)}{\mathrm{d}t} = ar(t) - b\dfrac{r(t)u(t)}{r(t)+u(t)} \\ \dfrac{\mathrm{d}u(t)}{\mathrm{d}t} = c\dfrac{r(t)u(t)}{r(t)+u(t)} \end{cases}, \tag{1}$$

in which $r(t)$ and $u(t)$ denote rural and urban populations at given time t, respectively, and a, b, and c represent three parameters of population transition. Please note that $r(t) > 0$, $u(t) > 0$. This model indicates that the rural–urban population interaction results in urbanization. According to Eq. (1), the growth rate of rural population depends on rural population size and the two-population interaction, while that of urban population growth rate only depends on the rural–urban interaction. If the study region is a close system, then the parameters b and c are equal to one another, i.e., $b = c$, or else they are not. Eq. (1) has a firm basis of statistical analysis. The model can be verified with the population data set of American census since 1790.

It can be proved that the system of differential equations on rural–urban interaction is equivalent to the logistic equation of urbanization curve. For simplicity, Eq. (1) can be rewritten as follows:

$$\begin{cases} \dfrac{\mathrm{d}r(t)}{\mathrm{d}t} = r(t)[a - b^*u(t)] \\ \dfrac{\mathrm{d}u(t)}{\mathrm{d}t} = c^*r(t)u(t) \end{cases}, \tag{2}$$

in which.

$$b^*(t) = \frac{b}{r(t)+u(t)}, \quad c^*(t) = \frac{c}{r(t)+u(t)}. \tag{3}$$

In urban geography, the level of urbanization is formulated as

$$L(t) = \frac{u(t)}{P(t)} = \frac{u(t)}{r(t)+u(t)} = 1 - \frac{r(t)}{r(t)+u(t)}, \tag{4}$$

where $L(t)$ denotes urbanization level at time t (obviously $0 \le L(t) \le 1$). The level of urbanization is an important measurement in urban study. Just because of the definition of urbanization level, the one-dimension map of logistic growth can be associated with the two-dimension map of rural–urban interaction. In fact, taking the derivative of Eq. (4) yields

$$\frac{\mathrm{d}L(t)}{\mathrm{d}t} = \frac{\mathrm{d}u(t)/\mathrm{d}t}{r(t)+u(t)} - \frac{u(t)}{[r(t)+u(t)]^2}\left[\frac{\mathrm{d}r(t)}{\mathrm{d}t} + \frac{\mathrm{d}u(t)}{\mathrm{d}t}\right]. \tag{5}$$

Substituting Eq. (2) into Eq. (5) gives

$$\frac{\mathrm{d}L(t)}{\mathrm{d}t} = \frac{c^*r(t)u(t)}{r(t)+u(t)} - \frac{u(t)}{[r(t)+u(t)]^2}[ar(t) - (b^* - c^*)r(t)u(t)]. \tag{6}$$

For simplicity, we can postulate that the region is a close system, which has no population exchanged with outside. In this case, we have $b = c$ and $b^* = c^*$, and thus we have

$$\frac{\mathrm{d}L(t)}{\mathrm{d}t} = \frac{c^* r(t)u(t)}{r(t)+u(t)} - \frac{ar(t)u(t)}{[r(t)+u(t)]^2} = c^* r(t)L(t)\left[1 - \frac{a}{c^* u(t)}L(t)\right]. \tag{7}$$

As indicated above, $c^* = c/[r(t) + u(t)]$, Eq. (7) can be reduced to

$$\frac{\mathrm{d}L(t)}{\mathrm{d}t} = c\frac{r(t)}{r(t)+u(t)}L(t)\left[1 - \frac{a}{cu(t)/[r(t)+u(t)]}L(t)\right]. \tag{8}$$

Based on the level of urbanization defined by Eq. (4), the logistic equation is readily derived as below:

$$\frac{\mathrm{d}L(t)}{\mathrm{d}t} = c\left(1 - \frac{a}{c}\right)L(t)\left[1 - \frac{u(t)}{r(t)+u(t)}\right] = (c-a)L(t)[1-L(t)]. \tag{9}$$

In literature, Eq. (9) is always expressed as follows:

$$\frac{\mathrm{d}L(t)}{\mathrm{d}t} = kL(t)[1-L(t)], \tag{10}$$

in which k is just the original rate of growth in the logistic model ($k = b$-$a = c$-a). Discretizing Eq. (10) yields a one-dimension logistic mapping. By means of the one-dimension mapping, May [1] created the period-doubling bifurcation and chaotic patterns, which are familiar to many scientists of chaos and complexity.

2.2. Bifurcation and chaos based on two-dimensional map

Discretizing the rural–urban population interaction model yields a two-dimensional map, which can be employed to make numerical analysis. Since Eq. (10) can be derived from Eq. (1) through mathematical transformations, we expect that the complicated dynamical behaviors such as period-doubling oscillation and chaos can also be created by the two-dimension maps based on Eq. (1). Discretizing Eq. (1) yields a pair of iterative functions such as

$$\begin{cases} r(t+1) = (1+\alpha)r(t) - \beta\dfrac{r(t)u(t)}{r(t)+u(t)} \\ u(t+1) = u(t) + \gamma\dfrac{r(t)u(t)}{r(t)+u(t)} \end{cases}, \tag{11}$$

in which the parameters α, β, and γ for discrete form correspond to a, b, and c for continuous form in Eq. (1), respectively. The parameters in Eq. (11) will vary slightly after continuous-discrete transformation. If the region is a close system, we will have $\beta = \gamma$. In light of the US urbanization model as well as the American census in 1790, the parameter α can be set as

$\alpha = 0.025$, and the initial values can be set as $r(0) = 3.727559$ and $u(0) = 0.201655$. Thus the behavior of Eq. (11) will depend on the values of the parameters β and γ. The numerical computation can be fulfilled through a common computer with mathematical software. It is expected that the numerical behavior of the two-dimension maps on the base of Eq. (11) is really identical in form to the complicated performance of the one-dimension map based on the logistic function in ecology (**Figure 1**).

The numerical iterations can be fulfilled by mathematical software such as MATLAB or even by the well-known spreadsheet, Microsoft Excel. In order to correspond the two-dimension rural–urban maps to the one-dimension logistic map, a limiting condition is set as $\beta = \gamma$. The iterative values represent the rural and urban population in different times. Using Eq. (4),

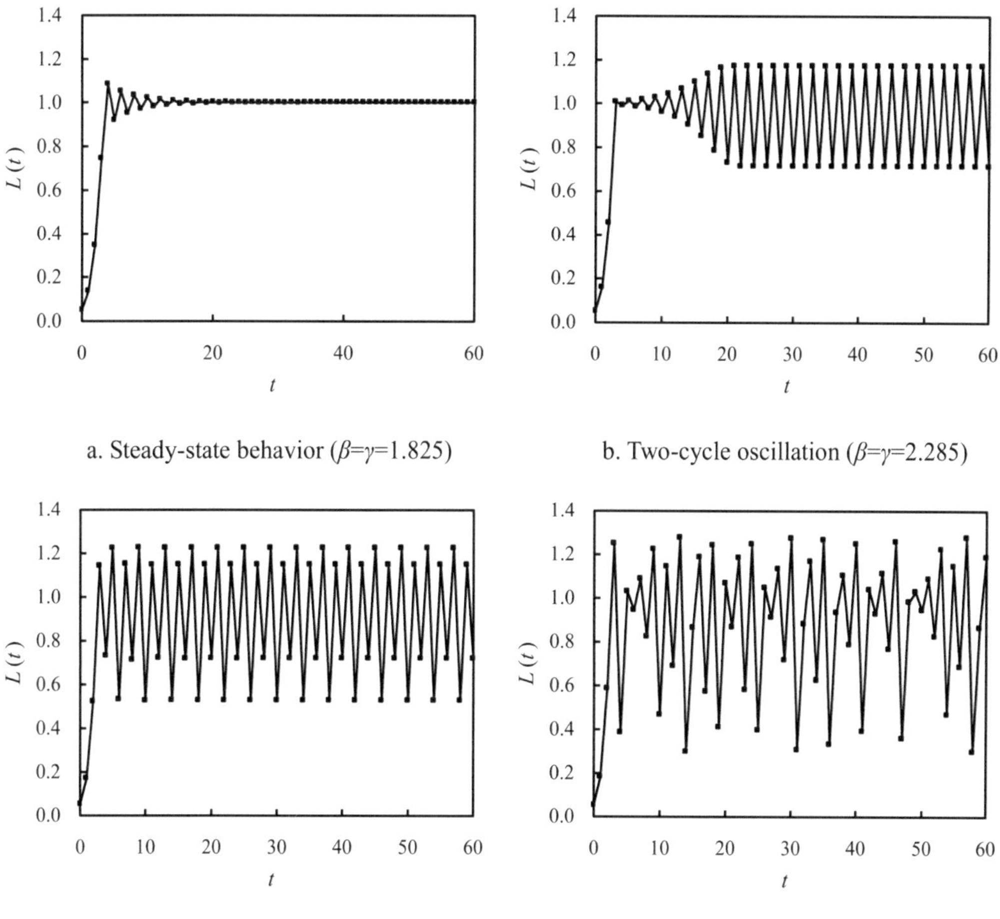

a. Steady-state behavior (β=γ=1.825)

b. Two-cycle oscillation (β=γ=2.285)

c. Four-cycle oscillation (β=γ=2.545)

d. Chaotic behavior (β=γ=2.785)

Figure 1. The urbanization curves resulting from the two-dimension mapping based on the rural–urban interaction model (Note: the parameter value of the model is $a = 0.025$, and initial values of the iteration are $r(0) = 3.727559$ and $u(0) = 0.201655$. The unit of the initial values is million. See Ref. [8]).

we can convert the rural and urban population into the level of urbanization and obtain the urbanization curve. The main results can be summarized as follows. (1) Logistic decay and growth. When $\beta = \gamma < 0.025$, the urbanization curve takes on a monotonous decreasing graph, and the final value is $L_{min} = 0$; when $0.025 < \beta = \gamma < 1.032$, it displays a monotonous increasing graph, and the final value is $L_{max} = 1$. The latter represents the common logistic curve that is familiar to geographers. (2) Steady-state behavior. When $1.033 < \beta = \gamma < 2.025$, the urbanization curve exhibits an alternating change and finally changes to unit (**Figure 1a**). (3) Period-doubling bifurcation. When $2.025 < \beta = \gamma < 2.475$, the urbanization curve shows an oscillation of period 2 (**Figure 1b**); when $2.475 < \beta = \gamma < 2.571$, the curve displays an oscillation of period 4 (**Figure 1c**); and with β and γ increasing, an oscillation of period 8 ($b = c > 2.571$) and period 16 ($b = c > 2.591$) and period 2^n (the natural number $n > 4$) emerges step by step. Finally, when $\beta = \gamma > 2.61$, the urbanization curve evolves into chaotic state, in which no 2^n cycle can be detected. The upper limit of the parameters β and γ is about 3.033. That is, if $\beta = \gamma \geq 3.033$, the numerical iteration will break down [8].

A comparison can be drawn between the results from the one-dimension logistic mapping and those from the two-dimension rural–urban interaction mappings. An interesting finding comes from the comparative analysis. In fact, Eq. (10) can be discretized as a one-dimension mapping such as $L(t + 1) = (1 + K)L(t)\text{-}KL(t)^2$, where the parameter K corresponds to the parameter k in Eq. (10). Then we have $K\sim\beta\text{-}\alpha$. Using this one-dimension logistic mapping, we can obtain various urbanization curves. The common characters of the bifurcation and chaos from the one-dimension mapping and the two-dimension mappings are the same with one another. What is more, the critical values of the model parameters for the period-doubling bifurcation and chaos are approximate to those of the logistic model. In particular, according to the process of numerical experiments, if the parameter α value becomes small enough, the critical value of the periodic oscillation to chaos based on the rural–urban interaction is close to the value based on the logistic growth. This discovery suggests a new way of looking at the origin and essence of bifurcation and chaos. It is the interaction rather than the intrinsic randomicity that causes the complicated behaviors of a simple dynamic system.

Another finding is the inherent relation between order and chaos. There are narrow ranges of periodic solutions in the chaotic "band." If $\beta = \gamma > 2.857$, the urbanization curve takes on an oscillation of period 3. Further, when $\beta = \gamma > 2.871$, an oscillation of period 5 or period 6 or period 7 appears. All in all, a non-2^n cycle can be found in the chaotic state. Finally, when $\beta = \gamma > 2.88$, the urbanization curve will get into a random state once again. However, the periodic oscillations in the chaotic belt are different from the cycles in the process of period-doubling bifurcation. The period in bifurcation is of 2^n cycle, while the oscillation in chaos is of non-2^n cycle. The varied non-2^n cycles such as the period 5 and the period 6 indicate chaos rather than bifurcation. The typical non-2^n cycle is period 3 [15]. In short, the limited chaos can be regarded as the sum of randomicity and the cycles of non-doubling period [8]. One the other hand, some slight disorder can be found during the 2^n cycles, which can be revealed by spectral analysis. This suggests that chaos and order cannot be absolutely separated, and they contain one another or are interwoven with each other.

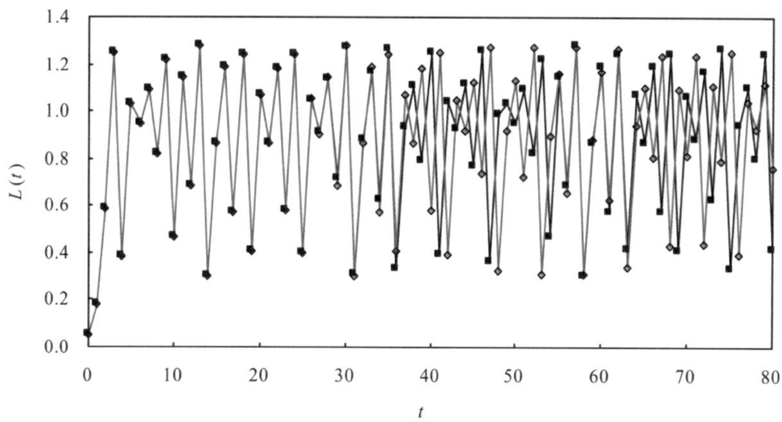

Figure 2. Two urbanization curves display the sensitive dependence on the initial conditions of rural–urban interaction (Note: the square solid dots represents the typical values of the old urbanization curve, in which the initial rural population is $r(0) = 3.727559$; the rhombic hollow dots denotes the typical values of the new urbanization curve, in which the initial rural population is $r(0) = 3.727558$).

One of properties of chaos is the sensitive dependence on the initial conditions. The property can be testified by the urbanization curve based on the rural–urban interaction mapping. Suppose that the parameter values are given as $\alpha = 0.025$ and $\beta = \gamma = 2.785$. Let us change the initial rural population from $r(0) = 3.727559$ to $r(0) = 3.727558$ (million) but keep the initial urban population $u(0) = 0.201655$ unchanged. In this case, the numerical iterative curve shows a new urbanization trace. At the beginning, the new urbanization curve and the old urban curve almost coincide with one another; but gradually, the new curve deviates from the old one (**Figure 2**). The difference between the two urbanization curves becomes bigger and bigger over time. It should be noted that only one person is reduced from the initial rural population. A minimal error results in wide divergence. This just reflects the sensitive dependence on the initial conditions of the rural–urban interaction.

Urban chaos is an interesting issue, but it seems to appear in the mathematical world instead of the physical world. The model parameter values such as $\alpha = 0.025$ are determined by the US census data. In terms of Eq. (4), the level of urbanization ranges from 0 to 1, i.e., $0 \le L(t) \le 1$. It will make no sense if $L(t) < 0$ or $L(t) > 1$. On the other hand, according to the observational data from the real world, the parameter β and γ values should come between 0.025 and 1.032. Otherwise, the urbanization level $L(t)$ will be less than 0 or greater than 1. Unfortunately, if the parameter β and γ values are confined into 0.025 and 1.032, no bifurcation and chaos will emerge in the rural–urban mapping process. If and only if $\beta = \gamma > 1.032$, we can create the period-doubling bifurcation and chaos, and thus the level of urbanization will exceed 1. This is absurd in both mathematics and urban geography. It is one of the necessary conditions of urban complicated behaviors. This suggests that the urban bifurcation and chaos emerge in the possible world, and we cannot find them in the real world for the time being.

2.3. Phase portraits of two-dimension map

Using the two-dimensional map, we can draw the phase portraits of the logistic process based on the one-dimensional map. The spatiotemporal feature of urbanization dynamics can be revealed with the phase portraits. Taking rural population $r(t)$ as x-axis and urban population $u(t)$ as y-axis, we can create a set of scatterplots for the period-doubling bifurcation and chaotic behavior of urbanization. The plots show the rural–urban relationships defined in the phase space based on Eq. (11). Consequently, the period-doubling process can be characterized by 2^n radials (n = 1, 2, 3, …), and the cross point of the rural and urban radials is just the origin of coordinate (**Figure 3a–c**). If the level of urbanization evolves from bifurcation into chaos, all the scattered points are randomly confined in the triangular region defined by the intersectant rural and urban radials (**Figure 3d**). For the chaotic state, the radials indicative of non-2^n cycle

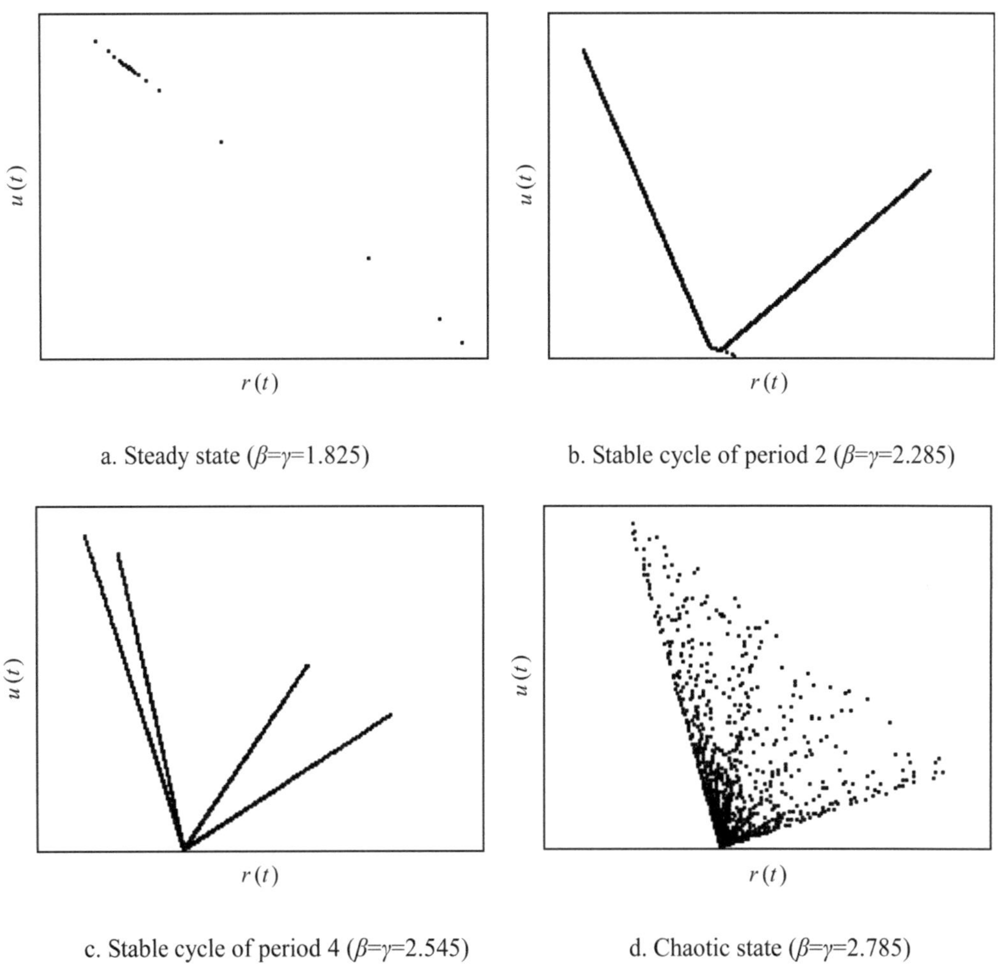

Figure 3. The phase portrait of the period-doubling bifurcation and chaos of rural–urban population interaction (Note: the times of iterations are 2500. The four subplots in **Figure 3** correspond to the four subplots in **Figure 1**, respectively. See [8]).

may appear in the phase portraits. The feature of phase portrait is independent of the times of iteration. The spatial distribution of scattered points never converge, and this suggests that there is no strange attractor in the phase space of urban chaos. This inference differs from the traditional understanding on the chaotic dynamics based on logistic growth.

Despite the fact that no chaotic attractor can be found, these scatter points follow certain mathematical rule. The distance from a data point ($r(t)$, $u(t)$) to the origin (0, 0), i.e., the cross point of radicals which act as boundaries of these points, can be formulated as

$$d = \left[r(t)^2 + u(t)^2\right]^{1/2}, \tag{12}$$

which quantifies the spatial relationships of the scattered points. Thus the distribution of the scattered points in the phase space meets a logarithmic relation as below:

$$N(d) = A\ln d - B, \tag{13}$$

in which $N(d)$ refers to the cumulative number of the scattered points within the distance d, and A and B are two parameters representing the slope and intercept, respectively. Now, let us examine mathematical structure of the phase space from the perspective of statistics. The distance is taken as $d = 4^n$, where n is a natural number, and the number of iterations is set as 5000. As an example, if the parameter value $\beta = \gamma = 2.785$ as given, the estimated values of the parameters in Eq. (13) are $A = 369.87$ and $B = 509.33$, respectively, the regression degree of freedom is $df = 8$, and the coefficient of determination is about $R^2 = 0.9999$ (**Figure 4**). Changing the parameter values in Eq. (11) results in different values of A and B, but the logarithmic relation will not change with it.

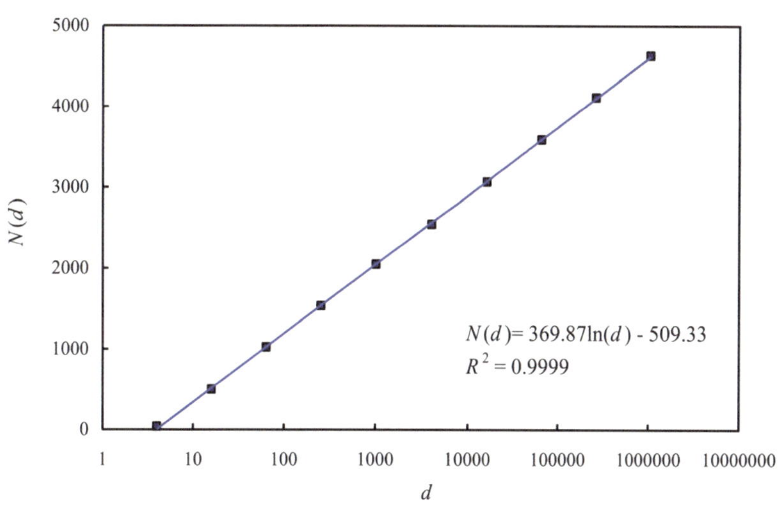

Figure 4. The logarithmic distribution of the scattered points in the phase space of urban chaos (Note: the plot corresponds to the fourth subplot in **Figure 3**, and the parameter values are $\beta = \gamma = 2.785$).

The derivative of the logarithmic function is a hyperbolic function. This implies that the density of the points in the phase portrait of chaotic state decays gradually from the origin, and the density change can be characterized by a hyperbolic curve. Despite the fact that both a city and a system of cities bear fractal structure [3–5, 16, 17], the phase portrait of the urban chaos does not display self-similar pattern. The reciprocal function of the logarithmic function is just an exponential function. This suggests that the basic property of the logarithmic distribution can be understood through the exponential distribution. Compared with the Gaussian distribution, the exponential distribution implies complexity [18], while compared with the exponential distribution, the power-law distribution implies complexity [19, 20]. This suggests that complexity seems to be a relative concept. Exponential distribution falls between the simplicity based on normal distribution and the complexity based on power-law distribution. According to the dual relation between the exponential function and the logarithmic function, the logarithmic distribution of the scattered points in the phase space of urban chaos indicates a process appearing between simplicity and complexity.

3. Empirical analysis

3.1. Data and method

The above-shown numerical iterations are based on the two-dimensional map from the rural–urban population interaction model. It is necessary to make empirical analysis using the dynamic equations of urbanization and observational data. There are two central variables in the study of spatial dynamics of city development: population and wealth [21]. According to the aim of this study, only the first variable, population, is chosen to test the models on urban chaos. In fact, population represents the first dynamics of urban evolution [22]. Generally speaking, the population measure falls roughly into four categories: rural population $r(t)$, urban population $u(t)$, total population $P(t)$, and the level of urbanization indicative of the ratio of urban population to the total population, $L(t)$. The measure relations are as follows—$P(t) = r(t) + u(t)$ and $L(t) = u(t)/P(t)$—which can be found in Eq. (4).

The American rural and urban data comes from the US ten-yearly population censuses. There are 23 times of census data from 1790 to 2010 available on the website of American population census. However, only the data from 1790 to 1960 are adopted in this work (**Table 1**). In fact, the definition of cities in America was changed in 1950, and the new definition came into use since 1970. The US urban population caliber after 1970 may be inconsistent with that before 1960. The observational data can be fitted to the discretization expressions of the United Nations model [23] and the generalized Lotka-Volterra model [24–26], respectively. The parameters of models are estimated by the multiple linear regression based on the ordinary least squares (OLS) method. The advantage of the OLS method is to keep the key parameters, slopes, come into a proper range. Two sets of tests can be made after parameter estimation: one is statistical tests and, the other, logical tests. The latter is usually neglected in literature. First, failing to pass the statistical tests indicates that it has some problems like incomplete or redundant variables, inaccurate parameter values, and so on. If so, the modeling process should be reconsidered. Second, failing to pass the logical

Time (year) [t]	Interval (years) [Δt]	Rural population [$r(t)$]	Urban population [$u(t)$]	$\frac{r(t)u(t)}{r(t)+u(t)}$	Rural rate of growth [$\Delta r(t)$]	Urban rate of growth [$\Delta u(t)$]
1790	10	3,727,559	201,655	191305.67	125855.30	12071.60
1800	10	4,986,112	322,371	302794.21	172831.00	20308.80
1810	10	6,714,422	525,459	487322.03	223077.60	16779.60
1820	9.8125	8,945,198	693,255	643391.97	284153.58	44228.48
1830	10	11,733,455	1,127,247	1028443.23	348484.30	71780.80
1840	10	15,218,298	1,845,055	1645549.78	439908.20	172944.10
1850	10	19,617,380	3,574,496	3023569.39	560942.30	264202.20
1860	10	25,226,803	6,216,518	4987478.10	342920.70	368584.30
1870	10	28,656,010	9,902,361	7359287.97	740346.40	422737.40
1880	10	36,059,474	14,129,735	10151800.00	481402.70	797653.00
1890	10	40,873,501	22,106,265	14346837.12	512383.50	810856.70
1900	9.7917	45,997,336	30,214,832	18235956.49	425582.20	1210127.90
1910	9.7917	50,164,495	42,064,001	22879255.97	163788.26	1244862.74
1920	10.25	51,768,255	54,253,282	26490822.68	221831.22	1454372.39
1930	10	54,042,025	69,160,599	30336844.29	341720.60	554473.90
1940	10	57,459,231	74,705,338	32478532.68	373837.30	1542285.60
1950	10	61,197,604	90,128,194	36448706.03	506197.80	2293539.90
1960	10	66,259,582	113,063,593	41776788.81		

Source: http://www.census.gov/population

Table 1. The US rural and urban population and the relevant processed data (1790–1960).

tests indicates some structural problem. In this instance, the model cannot explain the situation at present and cannot predict the tread of development in the future. Statistical tests bear conventional procedure. However, the logical tests must be made by means of mathematical reasoning and numerical analyses.

3.2. Parameter estimation and model selection

The above-stated model on rural–urban interaction is an equation system coming from empirical analysis. One of the general forms of urbanization dynamics models can be expressed as

$$\begin{cases} \frac{\mathrm{d}r(t)}{\mathrm{d}t} = ar(t) + \varphi u(t) - b\frac{r(t)u(t)}{r(t)+u(t)} \\ \frac{\mathrm{d}u(t)}{\mathrm{d}t} = \omega r(t) + \psi u(t) + c\frac{r(t)u(t)}{r(t)+u(t)} \end{cases}. \tag{14}$$

This is in fact the urbanization model of United Nations [23], in which a, b, c, ϕ, ψ, and ω are parameters. In order to make statistical analysis based on the observational data, we must discretize differential equations, Eq. (14), into difference expressions. As a result, the analytical process based on continuous dynamics is converted into the process based on discrete dynamics. Given that $\Delta x/\Delta t \sim dx/dt$, in which the time difference is $\Delta t = 10$. The independent variables include $r(t)$, $u(t)$, and $r(t)^*u(t)/[r(t) + u(t)]$, and the dependent variables are $\Delta r(t)/\Delta t$ and $\Delta u(t)/\Delta t$, respectively. The model can be fitted to the American census data of rural and urban population. A multivariate stepwise regression analysis based on the least squares calculation gives the following model:

$$\begin{cases} \dfrac{\Delta r(t)}{\Delta t} = 0.02584 r(t) - 0.03615 \dfrac{r(t)u(t)}{r(t) + u(t)} \\ \dfrac{\Delta u(t)}{\Delta t} = 0.05044 \dfrac{r(t)u(t)}{r(t) + u(t)} \end{cases} . \tag{15}$$

which corresponds to Eq. (1). Clearly, the model parameters $\varphi = \psi = \omega = 0$. Eq. (15) is a pair of difference equations. Given a significance level of $\alpha = 0.01$, the important statistics such as F value, T value, variance inflation factor (VIF) value, and Durbin-Watson (DW) value can pass the common tests. In theory, as indicated above, we have $b = c$. However, in the empirical modeling, the two parameters are not equal to one another. The main reasons are as below. First, America is not a truly closed system. It has mass foreign migration. Second, the natural growth of urban population relies heavily on the rural–urban interaction. The latter reason seems to be more important than the former one. All things considered, as a special case of the United Nations model, Eq. (15) can describe the rural and urban population migration and transition of America in the recent 200 years in a better way.

To examine the relationship between the one-dimensional map and the two-dimensional mapping of urbanization, we can investigate the US urbanization curve. According to Eq. (9), the level of urbanization should follow the logistic curve. It is easy to calculate the urbanization ratio using the data in **Table 1**. For convenience, we set time dummy t = year-1790. A least squares computation involving the percentage urban data gives the following results:

$$L(t) = \frac{1}{1 + 20.4157 e^{-0.0224t}} . \tag{16}$$

The goodness of fit is about $R^2 = 0.9839$. According to Eq. (16), the intrinsic growth rate is about $k = 0.02238$. On the other hand, according to Eq. (15), the intrinsic growth rate has two estimated values: the first is $k_1 = b\text{-}a \approx 0.03615\text{–}0.02584 = 0.01031$, and the second is $k_2 = d\text{-}a \approx 0.05044\text{–}0.02584 = 0.02460$. The number comes between 0.01031 and 0.02460. This suggests that the parameter value based on Eq. (15) is consistent with that based on Eq. (16). The subtle difference between different estimated results can be attributed to three reasons, that is, non-closed geographical region, imprecise observational data, and the computation error stemming from the conversion from continuous function to discrete equation.

As a reference, the American rural and urban data can be fitted to the predator–prey interaction model. The independent variables include $r(t)$, $u(t)$, and $r(t)^*u(t)$, while the dependent variables are $\Delta u(t)/\Delta t$ and $\Delta r(t)/\Delta t$, respectively. The multivariate stepwise regression based on the OLS method yields an unacceptable result [27]. If the statistical standard for modeling is lowered, then the US urbanization can be described by the Keyfitz-Rogers model [28, 29]. Unfortunately, this model bears two vital deficiencies and is not acceptable for urbanization analysis [27]. All in all, both the linear model proposed by Keyfitz and Rogers and the nonlinear model presented by Lotka and Volterra are inferior to the special case of the United Nations model, Eq. (1).

3.3. Numerical experiment

As a complement analysis, the US census data of urban, rural, and total population as well as the level of urbanization can be generated using the rural–urban interaction model. A comparison between the simulation value and observed data shows the effect of urban modeling. The numerical simulation results are based on Eq. (15) and are displayed in **Figures 5** and **6**, respectively. Clearly, the change of the urban and total population takes on of the sigmoid curves, while the rural population takes on a unimodal curve (**Figure 5**). What is more, the urbanization level is also an S-shaped curve, which can be described with the logistic function (**Figure 6**). The changing trends of four types of curves based on the numerical simulation are supported by the observation data from the real world [4, 27]. In the model, the capacity parameter of the urbanization level is evaluated as 100%, and this does not accord with reality of urban evolution. Nevertheless, the basic characters of the rural and urban development can be brought to light by Eq. (15). Anyway, there is no logical contradiction in the results from the numerical computation based on the rural–urban mapping.

So far, we have finished the building work of the model of urbanization based on the population observation in the real world. To sum up, the calculation results lend empirical support to the theoretical models and relations. First, the rural–urban population interaction model is testified, at least for a number of developed countries. The American model of rural–urban population interaction can be expressed by Eq. (1). This is the experimental foundation of theoretical analysis

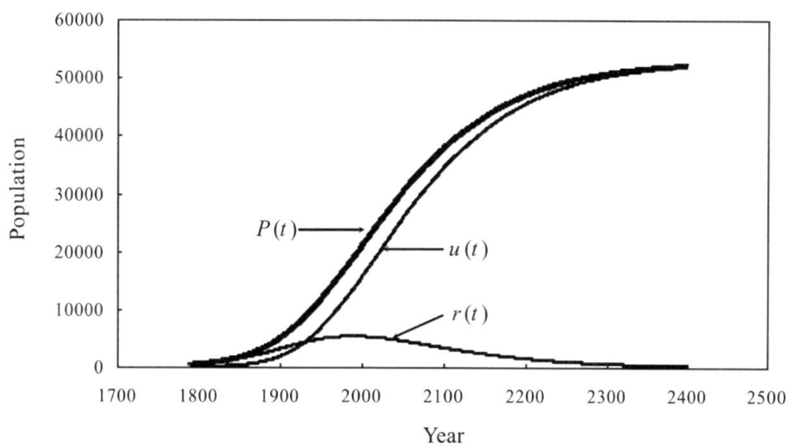

Figure 5. The predicted curves of the US rural, urban, and total population based on the two-dimension mapping of rural–urban interaction (Notes: the numerical iteration is fulfilled by Eq. (15), and the population unit is 10,000 persons. See [27]).

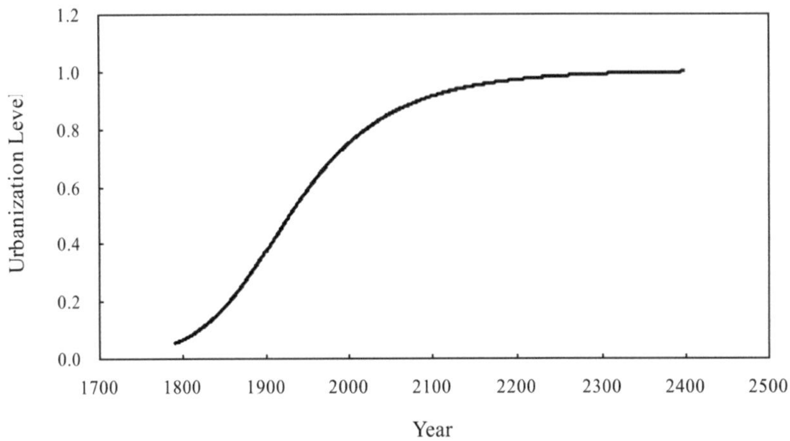

Figure 6. The numerical simulation curve of the US urbanization level (1790–2400) (Notes: the numerical simulation is based on Eq. (15), and the capacity parameter is 1. The curve is identical in shape to that of logistic growth indicated by Eq. (16). See [27]).

of discrete urbanization dynamics. Second, the relationship between the one-dimensional map of logistic growth and the two-dimensional map of rural–urban interaction is verified. By using the system of rural–urban interaction models, we can produce the logistic curve of urbanization. What is more, the curves of urban population, rural population, and total population are empirically acceptable. In the following section, I will discuss the related questions about bifurcation, chaos, complexity, and scaling law from the theoretical angle of view.

4. Questions and discussion

4.1. Generalization and supposition

According to the theoretical derivation, numerical experiments, and empirical analysis, an inference can be reached that chaos originates from nonlinear interaction between two coupling elements. The reasons are as below. First, a one-dimensional logistic map is actually based on a two-dimensional interaction map between two populations. Second, both the one-dimensional map and the two-dimensional map processes can create the same patterns of bifurcation and chaos. Further, the theoretical findings can be generalized to the other scientific fields. Where dynamical behaviors are concerned, urban systems bear analogy with ecosystems [21]. Both the logistic equation and the predator–prey interaction model coming from ecology and can be applied to urban studies [24]. The predator–prey system can be modeled by different mathematical expressions, which can produce period-doubling bifurcation and chaos [9, 30–32]. On the one hand, the bifurcation and chaos proceeding from the two-dimension mapping of urbanization dynamics remind us of the complicated behaviors shown by the one-dimension logistic mapping of insect population. On the other, the model of rural–urban interaction reminds us of the Lotka-Volterra model for the predator–prey interaction [25, 26]. Therefore, the conclusions drawn from urban studies may be generalized to ecological

Model	Dynamical equation	Urban system	Ecosystem
Allometric growth	$\begin{cases} dx(t)/dt = ax(t) \\ dy(t)/dt = by(t) \end{cases}$	Allometric scaling relations	Two-population competition
Two-population interaction	$\begin{cases} dx(t)/dt = ax(t) - bx(t)y(t) \\ dy(t)/dt = cx(t)y(t) - dy(t) \end{cases}$	The rural–urban interaction	The predator–prey interaction
Generalized two-population interaction	$\begin{cases} \frac{dx(t)}{dt} = ax(t) - b\frac{x(t)y(t)}{x(t)+y(t)} \\ \frac{dy(t)}{dt} = c\frac{x(t)y(t)}{x(t)+y(t)} - dy(t) \end{cases}$	The rural–urban interaction and logistic growth	Two-population competition and predator–prey interaction

Notes: In these equations, a, b, c, and d are parameters. The equations of allometric growth suggest simplicity, while the two-population interaction models indicate complexity.

Table 2. The typical dynamical equations for modeling urban and ecological systems.

field and vice versa (**Table 2**). A speculation is that the logistic growth in ecology can be interpreted by the two-population interaction, and the Lotka-Volterra model can be revised as below [8]:

$$\begin{cases} \frac{dx(t)}{dt} = ax(t) - b\frac{x(t)y(t)}{x(t)+y(t)} \\ \frac{dy(t)}{dt} = c\frac{x(t)y(t)}{x(t)+y(t)} - dy(t) \end{cases}, \tag{17}$$

in which $x(t)$ and $y(t)$ denote the numbers of prey and predators at time t, respectively. The symbols a, b, c, and d are all parameters. Eq. (17) represents a generalized predator–prey interaction model. Given $x(t) + y(t) = constant$, Eq. (17) will return to the original form of the Lotka-Volterra model. The dynamical behaviors of Eq. (17) are more plentiful than those of Eq. (1). In fact, Eq. (1) can be treated as a special case of Eq. (17). Suppose that the percentage of predator population is defined by

$$z(t) = \frac{y(t)}{x(t) + y(t)}. \tag{18}$$

Thus, we can derive a logistic equation from Eqs. (17) and (18) as follows:

$$\frac{dz(t)}{dt} = (c - a - d)z(t)[1 - z(t)]. \tag{19}$$

Discretizing Eq. (19) yields a one-dimension mapping of logistic growth as below:

$$z(t) = (k+1)z(t-1) - kz(t-1)^2, \tag{20}$$

where the parameter k~c-a-d. Both the one-dimension mapping based on Eq. (19) and the two-dimension mapping based on Eq. (17) can create the same complicated dynamics as those displayed in **Figure 1**. This implies that the two-population interaction leads to the logistic growth, periodic oscillations, and chaotic behavior in ecosystems.

A conjecture is that the logistic growth of population in ecology is just an approximate expression. It is the ratio of the predator population to the total population rather than the predator population itself that follows the law of logistic growth. Using the two-dimension mapping based on Eq. (17), we can carry out a numerical simulation experiment. The results show that if the percentage of predator population $z(t)$ takes on a logistic growth, the predator population $y(t)$ will grow according to an J-shaped curve in form (**Figure 7**). However, the latter is a quadratic or fractional logistic growth rather than the conventional logistic growth. What is more, the oscillations of population and the total population can mirror the period-doubling bifurcation and chaos of percentage population. All in all, the generalized predator–prey interaction can account for more ecological phenomena than the classical Lotka-Volterra model does [8]. Anyway, the studies on urban chaos can help us understand John Holland's question. After discussing the Lotka-Volterra model, Holland [33] said: "In the long run, extensions of such models should help us understand why predator-prey interaction exhibit strong oscillations, whereas the interactions that form a city are typically more stable."

4.2. Scaling in bifurcation diagrams

Chaos and fractals are often placed in the same category in literature, although there is no essential correlation between them. A fractal is a hierarchy with cascade structure, which can be testified by urban systems. In fact, a period-doubling bifurcation diagram contains self-similar hierarchy. So, the period-doubling bifurcation route to chaos of urbanization dynamics can be compared with the hierarchical structure of cities. The general character of varied bifurcation diagrams can be reflected by Feigenbaum's number, which is a universal constant found by Feigenbaum [34]. This constant can also be figured out through the rural–urban interaction mapping. Based on a bifurcation diagram, we can draw the tent map [35] (**Figure 8**).

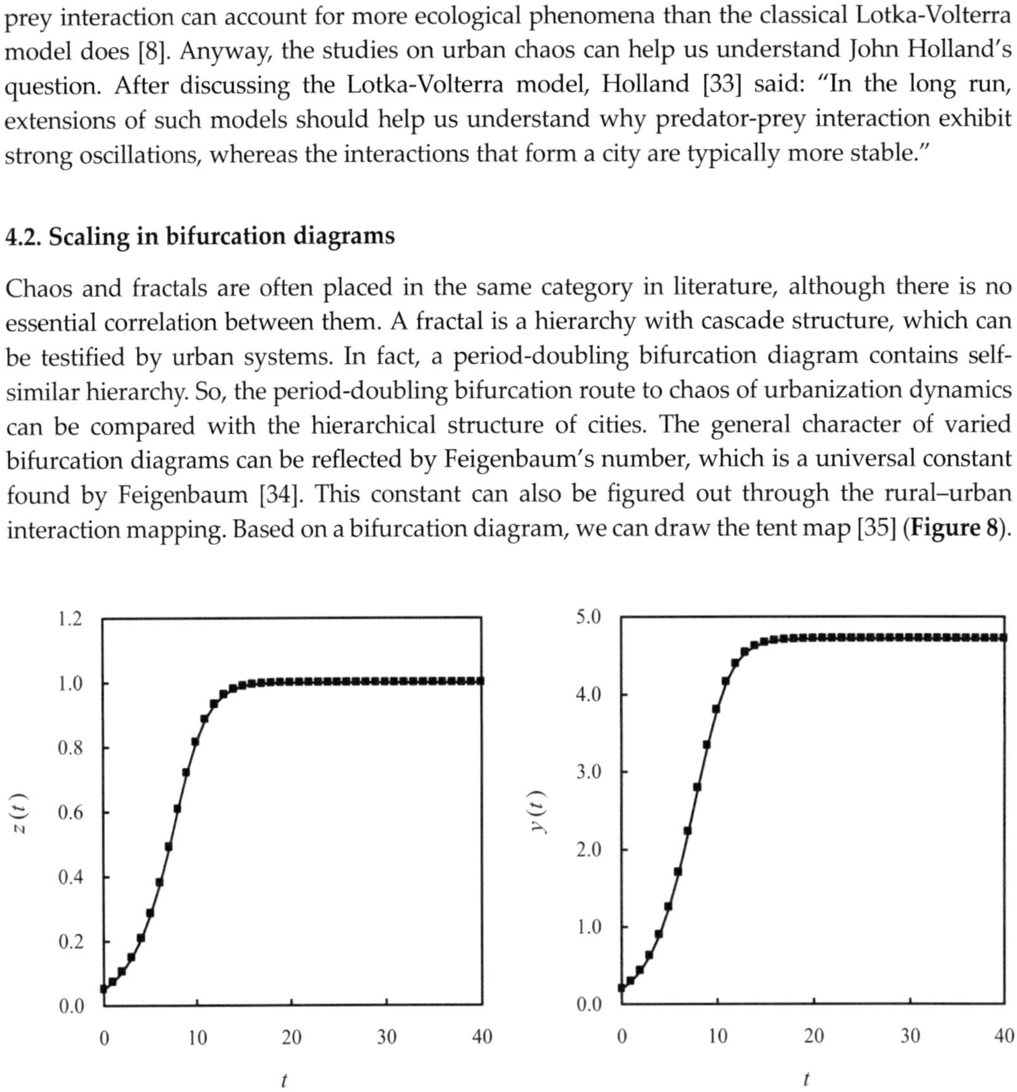

Figure 7. The logistic growth of the percentage of predator population and the quasi-logistic growth of the predator population (Note: if the percentage of predator population takes on the S-shaped logistic growth, then the predator population growth will take on an J-shaped curve. See [8]). (a) Percentage of predator population. (b) Predator population.

http://dx.doi.org/10.5772/intechopen.71035

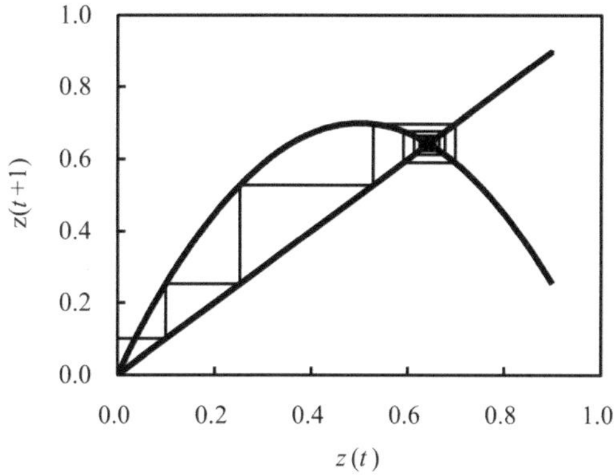

a. Steady-state behavior (β-α+1=2.80)

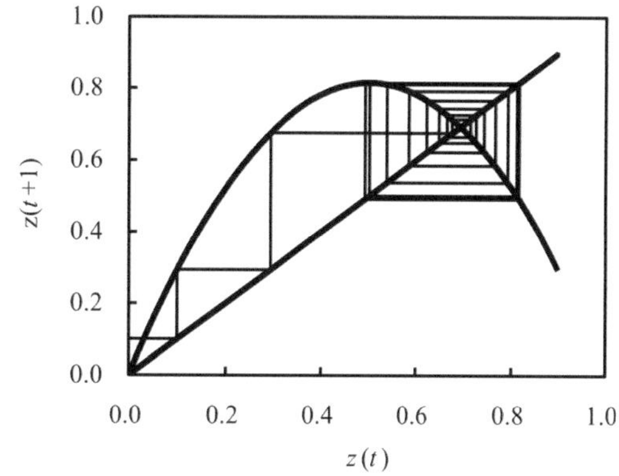

b. Two-cycle oscillation (β-α+1=3.26)

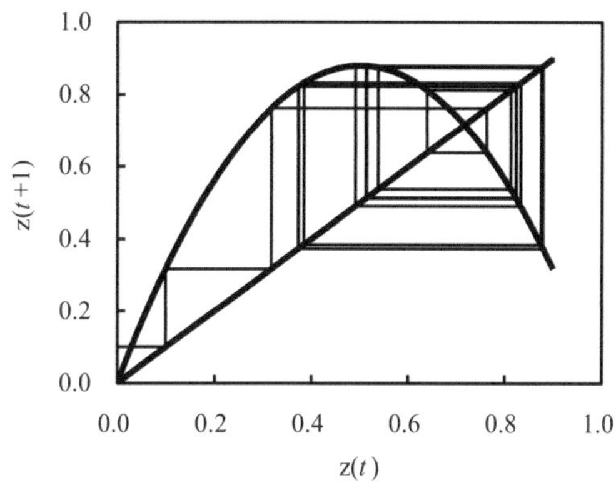

c. Four-cycle oscillation (β-α+1=3.52)

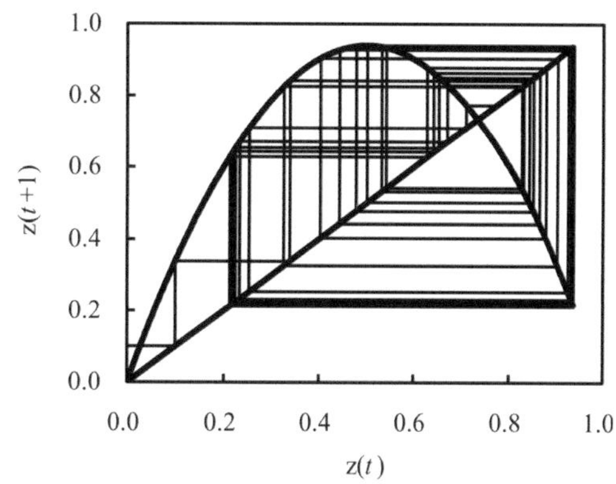

d. Chaotic behavior (β-α+1=3.76)

Figure 8. Tent map: From steady state to chaos (the initial value is $L_0 = 0.01$) (Note: the graph of tent map is also termed "spider diagram," which can be seen in literature such as ref. [35]. The diagrams are created by using the two-dimensional rural–urban interaction map based on Eq. (11). These subplots correspond to the subplots in **Figures 1** and **3**).

If we give up the hypothesis of regional closure, the parameter equation $\beta = \gamma$ in Eq. (11) will break. Then more complex and plentiful dynamics can be revealed by the rural–urban interaction mapping.

The period-doubling bifurcation process of urbanization and the cascade structure of systems of cities share the same hierarchical scaling. The bifurcation can be described with three exponential functions such as

$$N_m = N_1 r^{m-1}, \tag{21}$$

$$L_m = L_1 \delta^{1-m}, \tag{22}$$

$$W_m = W_1 a^{1-m}, \tag{23}$$

where m denotes the order of hierarchy of bifurcation, N_m refers to period number (or bifurcation number), L_m is the range for the stable periodicity, and W_m is the span between two bifurcation points of order m. As for the parameters, $N_1 = 1$, L_1 and W_1 are constants, $r = 2$, $\delta \approx 4.6692$, and $a \approx 2.5029$ [34, 36, 37]. In fact, Eq. (22) represents "the bifurcation-rate scaling law" and Eq. (23) "the fork-width scaling law" [38]. Accordingly, Eq. (21) represents "period-number scaling law." These what is called scaling laws are linear scaling laws, but they can be transformed into nonlinear scaling laws, i.e., power laws [4]. From Eqs. (22) and (23), it follows an allometric scaling relation between the periodical range (L_m) and the fork width (W_m), and the expression is

$$L_m = \mu W_m^b, \tag{24}$$

where the proportionality constant is $\mu = L_1 W_1^{-b}$ and b denotes a scaling exponent as below:

$$b = \frac{\ln \delta}{\ln a} \approx 1.6796. \tag{25}$$

The physical meaning of this number is not yet clear for the time being and remains to be brought to light in future studies.

The three exponential equations reflect the universal cascade structure of nature and society. An analogy can be drawn between the cascade structure of the bifurcation diagram and the hierarchical structure of urban systems (**Table 3**). The scaling laws behind the period-doubling bifurcation can be employed to describe the nonlinear process of urbanization, and the variants of the scaling laws can be adopted to characterize the cascade structure of a hierarchy of cities [10–12, 39]. Moreover, the allometric scaling relation, Eq. (24), bears an analogy with the fractal relation between urban area and population. The allometric growth law asserts that the rate of relative growth of an organ is a constant fraction of the rate of relative growth of the total organism [40–42]. In urban studies, the allometric scaling law can be utilized to describe the measure relation between the urban area (A_m) of a city and its population (P_m) in the urbanized area [4, 16, 42]. The similarity between urban scaling and bifurcation scaling lends further support to the inference that urban evolution falls between order and chaos [43].

Linear scaling law	**Period-doubling bifurcation**	**Hierarchy of cities**
The first law—number law	$N_m = N_1 r^{m-1}$	$N_m = N_1 r_n^{m-1}$
The second law—length/size law	$L_m = L_1 \delta^{1-m}$	$P_m = P_1 r_p^{1-m}$
The third law—width/area law	$W_m = W_1 a^{1-m}$	$A_m = A_1 r_a^{1-m}$

Notes: (1) The scaling laws of hierarchy of cities are illuminated by [4]. (2) The period-doubling bifurcation in this work comes from the two-dimension mapping based on the rural–urban interaction model, which differs from the one-dimension logistic mapping in form.

Table 3. A comparison between the linear scaling laws of period-doubling bifurcation and the exponential laws of hierarchy of cities.

4.3. Dynamics of fractal dimension evolution of urban growth

The nonlinear dynamics of urbanization corresponds to the complex dynamics of urban growth and morphology. Urban growth can be measured with the time series of fractal dimension of urban form. The common fractal dimension can be obtained by box-counting method. In theory, the box dimension of urban form ranges from 0 to 2. However, in practice, the box dimension always comes between 1 and 2. Boltzmann's equation can be employed to describe the fractal dimension growth of cities [13]. In fact, Boltzmann's equation was used to model urban population evolution by Benguigui et al. [44]. Urban population is associated with urban form and urbanization. The Boltzmann model of fractal dimension evolution is as follows:

$$D(t) = D_{\min} + \frac{D_{\max} - D_{\min}}{1 + \left[\frac{D_{\max} - D_{(0)}}{D_{(0)} - D_{\min}}\right] e^{-kt}} = D_{\min} + \frac{D_{\max} - D_{\min}}{1 + \exp\left(-\frac{t - t_0}{p}\right)}, \tag{26}$$

where $D(t)$ refers to the fractal dimension of urban form in time of t; $D_{(0)}$ to the fractal dimension in the initial time/year; $D_{\max} \leq 2$ to upper limit of fractal dimension, i.e., the capacity of fractal dimension; $D_{\min} \geq 0$ to the lower limit of fractal dimension; p is a scaling parameter associated with the initial growth rate k; and t_0 a temporal translational parameter indicative of a critical time, when the rate of fractal dimension growth indicating city growth reaches its peak. The scale and scaling parameters can be, respectively, defined by $p = 1/k$, $t_0 = \ln[(D_{\max}\text{-}D_{(0)})/(D_{(0)}\text{-}D_{\min})]^p$. For the normalized variable of fractal dimension, Eq. (26) can be reexpressed as a logistic function:

$$D^*(t) = \frac{D(t) - D_{\min}}{D_{\max} - D_{\min}} = \frac{1}{1 + \left(1/D^*_{(0)} - 1\right) e^{-kt}}, \tag{27}$$

where $D_{(0)}^* = (D_{(0)}\text{-}D_{\min})/(D_{\max}\text{-}D_{\min})$ denotes the normalized result of $D_{(0)}$, the original value of fractal dimension. Empirically, Eqs. (26) and (27) can be supported and thus validated by the dataset of London from Batty and Longley [16], the datasets of Tel Aviv from Benguigui et al. [45], and the dataset of Baltimore from Shen [46]. The derivative of Eq. (27) is just the logistic equation:

$$\frac{\mathrm{d}D^*(t)}{\mathrm{d}t} = kD^*(t)[1 - D^*(t)], \tag{28}$$

which is actually based on the normalized fractal dimension. Without loss of generality, let the time interval $\Delta t = 1$. Thus, discretizing Eq. (28) yields a one-dimensional map such as

$$D^*_{t+1} = (1 + k)D^*_t - kD^{*2}_t. \tag{29}$$

Defining $D_t^* = (1 + k)x_t/k$, we can transform Eq. (29) into the following form:

$$x_{t+1} = (1 + k)x_t(1 - x_t) = \mu x_t(1 - x_t), \tag{30}$$

where x_t is the substitute of D_t^* and $\mu = k + 1$ is a growth rate parameter. Eq. (30) is just the well-known logistic map [1]. If the fractal dimension of urban form can be fitted to Boltzmann's equation, it implies that urban evolution can be associated with spatial chaotic dynamics.

The process of urban growth is a dynamic process of urban space filling. An urban region falls into two parts: filled space and unfilled space. We can define a spatial filled-unfilled ratio (FUR) for urban growth [13], that is:

$$O = \frac{D^*}{1 - D^*} = \frac{U}{V}. \tag{31}$$

Thus we have

$$D^* = \frac{O}{O + 1} = \frac{U}{U + V} = \frac{U}{S}, \tag{32}$$

where U refers to the filled space area with various buildings (space-filling area), measured by the pixel number of built-up land on digital maps, and V to the unfilled space area without any construction or artificial structures (space-saving area). Thus the total space of urbanized region is $S = U + V$. Obviously, the higher the O value is, the higher the degree of urban spatial filling will be. The normalized fractal dimension can be termed level of space filling (SFL) of cities, implying the degree of spatial replacement.

Based on a digital map with given resolution, the filled space can be measured with the pixels indicating urban and rural built-up area such as structures, outbuildings, and service areas. In contrast, the unfilled space is the complement of the filled space of built-up area. On the digital map, the unfilled space is just the blank space of an urban figure. If a region is extensively developed and is already occupied by various urban infrastructures and superstructures, it is transformed, and the unfilled space is replaced by filled space. This spatial replacement dynamics can be described by a pair of differential equations:

$$\begin{cases} \frac{\mathrm{d}U(t)}{\mathrm{d}t} = \alpha U(t) + \beta \frac{U(t)V(t)}{U(t) + V(t)} \\ \frac{\mathrm{d}V(t)}{\mathrm{d}t} = \lambda V(t) - \beta \frac{U(t)V(t)}{U(t) + V(t)} \end{cases}, \tag{33}$$

where α, β, and λ are parameters. This implies that the growth rate of filled space, $\mathrm{d}U(t)/\mathrm{d}t$, is proportional to the size of filled space, $U(t)$, and the coupling between filled and unfilled space, but not directly related to unfilled space size; the growth rate of unfilled space, $\mathrm{d}V(t)/\mathrm{d}t$, is proportional to the size of unfilled space, $V(t)$, and the coupling between unfilled and filled space, but not directly related to filled space size. From Eq. (33), we can derive Eq. (28). Discretizing Eq. (33) yields a two-dimensional map of urban growth, which can be used to created periodic oscillation chaos similar to the patterns shown in **Figure 1** [13].

4.4. Replacement dynamics

The logistic growth model and the rural–urban interaction model can be employed to develop the theory of replacement dynamics. Dynamical replacement is one of the ubiquitous general empirical observations across the individual sciences, which cannot be understood in the set of references developed within the certain scientific domain. We can find the replacement processes associated with competition everywhere in nature and society. The theory of replacement dynamics should be developed in the interdisciplinary perspective. It deals with the replacement of one activity by another. One typical substitution is the replacement of old technology by new; another typical substitution is the replacement of rural population by urban population. Urbanization is a process of population replacement, that is, the urban population substitutes for the rural population [47, 48]. The components in a self-organized system, generally speaking, can be distributed into two classes, and the process of a system's evolution is a process of discarding one kind of component in favor of another kind of component. This process is termed "replacement" [13, 14]. For example, the population in a geographical region can be divided into urban population and rural population, and urbanization is a process of rural–urban replacement of population [48]; the technologies can be divided into new ones and old ones, and technical innovation is a process of new-old technology replacement [49, 50]. In fact, people can be divided into the rich and the poor, the geographical space can be divided into natural space and human space, and so on. Where there are self-organized systems, there is evolution, and where there is evolution, there is replacement. Replacement results from competition and results in evolution. Replacement analysis is a good approach to understanding complex systems and complexity.

The basic and simplest mathematical model of replacement is the logistic function, which can be employed to describe the processes of growth and conversion. Besides, other sigmoid functions such as the quadratic logistic function and Boltzmann's equation may be adopted to model the replacement dynamics. A number of mathematical methods such as allometric scaling can be applied to analyzing various types of replacement. In fact, the allometric scaling can be used to analyze the relationships between the one thing/group (e.g., urban population) and another thing/group (e.g., rural population). A replacement process is always associated with the nonlinear dynamics described by two-group interaction model. The discrete expression of the nonlinear differential equation of replacement is a one-dimensional map, which is equivalent to a two-dimensional map. The maps can generate various simple and complex behaviors including S-shaped growth, periodic oscillations, and chaos. If the rate of replacement is lower, the growth curve is a sigmoid curve. However, if the replacement rate is too high, periodic oscillations or even chaos will arise. This suggests, no matter what kind of replacement it is—virtuous substitution or vicious substitution—the rate of replacement should be befittingly controlled. Otherwise, catastrophic events may take place, and the system will likely fall apart. The studies on the replacement dynamics are revealing for us to understand the evolution in nature and society, and the relationship between the one-dimension map and the two-dimension map is revealing for our understanding of the replacement dynamics.

5. Conclusions

Researching the origin and essence of bifurcation and chaos in urbanization process offers a new way of looking at complicated dynamics of simple systems. The pattern of phase space cannot be revealed by the one-dimension mapping diagram based on ecological systems, but it can be displayed by the two-dimension mapping diagram based on the rural–urban population migration and transition. This suggests that urban evolution is a good window for examining bifurcation and chaos. Moreover, the similarity between urban dynamics and ecological dynamics will inspire us to explore the implicit substance of natural laws. By the study of urbanization dynamics, we can obtain three aspects of new knowledge about bifurcation and chaos. *First, it is interaction rather than the intrinsic randomicity of dynamic systems that leads to bifurcation and chaos.* Period-doubling bifurcation and chaos used to be regarded as inherent randomness of determinate systems due to the complicated behaviors of the one-dimension logistic mapping. The people with this viewpoint ignore the following fact: the logistic growth is always based on two-population interaction. However, because of the absence of effective measurement linking the logistic function and the two-population interaction model, the relationships between chaos and interaction cannot be revealed in ecological fields. *Second, the chaotic behaviors of the logistic model do not indicate a chaotic attractor, and the relationship between chaos and fractals is scaling.* A strange attractor with fractal structure in the phase space used to be treated as a typical sign of chaos. The phase portrait of the logistic growth cannot be demonstrated by the one-dimension mapping. The two-dimension mapping based on rural–urban interaction can be employed to illustrate the phase space of the logistic process. The result shows that the whole trajectory fails to converge into a limited area. No strange attractor or even no fractal structure can be found in the phase portrait of the two-population mapping. However, both fractal structure and the route from bifurcation to chaos can be characterized by hierarchical scaling law. *Third, the predator–prey interaction model can be developed to interpret the logistic growth and sigmoid curves.* By analogy, we can infer that the predator–prey interaction causes the complicated behaviors of the logistic process in ecological field. In fact, the classical Lotka-Volterra model can be restructured by referring to the expression of the rural–urban interaction model. Consequently, we can get a normalized predator–prey interaction model. Using the revised predator–prey model, we can derive the logistic function for population growth. Finally, where urban geography is concerned, the models of urbanization dynamics can be generalized to describe the spatial dynamics of urban morphology by means of fractal dimension growth. Moreover, both the models of urbanization and urban form evolution can be applied to developing the theory of spatial dynamics of replacement.

Acknowledgements

This research was sponsored by the National Natural Science Foundations of China (Grant No. 41590843 & 41671167). The support is gratefully acknowledged.

Author details

Yanguang Chen

Address all correspondence to: chenyg@pku.edu.cn

Department of Geography, College of Urban and Environmental Sciences, Peking University, Beijing, PR China

References

[1] May RM. Simple mathematical models with very complicated dynamics. Nature. 1976;**261**: 459-467

[2] Albeverio S, Andrey D, Giordano P, Vancheri A, editors. The Dynamics of Complex Urban Systems: An Interdisciplinary Approach. Heidelberg: Physica-Verlag; 2008

[3] Batty M. New ways of looking at cities. Nature. 1995;**377**:574

[4] Chen YG. Fractal Urban Systems: Scaling, Symmetry, and Spatial Complexity. Beijing: Scientific Press; 2008 [In Chinese]

[5] Dendrinos DS, El Naschie MS, editors. Nonlinear dynamics in urban and transportation analysis. Chaos, Soliton & Fractals (Special Issue). 1994;**4**:497-617

[6] Portugali J. Complexity, Cognition and the City. Heidelberg: Springer; 2011

[7] Wilson AG. Complex Spatial Systems: The Modelling Foundations of Urban and Regional Analysis. Pearson Education: Singapore; 2000

[8] Chen YG. Spatial interaction creates period-doubling bifurcation and chaos of urbanization. Chaos, Solitons & Fractals. 2009;**42**(3):1316-1325

[9] Chen YG. Urban chaos and perplexing dynamics of urbanization. Letters in Spatial and Resource Sciences. 2009;**2**(2):85-95

[10] Chen YG. Modeling fractal structure of city-size distributions using correlation functions. PLoS One. 2011;**6**(9):e24791

[11] Chen YG. Zipf's law, 1/*f* noise, and fractal hierarchy. Chaos, Solitons & Fractals. 2012; **45**(1):63-73

[12] Chen YG. The rank-size scaling law and entropy-maximizing principle. Physica A: Statistical Mechanics and its Applications. 2012;**91**(3):767-778

[13] Chen YG. Fractal dimension evolution and spatial replacement dynamics of urban growth. Chaos, Solitons & Fractals. 2012;**45**(2):115-124

[14] Chen YG. Urban chaos and replacement dynamics in nature and society. Physica A: Statistical Mechanics and its Applications. 2014;**413**:373-384

[15] Li TY, Yorke JA. Period three implies chaos. American Mathematical Monthly. 1975;**82**: 985-992

[16] Batty M, Longley PA. Fractal Cities: A Geometry of Form and Function. London: Academic Press; 1994

[17] Frankhauser P. La Fractalité Des Structures Urbaines (The Fractal Aspects of Urban Structures). Paris: Economica; 1994

[18] Goldenfeld N, Kadanoff LP. Simple lessons from complexity. Science. 1999;**284**(2):87-89

[19] Barabási A-L. Linked: The New Science of Network. Massachusetts: Persus Publishing; 2002

[20] Barabási A-L, Bonabeau E. Scale-free networks. Scientific American. 2003;**288**(5):50-59

[21] Dendrinos DS. The Dynamics of Cities: Ecological Determinism, Dualism and Chaos. London and New York: Routledge; 1992

[22] Arbesman S. The Half-Life of Facts: Why Everything We Know Has An Expiration Date. New York: Penguin Group; 2012

[23] United Nations. Patterns of Urban and Rural Population Growth. New York: U.N. Department of International Economic and Social Affairs, Population Division; 1980

[24] Dendrinos DS, Mullally H. Urban Evolution: Studies in the Mathematical Ecology of Cities. New York: Oxford University Press; 1985

[25] Lotka AJ. Elements of Mathematical Biology. New York: Dover Publications; 1956

[26] Volterra V. Variations and fluctuations of the number of individuals in animal species living together. In: Chapman RN, editor. Animal Ecology. New York: McGraw-Hill; 1931. pp. 409-448

[27] Chen YG, Xu F. Modeling complex spatial dynamics of two-population interaction in urbanization process. Journal of Geography and Geology. 2010;**2**(1):1-17

[28] Keyfitz N. Do cities grow by natural increase or migration? Geographical Analysis. 1980;**12**:142-156

[29] Rogers A. Matrix Analysis of Interregional Population Growth and Distribution. Berkeley, CA: University of California Press; 1968

[30] Jing ZJ, Yang JP. Bifurcation and chaos in discrete-time predator–prey system. Chaos, Solitons & Fractals. 2006;**27**(1):259-277

[31] Krise S, Choudhury SR. Bifurcations and chaos in a predator–prey model with delay and a laser-diode system with self-sustained pulsations. Chaos, Solitons & Fractals. 2003;**16**(1): 59-77

[32] Wang FY, Zeng GZ. Chaos in a Lotka–Volterra predator–prey system with periodically impulsive ratio-harvesting the prey and time delays. Chaos, Solitons & Fractals. 2007;**32**(4): 1499-1512

[33] Holland J. Hidden Order: How Adaptation Builds Complexity. Reading, MA: Addison-Wesley; 1995. p. 18

[34] Feigenbaum MJ. Quantitative universality for a class of nonlinear transformations. Journal of Statistical Physics. 1978;**19**(1):25-52

[35] Messel H, editor. The Study of Population. New York: Pergamon Press; 1985

[36] Feigenbaum MJ. The universal metric properties of nonlinear transformations. Journal of Statistical Physics. 1979;**21**(6):669-706

[37] Feigenbaum MJ. Universal behavior in nonlinear systems. Los Alamos. Science. 1980;**1**:4-27

[38] Williams GP. Chaos Theory Tamed. Washington, DC: Joseph Henry Press; 1997

[39] Jiang B, Yao X, editors. Geospatial Analysis and Modeling of Urban Structure and Dynamics. Berlin: Springer; 2010

[40] Beckmann MJ. City hierarchies and distribution of city sizes. Economic Development and Cultural Change. 1958;**6**:243-248

[41] Bertalanffy L. General System Theory: Foundations, Development, and Applications. New York: George Breziller; 1968

[42] Lee Y. An allometric analysis of the US urban system: 1960-80. Environment and Planning A. 1989;**21**:463-476

[43] White R, Engelen G. Urban systems dynamics and cellular automata: Fractal structures between order and chaos. Chaos, Solitons & Fractals. 1994;**4**(4):563-583

[44] Benguigui L, Czamanski D, Marinov M. City growth as a leap-frogging process: An application to the Tel-Aviv metropolis. Urban Studies. 2001;**38**(10):1819-1839

[45] Benguigui L, Czamanski D, Marinov M, Portugali J. When and where is a city fractal? Environment and Planning B: Planning and Design. 2000;**27**(4):507-519

[46] Shen G. Fractal dimension and fractal growth of urbanized areas. International Journal of Geographical Information Science. 2002;**16**(5):419-437

[47] Karmeshu. Demographic models of urbanization. Environment and Planning B: Planning and Design. 1988;**15**(1):47-54

[48] Rao DN, Karmeshu JVP. Dynamics of urbanization: The empirical validation of the replacement hypothesis. Environment and Planning B: Planning and Design. 1989;**16**(3): 289-295

[49] Fisher JC, Pry RH. A simple substitution model for technological change. Technological Forecasting and Social Change. 1971;**3**:75-88

[50] Hermann R, Montroll EW. A manner of characterizing the development of countries. Proceedings of the National Academy of Sciences. 1972;**69**(10):3019-3024

Chapter 2

Chaos Theory and Butterfly Effects in Times of Corruption and a Bank Crash in 1886: The Case of Arendal (Norway) Illustrated through a Regional-Globalized Model

Carsten Martin Syvertsen

Additional information is available at the end of the chapter

http://dx.doi.org/10.5772/intechopen.72657

Abstract

The chapter focuses at corruption practices in the bank crash in the town of Arendal in Southern Norway in 1886 using insights from chaos theory and butterfly effects as theoretical frameworks. Using secondary sources from reports and documents, we illustrate that the bank crash can be explained by corrupt practices of the business and political elite involving manipulation of accounting figures, financial guarantees given in closed and secret circles, and banks giving credit without sufficient security. These activities led the town into a large bank crash in the fall of 1886 having negative effects on business performance, large unemployment, and falling living standards for decades illustrated through a regional-global model discussed in the chapter. The findings can be of interest when studying other bank crashes such as the global bank crisis setting in fall 2008 having negative consequences for leading OECD countries up to present times.

Keywords: Chaos theory, butterfly effects, corruption, shipping, bank crash, economic history

1. Problem statement

The problem statement is defined as how the bank crash in Arendal (Southern Norway) in 1886 can be explained by corrupt practices from the business and political elite in the town.

2. Plan for the chapter

We ask if the bank crash in Arendal (Norway) in 1886 can be explained by corrupt practices from the business and political elite in the town. For this purpose, we use a regional-global organizational model as illustration. Chaos theory is used to illustrate corrupt practices using the theory in an untraditional way focusing on bounded rationality as a part of humanistic research from organizational thinking. Thereafter, general principles for the research project are introduced focusing on chaos theory and how reports and documents are used as secondary sources in the data collection process. Findings confirm that corruption took place in the bank crash in 1986 initiated and implemented by the business and political elite in the town. The problem definition is confirmed leading us to believe that the study might be used as a candidate to explain other bank crashes such as the global bank crises setting in fall 2008 having negative effects up to this day with no clean-cut suggestions for how the bank crisis can be solved.

3. Introduction: the Norwegian shipping industry, a regional-global model, and the use of chaos theory

3.1. Norwegian shipping expansion in the 1800s

The historical background. Norwegian shipping has a long and proud history in international trade. From the Viking times, it has transported goods from the long coast to Greenland and the Southern Europe stimulating trade and economic growth.

Holland became a large economy in the 1500 and 1600 centuries. Norwegian timber was used to build Amsterdam and Rotterdam as large cities. Trade leads to a large immigration from Norway to Holland, and the opposite [55]. United Kingdom was also a leading player in international trade meaning that new trading routes for Norwegian ships were established and developed.

The First Industrial Revolution, which spanned from the mid-1700s to the mid-1800s, was largely driven by the drivers of international trade in few commodities (particularly cotton). Most businesses tended to remain small and to employ as little fixed capital as possible. The chaotic markets of this area led economists such as Smith [48] to describe market forces as an "invisible hand" that remained largely beyond the control of individual firms, leading to less interest for strategic thinking.

The Second Industrial Revolution, which began in the last half of the nineteenth century in the United States and rapidly expanded to Europe, saw the emergence of strategy as a way to shape market forces and affect the competitive environments. In the United States, the construction of the main railways after 1850 made it possible to build mass markets for the first time [4]. In some capital industries, such as shipping and banking which is the empirical setting of this research, Smith's "invisible hand" cam was supplemented by what Chandler [5] termed the "visible hand" of professional managers.

Norwegian shipping from 1814 until 1849. Norway got her own constitution, the 17th of May 1814. After the poor country was significantly hurt by the Napoleon War (1807–1814), Norway gradually managed to catch up in the capitalist race far behind super powers like United Kingdom and United States basing their economies on decentralized organizational solutions from the First Industrial Revolution up to modern times ([4, 5, 52, 58]; 105) formalizing the use of explicit and tacit knowledge putting economic growth in the center of attention. The fundaments were laid for an expansion in the shipping industry with Arendal, one of the leading Norwegian towns.

Norwegian shipping expansion from 1850 until 1886 with a focus on Arendal. The Norwegian shipping industry expanded rapidly from 1850 until 1874. There was a great demand for products such as timber from Arendal when the United Kingdom was an engineer of economic growth in Europe, leading to possibilities for business people to take advantage of both economics of scale and economics of scope [4, 5].

Arendal took advantage of the new business environment and expanded the fleet rapidly. From 1850 until 1870, Arendal's fleet increased by 260% while it barely doubled from 1810 until 1849 [56]. Arendal was the largest shipping town in Norway.

In 1875, Arendal was the richest town in Norway mainly due to an expanding shipping industry ([22], p. 156).

United Kingdom decided to drop the Navigation laws in 1849 as a result of more trade stimulating trade in many parts of the world. Lack of protective steps from United Kingdom meant that it opened up markets also for small countries like Norway. The change in attitude from United Kingdom meant that Norway and Sweden were regarded as one country being involved in a union until 1905 when Norway got her independence. This made trade much easier stimulating shipping between Norway and the United Kingdom [56].

In 1850, Norway had a fleet of 284,000 death weight tons and 1156 ships mainly consisting of sailing ships. The number of crews in the shipping industry this year consisted of 19,000 persons. Twenty-eight years later (1878), the number of death weight tons was 1.5 millions. The number of crew working in the shipping industry was about 62,000 persons. For ships, this meant a yearly growth rate of 5.7%, for the crew an annual growth rate of 4.5% ([22], p. 136).

In the time period 1850 until 1880, Norway went from number eight in the world of shipping to number three in the world, with USA and United Kingdom in the front, a remarkable achievement given the small size of the country ([22], p. 136).

Economic and political turbulence often have positive effects on shipping markets. The Crimean War (1853–1856), the American Civil War (1861–1865), and the Prussian War ("The

War of 1870") made it possible for the shipping industry to achieve handsome economic returns, a fact shipping people learn early in their careers often told by the elderly generation as an illustration as to how tacit knowledge is transferred [43].

3.2. Toward a regional-global organizational model in shipping with Arendal as the empirical setting

Arendal had a strong global orientation of her shipping activities paying attention to changing business regimes, political changes, and social unrest. The shipping industry is dynamic where profits are dependent upon economic, political and social changes (i.e., Blandley, 2000).

Flexibility may be the only option in a changing business landscape [46]. In order to adjust to changing market situations, it is necessary to disregard and even to overturn existing knowledge. Creating new knowledge requires theory building and conceptualization, experimentation and testing, involving successes as well as mistakes and dead ends [29], statement that many shipping executives might agree with.

Trade from Arendal was dependent upon a regional approach from Southern Norway. We build our reasoning based on research conducted by Drucker [10], Handy [18], Bartlett and Ghoshal (1995), and Syvertsen [50, 51] relating regionalization to globalization.

A study of a regional – global model can have a certain degree of validity when studying Arendal in the years from 1850 until 1885. Globalization opens up trading opportunities and the same time as regionalization can support personal and business identity and stimulate trade. It can be wise to have a mental home in global business.

Studies of regionalization have become a popular research approach in the last decades consisting of specialized production, close cooperation, personal contact, and a strong culture, well-defined geographical areas as elements ([39]; Cappchi, 1990).

In the world of regionalization, the value to craftwork becomes an asset in itself as it helps business firms offer tailor-made solutions to carefully targeted market segments (Boynton, 2000). The time of mass production and mass distribution is over, putting regional identity in the center for ship building, ownership over ships, and the operation of the ships, as illustrated in this study using a historical study of the town Arendal in Southern Norway as the empirical setting. In many ways, the idea of market novelty is consistent with the classis market position of differentiation, wherein a firm tries to garner a premium price with a product or a service that customers regard as unique and customized [40].

Business practices often have their own dynamics where contributions from the academic world can give limited insights. Management can thus in many situations be more regarded as an art than a science, by Mintszberg [36] called crafting:

> *"Craft evolves traditional skill, dedication, perfection through mastery of detail.*
>
> *What springs to mind is not so much thinking and reason as involvement, a feeling of.*
>
> *intimacy and harmony with the materials at hand, developed through long experience and commitment. Formulation and implementation merge into a fluid process of learning though which creative strategies evolve."*

3.3. Chaos theory used in the shipping industry

Why we use chaos theory in this study? Due to the dynamic character of the shipping industry, well-established theories such as forecasting and behavior patterns of clients seem to change rapidly. Economic turbulence coupled with accelerating globalization, continuous improvements in technologies, and deregulation of markets have a profound impact on business firm's competition. As a consequence, firms have to organize their operations in new ways and use new mental models when analyzing a changing business environment.

Chaos theory is an approach with a relatively long history with most contributions from natural science, less with a focus on economics and business administration. Still, it can be regarded as a flexible theory chosen as the theory to use in this research project.

What is meant by chaos theory? Chaos theory is a study of complex systems, nonlinear dynamic systems, dislodged from its steady-state condition by trigging events, where outcomes can lead to both harmony and increased tensions [20].Chaos describes a situation where the system is dislodged from its steady-state condition by trigging events [33]. It involves regrouping of elements of a system, for which a new order eventually emerges arising spontaneously from the internal structures [16].

It is possible that economic models can be improved through the application of chaos theory by studying and applying which factors can influence processes leading to economic growth or decline. It has shown to be a difficult task. The results in the field give mixed results in part due to confusion between specific tests for chaos and a more general test for nonlinear relationships [3].

Chaos theory can in our point of view, in contrast to much as the writing on chaos theory, be judged from a humanistic perspective in the way that the concept of bounded rationality [47] is central. This logic breaks with neoclassical economic thinking assuming that actors are rational which often is hard to believe analyzing our daily lives and taking a critical look at strategic decisions such as job changes and buying a new home?

We believe that actors are unable to take decisions in a completely rational manner due to both mental limitations and information-processing constraints [12]. Decisions from the practical world of business are often so complex to comprehend and therefore it is difficult to judge the different alternatives when a decision has to be made. Relatively simple and heuristic decision rules, rules of thumbs and easy procedures and routines are used in order to respond rapidly to a changing shipping market where it can look like that the only constants are uncertainty and short-term competitive advantages (Spencer, 1996).

Why butterfly effects are important in chaos theory? The field of chaos theory was pioneered by Lorentz [33] who studied the dynamics of turbulent flows. It is when a system is in a state of chaos that it is most vulnerable to butterfly effects, which states that small causes can have large effects [33].

This metaphor explains that a butterfly in Amazon can, certainly theoretically, cause a swelling ripple that, in turn, can lead to a gigantic dust storm in Texas. Lorentz [33] discovered the effect when he observed the runs of a weather model with initial condition data that behaved in a perceived inconsequential manner that failed to reproduce results in a consistent manner. The butterfly effect presents a challenge of prediction since initial conditions for a system can never be known to complete accuracy.

On the other hand, scientists have since the contribution of Lorentz [33] argued that the weather system is not as sensitive to initial conditions as previously believed [2, 34]. Research has suggested that the Lorentz equilibriums are highly simplified, seen from a natural science point of view [38].

4. Closer description of the research project

4.1. The research design

The objective of the research is to analyze if corruption took place in the bank crash in Arendal in the year 1886 caused by the business and political elite.

In order to draw conclusions, we had to find indicators of corruption using reports and documents as sources in the data collection process. This way of approaching research is consistent with the argument to search for relationships that repeat themselves [11].

Kuhn [29] introduced the concept of paradigm shift in order to focus on changes in thinking that can take place over time. He defines a paradigm as a "scientific umbrella" that might manage to unify theories that might seem to be contradictorily. Chaos theory is new enough and flexible enough so that it can be used for a study of the bank crash in Arendal in 1886, where more research is needed.

According to Howe and Eisenhardt [23], the research questions should drive the research design and not the opposite. Platt [41, 42] warns about becoming "method oriented" rather than "problem orientated." We have played attention to these advices by having an applied approach on the current study. For us, theory has no value in itself. Theory should confirm or reject the claim found in the problem statement.

Validity refers to the relevance of measures and variables. Cook and Campbell [6] present four types of validity: internal, external, statistical, and construct validity. In an ideal world, one should design one's study to ensure that all forms of validity are ensured. However, this is not always possible in social science. Internal validity refers to causality between two variables, whether variable A has an effect on variable B. In this research chapter, we ask if the there is a relationship between corrupt practices and the bank crash in Arendal in 1886.

According to Calder et al. (1981), generalizability can be distinguished by effect application and theory application. The two types of application lead to different priorities when designing studies. This study belongs to the first category; this means that the study is more practical oriented than theory driven. We ask if the study can be of interest for other bank crashes. We are particularly interested if the current study can be of interest when studying the global bank crisis from 2008 until the current times.

4.2. Data collection through analysis of records and documents

Since this is a historical study with implications for bank crashes in recent decades, it was necessary to research and draw conclusions from both records and documents ([32], p. 277).

In this research project records included banking statements and shipping contracts. Documents are prepared for personal rather than for official reasons and include diaries, memos, letters, field notes, and so on. Documents, closer to speech, require more contextual interpretations. Records may have local uses that may become distant from officially sanctioned meanings [7].

It has often been assumed that written texts provide a "truer" indication of original meanings than other types of evidence. Indeed, Western social science has long privileged spoken over the written and the written over the non-verbal [7]. Somehow, it is assumed that the words get closer to the minds ([32], p. 277).

However, as Derrida [7] has suggested, meaning does not reside in a text but in the writing and reading it. As the text is reread in different contexts, it is given new meanings, often contradictory and always socially embedded, giving room for subjective interpretations of observations and findings.

4.3. A flexible research approach

Given the explorative way the research took place, we preferred to use a flexible research approach. As the study processed, a similar process outlined by Meyer et al. [35], whereby concepts and research methods were constantly rethought and updated following analysis and findings, followed. Similarly, [24], 99) argued that the researcher has to modify theoretical frameworks during the life of the project.

It has been recognized that the conventional research cycle conceptualization, design, measurement, analysis, and reporting do not hold well in hyperturbulent environments (Chiaburu, 2006, 744). In order to understand organizational phenomena at a more than superficial level, the scholarly literature has called for a more in-depth process research [30].

In our research, we consider change to be a continual process of becoming, rather than a succession of stable states. This viewpoint suggests that social reality is not a steady state, but rather can be regarded as a dynamic process (Beech and Johnson, 2005). Thus, there is a need to observe events and interactions as they unfold over time. This approach suggests that dynamic construction, deconstruction, and reconstruction of meaning make sense over time as contextual forces evolve and as organizational restructuring takes place.

An interpretive approach is regarded as suitable for the investigation of complex and poorly understood phenomena [9] since such an approach implies that the researcher's task is to "make sense of local actors' activities" ([49],1426). Thus, the important criterion for assessing interpretive data analysis is its ability to provide reasonable insights into phenomena that demand deeper understandings. Empirical findings illustrate, rather than validate, the theories they reflect [1].

4.4. Data collection through records and documents

We collected data through secondary sources using records and documents. We collected these data from October 2016 until June 2017, using the Kuben (Aust-Agder Museum and Achieves) in Arendal (Norway) as the main site in the data collection process.

Records can include banking statements and shipping contracts, and intentions of going business. Documents are prepared for personal rather than official reasons and include diaries, memos, letters, field notes and so on. Documents, closer to speech, require more contextual interpretations. Records may have local uses that may become distant from officially sanctioned meanings. ([32], p. 277).

It has often been assumed that what written texts provide a "truer" indication of original meanings than other types of evidence. Indeed, Western social science has long privileged the spoken over the written and the written over the non-verbal. Somehow it is assumed that the words get closer to the minds [7].

However, as Derrida [7] has suggested, meaning does not reside in a text but in the writing and reading it. As the text is reread in different contexts, it is given new meanings, often contradictory and always socially embedded. Thus, there is no "ordinal" or "true" meaning of a text outside the specific historical context. In a similar fashion, different types of texts have to be understood in the context of their conditions of reading and production [57].

5. The bank crash in Arendal (southern Norway) in 1886 explained using insights from chaos theory and butterfly effects

In order to analyze the bank crash, we will distinguish between the years before the crash (1872–1886), the crash itself in 1886, and the time after the crash.

5.1. The time before the crash 1872–1885: butterfly effects illustrate the coming harder economic times

The traditional view on the crash. The traditional approach to the decline is that United Kingdom as the main trading partner of Norway went into a decline in 1872 due to high costs in production and distribution and a country not being able to change technology to a more modern capitalist tradition found in Germany and Holland [56]. This led to major decline in supply from Norway, for example, timber to the United Kingdom, having negative effects on the town of Arendal [17].

Sailing ships was a Norwegian trade mark as the people had a competence in both building, owning, and operating such ships. This was to a large extent the case in Arendal where this research takes place. When sailing ships became outcompeted by the dampers, the strategic advantage of sailing ships became less dominating ([22], p. 155).

The traditional point of ship owners from Arendal was to show in the transformation from sailing ships to dampers leading to the bank crash in 1886. Our findings are not in accordance with this argument.

The argument of corruption from the business and political elite in Arendal leads to the crash. The argument is that the elite controlled the business bank Arendal Privatbank, established in 1884 in order to support the business interests of local and regional business. This view point supports the idea that business people were involved in opportunistic behavior manipulating accounts in order to attract more investors and ordinary people to take part in new ventures in Arendal, for example, in shipping, insurance, and wood processing.

Our findings support the argument that the brothers Axel and Oscar Herlofson were involved in business practices allocated through Arendal Privatbank, putting their interests first as investors in a number of industries in Arendal, other parts of Norway and abroad. Our results are in accordance with writings of Torstveit [53, 54] claiming that business practices of the business and political elite had direct effects on the bank crash in Arendal in 1886.

The 1860, 1870s, and 1880s were the swinging years of Arendal. Arendal was the town with the highest incomes in Norway with many people being involved in the shipping industry as investors. The years from 1870 until 1874 ship owners gave an annual dividend on 17% of invested capital on average ([54]).

High earnings in shipping led to unrealistic attitudes toward risk in both business and privately. In the late 1870s, business people had easy access to credit without good security. People guaranteed for each other. Rules and procedures for sound banking were no longer so carefully followed. Shortcuts were taken in conflict with good banking practices. The banks also had far too low capital in relation to the assets not being able to meet toucher market situations [27, 28].

The Herlofson family played a main role in the crash of 1886. With ownership and management in many industries, the family was central in the crash of Arendal in 1886. Axel Herlofson was also involved in politics. He was a member of tax commission from 1874 on, and from 1878 he had a similar position in Barbu, which was at that time a village close to Arendal, now a natural part of the town. He won confidence of ordinary people writing off small amounts of debts in appeals.

Axel Herlofson was a key person in a network of young businessmen called the "Arendal Ring." They supported each other in business and in social activities operating as a closed group of people with concentration of economic and political power.

5.2. The bank crash of 1886

At times of increased debt, falling freight rates, and ships of falling quality in 1885, it was only a question of time before a financial collapse would occur. So it did.

Arendal Privatbank went bankrupt the 30th of September 1886. For the first time in Norwegian history, a business bank went bankrupt. It was revealed that Axel and Oscar Herlofson's debt was 12.5 million croners, more than the annual budget in the larger town in Southern Norway Kristiansand [54].

Axel Herlofson had to quit his job when corrupt business practices were found to be of great disappointment for many people in Arendal. He was arrested in the town of Kristiansand trying to leave the country with money from the bank making the scandal even larger. Corruption was confirmed leaving a prison sentence of 6 years for Mr. Aksel Herlofson [54].

The situation in the savings Arendal Sparebank was also led to bankruptcy; 1.7 million croners were given in credit to business clients with limited degree of financial security. Other clients, particularly from the villages, lost the confidence to the bank and rushed to the bank trying to withdraw cash. A total of 800,000 croners were withdrawn until December 1886, of these 75% where from clients in the villages. Accounts for 600,000 were canceled from the clients. The Board of Directors came to the conclusion that it was not possible to continue in business. The bank went bankrupt on the 13th of December 1986. The same occurred the next day with the financial group Arendl Haanværkeres Laaneindretning. The only bank that survived the financial crisis in Arendal was the small savings bank Tromø Sogn Sparebank [56].

A successful town went into a recession with large negative consequences. Workers from all industries came unemployed. In October 1986, Arendal was at the edge of revolt. Fundraising campaigns and emergency work were started to reduce the disappointment by ordinary people [54].

The working class emerged as a powerful forces leading to the foundation of the Norwegian Labor Party in August 1887 in Arendal. Other consequence of the bank crash in Arendal in 1886 was changes in the bank legislation. The huge corruption in Arendal taking place meant that public authorities were of the opinion that business people had to be controlled to a large extent [54].

6. Consequences of the bank crash of 1886: long-term effects as a result of butterfly effects prior to the crash

The crash in Arendal in 1886 had large negative effects. It is argued by the people of Arendal that the town, de facto, never recovered from the decline. The neighboring town of Kristiansand in Southern Norway has expanded while Arendal has not had the same positive development.

The bank failure in Arendal had consequences far beyond the local community. The region of Southern Norway was pushed into recession leading to immigration to the USA, particularly to New York and the surrounding areas.

The socialist movement became a strong source of influence in Norway changing the political landscape from the 1920s on broke with the communist bloc within the party in 1923. The Labor Party has since played a major role in Norwegian politics.

As a part of the new political regime, the bank failure in Arendal, the Norwegian Parliament adapted stricter banking laws. The new legislation stipulated requirements for credits and restrictions for how clients could organize loans in the financial sector [54].

7. Findings

7.1. Corrupt business practices confirmed

The findings must be regarded as preliminary due to little research conducted using the regional-global model as a new to historical events as we have done in this piece of research.

Overall, the research confirms that corruption leads to economic decline in Arendal with large regional negative consequences not only for Arendal as a town but also for the region of Southern Norway.

In order to study the corruption, the regional-global model [51] made sense describing Arendal as a center for shipping until the decline set in the beginning of the 1870s. In the industrialization and urbanization of large countries such as Germany, United Kingdom, and United States, Arendal as a town and Southern Norway as a region had the timber, ice, fish, and other resources that meet the demand internationally.

However, the study of corruption practices is limited to the business elite in Arendal in the 1870 and 1880s. Corruptions might also have taken part in other towns and villages in the region but we have not enough data to draw any conclusions. This is neither the case when it comes to business associates at international markets.

The global part of the regional-global model probably made it possible to hide business practices to a certain extent. In the time period the research project focuses at the 1870s and 1880s in Arendal in Southern Norway, it was probably easier than today to avoid paying taxes in international deals due to less control, also from the public sector. In those years, people from over the class had probably greater possibilities to take advantage of a favorable position. Today with stronger means of social control and an active press, opportunistic behavior have been reduced to a large extent.

7.2. Can the study have external validity?

The study of the Arendal bank crash in 1886 can have a certain degree of external validity as the bank crash in the USA in 2008 led to a global recession that has negative effects on the economic situation such as employment and loss of main industries.

The case of the Arendal crash in 1886 was a result of adaptive expectations, meaning that price increases, for example, in real estate and on stocks would continue to increase. The assumptions were not illustrated through a fall on the US real estate market. Loans were not possible to be met leading to dramatic consequences for the private households and firms, alike [26].

Many of the loans were given with bad security to clients with weak financial standings, the so-called pub-prime loans. Many banks and other financial institutions ran into problems in many situations leading to bankruptcy [26].

Greed was the main motivation for many of the banks leading poor people with limited financial security into deep trouble. In the years from 2005 until 2007, more than 50% of the allocated loans in the US belonged to the prime loan category indicating opportunistic behavior and maybe also corruption [26].

7.3. The argument of random growth confirmed

The research confirms the findings of Geroski et al. [14] arguing that growth rates vary more or less randomly across firms over time. As such, it might be argued that corporate growth is unpredictable. However, their data also indicate that firms' current period of high growth rates is a reasonable predictor of increases in long-term predictability. Our study confirm such as logic.

7.4. The importance of crowd practices confirmed

The study shed light on the importance of crowd practices when business decisions are taken in closed and secret circles. The important role of the brothers Axel and Oscar Herlofson is mentioned in the chapter in order to explain how corruption could take place and lead to the bank crash.

Crowd-related practices and seemingly new, more "open" organizational form are receiving increased attention in the strategy, organizational design, and innovation literature (Harhoff and Lakhani [19]. In this research line, the current research might help to give a contribution to how crowds function, both as an organization and how such organization helps to understand the environment in which the organization operates (i.e., [13]).

7.5. Limitations of the study

The results must be regarded as pre-limitary. It is the first study that tries to combine a bank crash and corruption to chaos theory and how the regional-global model can be used.

More research in public registers and shipping registers can lead to new insight on how corruption can have led to the bank crash in Arendal in 1886. We are of the opinion that more insights can lead to more insights on other bank crashes, also studies as to how the chances of large bank crashes in the future.

On this journey, chaos theory and butterfly effects can be a candidate for further studies on bank crashes. Deeper insights on chaos theory can give possibilities to gain more insights on bank crashes combining theory with practice, an adequate research tradition from chaos theory building on Greek thinking from the early antique.

8. Conclusion

8.1. Corruption confirmed with its negative effects

Corruption was confirmed studying the bank crash in Arendal (Norway) in 1886. Opportunistic behavior of the business and political elite lead the town into a deep economic recession with negative long-term consequences.

8.2. Future research

More research on the relationship between bank crashes and corruption can give new insights.

We will suggest certain areas that can push research to new levels of knowledge.

The ambidexterity organization literature and corruption? More research on banking crashes linked to corporate practices can use insights from the ambidexterity organization literature (Birkinshaw and Gupta, 2013, [37]), focusing at strategic decisions and operation in running a company, for example, a business bank or a ship owner company.

Blue ocean strategy and corruption? We are of the opinion that in our search for corrupt business practices, chaos theory can be combined with a blue ocean strategy [25] looking at the business world through untraditional approaches, expanding for mental processes. We believe that people who wish to fight corruption can benefit handsomely from using such a way of approaching corporate practices.

Coase and corruption? Shipping executives must be brave and ask why they exist at all, as Coase [8] did in his article. Coase's [8] theory of the firm can be regarded as a landmark contribution to help understand organizational boundaries and the competitive dynamics between organizations and markets [15, 44, 45, 59].

Coase, in short, argued that the existence of transaction costs in markets leads to the "emergence of the firm." His seminal contribution was to highlight how the visible hand of an entrepreneur or a manager ([5, 31]; Baldwin and Von Hippel, 2012) intervenes in markets through price mechanism [21].

While Coese's theory (1937) made significant contributions to the understanding of firms and markets, it might be argued that Coase has a rather limited view on social processes in his study. We are of the opinion that future studies on corruption in bank crashes can benefit from paying more attention to environmental factors, in accordance with current political winds found in many parts of the world, for example, in Germany, France, and the USA.

More research on bank crashes using the regional-global model. We assume that bank crashes will become a more researched area given the more complex and turbulent business environments. We believe that the regional-global model can be a suitable candidate when researching on bank crashes.

Acknowledgements

The author wishes to thank his children Alexander and Christina for all the inspiration in this research project. I follow the progress of the kids with great pride and surprise. I am without doubt a very proud father. The gifts of life. Nothing less.

Author details

Carsten Martin Syvertsen

Address all correspondence to: carsten.m.syvertsen@hiof.no

Østfold University College, Norway

References

[1] Astley WG, Zammuto RF. Organization science, managers and language games. Organizational Science. 1992;**3**(4):443-460

[2] Basener WF. Topology and its Application. New York: Wiley & Sons; 2006

[3] Brooks C. Chaos in foreign exchange markets. A special view. Computational Economics. 1998;**11**:265-281

[4] Chandler AD Jr. Strategy and Structure. Cambridge, MA: MIT Press; 1963

[5] Chandler AD Jr. Scale and Scope. Cambridge, MA: Harvard University Press; 1990

[6] Cook TD, Campell DT. Quasi-Experimentation. Design and Analysis Issues of Field Settings. Boston: Houghton Mifflin Company; 1979

[7] Derrida J. Writing and Difference, Rence. London: Routledge & Kegan Paul; 1978

[8] Coase RS. The Nature of the Firm. Economica. 1937, N.S;**4**:386-405. reprinted in Stigler GJ, Boldings KE. eds. Readings in Price Theory 1952, Richard D. Irwin, Homewood, IL

[9] Dixon S, Meyer KE, Day M. Exploitation and exploration learning and the development of organizational capabilities: A cross-case analysis of the Russian oil industry. Human Relations. 2007;**60**(10):1493-1523

[10] Drucker P. The Practice Management. New York: Harper and Row; 1954

[11] Dublin R. Theory Building. New York: Free Press; 1969

[12] Eden C, Spender JC. Managerial and Organizational Cognition, Theory, Methods and Research. Sage Publications Ltd; 1998

[13] Fedin T, Lakhani KR, Tushman ML. Firms, crowds, and innovation. Strategic Organization. 2017;**15**(2):119-140

[14] Geroski PA, Machin SJ, Walters CF. Corporate growth and profitability. Journal of Industrial Economics. 1997;**45**(2):171

[15] Gibbons R. Four formal(izable) theories of the firm? Journal of Economic Behavior and Organization. 2005;**58**(2):200-245

[16] Gleick J. Chaos: Making a New Science. London: Heineman; 1987

[17] Gjerstad JO. Arendal's decline as a shipping town from 1880 until 1900, Master Thesis the Norwegian School of Economics and Business Administration (Norges Handelshøyskole). Norway: Bergen; 1975

[18] Handy C. Balancing corporate power: A new federalist paper. Harvard Business Review. 1992, nov./dec.:59-72

[19] Harhoff D, Lakhani K. Revolutionizing Innovation: Users, Communities and Open Innovation, MA. Cambridge: MIT Press; 2016

[20] Hassard J, Parker M. Postmodernism and Organizations. Thousand Oarks, CA: Sage; 1993

[21] Hayek FA. The use of knowledge in society. American Economic Review. 1945;**35**(4): 519-530

[22] Hodne F. The economic history of Norway, 1815-1970. Oslo: J.W. Cappelen Publishing Company; 1981

[23] Howe K, Eisenhardt M. Standards for qualitative (and quantitative) research: A prolegomenon. Educational Researcher. 1990;**19**(4):2-9

[24] Hindings CR, Greenwood R. The Dynamics of Strategic Change: Basel. Oxford: Blackwell; 1988

[25] Kim WC, Mauborgne R. Blue Ocean Strategy, how to Create Uncontested Market Space and Make the Competition Irrelevant. Boston, Mass: Harvard Business School Publishing Corporation; 2005

[26] Knudsen S. Financial crisis at present and in a historical perspective", in financial lack of balance, special issue. Magma. 2008;**11**(3):37-46

[27] Kreps GL, Ferndon, Arnesson P. The power of qualitative research to address organizational issues. In: Herndon SE, Kreps GL, editors. Qualitative Research: Application in Organizational Communication. USA: Hampton Press; 1993

[28] Knudsen L. From N.B. Herlofson's Memoirs- The way things where. 2007. Arendal Historical Society, No. 13, 65-75, printed in Arendal (Norway)

[29] Kuhn T. Scientific Paradigms. In: Barnes B. ed. Sociology of Science. Hamondworth (UK): Penguin; 1972

[30] Langley A. Strategies or theorizing from process data. Academy of Management Review. 1999;**24**(49):691-710

[31] Langlois R. The vanishing hand: The changing dynamics of industrial capitalism. Industrial and Corporate Change. 2003;**12**:351-385

[32] Lincoln YS, Guba EG. Naturalistic Inquiry. Beverly Hills, CA: Sage; 1985

[33] Lorentz EN. Deterministic non-periodic flow. Journal of the Atmospheric Sciences. 1963;**20**(2):130-141

[34] Medio A, Marji L. Nonlinear Dynamics: A Primer. Mass: Cambridge University Press; 2001

[35] Meyer AD, Goes JB, Brooks GR. Organizations reaching to hyper turbulence. In: Huber CP, Glink WH, editors. Organizational Change and Redesign: Ideas and Insights for Improving Performance. Oxford: Oxford University Press; 1993

[36] Mintzberg H. Crafting Strategy. Boston, Mass: Harvard Business Review, July-August; 1987

[37] O'Reilly CA III, Harreld JB, Tushman ML. Organizational ambidexterity: IBM and emerging business opportunities. California Management Journal. 2008;**51**(4):75-99

[38] Ovchinnokov IV. Introduction to super symmetric theory of stochastics. Entropy. 2016;**18**

[39] Piore M, Sabel C. The Second Industrial Divide. New York: Basic Books; 1984

[40] Porter ME. Competitive Advantage. New York: Free Press; 1980

[41] Platt JR. Strong inference: Certain systematic methods of scientific thinking may produce much more rapid progress than others. Science. 1964;**146**(3642):347-353

[42] Pondy L. The role of metaphors and myths in organization and the facilitation of change. In: Pondy L, Frost P, Morgan G, Dandridge T, editors. Organizational Symbolism: Monographs in organizational and industrial relations. Vol. 1. Greenwich, CT: JAI Press; 1983. pp. 157-166

[43] Polanyi M. The Tacit Dimension. Mass: Gloucester; 1966

[44] Sanjek R, editor. Field Notes: The Making of Anthropology. Alberta: State University of New York; 1990

[45] Santos F, Eisenhardt K. Organizational boundaries and theories of organization. Organization Science. 2005;**16**:491-508

[46] Sennett R. A society of broken eggs. New Statesman. 2002, 17 December 1991-7 January 2002

[47] Simon HA. Rational Decision Making in Business Organizations, Lecture by Herbert A.Simon when receiving the Nobel Prize in Economic Science, December 8 (1978)

[48] Smith A, An Inquiry into the Nature and Causes of the Wealth of Nations; 1776. Glasgow

[49] Soulsby A, Clark E. Organization theory and the post-socialist transformation: Contributions to organizational knowledge. Human Relations. 2007;**60**(10):1419-1442

[50] Syvertsen CM. Towards the Business Federation in Management Consulting Firms", Doctoral thesis IESE Business School. Barcelona: University of Navarra; 2000

[51] Syvertsen CM. Towards a regional-global organizational model for leading research driven business schools, findings from a longitudinal study in China, Europe and the USA from 2010 until 2016. Problems and Perspectives in Management. 2017;**15**(2):36-44

[52] Taylor FW. The Principles of Scientific Management. New York: Norton; 1911

[53] Tilley C. ed. Discourse and power; the genre of the Cambridge inaugural. In: Miller D, Rowlands M, Tilley C. Domination and Resistance. London: Urwin Hyman; 1990. pp. 41-42

[54] Torstveit JG. Corruption and Bank Crash and New Political Party in Arendal 1886-88. Arendal (Norway): Arendal Tidende; 2012

[55] Wallin Weihe H-J. Turbulent Times and Tormod Torfæüs as a Historical Thinker-1636-1719. Stavanger, Norway: Hertervig Academic; 2015

[56] Wallin Weihe HJ, Syvertsen CM. The Frozen Water Trade. Stavanger, Norway: Hertervig Academic; 2012

[57] Webb EJ, Campell DT, Schwartz RC, Sechrest L. Unobtrusive Measures: Nonreactive Research in the Social Science. Chicago: University of Chicago Press; 1966

[58] Weber M. The Protestant Ethics and the Spirit of Capitalism. New York: Harper Collins Academy; 1991/1905

[59] Zenger T, Felin T, Bigelow L. Theories of the firm-market boundary. Academy of Management Annals. 2011;**5**:89-133

Chapter 3

A Colloidal Self-Organization of Impurities in a Liquid by Density Fluctuations

Alexander Shimkevich

Additional information is available at the end of the chapter

http://dx.doi.org/10.5772/intechopen.70459

Abstract

The two-parametric functional for weakly interacting fluctuations of liquid density and composition is studied within the theory based on Landau potential for these fluctuations in the kind of ensemble of phonons and compound clusters. Using the standard diagram technique, the task for weak-interacting phonons and clusters is reduced to solving the equations of proper-energetic functions of quasi-particle interaction by Neumann iterations of Feynman diagrams in "bootstrapping" of Fourier images (propagators) for correlation of the composition of liquid and its topological structure. It is shown that composition fluctuations as clusters are induced by phonons when impurity atoms being initially outside the dense part of liquid (introduction solution) become inherent constituents of the dense part (addition solution). By renormalizing parameters of the model, we have transformed weakly interacting fluctuations to free "dressed" phonons and clusters whose autocorrelation functions are characterized by various behaviors in small and large scales in comparison with the atomic spacing. In the first case, density fluctuations of liquid do not feel impurities. In the intermediate scale, the liquid matrix is inhomogeneous in the form of colloids, which is not observed at the large scales. Dynamics of such liquid is characterized by diffusion modes of solvent and oscillations of impurities.

Keywords: liquid, density and composition fluctuations, Feynman diagram, bootstrap, phonon, cluster, renormalization

1. Introduction

It is known that any liquid is characterized by a random chaotic packing of atoms. They are easily rearranged by little thermal fluctuations in contrast to a crystal whose topological structure is stable under any thermal fluctuations below the melting point [1].

At the same time, the topological structure of instantaneous dense part of any condensed matter (liquid, crystal, and amorphous) is represented as configurations of closely packed particles in Delaunay simplexes (dense triangular pyramids with particles in their vertices) that are connected by faces into ramified short-living tetrahedral clusters of density fluctuations [2, 3]. Using the topological criterion [3] in *molecular-dynamic* (MD) simulation of deterministic nonlinear system of many particles, one can exactly select these simplexes by defining a maximal length of their edges over the maximal number of obtained simplex clusters in the MD cell. The statistics of these clusters is gotten for any condensed matter [4] as their *two-dimensional* (2D) discrete distribution on *cardinality* (number of simplexes in the cluster) and on *connectivity* (number of their vertexes belonging also to other clusters).

For any crystal, these clusters consist of one and only one simplex, that is, their cardinality is equal to 1, but their connectivity is distributed normally in the interval of 7–23 (15 on average). In contrast to the crystal heated, the cluster cardinality of amorphous dense part achieves 10, and the connectivity of such clusters is more than 3 but less than 20 (11 on average). It means that the solid state (crystal and amorphous) is characterized by percolation of tetrahedral dense-part clusters of structural fluctuations.

The topological features of a liquid: (1) the cardinality of liquid dense-part clusters reaches 37, that is, almost four times more than the solid ones, and (2) there are almost 5% of dense-part clusters with zero connectivity sufficient for breaking off the percolation of solid dense-part clusters, providing a fluidity of liquid and forming long chains of liquid dense part. These clusters as dense configurations of particles are dynamically changed but statistically preserve the multifractal structure [3].

The existence in liquid metal of such chains with the fractal gyration radius of ~100 nm is confirmed by the experiments [5] on small-angle-scattering of neutrons. These data are obtained on the contrast of liquid-dense and nondense parts, which amount to 10–15% from the contrast of liquid boundary in vacuum.

Thus, a liquid is characterized by existence of dense-part clusters with zero connectivity in contrast to crystal and amorphous solid which have not such clusters. Moreover, the cardinality of dense-part clusters in any crystal is equal to 1, while amorphous solid occupies the intermediate position between crystal and liquid on the discrete 2D distribution of dense-part clusters [4]. At the same time, the tetrahedral clusters of dense-part open for impurity in principle two topologically differing positions in liquid and amorphous solid: (1) outside the dense-part simplexes and (2) in their clusters as compound constituents [6, 7]. The induced by density-fluctuations polymorphic transition of impurity between these positions is the subject of given theoretical consideration.

Revealing a mechanism of such self-organization of impurities in liquids will allow to have found an approach to their structural modification over chosen attributes by impurities.

2. The method of Green function

The method of Green function used in physics of phase transitions allows so to have formulated and disposed questions of theory that one can obtain topologically exact answers without knowing an explicit kind of the state equation [8]. This method bases on Landau potential [9] which usually is represented by a functional of generalized variables expressing parameters of the local order. Then, structural and phase changes are described by calculus variations of these parameters [8]. They mean by topological and compound (chemical) order. The first is understood as ordering of atoms regardless of the particles nature. The second is characterized by spatial correlation of different atoms and is responsible for the microstratification and clustering of the particles.

Besides the *compound parameter of order* (CPO), the two-parametrical fluctuation model of liquid alloy includes the *topological parameter of order* (TPO) which can induce by density fluctuations the clustering of impurity atoms far off from the phase change [10].

We consider the double system, $A_{1-x}B_x$, where $x = \overline{n_2/(n_1 + n_2)}$ is the average concentration of impurity component, B; n_i is the density of i-particles number (i = 1, 2) for representing Landau potential, ΔF, of this system by the functional of two parameters (n_1, n_2) [10]:

$$\Delta F = \int_V f\left(\Delta_i,\ \vec{\nabla}\Delta_i, n, x\right) d^3 r + \Delta F_0(n, x) \tag{1}$$

Here, $d^3 r$ is the differential of 3D space, f is the density of Helmholtz free energy, $\Delta_i = n_i - \overline{n}_i$ is the density fluctuation of i-particles number, $\vec{\nabla}$ is the gradient, n is the average density of particles, $\Delta F_0 = \Delta F(\Delta_i = 0)$ is the free energy of homogeneous system, and V is its volume.

The $\Delta_i(\vec{r})$ fluctuations are averaged in the neighborhood of point, $\vec{r}$, in a small volume which however contains sufficiently great number of particles as well as a distance, where $\Delta_i(\vec{r})$ function changes is appreciably more than the interatomic spacing, r_0 [8]. In this case, the other degrees of freedom (electronic, vibration et al) require a time far less than the configuration field, $\Delta_i(\vec{r})$, for reaching equilibrium. Therefore, one can apply the adiabatic approximation for describing the fluctuations fields of CPO and TPO in double system.

Then, one can limit Taylor expansion of $f(\Delta_i)$ as a function of small parameter, Δ_i, by the members of third-order infinitesimal: Δ_1^3, $\Delta_1^2\Delta_2$, and $\Delta_1\Delta_2^2$, which correct the second and third approximation of perturbation theory for F_0. One can also neglect the members of fourth-order infinitesimal: $\{\Delta_i\}^4$, because the coefficients of Δ_i^2 in Taylor expansion of $f(\Delta_i)$ are positive, and the Δ_i proportional members of Taylor series are equal to zero in (1) owing to the constant number of particles in the system.

Further for the isotropic liquid, the first derivatives, $\vec{\nabla}\,\vec{\Delta}_i$, can come into Taylor expansion of $f(\Delta_i,\ \vec{\nabla}\,\Delta_i)$ only in the scalar combination $(\vec{\nabla}\,\Delta_i \cdot \vec{\nabla}\,\Delta_k)$, and the second ones can be as products: *const* $\vec{\nabla}^2\,\Delta_i$ and $\Delta_i\vec{\nabla}^2\,\Delta_k$. The first of them gives the insignificant addition into the integral (1.1), which for the second is transformed into integral of $(\vec{\nabla}\,\Delta_i \cdot \vec{\nabla}\,\Delta_k)$ [11].

Thus, without limiting a task generality for liquid, one can present f as [10]

$$f=\frac{1}{2}\left(\frac{\partial\mu_1}{\partial n_1}\Delta_1^2+2\frac{\partial\mu_1}{\partial n_2}\Delta_1\Delta_2+\frac{\partial\mu_2}{\partial n_2}\Delta_2^2\right)+\frac{1}{6}\left(\frac{\partial^2\mu_1}{\partial n_1^2}\Delta_1^3+3\frac{\partial^2\mu_1}{\partial n_1\partial n_2}\Delta_1^2\Delta_2+3\frac{\partial^2\mu_1}{\partial n_2^2}\Delta_1\Delta_2^2\right)$$
$$+\frac{K_{11}}{2n}(\vec{\nabla}\Delta_1)^2+\frac{K_{12}}{n}(\vec{\nabla}\Delta_1\cdot\vec{\nabla}\Delta_2)+\frac{K_{22}}{2n}(\vec{\nabla}\Delta_2)^2 \tag{2}$$

Here, $\mu_i\ (n, x, T) \equiv (\partial f/\partial n_i)_{TV}$ is the chemical potential of i-component, T is Kelvin temperature, $K_{ik}=2|U_{ik}(r_0)|r_0^2 z$, $U_{ik}(r_0)$ is the pair-interaction potential of nearest particles of kind: i and k, and z is the average coordination number. Considering the homogeneous liquid of double system by the model of ideal solution, one can present the chemical potential, μ_i ($i = 1, 2$), in the form

$$\left.\begin{aligned}\mu_1&=\mu_{10}(T,n)+T\ln(1-x)\\ \mu_2&=\mu_{20}(T,n)+T\ln x\end{aligned}\right| \tag{3}$$

which, obviously, satisfies to Gibbs-Duhem relation

$$(1-x)\frac{\partial\mu_1}{\partial x}+x\frac{\partial\mu_2}{\partial x}=0 \tag{4}$$

Then, we will obtain [7]

$$\left.\begin{aligned}&\frac{\partial\mu_{10}}{\partial n}\equiv\frac{\partial\mu_{20}}{\partial n}=\frac{1}{n}\left(\frac{dP}{dn}\right)_T\\ &\frac{\partial\mu_1}{\partial n_1}=\frac{T}{n}\left(\beta+\frac{x}{1-x}\right)\\ &\frac{\partial\mu_1}{\partial n_2}=\frac{T}{n}(\beta-1)\\ &\frac{\partial\mu_2}{\partial n_2}=\frac{T}{n}\left(\beta+\frac{1-x}{x}\right)\\ &\frac{\partial^2\mu_1}{\partial n_1^2}=\frac{T}{n^2}\left(\beta'-\frac{x(2-x)}{(1-x)^2}\right)\\ &\frac{\partial^2\mu_1}{\partial n_2^2}=\frac{\partial^2\mu_1}{\partial n_1\partial n_2}=\frac{T}{n^2}(\beta'+1)\end{aligned}\right| \tag{5}$$

at the condition that the first bracket in (2) is the quadratic form positively defined. Here, $\beta=(n/T)(\partial\mu_{10}/\partial n)$, $\beta'=(n^2/T)(\partial^2\mu_{10}/\partial n^2)$, and P is the static pressure.

For simple liquids, $\beta \gg 1$ and $(\partial P/\partial n)_T$ weakly depends on the number density, n, of particles. Therefore, one can accept $\beta' \sim -\beta$ [7].

Transforming the quadratic forms in (2) to diagonal ones, one can present Landau potential as a sum of free-field Hamiltonians and the weak-interaction potential. Then, we will have the almost ideal Bose gas of two components [8].

Using relations (3)–(5), one can do (2) by diagonal square form by means of linear transformation

$$\left.\begin{array}{l}\Delta_1 = n(a_{11}\varphi + a_{12}\chi)\\ \Delta_2 = n(a_{21}\varphi + a_{22}\chi)\end{array}\right| \tag{6}$$

Substituting (6) into (2), we will find parameters

$$\left.\begin{array}{l}a_{11} = 1\\ a_{22} = x\\ a_{12} = -x\alpha_1[1 - x(\alpha_1 - \alpha_2/\alpha_1)\gamma]\\ a_{21} = x\left[1 + x\left(1 - \alpha_1\gamma - (1-\alpha_2)\beta\right)\right]\gamma\end{array}\right| \tag{7}$$

for $x < 1/\gamma$ and zero coefficients at $(\varphi \cdot \chi)$ and $(\vec{\nabla}\varphi \cdot \vec{\nabla}\chi)$ [10]. Here, $\alpha_1 = K_{12}/K_{11} \sim 1$, $\alpha_2 = K_{22}/K_{11} \sim 1$, and $\gamma = 1 - (1 - \alpha_1)\beta$ are the alternating-sign factor. As a result, Eq. (2) to x^2 becomes

$$f/\beta nT = \frac{(1+x\gamma)^2}{2}\varphi^2 + \frac{(1+x\alpha_1\gamma)^2}{2}\frac{K_{11}}{\beta T}\left(\vec{\nabla}\varphi\right)^2 + \frac{x\left[1+x(1-\alpha_1)^2\beta\right]}{2\beta}\chi^2 + \frac{x^2\left(\alpha_2-\alpha_1^2\right)}{2}\frac{K_{11}}{\beta T}\left(\vec{\nabla}\chi\right)^2$$
$$-\frac{(1+x\gamma)^3}{6}\varphi^3 - \frac{x(1-\alpha_1)+x^2(1-\alpha_2)\gamma}{2}\varphi^2\chi - \frac{x^2(1-\alpha_1)^2}{2}\varphi\chi^2 \tag{8}$$

Labeling $a_0 = 1 + x\gamma$, $b_0 = 1 + x\alpha_1\gamma$, $c = \left[1 + x(1-\alpha_1)^2\beta\right]/\beta$, $\lambda = 1 - \alpha_1 + x(1-\alpha_2)\gamma$, and $\vec{\rho} = \vec{r}\sqrt{\beta T/K_{11}}$, we will obtain

$$\Delta F(\varphi,\chi) = nK_{11}\sqrt{K_{11}/\beta T}\int\limits_{V\left(\frac{\beta T}{K_{11}}\right)^{3/2}} d^3\rho\left[\frac{a_0^2}{2}\varphi^2 + \frac{b_0^2}{2}\left(\vec{\nabla}\varphi\right)^2 - \frac{a_0^3}{6}\varphi^3\right.$$
$$\left. + x\left(\frac{c}{2}\chi^2 + x\frac{\alpha_2 - \alpha_1^2}{2}\left(\vec{\nabla}\chi\right)^2 - \frac{\lambda}{2}\varphi^2\chi - x\frac{(1-\alpha_1)^2}{2}\varphi\chi^2\right)\right] \tag{9}$$

What sense have the parameters of order, φ and χ? We obtain $\varphi \approx (\Delta_1 + \Delta_2)/n$ and $\chi \approx (\Delta_2/x - \Delta_1)/n$ out of (6) when $\alpha_i \approx 1$and $x < 1$. Then, φ is the reduced TPO of liquid, and χ expresses the reduced CPO for clustering the initially homogeneous liquid alloy to microregions of different composition, that is, the parameter, χ, describes the compound fluctuation field as opposed to the parameter, φ, which describes the topological fluctuation field.

Each of these fields can be presented as a set of oscillations of averaged corresponding collective modes that are Fourier images of topological and compound fluctuations of the liquid alloy. They are defined by Green functions, $G(\varphi)$ и $G(\chi)$ [12].

In the integral (9), Hamiltonian (2) defines the change of free energy of weak-interacting long-wave phonons and clusters in the double alloy. In the adiabatic approximation, one can take into account only the given ordering (φ, χ) without caring of other variables of the system. Then, we will define the equilibrium fields, $\varphi(\vec{\rho})$ and $\chi(\vec{\rho})$, in the minimum of $\Delta F(\varphi, \chi)$ [8]. This condition looks like Euler variation equation which for the entered parameters of order gives equations [10].

$$\left.\begin{aligned} -b_0^2\,\vec{\nabla}^{\,2}\varphi + a_0^2\varphi - a_0^3\varphi^2/2 &= x\left[\lambda\varphi\chi + x(1-\alpha_1)^2\chi^2/2\right] \\ x\left(\alpha_1^2 - \alpha_2\right)\vec{\nabla}^{\,2}\chi + c\chi - \lambda\varphi^2/2 &= x(1-\alpha_1)^2\varphi\chi \end{aligned}\right| \qquad (10)$$

Using the standard diagram techniques [11] for averaged collective variables, one can reduce the task for weak-interacting phonons and clusters to solve the equations of proper-energetic functions of interacting quasi-particles [10]. For this, we use an averaged correlator $\langle\phi(\vec{\rho})\cdot\phi(\vec{\rho}\,')\rangle$ which is Green function at $\vec{\rho}\,' = 0$ [8]:

$$G_\varphi\left(\vec{\rho}\right) = \left\langle\varphi\left(\vec{\rho}\right)\cdot\varphi(0)\right\rangle \qquad (11)$$

In such case, one can present the effects of alloy fluctuation nonhomogeneity as the integrals containing correlation functions, $G_\varphi(\vec{\rho})$ and $G_\chi(\vec{\rho})$ or their spectral densities

$$\left.\begin{aligned} \left\langle\varphi\left(\vec{k}\right)\cdot\varphi\left(\vec{k}\,'\right)\right\rangle &= G_{\vec{k}}(\varphi)\delta\left(\vec{k}-\vec{k}\,'\right) \\ \left\langle\chi\left(\vec{k}\right)\cdot\chi\left(\vec{k}\,'\right)\right\rangle &= G_{\vec{k}}(\chi)\delta\left(\vec{k}-\vec{k}\,'\right) \end{aligned}\right| \qquad (12)$$

obtained by Fourier conversion:

$$\left.\begin{aligned} \varphi\left(\vec{\rho}\right) &= \int e^{i\vec{k}\vec{\rho}}\varphi\left(\vec{k}\right)d^3k/(2\pi)^3 \\ \chi\left(\vec{\rho}\right) &= \int e^{i\vec{k}\vec{\rho}}\chi\left(\vec{k}\right)d^3k/(2\pi)^3 \end{aligned}\right| \qquad (13)$$

where $\varphi(-\vec{k}) = \varphi^*(\vec{k})$ and $\chi(-\vec{k}) = \chi^*(\vec{k})$. According to Wiener-Khinchin theorem, $G_i(\vec{\rho})$ and $G_{\vec{k}}(i)$ ($i = \varphi, \chi$) are equivalent functions because they are connected by Fourier conversion

$$G_i\left(\vec{\rho}\right) = \int G_{\vec{k}}(i)e^{i\vec{k}\vec{\rho}}d^3k/(2\pi)^3 \qquad (14)$$

Thanking δ-normalization of $\varphi(\vec{k})$ and $\chi(\vec{k})$, one can change the differential equations (10) to the algebraic ones for Fourier-images of Green functions: $G_{\vec{k}}\left(\varphi\right) = \langle|\varphi(\vec{k})|^2\rangle$. We will calculate them in approximation of the perturbation theory by means of iterations and Neumann series of Feynman diagrams [13].

3. The formalism of Feynman diagrams

For "bare" phonon propagator $G^0_{\vec{k}}(\varphi)$, determined by the first equation of system (10) without the member on the right ($x = 0$), we have [10]

$$\left(a_0^2 + b_0^2 k^2\right) G^0_{\vec{k}}(\varphi) = \left(a_0^3/2\right) F_{\vec{k}}\left[G^0_{\varphi}\left(\vec{\rho}\right)\right] \tag{15}$$

where $F_{\vec{k}}[G^0_{\varphi}(\vec{\rho})]$ is the iteration procedure presented by the chain

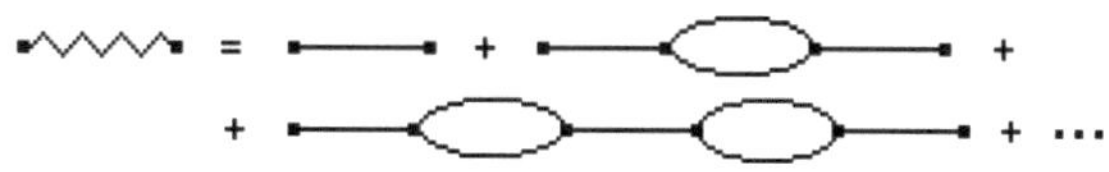

(16)

which is converted into the recurrence form [12]

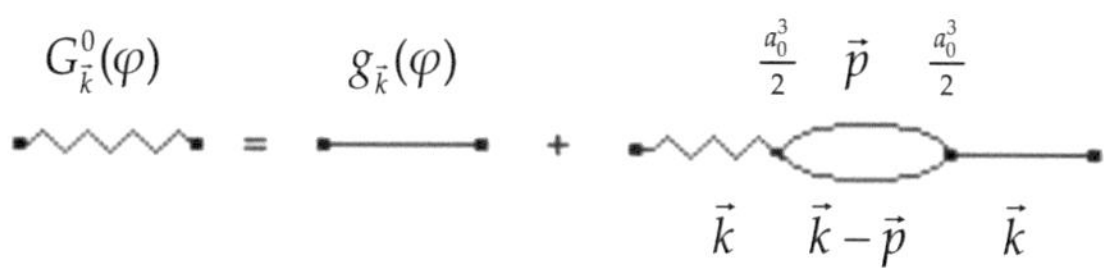

(17)

and has the analytic solution

$$G^0_{\vec{k}}(\varphi) = \left(a_0^2 + b_0^2 k^2 - \Sigma_0\left(\vec{k}\right)\right)^{-1} > 0 \tag{18}$$

under the condition: $|\Sigma_0(\vec{k})|/(a_0^2 + b_0^2 k^2) < 1$. Here, $\Sigma_0(\vec{k})$ is the proper-energetic function expressed by the equation [10]

$$\Sigma_0\left(\vec{k}\right) = \frac{a_0^6}{8}\int \frac{d^3p}{(2\pi)^3} g_{\vec{p}}(\varphi) g_{\vec{k}-\vec{p}}(\varphi) \tag{19}$$

and $g^{\vec{p}}(\varphi) = \left(a_0^2 + b_0^2 p^2\right)^{-1}$ as the solution of (15) with unit on the right. From the second equation of system (10) without the member on the right, we obtain the equation for "bare" cluster propagator, $G^0_{\vec{k}}(\chi)$ [10]:

$$\left[c + x\left(\alpha_2 - \alpha_1^2\right)k^2\right] G^0_{\vec{k}}(\chi) = \frac{\lambda}{2} F_{\vec{k}}\left[G^0_{\varphi}\left(\vec{\rho}\right)\right] \tag{20}$$

The solution of this equation converted into the recurrence form has the graphic form

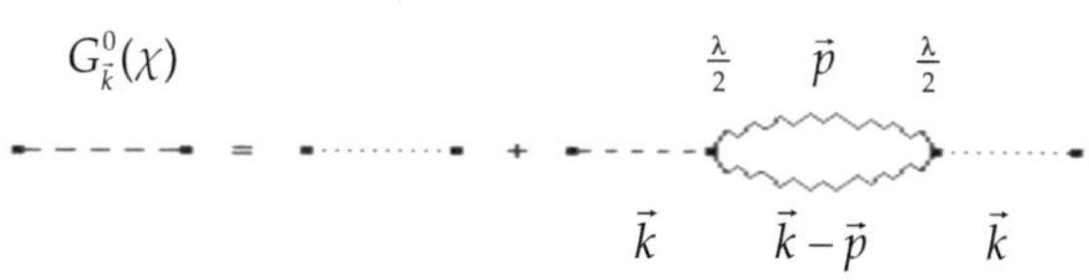

(21)

and the analytic one under the conditions, $|\Pi_0(\vec{k})|/[c + x(\alpha_2 - \alpha_1^2)k^2] < 1$ and $|\vec{k}| < 1$:

$$G^0_{\vec{k}}(\chi) = \left[c + x(\alpha_2 - \alpha_1^2)k^2 - \Pi_0\left(\vec{k}\right)\right]^{-1} > 0 \tag{22}$$

Here, $\Pi_0(\vec{k})$ is the phonon-proper-energetic function determined by the equation [10]

$$\Pi_0\left(\vec{k}\right) = \frac{\lambda^2}{8}\int \frac{d^3p}{(2\pi)^3} G^0_{\vec{p}}(\varphi) G^0_{\vec{k}-\vec{p}}(\varphi) \tag{23}$$

The solution (22) of the Eq. (20) defines the propagator of induced compound field entering in Hamiltonian (9), that is, the clusters are generated *forcedly by phonons* unlike their free field with the propagator, $G^0_{\vec{k}}(\varphi)$, whose fluctuations are formed spontaneously.

The natural development of this idea is the "bootstrap" hypothesis [14] which consists in the following. The fluctuations of CPO, χ, arising at the interaction of phonons deform partially the density-fluctuations field, φ, "dressing" the propagator, $G^0_{\vec{k}}(\varphi)$, by the proper-energetic function

$$\Sigma_1\left(\vec{k}\right) = x^2\lambda^2 \int \frac{d^3p}{(2\pi)^3} G^0_{\vec{p}}(\varphi) G^0_{\vec{k}-\vec{p}}(\chi) + \frac{x^4(1-\alpha_1)^4}{8}\int \frac{d^3p}{(2\pi)^3} G^0_{\vec{p}}(\chi) G^0_{\vec{k}-\vec{p}}(\chi) \tag{24}$$

defined by the members of the first equation of system (10) on the right. The graphic and analytic solution of this equation is [10]

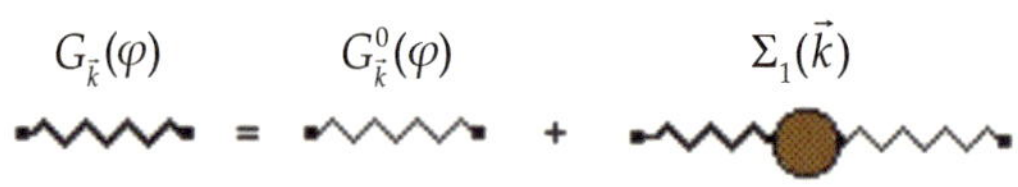

(25)

and

$$G_{\vec{k}}(\varphi) = \left[1/G^0_{\vec{k}}(\varphi) - \Sigma_1\left(\vec{k}\right)\right]^{-1} > 0 \tag{26}$$

This formula makes sense under the obvious condition $|\Sigma_1(\vec{k})| G^0_{\vec{k}}(\varphi) < 1$.

Now, one can analytically express the first (topological) bootstrapping of deformed CPO field by replacing function, $G^0_{\vec{k}}(\varphi)$, in (23) by "dressed" phonon propagator, $G_{\vec{k}}(\varphi)$:

$$\Pi_1\left(\vec{k}\right) = \frac{\lambda^2}{8}\int \frac{d^3p}{(2\pi)^3} G_{\vec{p}}(\varphi) G_{\vec{k}-\vec{p}}(\varphi) \tag{27}$$

and its substitution in the formula (22) instead of $\Pi_0(\vec{k})$. It is possible under the condition: $|\Pi_1(\vec{k})|/[c + x(\alpha_2 - \alpha_1^2)k^2] < 1$. Taking into account the member in the second equation of system (10) on the right gives for propagator, $G^0_{\vec{k}}(\chi)$, the proper-energetic function in the final form

$$\Pi_2\left(\vec{k}\right) = x^2(1-\alpha_1)^4\int\frac{d^3p}{(2\pi)^3}G^0_{\vec{p}}(\chi)G_{\vec{k}-\vec{p}}(\varphi) \tag{28}$$

This is expressed in graphic and analytic forms by

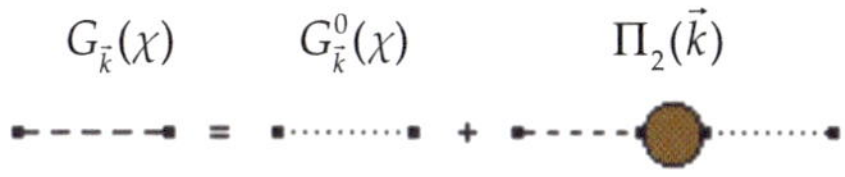

(29)

and

$$G_{\vec{k}}(\chi) = \left[1/G^0_{\vec{k}}(\chi) - \Pi_2\left(\vec{k}\right)\right]^{-1} > 0 \tag{30}$$

under the condition $|\Pi_2(\vec{k})|G^0_{\vec{k}}(\chi) < 1$.

Thus, one can find the fluctuation fields of the liquid density and compound in the form of autocorrelation functions of impurity concentration, x, and the parameters $(\alpha_1, \alpha_2, \beta)$ by means of the graphic, algebraic, and integral Eqs. (17)–(19) and (21)–(30).

4. The coherent propagators of phonons and clusters

One can find the solutions of the Eq. (10) in the form of phonons and clusters that are averaged on ensemble of the casual states defined by Hamiltonian (9). The representation of own functions of this Hamiltonian by flat waves with $k = |\vec{k}| < 1$ is a good approximation for the impurity content far from the saturation of liquid alloy.

For dilute solutions ($x << 1$), one can restrict the proper-energetic functions (19), (24), (27), (28) by the second degree of k and present the propagators (18), (22), (26), (30) in the form [10].

$$\left.\begin{aligned} G^0_{\vec{k}}(\varphi) &= \left(a^0 + b^0k^2\right)^{-1} \\ G_{\vec{k}}(\varphi) &= \left(a + bk^2\right)^{-1} \\ G^0_{\vec{k}}(\chi) &= \left(u^0 + v^0k^2\right)^{-1} \\ G_{\vec{k}}(\chi) &= \left(u + vk^2\right)^{-1} \end{aligned}\right| \tag{31}$$

At such restriction, it is easy to find all the proper energetic functions. For this, we will substitute (31) into (24), (27), and (28) and transform these multiple integrals to the kind

$$I_{lm}(k) = \int_0^\infty \left(\sigma_l + \tau_l p^2\right)^{-1}\left(\sigma_m + \tau_m|\vec{k} - \vec{p}|^2\right)^{-1} d^3p/(2\pi)^3 = arctg\left(\frac{\Lambda_l\Lambda_m k}{\Lambda_l + \Lambda_m}\right)/4\pi\tau_l\tau_m k \tag{32}$$

where $\Lambda_l = \sqrt{\tau_l/\sigma_l}$. Under the condition of $k < 1/\Lambda_l + 1/\Lambda_m$, one can transform (32) into Taylor expansion on k up to the second member [10]:

$$I_{lm}(k) \cong \frac{\Lambda_l \Lambda_m}{4\pi\tau_l\tau_m(\Lambda_l + \Lambda_m)} \left[1 - \left(\frac{\Lambda_l \Lambda_m}{\Lambda_l + \Lambda_m}\right)^2 \frac{k^2}{3}\right] \quad (33)$$

Substituting (33) into (19), (24), (27), and (28), we will obtain

$$\Sigma_0(k) = \frac{a_0^5}{64\pi b_0^3}\left(1 - \frac{b_0^2 k^2}{12 a_0^2}\right) \quad (34)$$

$$\Sigma_1(k) = \frac{x^2}{4\pi v^0}\left[\frac{\lambda^2}{b^0\left(\sqrt{\frac{a^0}{b^0}} + \sqrt{\frac{u^0}{v^0}}\right)} + \frac{x^2(1-\alpha_1)^2}{16\sqrt{u^0 v^0}}\right] - \frac{x^2 k^2}{12\pi v^0}\left[\frac{\lambda^2}{b^0\left(\sqrt{\frac{a^0}{b^0}} + \sqrt{\frac{u^0}{v^0}}\right)^3} + \frac{x^2 v^0 (1-\alpha_1)^2}{64\sqrt{(u^0)^3 v^0}}\right] \quad (35)$$

$$\Pi_1(k) = \frac{\lambda^2}{64\pi\sqrt{ab^3}}\left(1 - \frac{bk^2}{12a}\right) \quad (36)$$

$$\Pi_2(k) = \frac{x^2(1-\alpha_1)^2}{4\pi b v^0\left(\sqrt{\frac{a}{b}} + \sqrt{\frac{u^0}{v^0}}\right)}\left(1 - \frac{k^2}{3\left(\sqrt{\frac{a}{b}} + \sqrt{\frac{u^0}{v^0}}\right)^2}\right) \quad (37)$$

Now using formulas (18), (31), and (34), we will obtain

$$\left.\begin{aligned} a^0 &= a_0^2\left(1 - \frac{(a_0/b_0)^3}{64\pi}\right) \\ b^0 &= b_0^2\left(1 + \frac{(a_0/b_0)^3}{768\pi}\right) \end{aligned}\right| \quad (38)$$

The parameters (u^0, v^0) can be obtained by means of (22), (31), (36), and the comment to (27)

$$\left.\begin{aligned} u^0 &= c - \frac{\lambda^2}{64\pi\sqrt{ab^3}} \\ v^0 &= x(\alpha_2 - \alpha_1^2) + \frac{\lambda^2}{768\pi\sqrt{a^3 b}} \end{aligned}\right| \quad (39)$$

At last, the mutual solution of (26) and (30) gives the parameters of "dressed" phonon and cluster propagators, $G_{\vec{k}}(\varphi)$ and $G_{\vec{k}}(\chi)$:

$$\left.\begin{aligned} a &= a^0 - \frac{x^2}{4\pi v^0}\left(\frac{\lambda^2/b^0}{\left(\sqrt{\frac{a^0}{b^0}} + \sqrt{\frac{u^0}{v^0}}\right)} + \frac{x^2(1-\alpha_1)^2}{16\sqrt{u^0 v^0}}\right) \\ b &= b^0 + \frac{x^2}{12\pi v^0}\left(\frac{\lambda^2/b^0}{\left(\sqrt{\frac{a^0}{b^0}} + \sqrt{\frac{u^0}{v^0}}\right)^3} + \frac{x^2(1-\alpha_1)^2}{64\sqrt{(u^0)^3/v^0}}\right) \end{aligned}\right| \quad (40)$$

http://dx.doi.org/10.5772/intechopen.70459

$$\left.\begin{aligned} u &= u^0 - \frac{x^2(1-\alpha_1)^2}{4\pi b v^0\left(\sqrt{\frac{a}{b}} + \sqrt{\frac{u^0}{v^0}}\right)} \\ v &= v^0 + \frac{x^2(1-\alpha_1)^2}{12\pi b v^0\left(\sqrt{\frac{a}{b}} + \sqrt{\frac{u^0}{v^0}}\right)^3} \end{aligned}\right| \tag{41}$$

It means that the renormalization procedure of the model (9) parameters carries out isomorphic transformation of weak-interacting fields of TPO and CPO into the ensemble of free "dressed" phonons and clusters with Hamiltonian

$$\Delta F(\varphi,\chi) = nK_{11}\sqrt{K_{11}/\beta T} \int\limits_{V\left(\frac{\beta T}{K_{11}}\right)^{3/2}} d^3\rho\left[\frac{a}{2}\varphi^2 + \frac{b}{2}\left(\vec{\nabla}\varphi\right)^2 + x\left(\frac{u}{2}\chi^2 + \frac{v}{2}\left(\vec{\nabla}\chi\right)^2\right)\right] \tag{42}$$

under the condition $a > 0$ and $u > 0$. In this representation, the correlation functions for TPO and CPO functions look like:

$$\left.\begin{aligned} G_\varphi(\rho) &= \left(\frac{\beta T}{K_{11}}\right)^{3/2} \frac{\exp\left(-\frac{\rho}{\Lambda_\varphi}\right)}{4\pi\beta\rho n b} \\ G_\chi(\rho) &= \left(\frac{\beta T}{K_{11}}\right)^{3/2} \frac{\exp\left(-\frac{\rho}{\Lambda_\chi}\right)}{4\pi\beta\rho n v} \end{aligned}\right| \tag{43}$$

where $\Lambda_\varphi = \sqrt{b/a}$ and $\Lambda_\chi = \sqrt{v/u}$. It is easy to see that $G_i(\rho) \propto \rho^{-1}$ at $\rho < \Lambda_i$, and this function exponentially works for zero, when $\rho > \Lambda_i$.

It is clear that the Eq. (40) is obtained under the condition: $k < 1/\Lambda_\varphi^0 = \sqrt{a^0/b^0}$, that is equivalent to $|\vec{\rho}| > \Lambda_\varphi^0$, that is, the relation, $G_\varphi\left(\vec{\rho}\right) \sim |\vec{\rho}|^{-1}$, is valid for the interval, $\Lambda_\varphi^0 < |\vec{\rho}| < \Lambda_\varphi$.

Under the condition: $|\vec{\rho}| < \Lambda_\varphi^0$, it is necessary to replace the correlator, $G_{\vec{k}}(\varphi)$, by the "bare" propagator, $G_{\vec{k}}^0(\varphi)$, with the parameters (39).

Thus, the TPO fluctuations in the liquid alloy are characterized by various behaviors in small and large scales in comparison with Λ_φ^0. In the case of $|\vec{\rho}| < \Lambda_\varphi^0$, density fluctuations of liquid do not feel impurities. When $\Lambda_\varphi^0 < |\vec{\rho}| < \Lambda_\varphi$, the liquid matrix is inhomogeneous in the form of impurity colloids, and for $|\vec{\rho}| > \Lambda_\varphi$, such heterogeneity is not observed at all [10].

5. Stratification of impurity by density fluctuations of liquid alloy

The structural modification of the liquid alloy at varying the system parameters $(x, \alpha_1, \alpha_2, \beta)$ is characterized by changing the correlation radii Λ_ϕ and Λ_χ of Green functions (43). They define the characteristic ranges of observed TPO and CPO fluctuations [8]. Therefore, the concentration dependence, $\Lambda_i(x)$, is interested to consider for different $(x, \alpha_1, \alpha_2, \beta)$ of the model (9). At the same time, one should remember that this model is applied only in Taylor expansion (2) of $f(\Delta_i, \vec{\nabla}\Delta_i)$ under the conditions [11]: $x < 1/4|1 + (\alpha_i - 1)\beta|$ and $\langle |i|^2 \rangle_{\Lambda_i} << 1$ that are reduced to: $\sqrt{b^3/a}$, $\sqrt{v^3/u} >> (e-2)\sqrt{\beta(T/2z|J_{11}|)^3/e(1+z)}$ [10].

The solutions of Eqs. (38)–(41) obtained under these conditions are illustrated in **Figures 1–4** by the graphs of functions, $\Lambda_\varphi(x)$ and $\Lambda_\chi(x)$, in logarithmic coordinates for the ranges: $0.095 < \alpha_1^2 < \alpha_2 \leq 1.4$ and $10 \leq \beta \leq 150$. The last one characterizes liquid metals where the alloy components have a tendency for demixing at $\alpha_1^2 < \alpha_2$ in contrast to clustering at $\alpha_1^2 > \alpha_2$. The structural features of such alloy are discussed below.

One can see that the correlation radius of phonons (Λ_ϕ) is practically not changed with growing the impurity concentration as opposed to the correlation radius of impurity demixing (Λ_χ) which increases: the higher values of α_i at $\alpha_1^2 < \alpha_2$, the more is. At the same time, increasing β partially decreases this effect (compare **Figures 3** and **4**) [10].

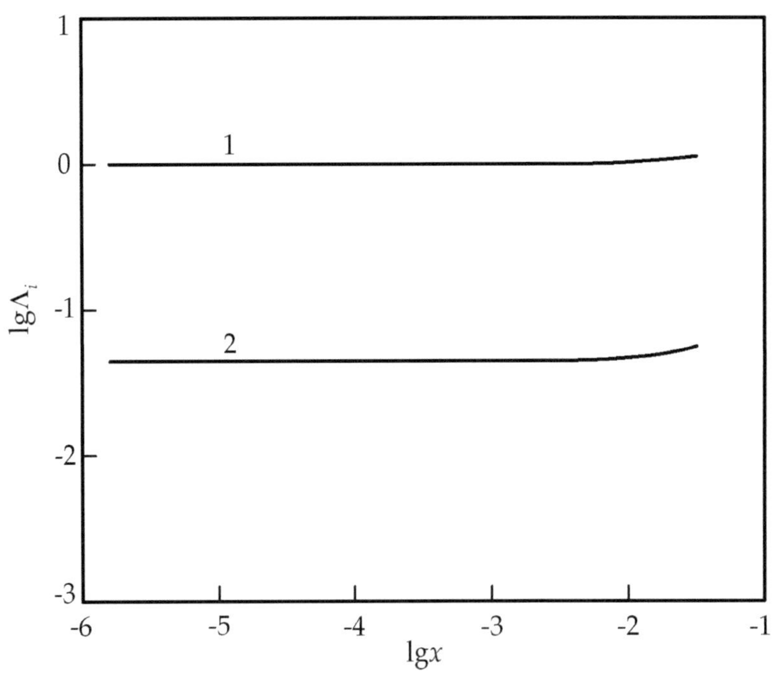

Figure 1. The graphs of lg $\Lambda_\varphi(1)$ and lg $\Lambda_\chi(2)$ as functions of the impurity concentration, lg$x$, at $\alpha_1 = 0.31$, $\alpha_2 = 0.1$, and $\beta = 10$.

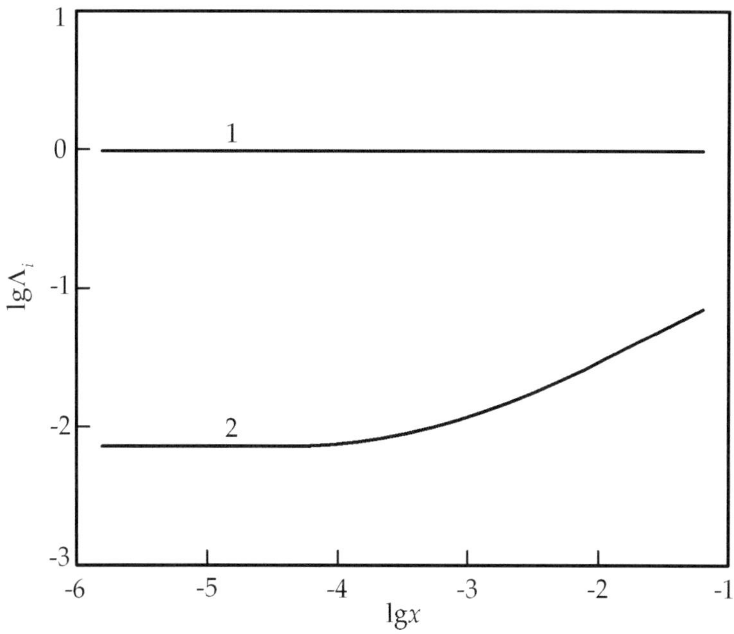

Figure 2. The graphs of lg $\Lambda_{\varphi}(1)$ and lg $\Lambda_{\chi}(2)$ as functions of the impurity concentration, lg$x$, at $\alpha_1 = 0.89$, $\alpha_2 = 0.8$, and $\beta = 10$.

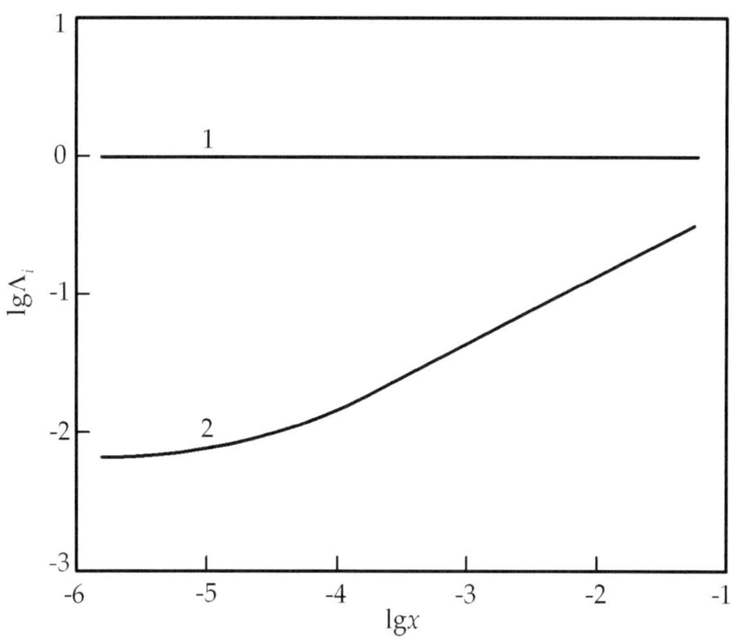

Figure 3. The graphs of lg $\Lambda_{\varphi}(1)$ and lg $\Lambda_{\chi}(2)$ as functions of the impurity concentration, lg$x$, at $\alpha_1 = 1.1$, $\alpha_2 = 1.4$, and $\beta = 10$.

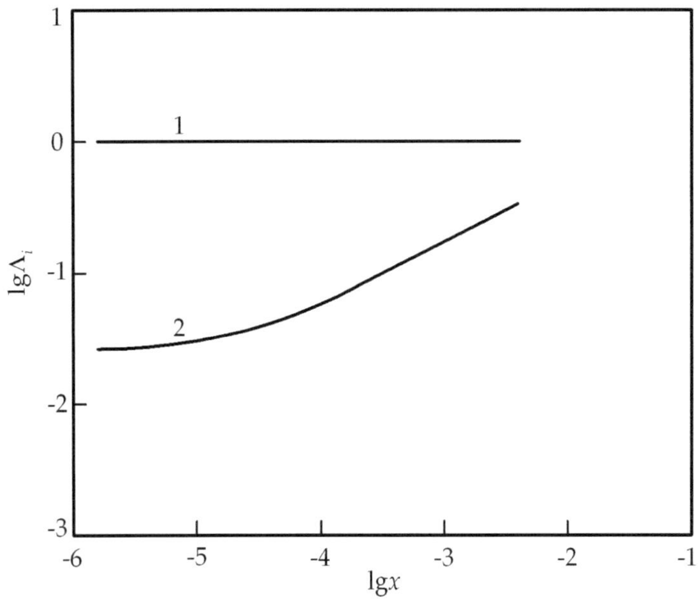

Figure 4. The graphs of lg $\Lambda_\varphi(1)$ and lg $\Lambda_\chi(2)$ as functions of the impurity concentration, lg$x$, at $\alpha_1 = 1.1$, $\alpha_2 = 1.4$, and $\beta = 150$.

6. Impurity clustering induced by alloy density fluctuations

At $\alpha_1^2 > \alpha_2$, the graphs of lg $\Lambda_\phi(x)$ and lg $\Lambda_\chi(x)$ are shown in **Figures 5–8** for $\alpha_1 = 0.6$, $\alpha_2 = 0.3$, and for four values of β in the range of 10–150.

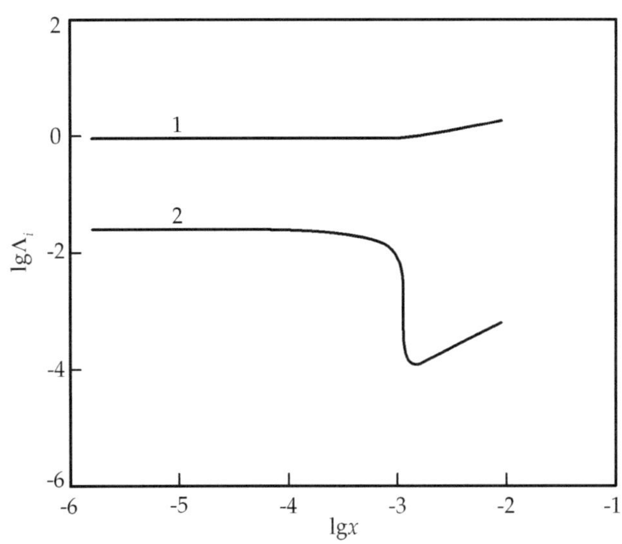

Figure 5. The graphs of lg $\Lambda_\varphi(1)$ and lg $\Lambda_\chi(2)$ as functions of the impurity concentration, lg$x$, at $\alpha_1 = 0.6$, $\alpha_2 = 0.3$, and $\beta = 10$.

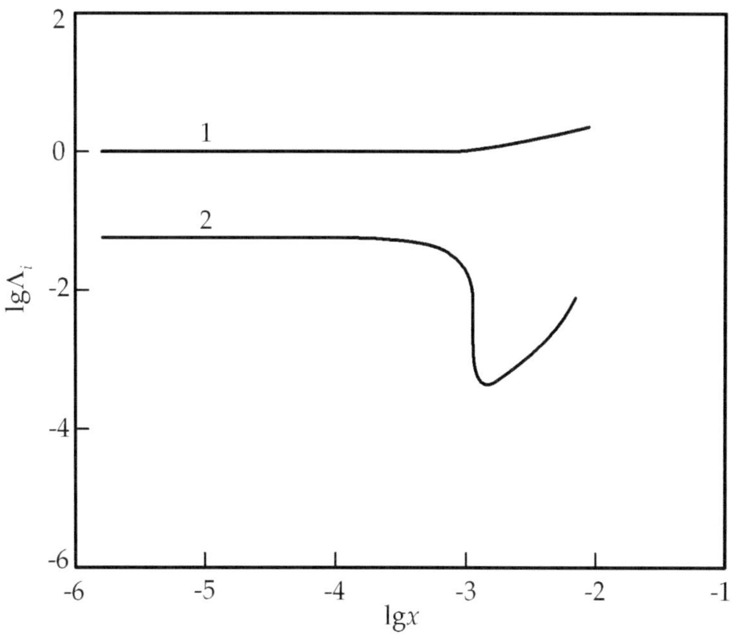

Figure 6. The graphs of lg $\Lambda_\varphi(1)$ and lg $\Lambda_\chi(2)$ as functions of the impurity concentration, lg$x$, at $\alpha_1 = 0.6$, $\alpha_2 = 0.3$, and $\beta = 50$.

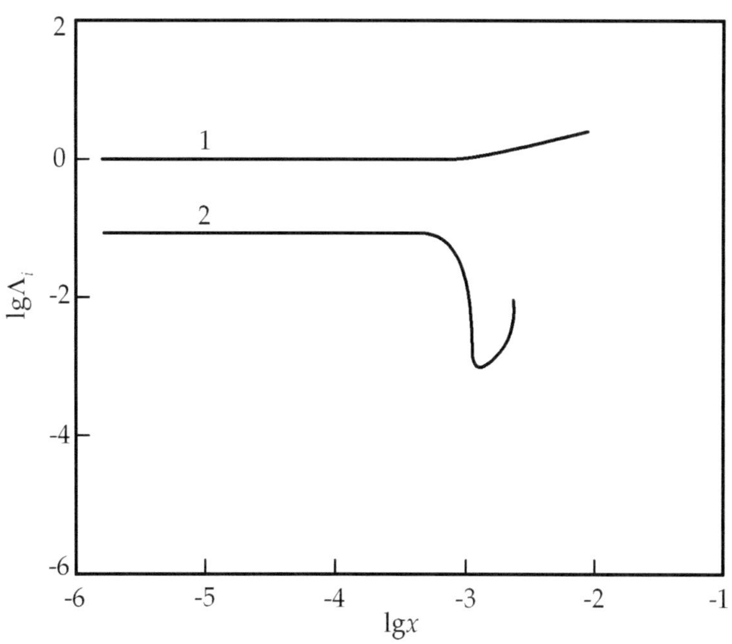

Figure 7. The graphs of lg $\Lambda_\varphi(1)$ and lg $\Lambda_\chi(2)$ as functions of the impurity concentration, lg$x$, at $\alpha_1 = 0.6$, $\alpha_2 = 0.3$, and $\beta = 100$.

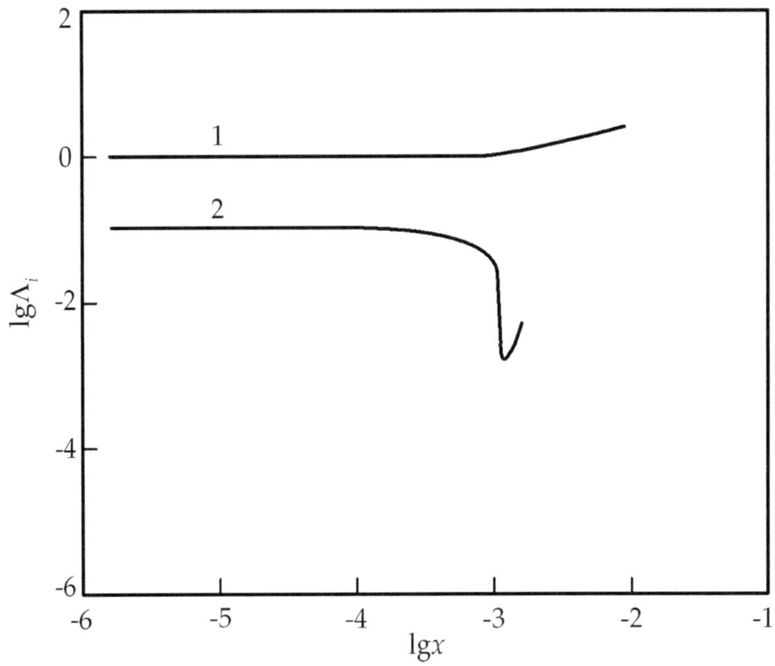

Figure 8. The graphs of lg $\Lambda_\varphi(1)$ and lg $\Lambda_\chi(2)$ as functions of the impurity concentration, lg$x$, at $\alpha_1 = 0.6$, $\alpha_2 = 0.3$, and $\beta = 150$.

It turned out that Λ_χ decreases sharply at some critical point, x_c. This indicates the decay of CPO fluctuations of double alloy into compound clusters on the background of long-wave density fluctuations of liquid. One can see that the range of impurity concentration of clusters existence decreases with growing the rigidity, β, of condensed matter.

At the same time, x_c does not practically change because this point is defined by the value of $\alpha_1^2 - \alpha_2$ which is constant. The following sharp increase of the CPO correlation radius (see **Figures 7** and **8**) is interpreted as aggregation of clusters [10]. The observed growing of TPO correlation radius, $\Lambda_\phi(x)$, can be caused by impurity precipitations that do more lengthy the density fluctuations.

7. Conclusions

According to the two-parametric model represented above, density fluctuations of liquid induce mono-ordering impurity in micro-regions at $\alpha_1^2 < \alpha_2$ (see **Figures 2–4**) and its clustering with basic component at $\alpha_1^2 > \alpha_2$ (see **Figures 5–8**). Such self-organization of liquid alloy has no thermodynamic singularities of the first-order phase transition because it has continuous character without the potential jump and concerns only to change the impurity state in liquid alloy, that is, it is interpreted as a component phase transition of the first order [15].

The scale of this transition increases with growing the concentration and bond force of impurity particles and it decreases with growing the rigidity of condensed matter inclined to stratification of components ($\alpha_1^2 < \alpha_2$). For opposite components inclined to clustering ($\alpha_1^2 > \alpha_2$), the composition fluctuations of double alloy decay to local states in the form of quasi-molecular fluctuations.

By renormalizing parameters of this model, we have transformed weakly interacting fluctuations to free "dressed" phonons and clusters whose autocorrelation functions are characterized by various behaviors in small and large scales in comparison with the atomic spacing. In the first case, density fluctuations of liquid do not feel impurities. In the intermediate scale, the liquid matrix is inhomogeneous in the form of colloids, which is not observed at the large scales. Dynamics of such liquid is characterized by diffusion modes of solvent and oscillations of impurities.

At the same time, any liquid can be composed from two structures. The first of them represents finite and ramified clusters from almost tetrahedrons having common faces in pairs. The second is locally less dense which includes micropores as elements of free volume of liquid.

Acknowledgements

The author thanks the colleagues for helping in this work and for useful discussion of the approach to forced modification of liquids by density fluctuations.

Author details

Alexander Shimkevich

Address all correspondence to: shimkevich_al@nrcki.ru

NRC Kurchatov Institute, Moscow, Russia

References

[1] Waseda Y. The Structure of Non-crystalline Materials: Liquids and Amorphous Solids. New York: McGraw-Hill; 1980. 326 p

[2] Bernal JD. The structure of liquids. Proceedings of Royal Society. 1964;**280A**:299-311

[3] Kolokol AS, Shimkevich AL. Topological structure of liquid metals. Atomic Energy. 2005;**98**:197-203

[4] Kolokol AS, Shimkevich AL. Topological structure of density fluctuations in condensed matter. Journal of Non-Crystalline Solids. 2010;**356**:220-223

[5] Kovalev YuS et al. The microstructure of Pb–K liquid alloy from small-angle neutron scattering experiments. Journal of Non-Crystalline Solids. 2007;**353**:3532-3541

[6] Kolokol AS et al. On composition converting liquid metal alloys. Journal of Physics: Conference Series. 2008;**98**:042021-5

[7] Shimkevich AL. The Composition Principles for Designing Nuclear-reactor Materials. N.N. Ponomarev-Stepnoi Edition. Moscow: IzdAt; 2008. 127 p

[8] Potashinsky AZ, Pokrovsky VL. The Fluctuation Theory of Phase Transitions. Moscow: Nauka; 1982. 381 p

[9] Landau LD. To theory of phase transitions. Collected Papers. Moscow: Nauka. 1969;**1**:234-252

[10] Shimkevich AL. The fluctuation theory of impurity micro-heterogeneity of liquid-metal coolants. Proceedings of the high school. Nuclear Power. 1999;**3**:6-16

[11] Landau LD, Lifshitz EM. The theoretical physics. Statistical Physics. Moscow: Nauka. 1976;**5**:583

[12] Lifshitz EM, Pitaevsky LP. The theoretical physics. Statistical Physics. Moscow: Nauka. 1978;**9**:477

[13] Royen RP. Scaling behaviour of second-order phase transitions. Physical Review B. 1976;**13**:4079-4092

[14] Chew GF. The Analytic S-Matrix. A Basis for Nuclear Democracy. New-York-Amsterdam: WA Benjamin; 1966. 103 p

[15] Ivanovsky MN, Morozov VA, Ponomarev-Stepnoi NN, Shimkevich AL. On the first-order component phase transition. Atomic Energy. 1988;**65**:319-321

Chapter 4

Chaos-Based Communication Systems

Nizar Al Bassam and Amer Zayegh

Additional information is available at the end of the chapter

http://dx.doi.org/10.5772/intechopen.71447

Abstract

The attractive properties of chaos signal that is generated from dynamic systems motivate the researchers to explore the advantage of using this signal type as a carrier in different communication systems. In this chapter, different types of digital chaos–based communication system are discussed; in particular, digital communications where reference signal and its modulated version are transmitted together. This type is called differential coherent systems. Brief surveys on the recently developed systems are presented.

Keywords: chaos, coherent systems, non-coherent systems, differentially coherent systems, DCSK, CDSK, HE-DCSK, TR-DCSK, EF-DCSK

1. Introduction

In digital communication systems, sinusoidal carriers with high frequency are used to carry information by modulation process where these carriers are deterministic with constant power over the time of transmission. Another proposed type of carriers is currently analyzed and is called chaotic. The chaotic signal is non-periodic, random-like, with low cross-correlation and impulse-like auto correlation. It is derived from dynamical systems, particularly from the independent state variables. The instantaneous value is often bounded between two constant peaks determined by the trajectory of the generated maps. To simplify the description of chaotic signal generation, let us consider the discrete time presentation for the iterative equation, that is, $x_n = f(x_{n-1}, u)$ where x_n is output vector of the state variable sampled at nth instant, $f(x_{n-1})$ is the iterative function determined by the map, finally μ is the parameter which controls the behavior of the chaotic function.

In chaos-based digital communications, bits are mapped to actual non-periodic output of chaotic circuits and the sample function for a given symbol is non-periodic and different from one bit to another [1]. Sample of chaos-based signal for symmetric tent map is shown in **Figure 1**.

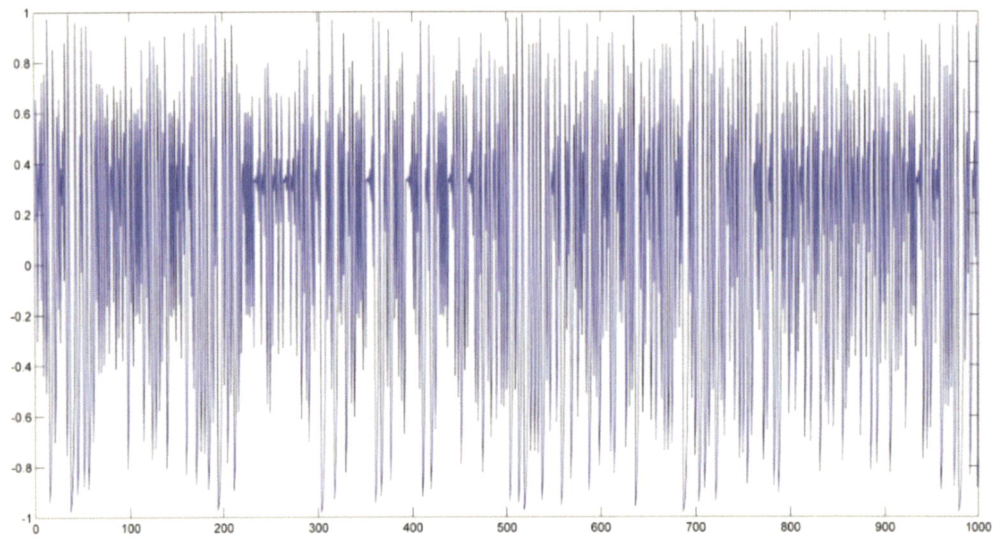

Figure 1. Chaotic signal generated by symmetric tent map.

Based on the previous discussion, receivers of digital chaotic communication systems can be broadly classified according to the receiver structures such as coherent, non-coherent and differentially coherent systems [2].

2. Types of chaos-based digital communication systems

2.1. Coherent systems

In coherent systems, a local synchronized copy of each sample function has to be produced at the receiver. When the transmitted signal is corrupted by the random noise, it will be challenging to synchronize the local generated carrier with that in the transmitters as in coherent shift keying (CSK) [1]. The idea of CSK is to map each information bit to chaos bases signal say f1 and f2. If "+1" is to be sent, then chaos signal from generator f1 is to be transmitted with one bit duration, and if "−1" is to be sent, chaos signal from generator f2 is transmitted with same bit duration. The receiver should generate exact copy from f1 and f2 to recover the information. This is done by using dedicated synchronization circuits [3].

2.2. Non-coherent systems

This type of chaos receivers offers simple solution for synchronization problem by estimating one unique parameter such as power. This is achieved by multiplying and integrating the product of received sample signal with itself to estimate the signal energy. Chaos ON OFF keying (COOK) and non-coherent chaos shift keying are a practical implementation of this idea [4]. In COOK, the signal is transmitted within bit duration only if information "+1" is to be transmitted. Otherwise, no transmission is taken place at "−1" bit duration. A bit control switch is used to control the emission of signal at the transmitter output. However, obtaining an optimum threshold to distinguish between signal sets does not depend only on signal power at the correlator output but also on the noise power estimation that is the major drawback of such systems [1].

2.3. Differentially coherent systems

Another scheme is developed where a reference signal is followed by another reference signal modulated by the information bit and called information carrying signal. This arrangement is known as differentially coherent systems. Here, every bit is presented by two sample functions. In the case of bit 1 transmission, the information is sent by transmitting two identical sample functions. For bit 0, the reference signal is transmitted and followed by an inverted copy of the sample function. General structure of the receiver is based on how to correlate the reference signal with information bearing signal.

Differentially coherent systems show better bit error rate (BER) performance among other existing chaos-based systems and in different channel conditions [5]. In spite of some structure complexity, hardware design is studied and tested.

In this chapter, standard differentially coherent schemes are described and tested by computer simulations, analytical expression to estimate BER in additive white Gaussian channel is obtained using Gaussian approximation method [6, 7]. A brief description of recently developed system is discussed.

3. Differential coherent systems

3.1. Differential chaos shift keying

Differential chaos shift keying (DCSK) transmitter structure is shown in **Figure 1**. Each information bit is represented by twin of successive chaotic signal slots with length of samples, where $2M$ represents the spreading factor. First time slot contains a reference signal and second slot contains the information bearing signal. That is simply a delayed version of the reference signal multiplied by the information bit. Thus, the instantaneous value of the transmitted signal at any instant can be written as

$$S_i = \begin{cases} x_i & 0 < i \le M \\ b\, x_{i-M} & M < i \le 2M \end{cases} \tag{1}$$

Average bit energy for a single bit can be given by:

$$E_b = 2MV(x_i) \tag{2}$$

where $V(.)$ is the variance operator.

There are many chaotic maps which can be used as a signal source [1, 8]. However, symmetric tent map is selected to produce the chaotic signal due to its simplicity. Its discrete form is given by the equation $x_{n+1} = 1 - 2|x_n|$ where x is uniformly distributed between 1 and -1. It can be easily shown that $E(x) = 0$, $V(x) = \frac{1}{3}$ and $V(x^2) = \frac{4}{45}$ [1] where $E(.)$ represents the average operator [6, 9, 10].

Received signal sample $r_i = s_i + \zeta_i$ is received via noisy channel characterized by Gaussian distribution where noise sample ζ_i is stationary random process with$E(\zeta) = 0$ and its power spectral density given by $V(\zeta) = \frac{N_o}{2}$. The received sample is multiplied by its delayed version r_{i-M} and the multiplication output is integrated over half bit duration M. Assuming that synchronization is achieved perfectly at the DCSK receiver shown in **Figure 3**. Then, the correlator output Z_{DCSK} at the end of bit duration can be described.

$$\begin{aligned} Z_{DCSK} &= \sum_{i=1}^{M} r_i r_{i-M} = \sum_{i=1}^{M} (S_i + \zeta_i)(S_{i-M} + \zeta_{i-M}) \\ &= b\sum_{i=1}^{M} x_i^2 + \sum_{i=1}^{M} x_i(\zeta_{i-M} + b\zeta_i) + \sum_{i=1}^{M} \zeta_i \zeta_{i-M} \end{aligned} \tag{3}$$

Average value of the correlator output can be determined by the value of information bit in the first term, while other terms will have mean value of zero due to their statistical independence [1, 6, 9, 11]. The correlator output is passed to the detector with zero threshold value to minimize BER as described in (4).

$$\tilde{b} = \begin{cases} 1 & Z_{DCSK} \geq 0 \\ -1 & Z_{DCSK} < 0 \end{cases} \tag{4}$$

As the chaotic signal x is stationary and x_i is statistically independent from ζ_j at any(i, j), correlator output Z_{DCSK} tends to have Gaussian distribution at sufficient value of M. Therefore, BER analytical evaluation of DCSK is obtained by calculating the means and variances of conditional probability of $P(Z_{DCSK}|\, b = 1)$ and $P(Z_{DCSK}|\, b = -1)$, respectively; then theoretical estimate of BER can be calculated as (5)

$$BER_{DCSK} = \frac{1}{2}\mathrm{erfc}\left(\sqrt{\frac{E_b}{4N_o}\left(1 + \frac{2}{5M}\frac{E_b}{N_o} + \frac{N_0}{2E_b}M\right)^{-1}}\right) \tag{5}$$

where $\mathrm{erfc}(y) = \frac{2}{\sqrt{\pi}}\int_y^{\infty} e^{-\frac{t^2}{2}} dt$.

Two major drawbacks of DCSK systems are as follows: (1) data rate is reduced by half because of the need of separate reference signal and (2) a technical issue can be generated from continuous change of switch position in **Figure 2**.

3.2. CDSK

Sending reference signal and information bearing signals in separate time slot will result in data rate reduction by half. Instead, orthogonality between each chaotic signal and its delayed

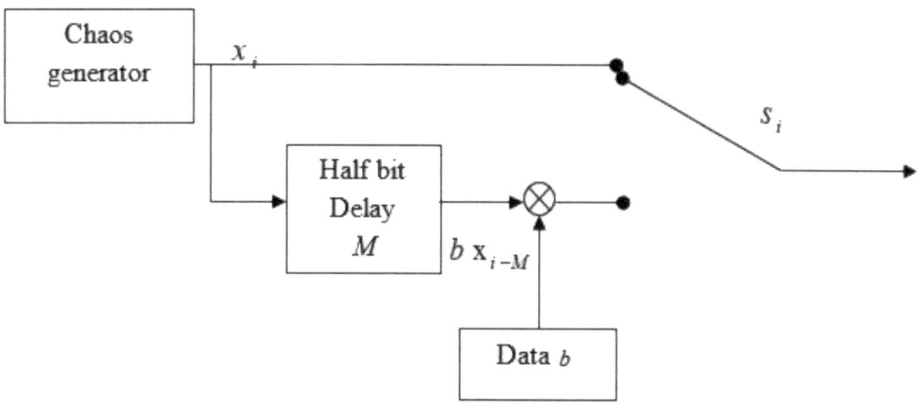

Figure 2. DCSK transmitter.

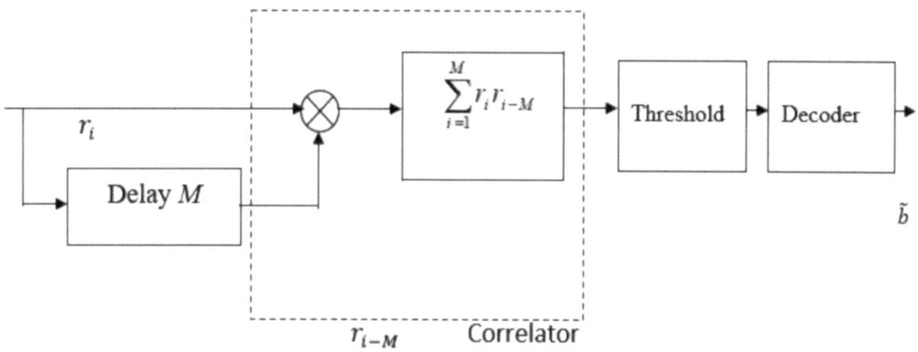

Figure 3. DCSK receiver.

version can be utilized efficiently by adding the generated chaotic signal with the modulated version of the previous signal. This scheme is known as correlation delay shift keying (CDSK) [6]. Information bit is sent by transmitting a signal as the sum of a chaotic sequence x_i and of the delayed chaotic sequence multiplied by the information signal $b_l x_{i-L}$, where l is the bit counter and L is the amount of sequence to be delayed. Hence, the transmitted signal of CDSK at any instant i is given by

$$s_i = x_i + b_l x_{i\_L} \qquad (l-1)M < i \leq lM \tag{6}$$

where $L \geq M$ and $E_b = 2MV(x)$.

Compared with structure of DCSK, structure of CDSK transmitter is characterized by replacing the switch by an adder as illustrated in **Figure 4**. Data rate is doubled when compared with DCSK because of reference time slot utilization [6]. Putting delay $L = M$, then the receiver of CDSK is similar to that DCSK and each received sample r_i segment is correlated with the previous one r_{i-M}. Hence, correlator output Z_{CDSK} can be computed as

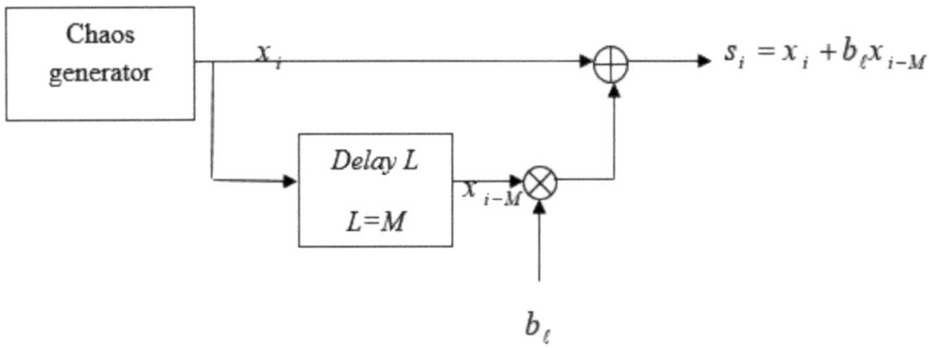

Figure 4. CDSK transmitter.

$$\begin{aligned} Z_{CDSK} &= \sum_{i=1}^{M} r_i r_{i-M} \\ &= \sum_{i=1}^{M} (x_i + b_l x_{i-M} + \zeta_i)(x_{i-M} + b_l x_{i-2M} + \zeta_{i-M}) \\ &= b_l \sum_{i=1}^{M} x_{i-M}^2 + \sum_{i=1}^{M} x_i x_{i-M} + b_{l-M} \sum_{i}^{M} x_i x_{i-2M} + \sum_{i=1}^{M} x_i \zeta_{i-M} + b_l b_{l-M} \sum_{i=1}^{m} x_{i-M} x_{i-2M} \\ &+ b_l \sum_{i=1}^{M} x_{i-M} \zeta_{i-M} + \sum_{i=1}^{M} x_{i-M} \zeta_i + b_{l-M} \sum_{i=1}^{M} x_{i-2M} \zeta_i + \sum_{i=1}^{M} \zeta_i \zeta_{i-M} \end{aligned} \tag{7}$$

It can be clearly observed that the correlator output Z_{CDSK} contains more intra-signal and noise terms compared to DCSK. Hence, BER performance is expected to be lower. The cross terms in (7) is statistically independent and Z_{CDSK} tends to have Gaussian distribution at sufficient value of M. Theoretical value of BER can be found by calculating the mean and variance of Z_{CDSK} when the transmitted bit is +1 and -1, respectively. Decoding is performed according to the same rule in (4) and BER is given by [6].

$$BER_{CDSK} = \frac{1}{2}\operatorname{erfc}\left(\sqrt{\frac{E_b}{8N_o}\left(1 + \frac{19}{20M}\frac{E_b}{N_o} + \frac{N_0}{4E_b}M\right)^{-1}}\right) \tag{8}$$

3.3. High efficiency-differential chaos shift keying (HE-DCSK)

To enhance the bandwidth efficiency of DCSK and CDSK, a pair of information bits can be modulated using same reference signal by reusing each reference signal twice [9]. First, reference signal is modulated with information bit after delay of M sequence as a standard DCSK. Second, information bit is modulated after the delay of *3 M*. Both modulated segments are added together in the second time slot. The scheme is illustrated in **Figure 5**. Thus, transmitted signal which is emitted from HE-DCSK transmitter can be written as:

$$S_i = \begin{cases} x_i & 2kM < i \le (2k+1)M \\ b_{2k} x_{i\_M} + b_{2k-1} x_{i-3M} & (2K+1)M < i \le (2K+1)M \end{cases} \tag{9}$$

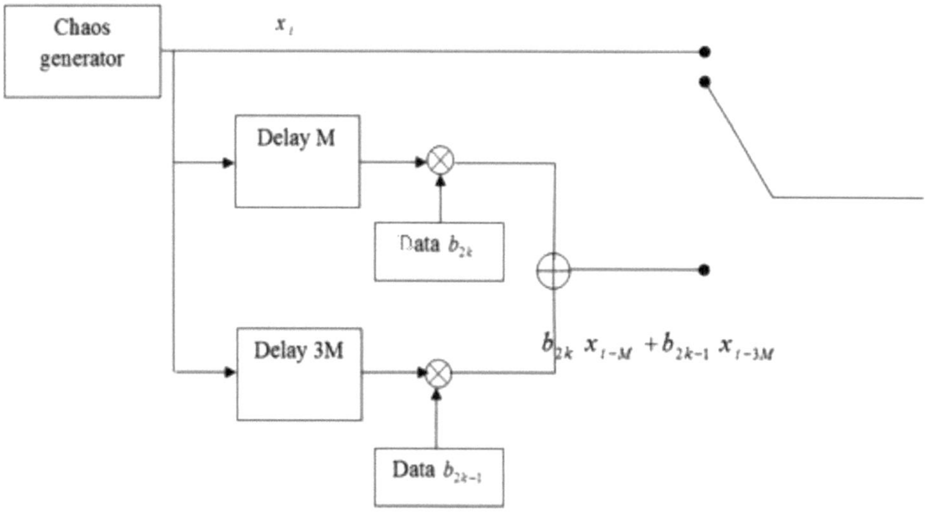

Figure 5. HE-DCSK transmitter diagram.

where k is the pair sequence number. Signal is received through AWGN where each received signal is delayed and correlated twice, first, after M samples delay and second, after $3M$ as shown in **Figure 6**. The scheme represents an extended version of DCSK receiver, therefore the output of first modulator Z_l can be given by:

$$\begin{aligned} Z_1 &= \sum_{i=1}^{M} r_i r_{i-M} = \sum_{i=1}^{M} (S_i + \zeta_i)(S_{i-M} + \zeta_{i-M}) = \sum_{i=1}^{M} (x_{i-M} + \zeta_i)(b_{2k}x_{i-M} + b_{2k-1}x_{i-3M} + \zeta_i) \\ &= b_{2k}\sum_{i=1}^{M} x_{i-M}^2 + b_{2k-1}\sum_{i=1}^{M} x_{i-M}x_{i-3M} + b_{2K}\sum_{i=1}^{M} x_{i-M}\zeta_{i-M} + b_{2K-1}\sum_{i=1}^{M} x_{i-3M}\zeta_{i-M} + \sum_{i=1}^{M} x_{i-M}\zeta_i + \sum_{i=1}^{M} \zeta_i\zeta_{i-M} \end{aligned} \tag{10}$$

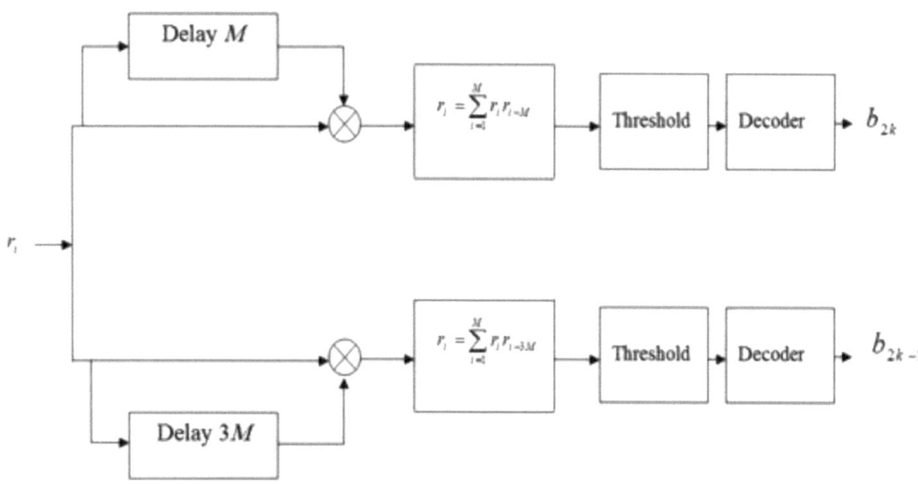

Figure 6. HE-DCSK receiver diagram.

Similarly, Z_2 can be calculated by $Z_2 = \sum_{i=1}^{M} r_i r_{i-3M}$. Average value of the first term in (10) contains the useful signal energy while the remaining terms are having zero mean. Information recovery is performed by comparing Z_1 and $Z_2$with zero-based threshold defined by the following equation.

$$\tilde{b}_{2k} = \begin{cases} 1 & Z_1 \geq 0 \\ -1 & Z_1 < 0 \end{cases} \tag{11}$$

$$\tilde{b}_{2k-1} = \begin{cases} 1 & Z_2 \geq 0 \\ -1 & Z_2 < 0 \end{cases} \tag{12}$$

Both correlator output Z_1 and Z_2 exhibit Gaussian distribution. BER of any correlator can be given as [9]

$$BER_{HE-DCSK} = \frac{1}{2}\text{erfc}\left(\sqrt{\frac{E_b}{4N_o}\left(\frac{9}{8} + \frac{9}{10M}\frac{E_b}{N_o} + \frac{9}{32}\frac{N_o}{2E_b}M\right)^{-1}}\right) \tag{13}$$

3.4. Time reversal-differential chaos shift keying (TR-DCSK)

The system is initially proposed [12] and developed by Albassam [13]. In this scheme, reference signal is generated and added to its time-reversed version. Hence, no separate time slot for reference signal is needed. This will generate a symmetric signal around the middle of bit duration. First half is transmitted directly and the second half is modulated with information bit. Provided that M is spreading factor, transmitted signal can be given by

$$S_i = \begin{Bmatrix} x_i + x_{M-i+1} & 0 < i \leq \frac{M}{2} \\ b(x_i + x_{M-i+1}) & \frac{M}{2} < i \leq M \end{Bmatrix} \tag{14}$$

Transmitter block diagram is illustrated in **Figure 7**.

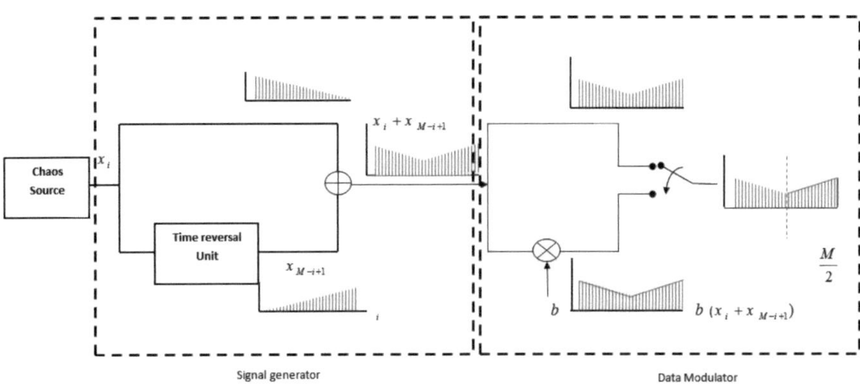

Figure 7. Time reversal DCSK transmitter.

Channel under investigation is AWGN and the received signal can be written as

$$r_i = \begin{cases} x_i + x_{M-i+1} + \zeta_i & 0 < i \le \frac{M}{2} \\ b(x_i + x_{M-i+1}) + \zeta_i & \frac{M}{2} < i \le M \end{cases} \tag{15}$$

At the receiver, each incoming noisy segment undergoes time reversal process. Hence, the output after the time reversal unit r_i' can be given as

$$r_i' = \begin{cases} b(x_{M-i+1} + x_i) + \zeta_{M-i+1} & 0 < i \le \frac{M}{2} \\ (x_i + x_{M-i+1}) + \zeta_{M-i+1} & \frac{M}{2} < i \le M \end{cases} \tag{16}$$

Perfect bit synchronization is assumed where each incoming signal r_i is correlated with time-reversed version r_i'. Due to signal symmetry, correlator output is integrated over the duration of $\frac{M}{2}$, which is twice as in DCSK and CDSK. This is to avoid the effect of redundant signal components in the second half (i.e., $> \frac{M}{2}$). The correlator output Z at the end of first bit duration can be given as

$$Z = \sum_{i=1}^{\frac{M}{2}} r_i r_i' = \sum_{i=1}^{\frac{M}{2}} (x_i + x_{M-i+1} + \zeta_i) b(x_{M-i+1} + x_i + \zeta_{M-i+1})$$

$$Z = b\sum_{i=1}^{\frac{M}{2}} x_i^2 + b\sum_{i=1}^{\frac{M}{2}} x_{M-i+1}^2 + 2b\sum_{i=1}^{\frac{M}{2}} x_i\, x_{M-i+1} + b\sum_{i=1}^{\frac{M}{2}} x_i\, \zeta_i + b\sum_{i=1}^{\frac{M}{2}} x_{M-i+1}\, \zeta_{M-i+1} + \sum_{i=1}^{\frac{M}{2}} x_i\, \zeta_{M-i+1} \tag{17}$$

$$+b\sum_{i=1}^{\frac{M}{2}} x_{M-i+1}\, \zeta_i + be\sum_{i=1}^{\frac{M}{2}} \zeta_{M-i+1}\zeta_i$$

Similarly, BER rate can be readily shown to have

$$BER_{TRDCSK} = \text{erfc}\left(\sqrt{\frac{E_b}{4N_o}\left(\frac{14}{10}\frac{E_b}{N_o} + 1 + \frac{M}{4}\frac{N_o}{E_b}\right)^{-1}} \right) \tag{18}$$

3.5. Energy efficient-differential chaos shift keying (EF-DCSK)

In all previous systems, each transmitted signal is composed of two separate segments such as reference signal and information bearing signal. A simplified system with minimum energy requirement is proposed in Ref. [14]. Simply, a chaos source generates a signal for one bit to be sent as a reference. Then, the transmitter will decide to send either same reference signal or newly generated one using a bit controlled switch as shown in **Figure 9**. For example, if information bit 1 is transmitted, delayed version of the reference signal is transmitted. Otherwise, the transmitter will generate a new signal. Therefore, each segment will play a dual role; one as information bearing signal at the time of bit generation and as a reference signal for the next bit duration. This eliminates the need for sending reference separately. Without loss of

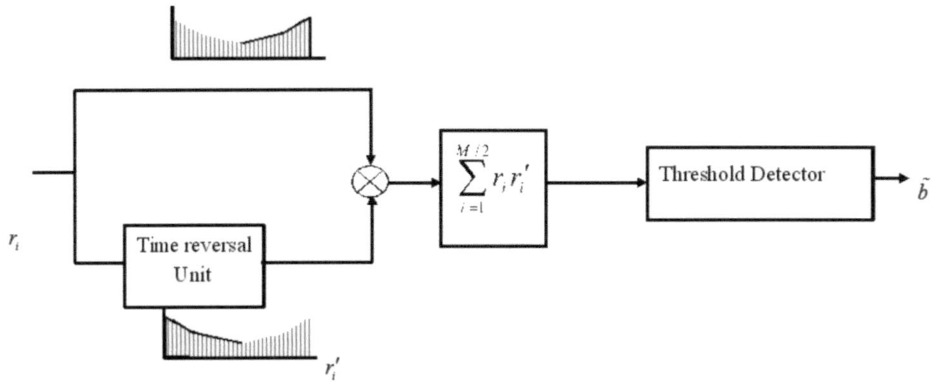

Figure 8. Time reversal DCSK receiver diagram.

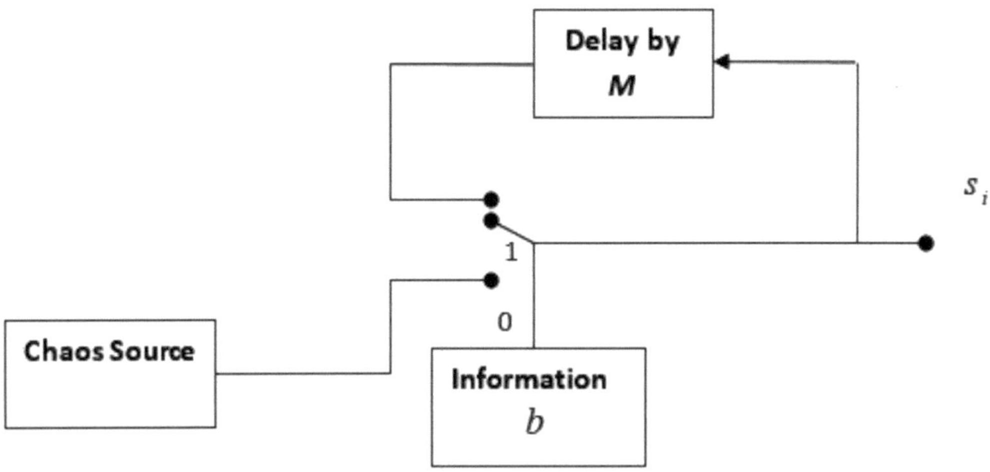

Figure 9. Energy efficient DCSK transmitter diagram.

generality, we will consider the analysis for the first bit b where $b \in \{1, 0\}$ and the transmitted signal S_i at the ith instant can be represented as

$$S_i = x_{i-bM} \tag{19}$$

The source emits M samples for each information bit in addition to the initial reference signal. Thus, the average bit energy transmitted can be found as.

$$E_b = \frac{l+1}{l} MVar(x^2) \approx MVar(x^2) \tag{20}$$

Information decoding is performed by correlating each incoming signal r_i with its delayed version and the correlation product is averaged over M. Information bit $\tilde{b}$ can be extracted by comparing correlator output with the predefined threshold as shown in **Figure 10**.

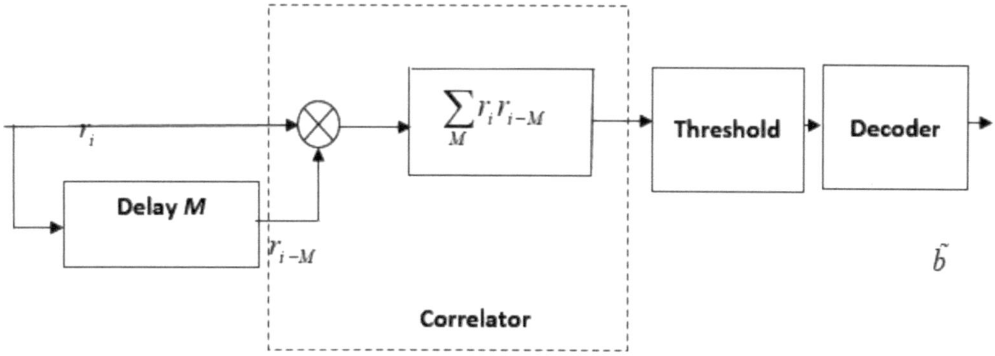

Figure 10. EF-CDSK receiver.

The received signal r_i can be described as $r_i = s_i + \zeta_i$ and the correlator output Z_{ef} can be formulated as

$$\begin{aligned} Z &= \sum_{i=1}^{M} r_i r_{i-M} = \sum_{i=1}^{M} (x_{i-bM} + \zeta_i)(x_{i-M}\zeta_{i-M}) \\ &= \sum_{i=1}^{M} (x_{i-bM} x_{i-M}) + \sum_{i=1}^{M} (x_{i-bM}\zeta_{i-M}) + \sum_{i=1}^{M} (x_{i-M}\zeta_i) + \sum_{i=1}^{M} (\zeta_i \zeta_{i-M}) \end{aligned} \tag{21}$$

Signal energy estimation can be obtained only by taking the mean value of first term in (7). Ideally, this will be either zero or $V_{ar(x)}$, all other terms are the zero mean. Obviously, it can be observed that the number of cross-terms of EF-CDSK correlator is less to that in CDSK. However, the distance between signal elements (average value of the correlator for each transmitted bit) is half compared to that in DCSK. Despite all that, the information can be decoded according to the following rule

$$\tilde{b} = \begin{cases} 1 & Z \geq \alpha_{th} \\ 0 & Z < \alpha_{th} \end{cases} \tag{22}$$

where α_{th} is the decoding threshold and it is given by $E_b/2$.

BER expression can be found by calculating mean and variance of the Gaussian distribution function of $P(Z | b = 1)$ and $P(Z | b = -1)$ and can be formulated as

$$\begin{aligned} BER_{EFCDSK} &= \frac{1}{2} \text{erfc}\left(\frac{E_b}{2\sqrt{2}\sqrt{\left(\frac{E_b^2}{M} + E_b N_o + \frac{M N_o^2}{4} \right)}} \right) \\ &= \frac{1}{2} \text{erfc}\left(\sqrt{\frac{E_b}{8N_o}\left(1 + \frac{1}{M}\frac{E_b}{N_o} + \frac{M}{4}\frac{N_o}{E_b} \right)} \right) \end{aligned} \tag{23}$$

4. Performance evaluation

A simulation result of BER for DCSK, CDSK, HE-DCSK and TR-DCSK schemes BER versus $\frac{E_b}{N_o}$ is presented in **Figures 11–14** with typical values of M, respectively. For all the systems, it can be clearly observed that BER performance is decreased by increment of spreading factor M. This is due to the nonlinear contribution of the last term in (3), (7), (10), and (17) with respect to other terms which exhibit linear contribution with respect to M.

In **Figure 15**, an overall comparison between an optimum differentially coherent systems performance is shown. With respect to DCSK, CDSK system has degradation in performance by 2–3 dB. This is due to two fundamental reasons: (1) number of cross terms in CDSK correlator is more than in DCSK and (2) incomplete orthogonality between intra-signal terms [1, 6, 9], which can affect the correlator output negatively. Additionally, HE-DCDK outperform DCSK at $M = 100$ and when $\frac{E_b}{N_o}$ is below 17 db. The fact behind this is the reduction in average bit from $2MVar(x)$ to $3\frac{M}{2}Var(x)$ which result in improvement by 1.25 dB. However, this improvement is vanished due to signal to signal contribution. TR-DCSK always shows better performance against DCSK, CDSK and HE-DCSK by an average of 2 dB.

In **Figure 14**, theoretical estimation of BER for all the above mentioned systems in (5), (8), (13) and (18) is plotted against simulation result. Clearly, there is an acceptable matching between theoretical expression and simulated version. However, these expressions are derived based on GA approximation method, which is suitable for the system operating in large spreading factor. To have more accurate derivation, it is preferred to implement integration method [15].

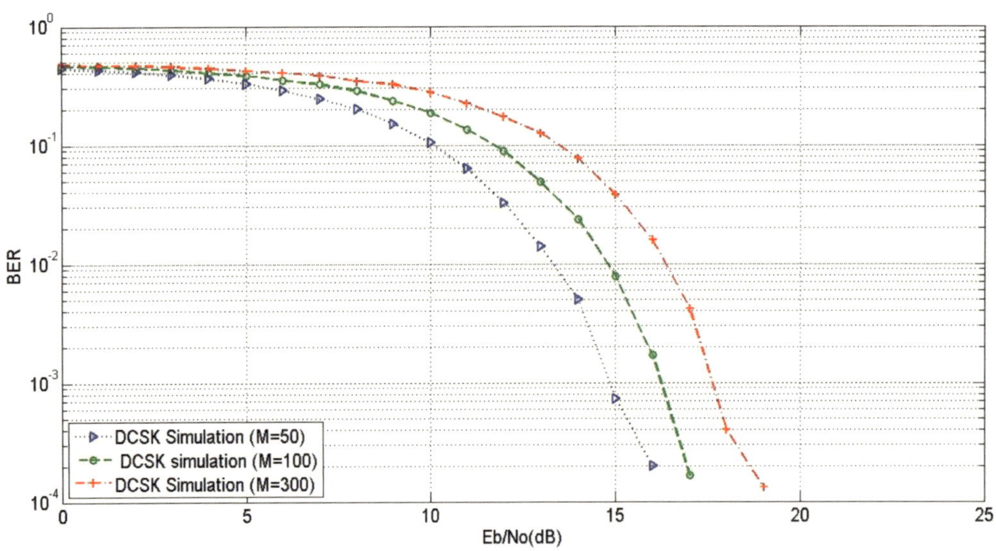

Figure 11. BER vs. Eb/N for DCSK system at M = 50,100 and 300.

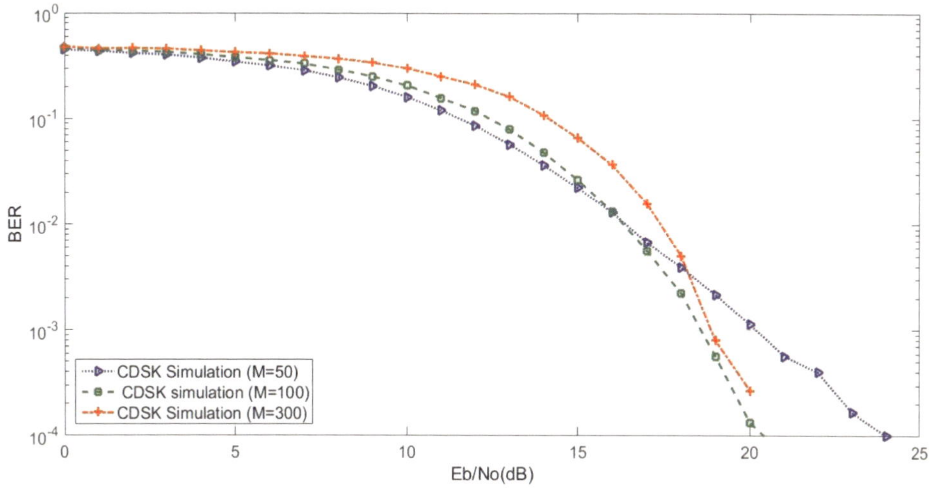

Figure 12. BER vs. Eb/N for CDSK system at $M = 50,100$ and 300.

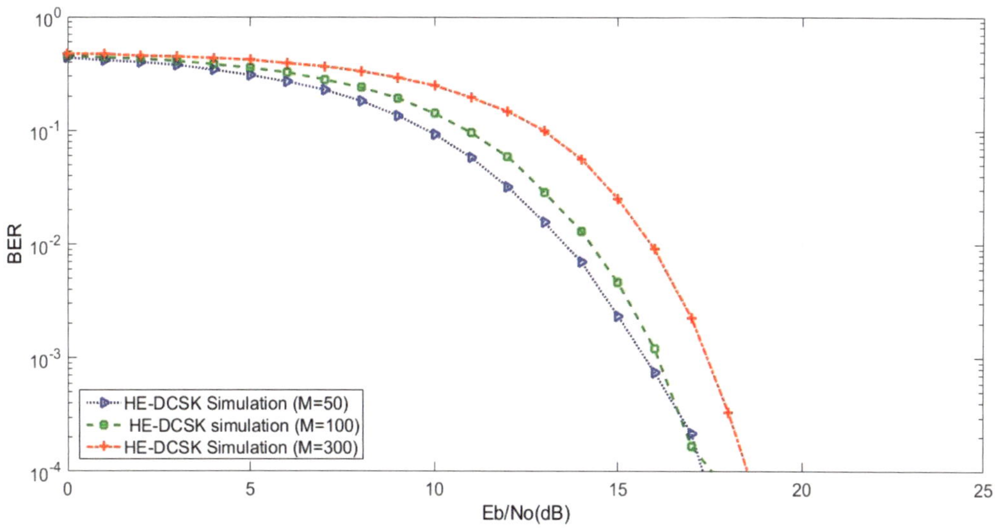

Figure 13. BER vs. Eb/N for HE-DCSK system at M = 50,100 and 300.

5. Other differential coherent systems

Many chaotic systems have been suggested to enhance BER and bandwidth efficiency of DCSK. Single reference segment is used as a reference to modulate and demodulate multiple successive bits in Ref. [16]. Average bit energy is reduced with bit error rate enhancement. However, the system is not suitable for secure communications due to easy spectrum prediction

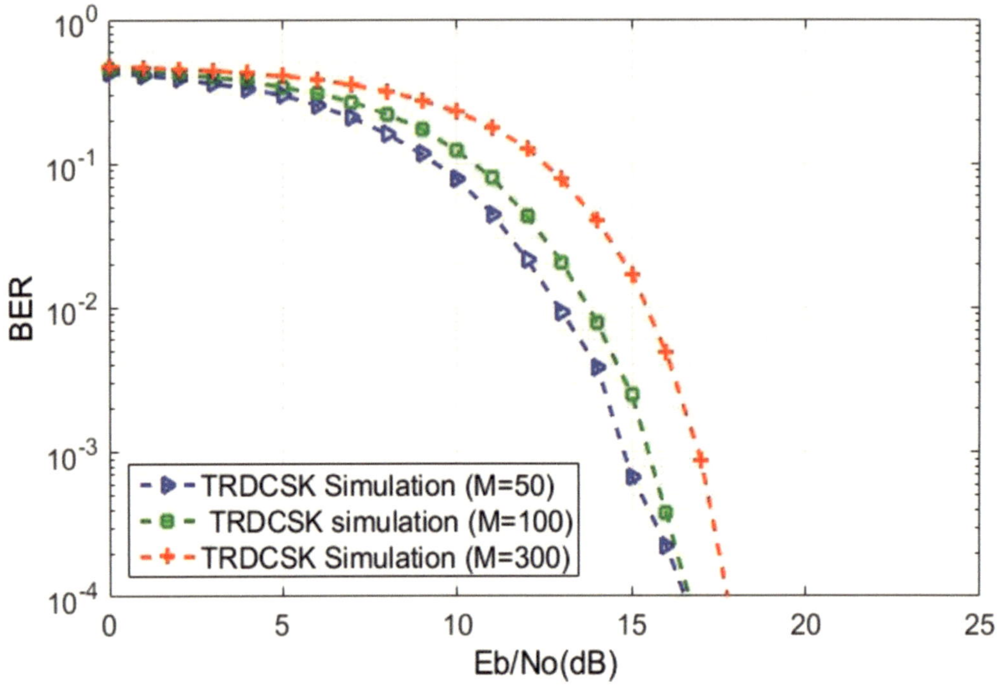

Figure 14. BER vs. Eb/N for TR-DCSK system at M = 50,100 and 300.

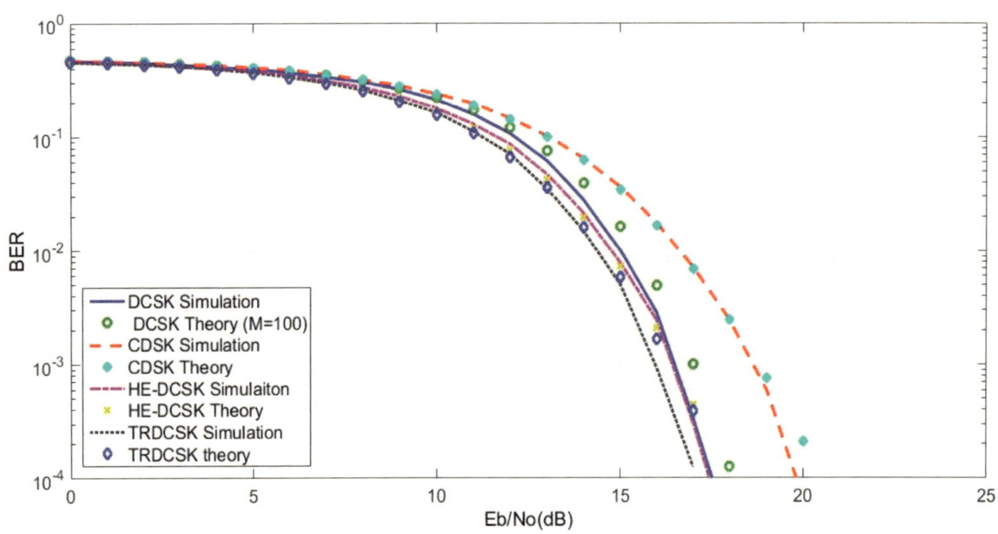

Figure 15. Simulation result and theoretical evaluation for DCSK, CDSK, HE-DCSK and TR-DCSK at M = 500.

in addition to the need for multiple delay elements in both transmitter and receiver which increase the system complexity. Chaotic signals have fluctuated energy due to randomness nature of the signal. To have fixed energy, FM-DCSK is proposed in Ref. [17] as a possible solution. Permutation between chaotic samples is implemented to destroy the similarity between the reference signal and information signal in DCSK. Moreover, permutation is used to reduce the interference between different users in multiple access-DCSK (MA-DCSK).

Sending both reference and information bearing signal in separate time slot causes a reduction in bandwidth efficiency of differential coherent systems such as DCSK. Hence, many systems have been designed to combine both reference signal and information bearing signal in one time slot. Xu and Wang proposed a code-shifted DCSK (CS-DCSK) system [18]. System is based on using Walsh code to combine reference signal and information bearing signal in single time slot rather than sending them separately. An extend version of CS-DCSK which sent multiple bits using single reference is named as (high data rate-DCSK) [19]. Another scheme which is based on mapping series of bits into two channels and each encoded output is consider as an initial condition value for the sequence generator pairs and their outputs are added and up converted [20]. Implementation of delay diversity scheme as a basic building block for space time block coder (STBC) is suggested in ref. [21]. Here, bits stream is converted from series to parallel; an each bit in parallel channel is modulated by DCSK modulators and followed by analogue space time block coder (STBC). This arrangement gains advantage of transmission by 5 dB at BER of 1×10^{-4} compared with the single input-single output DCSK.

Efficiency of multicarrier modulation has been used to send multiple bits of modulating each information bits with subcarrier using multicarrier modulation-DCSK. The system provides a considerable saving in bandwidth [22]. However, the cost which needs to pay is the complexity of having multiple carrier multipliers in the transmitter side and bank of matched filter on the receiver side.

Transmitting reference signal followed by information bearing signal is the common signal format for most of the differential coherent spread spectrum systems which can be affected by fast fading channel. A suggested scheme to send only one sample form reference signal followed directly by one sample from information bearing signal is analyzed and tested in Ref. [23]. The system provides immunity against fading in continuous mobility environment. System block diagram is almost similar to standard DCSK except for switching timing.

Major drawback of DCSK system is the addition of channel random noise in both signal segments reference and information bearing signal. Therefore, a noise reduction technique has been introduced to reduce the noise variance by sending a repeated subsegment of samples inside one bit duration rather than sending continuous stream of samples. At the receiver, averaging operation is performed over the repeated segment before the standard correlation procedure [24]. This enhances the BER performance over other newly developed segments.

Author details

Nizar Al Bassam* and Amer Zayegh

*Address all correspondence to: nazarhooby@yahoo.co.uk

Middle East College, Affiliated with Coventry University, Muscat, Oman

References

[1] Lau FCM, Tse CK. Chaos-Based Digital Communication Systems: Operating Principles, Analysis Methods, and Performance Evaluation. Berlin, Germany: Springer; 2003

[2] Kolumban G, Kennedy MP, Chua LO. The role of synchronization in digital communications using chaos. II. Chaotic modulation and chaotic synchronization. IEEE Transactions on Circuits and Systems I: Fundamental Theory and Applications. November 1998;**45**(11): 1129-1140

[3] Lau F, Tse C. Optimum Correlator-type receiver design for CSK communication systems. International Journal of Bifurcation and Chaos. 2002;**12**:1029-1038

[4] Kis G, Jako Z, Kennedy MP, Kolumban G. Chaotic communications without synchronization. In: Proceedings of the 6th IEE Conference on Telecommunications. IEE; April 1998. p. 49-53

[5] Sushchik M, Tsimring LS, Volkovskii AR. Performance analysis of correlation-based communication schemes utilizing chaos. IEEE Transactions on Circuits and Systems I: Fundamental Theory and Applications. 2000;**47**(12):1684-1691

[6] Kolumbán G, Kennedy MP, Jákó Z, Kis G. Chaotic communications with correlator receivers: Theory and performance limits. Proceedings of the IEEE. 2002;**90**(5):711-732

[7] https://link.springer.com/article/10.1007/BF01200500

[8] Larson LE, Tsimring LS, Liu J-M. Digital Communications Using Chaos and Nonlinear Dynamics. New York, NY: Springer; 2006

[9] Yang H, Jiang G-P. High-efficiency differential-chaos-shift-keying scheme for chaos-based noncoherent communication. IEEE Transactions on Circuits and Systems II: Express Briefs. 2012;**59**(5):312-316

[10] Yang H, Jiang G-P. Reference-modulated DCSK: A novel chaotic communication scheme. IEEE Transactions on Circuits and Systems II: Express Briefs. 2013;**60**(4):232-236

[11] Chernov NI. Limit theorems and Markov approximations for chaotic dynamical systems. Probability Theory and Related Fields. Sep. 1995;**101**(3):321-362

[12] Albassam Nizar N. Reference flipped-differential chaos shift keying scheme for chaos-based communications. International Journal of Engineering & Technology. April 2015;**4**(2):320-326

[13] Albassam N. Design of DCSK based on modified time reversal technique. Cogent Engineering, **4**(1):1365576. https://doi.org/10.1080/23311916.2017.1365576

[14] Albassam. Energy efficient scheme for differential coherent chaos based communication system. In: International Conference on Control, Decision and Information Technologies 34 (CoDIT2017), Spain; 2017

[15] Kaddoum G, Chargé P, Roviras D. A generalized methodology for bit-error-rate prediction in correlation-based communication schemes using chaos. IEEE Communications Letters. 2009;**13**(8):567-569

[16] Kolumban G, Jako Z, Kennedy MP. Enhanced versions of DCSK and FM-DCSK data transmission systems. In: Proceedings of the IEEE International Symposium on Circuits and Systems (ISCAS '99), Vol. 4. Orlando, FL, USA: IEEE; June 1999. p. 475-478

[17] Lau FCM, Cheong KY, Tse CK. Permutation-based DCSK and multiple-access DCSK systems. IEEE Transactions on Circuits and Systems I: Fundamental Theory and Applications. June 2003;**50**(6):733-742

[18] Xu WK, Wang L, Kolumbán G. A novel differential chaos shift keying modulation scheme. International Journal of Bifurcation and Chaos. 2011;**21**(03):799-814

[19] Xu W, Wang L, Chen G. Performance analysis of the CS-DCSK/BPSK communication system. IEEE Transactions on Circuits and Systems I. 2014;**61**(9):2624-2633

[20] Xu M, Leung H. A novel high data rate modulation scheme based on chaotic signal separation. IEEE Transactions on Communications. October 2010;**58**(10):2855-2860

[21] Chen P, Wang L, Lau FCM. One analog STBC-DCSK transmission scheme not requiring channel state information. IEEE Transactions on Circuits and Systems I: Regular Papers. 2013;**60**(4):1027-1037

[22] Kaddoum G, Richardson F-D, Gagnon F. Design and analysis of a multi-carrier differential chaos shift keying communication system. IEEE Transactions on Communications. 2013;**61**(8):3281-3291

[23] Escribano FJ, Kaddoum G, Wagemakers A, Giard P. Design of a new differential chaos-shift-keying system for continuous mobility. IEEE Transactions on Communications. May 2016;**64**(5):2066-2078

[24] Kaddoum G, Soujeri E. NR-DCSK: A noise reduction differential chaos shift keying system. IEEE Transactions on Circuits and Systems II: Express Briefs. July 2016;**63**(7):648-652

Chapter 5

Nonlinear Filtering of Weak Chaotic Signals

Valeri Kontorovich, Zinaida Lovtchikova and
Fernando Ramos-Alarcon

Additional information is available at the end of the chapter

http://dx.doi.org/10.5772/intechopen.70717

Abstract

In recent years, the application of nonlinear filtering for processing chaotic signals has become relevant. A common factor in all nonlinear filtering algorithms is that they operate in an instantaneous fashion, that is, at each cycle, a one moment of time magnitude of the signal of interest is processed. This operation regime yields good performance metrics, in terms of mean squared error (MSE) when the signal-to-noise ratio (SNR) is greater than one and shows moderate degradation for SNR values no smaller than −3 dB. Many practical applications require detection for smaller SNR values (weak signals). This chapter presents the theoretical tools and developments that allow nonlinear filtering of weak chaotic signals, avoiding the degradation of the MSE when the SNR is rather small. The innovation introduced through this approach is that the nonlinear filtering becomes multimoment, that is, the influence of more than one moment of time magnitudes is involved in the processing. Some other approaches are also presented.

Keywords: nonlinear filtering, chaotic systems, Rossler attractor, Lorenz attractor, Chua attractor, Kalman filter, weak signals, mean squared error

1. Introduction

The detection of chaotic (stochastic) weak signals is relevant (among others) for applications such as biomedical telemetry [1, 2], seismological signal processing [3], underwater signal processing [4], interference modeling [5], etc. Effective detection of weak and rather weak chaotic signals (−3 dB or less) is a challenge whose solution can improve, for example, the link budget (communication distance). Among different approaches to this problem, one can mention techniques such as stochastic resonance [4], instantaneous spectral cloning [6], etc. The problem in this chapter is addressed from the standpoint of nonlinear filtering techniques which earlier was designed to operate with signal-to-noise ratio (SNR) values bigger than one or at least rather close to one (with an acceptable slight degradation as the SNR approaches −3 dB [7]. Far down −3 dB, the performance of the available filtering methods drops down sharply and becomes ineffective. One of the possible explanations for this issue is that current nonlinear filtering algorithms can be considered as one moment in the sense that they operate in an instantaneous fashion, that is, during each operation cycle, they process an instantaneous one moment of time magnitude of the received aggregate signal; in the next cycle, a new instantaneous one moment of time magnitude is processed and so on. This is precisely the operation rule for all known optimum algorithms and their quasi-optimum versions as well, for instance, the extended Kalman filter (EKF) [7], but it can also be found in strategies such as unscented Kalman filter (UKF), Gauss-Hermite filter (GHF), and quadrature Kalman filter (QKF), among others. One of the goals of this chapter is to describe the detection of weak chaotic signals applying the principles of noninstantaneous filtering in a block way, that is, multimoment filtering theory [8], through a real-time implementation in a digital signal processing (DSP) block. Moreover, some space of this chapter will be dedicated to the conditionally optimum approach for the nonlinear filtering methods as well, together with some asymptotic methods.

Theoretically, for many cases, the chaos might be represented as an output signal of dissipative continuous dynamic systems (strange attractors) [9]:

$$\dot{x} = f(x(t)), \quad x \in R^n, \quad x(t_0) = x_0, \tag{1}$$

where $f(\bullet) = [f_1(x), \ldots f_n(x)]^T$ is a differentiable vector function.

According to the idea of Kolmogorov, the equations for strange attractors (1) can be successfully transformed in the equivalent stochastic form as a stochastic differential equation (SDE) [9, 10]:

$$\dot{x} = f(x(t)) + \varepsilon\xi(t). \tag{2}$$

The influence of a weak external source of white noise is denoted by $\xi(t)$, and the noise intensities are given in a matrix form $\varepsilon = [\varepsilon_{ij}]^{nxn}$.

Note that a stationary distribution $W_{st}(x)$ exists even when the weak white noise component is tending to zero [11–13].

Nonlinear filtering of chaotic desired signals comes up naturally when SDE (2) is used as model of chaos. This follows straight from the classical theory of nonlinear filtering for Markov processes, proposed more than 50 years ago [14, 15] and extensively developed in subsequent studies [16–21], although those methods are still under development.

From the practical implementation point of view, the nonlinear filtering strategies are approximate (see the references above). This follows from the fact that, in general, there is no analytical solution for the a posteriori probability density functions when one attempts solving the Stratonovich-Kushner equations (SKE).

In the following, some of the numerous nonlinear filtering approximate approaches that have been developed will be presented.

2. Nonlinear filtering for Markovian processes

Let assume that filtering of the following received signal is required:

$$\boldsymbol{y}(t) = \boldsymbol{s}(t, \boldsymbol{x}(t)) + \boldsymbol{n}_0(t), \tag{3}$$

where $s\,(\cdot)$ is a vector function of the "message dependent" desired signal (which is subject of filtering) of dimension "m," the received signal is denoted by the vector $\boldsymbol{y}(t)$ (also of dimension "m"), and $\boldsymbol{n}_0$ is a vector of the white additive noises characterized by the intensity matrix $\mathbf{N}_0(m \times m)$. The following SDE is used to model the signal $\boldsymbol{s}\,(\cdot)$ as an n-dimensional Markov diffusion process [22]:

$$\dot{\boldsymbol{x}} = \boldsymbol{g}(t, \boldsymbol{x}) + \boldsymbol{\xi}(t). \tag{4}$$

Strictly speaking, Eqs. (4) and (2) are the same SDE, and the vector function $\boldsymbol{g}\,(\cdot)$ substitutes $\boldsymbol{f}\,(\cdot)$ in (2); for (4), $\boldsymbol{D}$ denotes the correspondent matrix of intensities for $\boldsymbol{\xi}(\cdot)$.

Under this assumption ([14, 22] and so on), one can use the so-called Fokker-Planck-Kolmogorov (FPK) equation in order to solve the a priori probability density function (a priori PDF), for $\boldsymbol{x}(t)$:

$$\frac{\partial W_{PR}(\boldsymbol{x}, t)}{\partial t} = -\sum_{i=1}^{n} \frac{\partial}{\partial x_i}\left[g_i(t, \boldsymbol{x}) W_{PR}(\boldsymbol{x}, t)\right] + \frac{1}{2}\sum_{i=1}^{n}\sum_{j=1}^{n} \frac{\partial^2}{\partial x_i \partial x_j}\left[D_{ij} W_{PR}(\boldsymbol{x}, t)\right], \tag{5}$$

where $W_{PR}(x,t_0) = W_0(x)$.

The Eq. (5) can be rewritten in another form [21, 23] as well:

$$\frac{\partial W_{PR}(\boldsymbol{x}, t)}{\partial t} = -\mathrm{div}\boldsymbol{\pi}(\boldsymbol{x}, t), \tag{6}$$

or

$$\frac{\partial W_{PR}(\boldsymbol{x}, t)}{\partial t} = L_{PR}\{W_{PR}(\boldsymbol{x}, t)\}, \tag{7}$$

where $\boldsymbol{\pi}(\boldsymbol{x}, t)$ is a probabilistic "*flow*" with components:

$$\boldsymbol{\pi}(\boldsymbol{x}, t) = g_i(\boldsymbol{x}, t) W_{PR}(\boldsymbol{x}, t) - \frac{1}{2}\sum_{j=1}^{n} \frac{\partial}{\partial x_j}\left[D_{ij} W_{PR}(\boldsymbol{x}, t)\right] \quad . \tag{8}$$

In Eqs. (5)–(8), $\{D_{ij}\}$ denote diffusion coefficients of the Markov process and $\{g_i(\boldsymbol{x}, t)\}_1^n$ are the correspondent drift coefficients, and both of them will be used in the Stratonovich sense [14, 22]; $L_{PR}\{\cdot\}$ denotes a FPK linear operator.

The integrodifferential equation for the a posteriori probability density function $W_{PS}(\boldsymbol{x}, t)$ is given by any of the two equivalent expressions (see [14]:

$$\frac{\partial W_{PS}(\boldsymbol{x},t)}{\partial t} = L_{PR}\{W_{PS}(\boldsymbol{x},t)\} + \frac{1}{2}\left[\boldsymbol{F}(\boldsymbol{x},t) - \int_{-\infty}^{\infty} \boldsymbol{F}(\boldsymbol{x},t) W_{PS}(\boldsymbol{x},t) d\boldsymbol{x}\right] W_{PS}(\boldsymbol{x},t) \tag{9}$$

or

$$\frac{\partial W_{PS}(\boldsymbol{x},t)}{\partial t} = -\mathrm{div}\widehat{\pi}(\boldsymbol{x},t) + \frac{1}{2}[\boldsymbol{F}(\boldsymbol{x},t) - < F(\boldsymbol{x},t) >] W_{PS}(\boldsymbol{x},t), \tag{10}$$

where $< F(\boldsymbol{x},t) >$ denotes the averaging of $F(\boldsymbol{x},t)$ given by $< F(\boldsymbol{x},t) >= \int_{-\infty}^{\infty} \boldsymbol{F}(\boldsymbol{x},t) W_{PS}(\boldsymbol{x},t) d\boldsymbol{x}$; $\widehat{\pi}(\boldsymbol{x},t)$ is (5), $W_{PR}(\boldsymbol{x}, t)$ is substituted by $W_{PS}(\boldsymbol{x}, t)$, and

$$\boldsymbol{F}(\boldsymbol{x},t) = \left[\boldsymbol{y}(t) - \frac{1}{2}s(\boldsymbol{x},t)\right]^T \boldsymbol{N}_0^{-1} \left[\boldsymbol{y}(t) - \frac{1}{2}s(\boldsymbol{x},t)\right]. \tag{11}$$

The combination of Eqs. (9)–(11) is known as the Stratonovich-Kushner nonlinear equations (SKE), and they have an appealing physical sense: the first term in (9) represents the dynamics of the a priori data of $\boldsymbol{x}(t)$. For the second term, the analysis of observations is used to drive the innovation of the a priori data.

Using any optimization criteria, one can get $\widehat{\boldsymbol{x}}(t)$ (the optimum estimation of $\boldsymbol{x}(t)$) which comes as a solution of (9), when $y(t)$ is the input signal, that is, filtering of $x(t)$.

Here, one has to note that Eq. (9) turns into FPK (6) if the intensity of the additive noises $\boldsymbol{N}_0$ grows (the first term in (9) is dominant), and as a consequence, the filtering accuracy diminishes drastically. In the opposed scenario (large signal-to-noise ratio), the $W_{PS}(\boldsymbol{x}, t)$ tends to the unimodal Gaussian PDF [14, 20].

Note that the time evolution of $W_{PS}(\boldsymbol{x}, t)$ is completely described by the SKE but, as it was mentioned earlier, does not provide exact analytical solutions. There are very few exceptions: linear SDE (4) which yields the well-known Kalman filtering algorithm [14–24], the Zakai approach [25], and so on. Due to this, the nonlinear filtering algorithms are practically always approximate. As it was mentioned before, during almost 50 years of intensive research, the bibliography for nonlinear filtering algorithms has become enormous; in the next section, we will consider only few of those works taking into account the following considerations:

- the models applied for filtering of chaos correspond to the equations for Rössler, Chua, and Lorenz strange attractors with $n = 3$, that is, low dimensional;
- the algorithms for nonlinear filtering have to be of reduced computational complexity in order to satisfy real-time application requirements;
- the algorithms for nonlinear filtering, according to the aim of the material of the chapter, have to be able to perform satisfactorily in scenarios with low or very low signal-to-noise ratios (SNR), although the Gaussian assumption for $W_{PS}(\boldsymbol{x})$ is not always valid;
- $$s(\boldsymbol{x}(t),t) \cong \boldsymbol{x}(t); \tag{12}$$
- All D_{ij} are equal to zero, except $D_{11} \cong D_1$ [11].

2.1. Approximate approaches for nonlinear filtering

For the sake of simplicity, it is "easier" to approximate the a posteriori PDF $W_{PS}(\boldsymbol{x}, t)$ than the nonlinearity at (4) and (9) [16, 17, 19]. In this sense, let us just list some of the approximate approaches for $W_{PS}(\boldsymbol{x}, t)$:

- Integral or global approximations for $W_{PS}(\boldsymbol{x}, t)$ [20];
- Functional approximations for $W_{PS}(\boldsymbol{x}, t)$ [16, 21];
- Higher Order Statistics (HOS) approximations for $W_{PS}(\boldsymbol{x}, t)$, and so on;
- Gaussian approximations: extended Kalman filter (EKF) [14–24]; unscented Kalman filter (UKF) [19]; quadrature Kalman filter (QKF) [17]; iterated Kalman filter (IKF), etc.

It is hardly feasible to give a complete overview of all those methods; moreover, not all of them are adequate, taking into account the observations introduced at the end of the previous section.

Let us start with the extended Kalman filter (EKF): considering $W_{PS}(\boldsymbol{x}, t)$ as a three-dimensional Gaussian PDF- $\widehat{W}_G(\boldsymbol{x}, t)$, from (9), it is possible to obtain the following equations for per-component of the mean estimates $\{\widehat{x}_i\}_1^3$ and for estimates of the elements of the a posteriori covariance matrix $\left\{\widehat{R}_{ij}\right\}_{i,j=1}^{3}$:

$$\begin{aligned}\dot{\widehat{x}}_i &= \int_{-\infty}^{\infty}\left(\widehat{\boldsymbol{\pi}}^{\mathrm{T}}(\boldsymbol{x}, t)\,\mathrm{grad}\,x_i\right)d\boldsymbol{x} + \frac{1}{2}\left[\int_{-\infty}^{\infty} x_i \boldsymbol{F}(\boldsymbol{x}, t)\widehat{W}_G(\boldsymbol{x}, t)d\boldsymbol{x} - \widehat{x}_i\int_{-\infty}^{\infty}\boldsymbol{F}(\boldsymbol{x}, t)\widehat{W}_G(\boldsymbol{x}, t)d\boldsymbol{x}\right]\\ \dot{\widehat{R}}_{ij} &= \int_{-\infty}^{\infty}\left(\widehat{\boldsymbol{\pi}}^{\mathrm{T}}(\boldsymbol{x}, t)\,\mathrm{grad}\,\mathring{x}_i\mathring{x}_j\right)d\boldsymbol{x} + \frac{1}{2}\left[\int_{-\infty}^{\infty}\mathring{x}_i\mathring{x}_j\boldsymbol{F}(\boldsymbol{x}, t)\widehat{W}_G(\boldsymbol{x}, t)d\boldsymbol{x} - \widehat{R}_{ij}\int_{-\infty}^{\infty}\boldsymbol{F}(\boldsymbol{x}, t)\widehat{W}_G(\boldsymbol{x}, t)d\boldsymbol{x}\right],\end{aligned} \tag{13}$$

where $\mathring{x}_i = x_i - \widehat{x}_i$ and $\mathring{x}_j = x_j - \widehat{x}_j$.

The matrix form [14–16, 20] can be used to represent Eq. (13); however, for some specific applications, per-component representation (13) could be more adequate (see the following).

It is reasonable to assume convergence to the stationary values $\overline{R_{ij}}$ for $\forall\widehat{R}_{ij}(t)$ when $t\rightarrow\infty$, and as a result, the second equation in (13) can be expressed as a system of nonlinear algebraic equations, with standard numerical solutions. This consideration is relevant for real-time scenarios, as it significantly simplifies the implementation of the related EKF algorithms.

Functional approximation for $W_{PS}(\boldsymbol{x}, t)$ is, as it was described in [16, 21],

$$W_{PS}(\boldsymbol{x}, t) = \prod_{i=1}^{3} W_{PS}(x_i)\left[1 + \sum_{q=2}^{3}\sum_{j=1}^{q-1}\frac{R_{qj}}{R_{qq}R_{ji}}\left(x_q - \widehat{x}_q\right)\left(x_j - \widehat{x}_j\right)\right]. \tag{14}$$

From (14), we see that the functional approximation for the PDF is sufficiently non-Gaussian (marginal $W_{PS}(x_i)$ is arbitrary), but for "joint" characterization of the vector $\widehat{\boldsymbol{x}}$, only elements of the a posteriori covariance matrix $\widehat{R}_{ij}$ are considered.

It can be shown that the equations for $\{\widehat{x}_i\}_1^n$ and $\left\{\widehat{R}_{ij}\right\}$ coincide with those in (13), and the unique difference would be that one has to apply in (13) the approximation for $W_{PS}(\boldsymbol{x}, t)$ instead of $\widehat{W}_G(\boldsymbol{x}, t)$. The resulting integrals can be solved either through the Gauss-Hermit quadrature formula [17, 18] or analytically.

The integral or Global approximation for $W_{PS}(\boldsymbol{x}, t)$ is another approach for approximate solution. Maybe the experienced reader already noticed that the last two approximations for $W_{PS}(\boldsymbol{x}, t)$ can be considered as "local" as they offer maximum of $W_{PS}(\boldsymbol{x}, t)$, estimation of $\{\widehat{x}_i\}$, and $\left\{\widehat{R}_{ij}\right\}$.

For conditions of significantly large SNR, this is sufficient, but for low SNR, one has to find a different approach, known as integral approximation. This strategy was suggested as an adequate approximation of $W_{PS}(\boldsymbol{x}, t)$ together with the PDF's "tails," that is, for the whole span of $\boldsymbol{x}$.

Let us suppose that $W_{PS}(\boldsymbol{x}, t)$ can be characterized as:

$$W_{PS}(\boldsymbol{x}, t) = W_{PS}(\boldsymbol{x}, \boldsymbol{\alpha}(t)). \tag{15}$$

Here $\boldsymbol{\alpha}$ is an unknown vector of approximation parameters. As an approximation criterion for PDF, it is possible to use the Kullback measure; thus, one might obtain the following equation for the unknown vector $\boldsymbol{\alpha}$:

$$\dot{\boldsymbol{\alpha}} = \left\langle L_{PR}^{+}\{\boldsymbol{h}(\boldsymbol{x}, t)\}\right\rangle + \boldsymbol{V}^{-1}(t)\langle \boldsymbol{h}(\boldsymbol{x}, t)\boldsymbol{F}(\boldsymbol{x}, t)\rangle, \tag{16}$$

where $\boldsymbol{h}(\boldsymbol{x}, t) = \frac{\partial \ln W_{PS}(\boldsymbol{x}, \boldsymbol{\alpha}(t))}{\partial \boldsymbol{\alpha}}$, $\boldsymbol{V}(t) = \int\limits_{-\infty}^{\infty} \left[\frac{\partial \ln W_{PS}(\boldsymbol{x}, \boldsymbol{\alpha}(t))}{\partial \boldsymbol{\alpha}}\right]^T W_{PS}(\boldsymbol{x}, \boldsymbol{\alpha}(t))dx = \frac{\partial^2 W_{PS}(\boldsymbol{x}, \boldsymbol{\alpha}(t))}{\partial \boldsymbol{\alpha} \partial \boldsymbol{\alpha}^{\mathrm{T}}}$, $L_{PR}^{+}\{\bullet\}$ is a self-adjoint operator to the FPK operator [22].

Now, as an integral approximation of $W_{PS}(\boldsymbol{x}, \boldsymbol{\alpha}(t)$, let us choose the so-called "Dynkin PDF" with $\boldsymbol{\alpha}(t)$ is the vector of sufficient statistics for $W_{PS}(\cdot)$:

$$W_{PS}(\boldsymbol{x}, \boldsymbol{\alpha}(t)) = C\exp\left\{\sum_{p=1}^{K} \alpha_p(t)\phi_p(\boldsymbol{x}) + \phi_0(\boldsymbol{x})\right\}, \tag{17}$$

where $\{\varphi_p(\boldsymbol{x})\}$ are orthogonal multidimensional operators: Laguerre, Hermite, and so on.

One can notice that there is a significant coincidence between (17) and the orthogonal series characterization of $W_{PS}(\boldsymbol{x}, \boldsymbol{\alpha}(t)$ [22]: even though both apply series of orthogonal functions, in (17), it is not used for $W_{PS}(\boldsymbol{x}, \boldsymbol{\alpha}(t))$ but for its monotonical transform $\ln\{W_{PS}(\boldsymbol{x}, \boldsymbol{\alpha}(t)\}$. So, the coefficients $\{\alpha_p(t)\}$ can be expressed by means of the cumulants of $W_{PS}(x)$ [22]. Thanks to this, instead of searching for a solution of (17), hardly possible in an analytically way, one can search directly equations for the cumulants (HOS) of $W_{PS}(\boldsymbol{x}, t)$ [16, 26].

Here, the HOS approach will be presented because the last problem was addressed in the cited references. It is worth noticing the following: for real-time scenarios when $n > 1$, equations for HOS and Eq. (16) are significantly complex; for $n = 1$, both strategies are equivalent [26].

3. Multimoment filtering of chaos

As it follows from the material of Section 2, all the algorithms are "one-moment" in the sense that they are operating only with the data at each time instant, that is, they are tracking instantaneously one moment magnitude of the received aggregate signal. As it was shown at [27], the adequate filtering algorithm (for the one-moment case) is an Extended Kalman Filter (EKF).

This choice is more or less expected, due to the experience which is already known from the available references (see above). EKF shows rather good performance for the filtering of chaotic signals: the mean squared error (MSE) is less than 1% when SNR is about −3 dB, and for SNR bigger than −3 dB, the results are much better.

In this regard, a question arises: is it possible to improve this approach in the sense of getting still rather good MSE's for successively lower thresholds of the SNR with an algorithm of reasonable complexity? The following material attempts to prove that the answer is "yes," if one can apply some additional information from the received aggregate signal taken on several sequential time instants.

It means that the information has to be considered in the block manner by aggregating data, in our case, for several time instants ([8, 16, 27], and so on.). The difference between the following approach and that from the cited references is precisely the aggregated data obtained for many time instants: multimoment algorithms are carried out through the generalization of the Stratonovich-Kushner equations (SKE) for the corresponding multimoment data, and therefore, in the following, all heuristics for the simplification, considered as Generalized SKE (GSKE), are not arbitrary but can be taken as generalized heuristics from the "standard" one-moment SKE (see below). This gives a "hope" to achieve the abovementioned improvement for the SNR threshold with less complex tools.

It follows from the fact that, as it was shown in [8] (see also the references therein), the GSKE comes from the same structure as its one-moment prototype. So the way of its simplification (except for the limiting of the number of time instants) in order to get a quasi-optimum algorithm, could be done in a similar way as for the one-moment case: approximation of the a posteriori PDF (characteristic function) in SKE with a minimum set of significant parameters. Moreover, there is an additional way to improve the accuracy of the quasi-optimum solution for the GSKE: assume this quasi-optimum algorithm as a "given structure," as it was proposed in [16] and also considered in the following.

3.1. Generalization of SKE for the multimoment case

In the same way, as it was underlined earlier, the chaos is "generated" by the equation:

$$\dot{x} = f(x), \quad x \in R^n, \quad x(t_0) = x_0, \tag{18}$$

where $f(\bullet) = [f_1(x), \ldots f_n(x)]^T$ is a differentiable vector function and it can be considered as a degenerated Markov process from the following stochastic equation:

$$\dot{\boldsymbol{x}} = \boldsymbol{f}(\boldsymbol{x}) + \boldsymbol{\varepsilon}\boldsymbol{\xi}(t), \tag{19}$$

where $\boldsymbol{\xi}(t)$ is a vector of "weak" external white noise with the related positively defined matrix of "intensities" $\boldsymbol{\varepsilon} = [\varepsilon_{ij}]^{n\times n}$.

In the following, one can consider both the ordinary differential equation (ODE) (18) and the stochastic differential equation (SDE) (19) when the noise intensities tend equally to zero. Adding the $\boldsymbol{\varepsilon}$ term in (19) guarantees the existence of a stationary PDF for $\boldsymbol{x}(t)$ as well, no matter how small the elements of $\boldsymbol{\varepsilon}$ might be [28]. So, one can suppose that this stationary PDF, $W_{ST}(\boldsymbol{x})$, is known a priori. For our case in practical sense, one can deal actually only with the stationary PDF, which we assumed is modeled by means of a chaotic process (concretely let us say the first component, $x_1(t)$, of certain attractor model). Certainly $W_{ST}(\boldsymbol{x_1})$ can easily be obtained from $W_{ST}(\boldsymbol{x})$. If the two PDFs coincide in terms of certain fitness criteria, then only for simplicity in the subsequent developments, the SDE (19) can be substituted by its statistically equivalent one-dimensional SDE with the same $W_{ST}(\boldsymbol{x_1})$:

$$\dot{x}_1 = f(x_1) + \sqrt{\varepsilon}\xi(t), \tag{20}$$

where $f(x_1) = \frac{\varepsilon}{2}\frac{d}{dx_1}\ln W_{ST}(x_1)$ and ε in (20) can be considered here as a "scale factor" and can be chosen by equalizing the average powers of real $x_1(t)$ and solution of (20). Formally, there is no need for all those operations, but then the reader has to be extremely concentrated with "multiindex" definitions: one index for the number of applied components of the attractor and another index for the time instant, that is, $x^m(t_i)$, which might cause confusion in further developments, as $x_1(t)$ is an observable component whose dynamics depends on other "nonobservable" components. For those reasons, in the following, (20) will be considered as a model of the desired signal for filtering.

Let us introduce the following notation for the time instants (time moments): $t_1 < t_2 < t_3 \ldots < t_n$ and $x_i = x(t_i)$, $i = \overline{1,n}$. Then, $\{x(t_i)\}_1^n$ forms a vector $\boldsymbol{x}(t) = [x(t_1),\ldots, x(t_n)]^{\mathrm{T}}$ and $W_n(\boldsymbol{x}, t) \cong W_n(x_1, \ldots x_n; t_1, \ldots t_n)$; $W_n(\boldsymbol{x},t)$ is an a priori PDF for $\boldsymbol{x}(t)$. As it follows from ([16], ch. 5):

$$\frac{\partial W_n(\boldsymbol{x},t)}{\partial t_i} = L_i\{W_n(\boldsymbol{x},t)\} \tag{21}$$

where $L_i\{\bullet\} = -\frac{\partial}{\partial x_i}K_1(x_i) + \frac{1}{2}\frac{\partial^2}{\partial x_i^2}K_2(x_i)$ is the FPK operator [16] with $K_1(x_i) = f_1(x_i)$, $K_2(x_i) = \varepsilon^2$. It is easy to show that by consecutive differentiation one can obtain:

$$\frac{\partial^n W_n(\boldsymbol{x},t)}{\partial t_1 \ldots \partial t_n} = \prod_{i=1}^{n} L_i\{W_n(\boldsymbol{x},t)\}, \tag{22}$$

$$L_{PR}\{\bullet\} = \prod_{i=1}^{n} L_i\{\bullet\}. \tag{23}$$

Certainly, the adjoint operator [16, 22] for the multimoment case is:

$$\widehat{L}_{PR}\{\bullet\} = \prod_{i=1}^{n} \widehat{L}_i\{\bullet\}, \tag{24}$$

where $\widehat{L}_i = K_1(x_i)\frac{\partial}{\partial x_i} + \frac{K_2(x_i)}{2}\frac{\partial^2}{\partial x_i^2}$ is a Kolmogorov operator [22].

Let us then introduce the a posteriori n-dimensional PDF $W_{ps}(\boldsymbol{y}|\boldsymbol{x},t) \cong W_{ps}(\boldsymbol{x},t)$ for the multimoment case. Then, repeating formally the development for the SKE, but in this case generalized for the "n" time case (in the same way as it was done at [27]), one can get:

$$\frac{\partial^n W_{ps}(\boldsymbol{x},t)}{\partial t_1 \ldots \partial t_n} = L_{PR}\{W_{ps}(\boldsymbol{x},t)\} + \frac{1}{2}\left[\boldsymbol{F}(\boldsymbol{x},t) - \int\limits_{R^n} \boldsymbol{F}(\boldsymbol{x},t) W_{ps}(\boldsymbol{x},t) d\boldsymbol{x}\right] W_{ps}(\boldsymbol{x},t) \tag{25}$$

with $t = [t_1, \ldots, t_n]^T$,

$$\boldsymbol{F}(\boldsymbol{x},t) = \frac{\left[\boldsymbol{y}(t) - \frac{1}{2}\boldsymbol{x}(t)\right]^T}{N_0}\left[\boldsymbol{y}(t) - \frac{1}{2}\boldsymbol{x}(t)\right], \tag{26}$$

where $\boldsymbol{y}(t) = [y(t_1), \ldots, y(t_n)]^T$ is the vector of $\{x(t_i)\}_1^n$ taken from $y(t) = x(t) + n(t)$ and $n(t)$ is the AWGN with intensity N_0.

Analyzing (25) by comparing it with the standard form of the SKE (see Eqs. (9) and (10) in part II), one can see that there is a total "*structural*" identity! The same matter takes place for the a posteriori cumulants [16, 27], that is:

$$\frac{\partial \kappa^{ps}_{r_1,\ldots r_n}(t)}{\partial t_1 \ldots \partial t_n} = (-j)^k \frac{\partial^k}{\partial \lambda_1^{r_1}, \ldots \partial \lambda_n^{r_n}} \left\{ \left[\frac{M\left\{\widehat{L} \exp\{j\boldsymbol{\lambda}^T \boldsymbol{x}\} \boldsymbol{F}(\boldsymbol{x},t)\right\}}{M\{\exp\{j\boldsymbol{\lambda}^T \boldsymbol{x}\}\}}\right]_{\lambda=0} + \left[\frac{M\{\exp\{j\boldsymbol{\lambda}^T \boldsymbol{x}\} \boldsymbol{F}(\boldsymbol{x},t)\}}{M\{\exp\{j\boldsymbol{\lambda}^T \boldsymbol{x}\}\}}\right]_{\lambda=0} \right\} \tag{27}$$

where $r_1 + r_2 + \ldots + r_n = k$, $k = 1, 2, \ldots$.

One can see from (25) and (26) that those algorithms are rather complex for implementation in real-time regime. So, in addition to the one-moment SKE, they have to be modified in order to get the quasi-optimum solution.

3.2. Quasi-optimum solutions. Generalized EKF

One has to know that "quasi-optimum" solutions (for any problem) are based on some heuristics and those heuristics have to be reasonable and based on previous experience in solving similar problems. In the case of multimoment filtering, the analogies can be the following (of course implicit considerations for complexity have always to be taken into account):

- The priority will be given to the quasi-linear approximation for nonlinear functions in the same way as it was assumed for the "standard" one-moment filtering.

- All algorithms for block processing show that there is in some sense a reasonable block length for the processed data. Taking into account the complexity limits and that the covariance function of the chaos initially drops rather fast [29], let us take first $n = 2$.
- The approximation of the a posteriori PDF (characteristic function) has to apply the minimum set of first cumulants; one has to remind that, as the order of cumulants grows, their significance for PDF approximation vanishes [22];

Taking these observations into account, let us take $n = 2$, that is, two-moment filtering case, then [16, 22]:

$$\theta_{ps}(\boldsymbol{\lambda}) \cong \exp\left\{\sum_{s=1}^{2}\frac{js}{s!}\sum_{r_1, r_2}^{S}\kappa_s(t_1, t_2)\boldsymbol{\lambda}^{r_1}\boldsymbol{\lambda}^{r_2}\right\}, \tag{28}$$

and cumulants are:

$$\kappa_{r_1,\dots r_n}^{(ps)}(t) = (-j)^k\left[\frac{\partial^k}{\partial\lambda_1^{r_1},\dots\partial\lambda_n^{r_n}}\ln\theta_{ps}(\boldsymbol{\lambda})\right]_{\lambda=0}.$$

Another assumption is that the a posteriori process is supposed to be stationary; then, the one-moment cumulants for t_1 and t_2 have to be the same and the only mutual cumulant taken into account might be $\kappa_{11}(t_1, t_2)$. Next, for each moment "t_1" and "t_2" one-moment cumulants can be calculated applying Gaussian approximation for the a posteriori PDF, and for the two-moment case, the "functional approximation" could be applied. In a rigorous sense, the a posteriori variance κ_2^{ps} has to be evaluated as $\kappa_2^{ps}(t_1, t_2)$, considering the covariance among time instants "t_1" and "t_2"; in the following, the heuristic strategy will be introduced, which avoids the cumbersome calculations.

One can obtain the first two-moment cumulants:

$$\begin{aligned}\dot{\kappa}_1 &=< K_1(x) > +\frac{1}{2} < xF(x,t) > -\frac{\kappa_1}{2} < xF(x,t) > \\ \dot{\kappa}_2 &=< 2xK_1(x) > -\kappa_1 < K_1(x) > +\varepsilon + \frac{1}{2} < (x-\kappa_1)^2F(x,t) > -\frac{\kappa_2}{2} < xF(x,t) > ,\end{aligned} \tag{29}$$

where $<>$ is a symbol for the averaging procedure, $F(x,t) = \frac{1}{N_0}\left[y(t) - \frac{1}{2}x(t)\right]$, and $K_1(x)$ is the drift coefficient for (19).

One has to notice that at (29) $\kappa_1(t)$ is an estimation of the filtered signal (in our case, it is a chaotic signal); $\kappa_2(t)$ is a measure of the filtering accuracy. As it can be is seen from (29), those equations were written without any intention for linearization, that is, they are presented in a generalized form. For the quasi-linear algorithms, it is well known [27] that $\kappa_2(t)/N_0$ is the main part for the "*averaging coefficient*" of the second element in the first quasi-linear equation of (29), that is, it is an averaging value for the instantaneous information actualization from the entering desired signal plus noise. Thus, if one can reduce κ_2 through the two-moment processing, the accuracy of the quasi-linear method will grow and the challenge stated before will be almost solved. To achieve the latter, one can take into account that $\kappa_2(t)$ in the stationary regime is oscillating around its stationary value $\overline{\kappa_2(t)} = \lim_{t\to\infty} \kappa_2(t)$ which is commonly assumed as an accuracy measure in the one-moment case.

The value of $\overline{\kappa_2(t)}$ can be diminished applying the information from $\kappa_{11}(t)$ also in the stationary case, that is, $\overline{\kappa}_{11} = \lim_{t_1,\,t_2\to\infty} \kappa_{11}(t_1,t_2)$; then, it is known that $\widehat{\overline{\kappa}}_2 = \overline{\kappa}_2\left(1-\overline{\kappa}_{11}^2\right)$ and it is always less than $\overline{\kappa}_2$, if and only if the $\overline{\kappa}_{11} \geq 0$; In this way, $\widehat{\overline{\kappa}}_2$ can be used as a new weighting coefficient in (29). To find $\kappa_{11}(t_1,t_2)$ from (27), some cumbersome developments are required which finally yield to:

$$\frac{\partial\kappa_{11}(t_1,t_2)}{\partial t_1\partial t_2} = < K_1(x_1)K_1(x_2) > + < \frac{x_1x_2}{2}F(\mathbf{x},t) > - \frac{\kappa_{11}(t_1,t_2)}{2} < F(\mathbf{x},t) > \tag{30}$$

and

$$\overline{\kappa}_{11} = \frac{2\left[< \frac{x_1x_2F(\mathbf{x},t)}{2} + 2K_1(x_1)K_1(x_2) >\right]}{< F(\mathbf{x},t) >}. \tag{31}$$

First we would like to stress here that, as we are interested in covariance calculation, it is necessary to preserve the notations $x(t_1) = x_1$ and $x(t_2) = x_2$. Second, we want to "improve" the stationary value $\overline{\kappa}_2$ evaluated for the one-moment case through its indirect dependence on $\overline{\kappa}_{11}$ as if it was "evaluated" for the two-moment case.

Thus in doing so, the direct calculation of the quasi-linear algorithm for the two-moment case is bypassed (see (29) and (30)). For applications in real time, the formal calculus is almost impossible. Instead, we simplified it with a formal "ignorance" of the two-moment features. There might be for sure a compromise between the complexity and the improvement attempt for the "classic" EKF.

In order to avoid some additional complexities for the calculation of (31), let us make the following assumption: introduce the SNR of the filtering in the way: $h^2 = \frac{\overline{K}_1^2}{N_0} << 1$, that is, weak signal case. In this regard [16, 27], the a priori data are the main influence, that is, approximately only $<K_1(x_1)\ K_1(x_2)>$ can be applied. Or one can simply apply a Gaussian approximation for the second equation in (29) for the stationary regime ($\dot{\kappa}_2 \cong 0$)

$$2\left[\overline{K_1{}'(\kappa_1)} + \overline{\kappa}_{11}\right]\frac{\overline{\kappa}_2}{2} + \varepsilon + \frac{1}{4}\overline{F''(\kappa_1)}\overline{\kappa}_2^2 = 0. \tag{32}$$

In the case $h^2 < 1$, it is possible to achieve:

$$\overline{\kappa}_2 \sim \frac{1}{2\left[\overline{K'(\kappa_1)} + \overline{\kappa}_{11}\right]}, \tag{33}$$

and if $\overline{\kappa}_{11} > 0$, and $K'(\kappa_1) \geq 0$, κ_2 is always reduced compared with the one-moment approach. Formula (33) can be seen as another illustration about the usefulness of the heuristic approximation proposed above. Then, to evaluate the order of the $\overline{\kappa}_{11}$, let us apply for averaging of $<K_1(x_1)\, K_1(x_2)>$ the functional approximation of $W_{ps}(x_1, x_2)$ in the way:

$$W_{ps}(x_1,x_2) = \frac{1}{2\pi\overline{\kappa}_2} \exp\left[-\frac{(x_1-\kappa_1)^2}{2\overline{\kappa}_2}\right] \exp\left[-\frac{(x_2-\kappa_1)^2}{2\overline{\kappa}_2}\right] [1+\overline{\kappa}_{11}(x_1-\kappa_1)(x_2-\kappa_1)]. \quad (34)$$

As an approximate result, one can substitute (34) in (33), assume $h^2 < 1$ and see that the normalized value $\overline{\kappa}_{11}$ has the same order as h^2, that is, $\overline{\kappa}_{11} \sim O(h^2)$. This is an important consideration because usually the pure chaos has a low covariance interval [29] and one can obtain a very small MSE for two time instants t_1 and t_2 arbitrarily close. In this sense and fixing SNR $\sim$ 0.5 and MSE $\sim$ 0.1%, an equivalent MSE can be reached using the two-moment approach but with an SNR threshold 30% lower than for the one-moment case. Let us be emphatic and say that the approximation $\overline{\kappa}_{11} \sim O(h^2)$ is valid just for $h^2 < 1$, and calculation of $\widehat{\overline{\kappa}}_2 \sim \overline{\kappa}_2\left(1-\overline{\kappa}_{11}^2\right)$ has to be updated instantaneously because h^2 is varying in the interval $0 \le h^2 < 1$.

Of course this calculation is quite approximated and true superiority for the two-moment case of the modified quasi-linear strategy has to be verified by computer experiments. Anyway it is a strong sign indicating that the use of the two-moment strategy can be very opportunistic if and only if one can find strategies to reduce the computational complexity, for example, the generalized extended Kalman filter (GEKF) algorithm.

Finally, let us reiterate that the GEKF is yet a one-moment strategy for quasi-optimum filtering, but internally makes processing of the statistical features of the chaotic data (input) through the multimoment (two-moment) apparatus. That is why this modified GEKF improved accuracy in comparison with the standard EKF. In the following in order to additionally improve the accuracy of this one-moment modified EKF, it is convenient to apply the principles of the theory of so-called "conditionally optimum filtering" proposed in ([16], ch. 9), taking this generalized EKF as the "tolerance" or "admitted" filter.

4. Conditionally optimum filtering approach

The ideas and methods for conditionally optimum filtering are rather simple and are thoroughly described at ([16], ch. 9). So, let us first present the basic idea of this method. In the general case, the conditional optimum filter for the optimum estimation of the desired signal $x(t)$ in presence of AWGN $n(t)$ can be presented in the form [16]:

$$\dot{\kappa}_1 = \alpha\xi(y,\kappa_1,t) + \beta\eta(y,\kappa_1,t)y(t), \quad (35)$$

where $\kappa_1(t)$ is a filtered signal; $y(t) = x(t) + n(t)$; $n(t)$ is the AWGN with intensity N_0; α, β are some time-dependent coefficients which have to be found.

The representation (35) is a generalized representation of the filtering algorithms where $\dot{\kappa}_1$ is the expectation of the filtered signal. It is clear as well [16] that this form is valid also for the quasi-optimum nonlinear filtering algorithms. In the previous part, a modified EKF algorithm was proposed for the two-time-moment case, which shows rather opportunistic improvement of the filtering accuracy, applying some heuristics related to the simplified implementation of the two-moment principle of filtering. Sure those simplifications do not allow taking full advantage of the application of the two-moment principle. Once again, this simplification is reasonable for diminishing the dimension of the filtering algorithm in order to make it practical for real-time applications. Therefore, the hope for further improvement of the characteristics of this modified EKF might be based on further optimization in the framework of conditional optimality [16].

In the theory of conditional optimality, the structure of the filter is already chosen (in our case, it is the GEKF) and the only chance for further accuracy improvement is to optimize the coefficients $\alpha(t)$ and $\beta(t)$ in order to minimize the MSE. The structure which was chosen initially is a so-called admitted structure which actually belongs to a class of the admitted filters. The next step is to minimize the MSE. The minimization of the MSE is a strategy in which the admitted filter makes an optimal transition at the moment "s" ($s > t$, $s \to t$) from an initial stage, at moment "t," to a new stage at the moment "s" with the minimum MSE. The algorithm of such kind of filter is "conditionally optimum" according to Ref. [16].

Hereafter we are not going to present all the material related to this approach as it was comprehensively described at ([16], ch. 9), we will only apply the necessary final formulas from there. Unfortunately, full use of the abovementioned approach is not possible (as we will see in the following), and so, we will present some developments that allow to obtain the coefficients $\alpha(t)$ and $\beta(t)$ successfully.

4.1. Approach to find unknown coefficients $\alpha(t)$ and $\beta(t)$

It is possible to present an admitted structure of the conditionally optimum filter from (29) in two equivalent forms:

$$\dot{\kappa}_1 = \alpha\left[K_1(\kappa_1) + \frac{\widehat{\overline{\kappa}}_2}{2}K_1''(\kappa_1)\right] + \beta\frac{\widehat{\overline{\kappa}}_2}{N_0}[y(t) - \kappa_1(t)] \tag{36}$$

$$\dot{\kappa}_1 = \alpha\left[K_1(\kappa_1) + \frac{\widehat{\overline{\kappa}}_2}{2}K_1''(\kappa_1) - \frac{\widehat{\overline{\kappa}}_2\kappa_1}{N_0}\right] + \beta\frac{\widehat{\overline{\kappa}}_2}{N_0}y(t), \tag{37}$$

where, as it was proposed earlier,

$$\widehat{\overline{\kappa}}_2 = \overline{\kappa}_2\left(1 - \overline{\kappa}_{11}^2\right). \tag{38}$$

Then, from (36) and (37), one has

$$\xi(t) = K_1(\kappa_1) + \frac{\widehat{\overline{\kappa}}_2}{2}K_1''(\kappa_1), \quad \eta(t) = \frac{\widehat{\overline{\kappa}}_2}{N_0}[y(t) - \kappa_1(t)] \tag{39}$$

$$\xi(t) = K_1(\kappa_1) + \frac{\widehat{\overline{\kappa}}_2}{2}K_1''(\kappa_1) - \frac{\widehat{\overline{\kappa}}_2\kappa_1}{N_0}, \quad \eta(t) = \frac{\widehat{\overline{\kappa}}_2}{N_0}y(t). \tag{40}$$

One can see that in this regard, α and β are weighting coefficients of a priori information related to the desired chaotic signal and a posteriori data. This issue was thoroughly commented in [27]. For SNR < 1, the weight of $\xi(t)$ obviously prevails, because a posteriori data are strongly corrupted by the additive noise. Nevertheless, taking into account that $\widehat{\overline{\kappa}}_2$ is rather small for the modified EKF, in the following, $\widehat{\overline{\kappa}}_2$ (which is actually the MSE) will be considered as a "small parameter" in all the approximations.

In order to follow all definitions and notations from ([16], ch. 9), one has to use the Ito form in all the equations:

$$\begin{aligned} dy &= Xdt + dW_1 = \phi_1(y,x,t)dt + \psi_1(y,x,t)dW_1 \\ dx &= f(x)dt + dW_2 = \phi_1(x,t)dt + \psi(x,t)dW_2, \end{aligned} \tag{41}$$

where $\{W_i(t)\}$ are independent Wiener processes, $i = 1, 2$. It is obvious that:

$$\begin{aligned} \varphi_1(x,t) &= f(x) = \kappa_1(x) \\ \varphi_1(y,x,t) &= x \\ \psi_1(y,x) &= 1 \\ \psi(x,t) &= 1 \end{aligned} \tag{42}$$

Then, from ([16], ch. 9)

$$\widehat{x}_s - \widehat{x}_t \cong \kappa_s - \kappa_t = \alpha\xi_t\Delta\mathrm{t} + \beta\eta_t\left(\phi_{1_t}\Delta t + \phi_{1_t}\Delta W\right). \tag{43}$$

Unbiased conditions for the optimum estimation from (43) are [16]:

$$\alpha < \xi_t > + < \eta_t\phi_{1_t} > - < \phi_1 >= 0. \tag{44}$$

Taking ξ_t and η_t according to its definitions from (40), it is easy to get from (44):

$$\alpha m_1 + \beta m_2 = m_0, \tag{45}$$

where $m_0 = <\varphi_t>$, $m_1 = <\xi_t>$, $m_2 = <\eta_t\varphi_{1_t}>$.

Taking into account (42) with conditions $\widehat{\overline{\kappa}}_2 < 1$ and assuming that $K_1(\kappa_1) \approx K_1''(\kappa_1) \approx 0$[1], finally one gets:

$$\frac{\beta}{\alpha} = \frac{\kappa_2}{< x^2 >}. \tag{46}$$

The next step, as it was proposed in ([16], ch. 9), is focused on checking the correlation conditions for the error $(\kappa_s - x_s)$ with the vector $[\xi\Delta t, \eta\Delta y]$ which yields to [16]:

[1]This assumption follows from symmetry conditions for $f(x)$.

$$\beta = \kappa_{0_2}\kappa_{22}^{-1}, \tag{47}$$

where

$$\kappa_{0_2} = < (x_t - \kappa_{1_t})x_t \frac{\widehat{\widehat{\kappa}}_2}{N_0} y_t > + < \eta_t \cdot y_t > \frac{\widehat{\widehat{\kappa}}_2}{N_0}, \qquad \kappa_{22} = \left(\frac{\widehat{\widehat{\kappa}}_2}{N_0}\right)^2 < y_t^2 \cdot \eta_t > . \tag{48}$$

From the second equation in (48), it follows that $\beta \to \infty$ which is a clear absurd. So, why this happened and what is wrong? Is the approach in ([16], ch. 9) wrong? Definitively, no. It is possible to show that the estimate κ_1 is unbiased and decorrelated with both components $\xi(t)$ and $\eta(t)$, but for our special case, the condition that κ_{22} (a matrix in the general case) has to be invertible is violated. Opposed as it was stated in ([16], ch. 9), the approach is not working.

The solution might be found from direct calculation of $(x-\kappa_1)$ from the SDE of chaos and (29) and by minimization of $<(x-\kappa_1)^2>$ by α or β.

4.2. Direct evaluation of the MSE and its minimization

As a first step, let us calculate the difference between the solution of (20) and (39) by applying (46):

$$(x - \kappa_1) = \int_0^T \left\{ [K_1(x) - \alpha K_1(\kappa_1)] - \frac{\alpha \kappa_1 \widehat{\widehat{\kappa}}_2 n(t)}{< x^2 > N_0} \right\} dt. \tag{49}$$

Let us take the second power of (49) and make a statistical average. One has to notice that the second power of (49) is a double integral and $<n(t_1)\, n(t_2)> = N_0\delta(t_2-t_1)$. Then, applying finally the assumption $\widehat{\widehat{\kappa}}_2 < 1$, one can get for the MSE:

$$MSE \approx \; < K_1^2(x) > + \alpha^2 < K_1^2(\kappa_1) > - 2\alpha < K_1(x)K_1(\kappa_1) > + \frac{\alpha^2 \widehat{\widehat{\kappa}}_2}{< x^2 > N_0}. \tag{50}$$

Looking for the minimum of (50) in terms of "α", one easily finds:

$$\alpha = \frac{< K_1(\kappa_1)K_1(x) >}{< K_1^2(\kappa_1) > + \frac{\widehat{\widehat{\kappa}}_2}{<x^2>}}. \tag{51}$$

Assuming that still $\widehat{\widehat{\kappa}}_2$ is a "small parameter," it follows that $\alpha \approx 1$ and $\beta \cong \frac{\kappa_1}{<x^2>} \cong O\left(\frac{1}{\kappa_1}\right)$. In this regard,

$$MSE \sim \frac{\left(\widehat{\widehat{\kappa}}_2\right)^2}{< x^2 >}. \tag{52}$$

Comparing Eq. (52) with the MSE of the one-moment filtering which is κ_2, one can see that the conditional optimum filtering might significantly improve the MSE with the same SNR or significantly diminish the SNR threshold for a fixed MSE.

The authors consider that the two-moment filtering of chaos together with the conditionally optimum principle is a very opportunistic approach to significantly improve the MSE for chaos filtering.

Author details

Valeri Kontorovich[1]*, Zinaida Lovtchikova[2] and Fernando Ramos-Alarcon[1]

*Address all correspondence to: valeri@cinvestav.mx

1 Electrical Engineering Department, Communications Section, CINVESTAV-IPN, México D.F

2 Engineering and Advanced Technology Interdisciplinary Professional Unit, UPIITA-IPN, México D.F

References

[1] Rodriguez-Bermudez G, Garcia-Laencina PJ. Analysis of EEG signals using nonlinear dynamics and chaos: A review. Applied Mathematics & Information Sciences. 2015;**9** (5):2309-2321

[2] Wu G-Q, et al. Chaotic signatures of heart rate variability and its power spectrum in health, Aging and Heart Failure. PLoS ONE Journal. 2009 Feb;**4**(2)

[3] L. Yue, Baojun Y, et al. Ability to detect weak effective seismic signals by utilizing chaotic vibrator system, Chinese Science Bulletin, Vol. 51, No. 24, pp. 3010-3017, 2006 Dec

[4] Shu-Yao J, Fei Y, et al. Application of stochastic resonance technology in underwater acoustic weak signal detection. Conference OCEANS, 10–13 April, Shangai; 2016

[5] Eisencraft M, et al. White Gaussian chaos, IEEE Communication Letters, V. 21, No. 8, pp. 1719-1722, August, 2017

[6] Ataie V, Esman D, et al. Subnoise detection of a fast random event. Science Magazine. 2015 Dec;**350**(6266):1343-1345

[7] Arditti D, Alcocer A, Ramos F, Kontorovich V. Adaptive Mitigation of Platform-Generated Radio-Frequency Interference. Patent No. 14180219.9-1852; 2014

[8] Kontorovich V, Lovtchikova Z. Multi-moment statistical characterization and non-linear filtering of chaos. COMPEL The International Journal for Computation and Mathematics in Electrical Engineering. 2013;**32**(3):885-900

[9] Eckmann J, Ruelle D. Ergodic theory and strange attractors. Reviews of Modern Physics. July 1985;**57**:617-656

[10] Kontorovich V. Applied statistical analysis for strange attractors and related problems. Mathematical Methods in the Applied Sciences. 2007;**30**:1705-1717

[11] Anischenko VS, et al. Statistical properties of dynamical chaos. Physics-Uspekhi. 2005;**48** (2):151-166

[12] Kontorovich V, et al. Analysis of Rössler attractor and its applications Special Issue on Non-linear Dynamics and Synchronization. The Open Cybernetics and Systemics Journal. 2009

[13] Mijangos M, Kontorovich V, Aguilar-Torrentera J. Some statistical properties of strange attractors: Engineering view. Journal of Physics: Conference Series 012147. 2008 Mar;**96**:6

[14] Stratonovich R. Topics of the Theory of Random Noise; V.1 and V.2. Gordon and Breach; 1963

[15] Kushner H. Dynamic equations for optimal non-linear filtering. Journal of Differential Equations. 1971;**3**:179-190

[16] Pugachev V, Sinitsyn I. Stochastic Differential Systems. Analysis and Filtering, John Wiley & Sons, Chichester, New York, 1987

[17] Arasaratnan I, Haykin S, Elliot R. Discrete-time non-linear filtering algorithms using Gauss-Hermite quadrature. Proceedings of the IEEE. May, 2007;**96**(5):953-977

[18] Ito K, Xiong K. Gaussian filters for non-linear filtering problems. IEEE Transactions on Automatic Control. 2000 May;**45**(5):910-927

[19] Julier S, Uhlman J. Unscented filtering and non-linear estimation. Proceedings of the IEEE. 2000 Mar;**92**(3):401-422

[20] Jazwinski A. Stochastic Processing and Filtering Theory. NY: Academic Press; 1970

[21] Kazakov I, Artemiev V. Optimization of dynamic systems with random structure, Nauka, Moscow, Russia, 1980 (in Russian)

[22] Primak S, Kontorovich V, Lyandres V. Stochastic Methods and Their Applications to Communications: Stochastic Differential Equations Approach. John Wiley & Sons; 2004

[23] Van Trees H. Detection, Estimation and Modulation theory. John Wiley & Sons; 2001

[24] Kushner H, Budhiraja A. A non-linear filtering algorithm based on an approximation of the conditional distribution. IEEE Transactions on Automatic Control. March 2000;**45** (3):580-585

[25] Zakai M. On the optimal filtering of diffusion processes. Wahrscheinlikenheitstheorie-verngebiete. 1969;**11**:230-243

[26] Kontorovich V. Non-linear filtering for Markov stochastic processes using high-order statistics (HOS) approach. Non-linear Analysis; Theory, Methods and Applications. 1997;**30**(5):3165-3170

[27] Kontorovich V, Lovtchikova Z. Non-linear filtering of chaos for real time applications, Chapter 3 in the book *Selected topics in non-linear dynamics and theoretical electrical engineering*, Eds. K. Kyamanya, et al., Springer, Berlin Heidelberg 2013

[28] Anischenko VS, et al. Non-linear Dynamics of chaotic and stochastic systems, Springer, Berlin Heidelberg, 2007

[29] Kontorovich V, Lovtchikova Z, Ramos F. Correlation properties of chaos: Cumulant approach. Mathematical and Computational Applications. 2010;**15**(5):946-952

Chapter 6

Chaos on Set-Valued Dynamics and Control Sets[1]

Heriberto Román-Flores and Víctor Ayala

Additional information is available at the end of the chapter

http://dx.doi.org/10.5772/intechopen.72232

Abstract

The aim of this chapter is threefold. First, we show some advances in complexity dynamics of set-valued discrete systems in connection with the Devaney's notion of chaos. Secondly, we start to explore some relationships between control sets for the class of linear control systems on Lie groups with chaotic sets. Finally, through several open problems, we invite the readers to give a contribution to this beauty theory.

Keywords: chaos, set-valued maps, dynamic, Devaney, control sets

1. Introduction

Relevant classes of real problems are modelled by a discrete dynamical system

$$x_{n+1} = f(x_n)\ ,\quad n = 0, 1, 2, \ldots \tag{1}$$

where (X, d) is a metric space and $f : X \to X$ is a continuous function. The basic goal of this theory is to understand the nature of the orbit $O(x,f) = \{f^n(x)/\ n = 0, 1, 2, \ldots\}$ for any state $x \in X$, as n becomes large and, in general this is a hard task. The study of orbits says us how the initial states are moving in the base space X and, in many cases, these orbits present a chaotic structure. In 1989 in [1], Devaney isolates three main conditions which determine the essential features of chaos.

Definition 1 *Let X be a metric space and $f : X \to X$ a continuous map. Hence, f.*

a. is *transitive* if for any couple of non-empty open subsets U and V of X there exists a natural number k such that $f^k(U) \cap V \neq \emptyset$.

b. is *periodically dense* if the set of periodic points of f is a dense subset of X.

[1]Partially supported by Conicyt, Chile through Regular Fondecyt Projects no. 1151159 and no. 1150292 respectively.

c. has *sensitive dependence on initial conditions* if there is a positive number δ (a sensitivity constant) such that for every point $x \in X$ and every neighbourhood N of x there exists a point $y \in N$ and a non-negative integer number n such that $d(f^n(x), f^n(y)) \geq \delta$.

Next, we mention a remarkable characterisation of transitive maps. In fact, as a consequence of the Birkhoff Transitivity Theorem (see [2] for details), it is possible to prove.

Proposition 2 *Let X be a complete metric space which is also perfect (closed and without isolated points). If* $f : X \to X$ *is continuous, then f is transitive if and only if there exists at least one orbit* $O(x,f)$ *dense in X.*

Remark 3 *Also, other concepts very useful in this work are the following: i) f is weakly mixing iff for any non-empty open subsets U and V of X there exists a natural number k such that* $f^k(U) \cap V \neq \varnothing$ *and* $f^k(V) \cap V \neq \varnothing$. *ii) f is mixing iff given two non-empty open subsets U and V of X there exists a natural number k such that* $f^n(U) \cap V \neq \varnothing$ *for all* $n \geq k$. *iii) f is exact iff given a non-empty open subsets U there exists a natural number k such that* $f^k(U) = X$. *It is clear that f exact* $\Rightarrow$ *f mixing* $\Rightarrow$ *f weakly mixing* $\Rightarrow f$ transitive.

It is worth to point out that sensitivity dependence on initial conditions was widely understood as being the central idea in chaos for many years. However, in a surprising way, Banks et al. has proved that transitivity and periodically density imply sensitivity dependence (for details see [3]). Furthermore, for continuous functions on real intervals, Vellekoop and Berglund in [4] show that transitivity by itself is sufficient to get chaos. This last result is not necessarily true in other type of metric spaces (see Example 4.1 in [5]).

However, sometimes we need to know information about the collective dynamics, i.e. how are moved subsets of X via iteration or dynamics induced by f. For example, if X denotes an ecosystem and $x \in X$, then, by using radio telemetry elements, we can obtain information about the movement of x in the ecosystem X. In this form, it is possible to build an individual displacement function $f : X \to X$. Of course, this function could be chaotic or not. Eventually, we could also be interested to get information about the collective dynamics induced by f, means, to follow the dynamics of a group of individuals. Thus, in a natural way the following question appears: what is the relationship between individual and collective dynamics? This is the main topic of this chapter.

Given the system (1), consider the set-valued discrete system associated to f defined by

$$A_{n+1} = \overline{f}(A_n), \quad n = 0, 1, 2, \ldots \tag{2}$$

where $\overline{f}$ is the natural extension of f to the metric space $(\mathcal{K}(X), H)$ of the non-empty compact subsets of X endowed with the Hausdorff metric H induced by the original distance d of X.

In a more general set up, this work is strictly related with the following fundamental question: what is the relationship between individual and collective chaos?

As a partial response to this question, in this chapter we search the transitivity of a continuous function f on X in relation to the transitivity of its extension $\overline{f}$ to $\mathcal{K}(X)$. Our main result here establishes that $\overline{f}$ transitive implies f transitive. That is to say, collective chaos implies individual chaos under the dynamics of $\overline{f}$.

On the other hand, we propose a new approach to this problem: to study the dynamics induced by f on the subextension $\mathcal{K}_c(X)$ of $\mathcal{K}(X)$. Precisely, on the class of non-empty compact-convex subsets of X. We prove that the induced dynamics is less chaotic than the original one!

Finally, we mention that some relevant problems in the theory of control systems can be also approached by the theory of set-valuated map. In fact, to any initial state x of the system, one can associate its reachable set $\mathcal{A}(x)$. In other words, $\mathcal{A}(x)$ contains all the possible states of the manifold that starting from x you can reach in non-negative time by using the admissible control functions $\mathcal{U}$ of the system. The aim of this section is twofold. First of all, to apply to the class of linear control systems on Lie groups, the existent relationship between control sets of an affine control system Σ on a Riemannian manifold M with chaotic sets of the shift flow induced by Σ on $M \times \mathcal{U}$, [6]. In particular, we are looking for the consequences of this relation on the controllability property. At the very end, we propose a challenge to the readers to motivate the research on this topic through some open problem relatives to the mentioned relationship.

2. Preliminaries

In this section, we mention some notions and fundamental results we use through the chapter.

2.1. Extensions

If (X, d) is a metric space and $f : X \to X$ continuous, then we can consider the space $(\mathcal{K}(X), H)$ of all non-empty and compact subsets of X endowed with the Hausdorff metric induced by d and $\overline{f} : \mathcal{K}(X) \to \mathcal{K}(X)$, $\overline{f}(A) = f(A)\}$, the natural extension of f to $\mathcal{K}(X)$. Also, we denote by $\mathcal{K}_c(X) = \{A \in \mathcal{K}(X)/A \ is \ convex\}$. If $A \in \mathcal{K}(X)$ we define the "ϵ -dilatation of A" as the set $N(A, \epsilon) = \{x \in X/ \ d(x, A) < \epsilon\}$, where $d(x, A) = \inf_{a \in A} d(x, a)$.

The Hausdorff metric on $\mathcal{K}(X)$ is given by

$$H(A, B) = \inf\{\epsilon > 0/ \ A \subseteq N(B, \epsilon) \ \text{ and } \ B \subseteq N(A, \epsilon)\}.$$

We know that $(\mathcal{K}(X), H)$ is a complete (separable, compact) metric space if and only if (X, d) is a complete (separable, compact) metric space, respectively, (see [3, 7, 8]).

Also, if $A \in \mathcal{K}(X)$, the set $B(A, \epsilon) = \{B \in \mathcal{K}(X)/H(A, B) < \epsilon\}$ denotes the ball centred in A and radius ϵ in the space $(\mathcal{K}(X), H)$.

Furthermore, given a continuous function $(I, d) \xrightarrow{f} (I, d)$ on a real interval I, we also consider the extension $(\mathcal{K}_c(I), H) \xrightarrow{\overline{f}_c} (\mathcal{K}_c(I), H)$, where $\overline{f}_c$ is the restriction $\overline{f}|_{\mathcal{K}_c(I)}$.

2.2. Baire spaces

In this section, we review some properties of Baire spaces.

Definition 4 *A topological space X is a Baire space if for any given countable family of closed sets $\{A_n : n \in \mathbf{N}\}$ covering X, then $\text{int}(A_n) \neq \emptyset$ for at least one n.*

Definition 5 *In any Baire space X,*

1. $D \subset X$ *is called nowhere dense if* $\text{int}(cl(D)) = \emptyset$.
2. Any countable union of nowhere dense sets is called a set of first category.
3. Any set not of first category is said to be of second category.
4. The complement of a set of first category is called a residual set.

Remark 6 *It is important to note that:*

a. *Any complete metric space is a Baire space.*

b. *Every residual set is of second category in X.*

c. *Every residual set is dense in X.*

d. *The complement of a residual set is of first category.*

e. *If B is of first category and* $A \subseteq B$*, then* A is of first category.

(For details, see [8–10])

In particular, if $X = I$ is an interval, then $\mathcal{C}(X)$ and $\mathcal{C}(X, \mathbb{R})$, endowed with the respective supremum metrics, are Baire spaces.

In a Baire space X, we say that "most elements of X" verify the property (P) if the set of all $x \in X$ that do not verify property (P) is of first category in X. In this form, sets of second category can be regarded as "big" sets. A relevant area of the real analysis is to estimate the "size" of some sets associated to a continuous interval function f such as the set $\mathcal{P}(f)$ of periodic points of f, or the set $\mathcal{F}(f)$ of fixed points of f. Typically, continuous interval functions have a first category set of periodic points (see [11]) and, in particular, a first category set of fixed points. It has also been recently proved that a typical continuously differentiable interval function has a finite set of fixed points and a countable set of periodic points (see [12] and references therein). It is also well-known that the class of nowhere differentiable functions $\mathcal{ND}(I)$ is a residual set in $\mathcal{C}(I)$ (see [13, 14]). Also, a special class of functions in $\mathcal{C}(I)$ is the class $\mathcal{CNL}(I)$ of all continuous functions whose graphs "cross no lines" defined in a negative way as follows (see [10]):

Definition 7 *Let* $f : [a, b] \to [a, b]$ *a continuous map and* $L : \mathbb{R} \to \mathbb{R}$ *a function whose graph is a straight line. We say that L crosses f (or f crosses L) if there exists* $x_0 \in [a, b]$ *and* $\delta > 0$ *such that* $f(x_0) = L(x_0)$ *and either.*

(a) $L(x) \leq f(x)$ *for all* $x \in [x_0 - \delta, x_0] \cap [a, b]$ *and* $L(x) \geq f(x)$ *for all* $x \in [x_0, x_0 + \delta] \cap [a, b]$*; or.*

(b) $L(x) \geq f(x)$ *for all* $x \in [x_0 - \delta, x_0] \cap [a, b]$ *and new* $L(x) \leq f(x)$ *for all* $x \in [x_0, x_0 + \delta] \cap [a, b]$.

The following result can be found in [10]:

Theorem 8 ([10]) *The set* $\mathcal{CNL}(I) = \{f \in \mathcal{C}(I) / \ f \ \textit{crosses no lines}\}$ *is residual in* $\mathcal{C}(I)$.

The set $\mathcal{CNL}(I)$ will play an important role in the next sections.

2.3. The dynamics of control theory

In Section 7, we propose some challenges through the relationship between the notion of chaotic sets in the Devaney sense and control sets for the class of Linear Control Systems on Lie Groups, [15]. In particular, we explicitly show some results concerning the controllability property in terms of chaotic dynamics.

In the sequel, we follow the relevant book The Dynamics of Control by Colonius and Kliemann, [6]. Let M be a d dimensional smooth manifold. By an *affine control system* Σ in M, we understand the family of ordinary differential equations:

$$\Sigma : \dot{x}(t) = X(x(t)) + \sum_{j=1}^{m} u_j(t) Y^j(x(t)), \qquad u = (u_1, \ldots, u_m) \in \mathcal{U} \tag{3}$$

where X, Y^j, $j = 0, 1, \ldots, m$ are arbitrary C^∞ vector fields on M. The set $\mathcal{U} \subset L^\infty(\mathbb{R}, \Omega \subset \mathbb{R}^m)$ is the class of restricted admissible control functions where $\Omega \subset \mathbb{R}^m$ with $0 \in \text{int}\Omega$, is a compact and convex set.

Assume Σ satisfy the Lie algebra rank condition, i.e.

$$\text{for any } x \in M \Rightarrow Span_{\mathcal{LA}}\{X, Y^1, \ldots, Y^m\}(x) = d.$$

Of course, $\mathcal{LA}$ means the Lie algebra generated by the vector fields through the usual notion of Lie bracket. Furthermore, the *ad* -rank condition for Σ is defined as follows:

$$\text{for any } x \in M \Rightarrow Span\{ad^i(Y^j) : j = 1, \ldots, m \text{ and } i = 0, 1, \ldots\}(x) = d.$$

For each $u \in \mathcal{U}$ and each initial value $x \in M$, there exists an unique solution $\varphi(t, x, u)$ defined on an open interval containing $t = 0$, satisfying $\varphi(0, x, u) = x$. Since we are concerned with dynamics on Lie Groups, without loss of generality we assume that the vector fields X, $Y^1, \ldots, Y^m$ are completes. Then, we obtain a mapping Φ satisfying the *cocycle property*

$$\Phi : \mathbb{R} \times M \times \mathcal{U} \to M, \qquad (t, x, u) \mapsto \Phi(t, x, u) \text{ and } \Phi(t + s, x, u) = \Phi(t, \Phi(s, x, u), \Theta_s u)$$

for all $t, s \in \mathbb{R}$, $x \in M$, $u \in \mathcal{U}$. Where, for any $t \in \mathbb{R}$, the map Θ_t is the *shift* flow on $\mathcal{U}$ defined by $(\Theta_s\ u)(t) := u(t + s)$. Hence, Φ is a skew-product flow. The topology here is given by the product topology between the topology of the manifold and the weak* topology on $\mathcal{U}$.

It turns out the following results.

Lemma 9 [6] *Consider the set* $\mathcal{U}$ *equipped with the weak* topology associated to* $L^\infty(\mathbb{R}, \mathbb{R}^m) = (L^1(\mathbb{R}, \mathbb{R}^m))^*$ *as a dual vector space. Therefore,*

1. $(\mathcal{U}, d)$ is a compact, complete and separable metric space with the distance given by

$$d(u_1, u_2) = \sum_{n=1}^{\infty} \frac{1}{2^n} \frac{\left|\int_{\mathbb{R}} < u_1(t) - u_2(t), v_n(t) > dt\right|}{1 + \left|\int_{\mathbb{R}} < u_1(t) - u_2(t), v_n(t) > dt\right|}.$$

   Here, $\{v_n : n \in \mathbb{N}\} \subset L^1(\mathbb{R}, \mathbb{R}^m)$ is a dense set of Lebesgue integrable functions.

2. The map $\Theta : \mathbb{R} \times \mathcal{U} \rightarrow \mathcal{U}$ defines a continuous dynamical systems on $\mathcal{U}$. Its periodic points are dense and the shift is topologically mixing (and then topologically transitive).

3. The map Φ defines a continuous dynamical system on $M \times \mathcal{U}$.

On the other hand, the completely controllable property of Σ, i.e. the possibility to connect any two arbitrary points of M through a Σ-trajectory in positive time, is one of the most relevant issue for any control system. But, few systems have this property. A more realistic approach comes from a Kliemann notion introduced in [16].

Definition 10 *A non-empty set $\mathcal{C} \subset M$ is called a control set of (3) if.*

i. for every $x \in M$ there exists $u \in \mathcal{U}$ such that $\{\varphi(t, x, u) : t \geq 0\} \subset \mathcal{C}$

ii. for every $x \in \mathcal{C}$, $\mathcal{C} \subset \mathrm{cl}(\mathcal{A}(x))$

iii. $\mathcal{C}$ is maximal with respect to the properties (i) and (ii).

$\mathcal{A}(x)$ denotes the states that can be reached from x by Σ in positive time and cl its closure

$$\mathcal{A}(x) = \{y \in M : \exists u \in \mathcal{U} \text{ and } t > 0 \text{ with } y = \varphi(t, x, u)\}.$$

Moreover, for an element $x \in M$, the set of points that can be steered to x through a Σ-trajectory in positive time is denoted by

$$\mathcal{A}^*(x) = \underset{\tau > 0}{\cup} \{y \in M : \exists u \in \mathcal{U}, \quad e = \varphi_{\tau, u}(x)\}.$$

Finally, we mention that the Lie algebra rank condition warranty that the system is locally accessible, which means that for every $\tau > 0$,

$$\mathrm{int}(\mathcal{A}_{\leq \tau}(x)) \text{ and } \mathrm{int}\left(\mathcal{A}^*_{\leq \tau}(x)\right) \text{ are non empty, for any } x \in M.$$

3. $\overline{f}$ transitive implies f transitive

As we explain, in terms of the original dynamics and its extensions a natural question arises: what are the relations between individual and collective chaos? As a partial response to this question, in the sequel, we show that the transitivity of the extension $\overline{f}$ implies the transitivity of f. For that, we need to describe some previous results.

Lemma 11 [5] *Let A be a non-empty open subset of X. If $K \in \mathcal{K}(X)$ and $K \subset A$, then there exists $\epsilon > 0$ such that $N(K, \epsilon) \subset A$..*

Definition 12 *Let $A \subset X$ be. Then the extension of A to $\mathcal{K}(X)$ is given by $e(A) = \{K \in \mathcal{K}(X) / \ K \subset A\}$.*

Remark 13 $e(A) = \varnothing \Leftrightarrow A = \varnothing$..

Lemma 14 [5] *Let $A \subset X$ be, $A \neq \varnothing$, an open subset of X. Then, $e(A)$ is a non-empty open subset of $\mathcal{K}(X)$.*

Lemma 15 [5] *If* $A, B \subset X$, *then: i)* $e(A \cap B) = e(A) \cap e(B)$, *ii)* $\overline{f}(e(A)) \subseteq e(f(A))$, *and iii)* $\overline{f}^p = \overline{f^p}$, *for every* $p \in \mathbb{N}$.

Now, we are in a position to prove the following results

Theorem 16 *Let* $f : X \to X$ *be a continuous function. Then,* $\overline{f}$ *transitive implies* f *transitive.*

Proof: Let A, B be two non-empty open sets in X. Due to Lemma 13, $e(A)$ and $e(B)$ are non-empty open sets in $\mathcal{K}(X)$. Thus, by transitivity of $\overline{f}$, there exists some $k \in \mathbb{N}$ such that

$$\overline{f}^k(e(A)) \cap e(B) = \overline{f^k}(e(A)) \cap e(B) \neq \varnothing$$

and, from Lemma 14, we obtain

$$e\left(f^k(A)\right) \cap e(B) = e\left(f^k(A) \cap B\right) \neq \varnothing$$

which implies $f^k(A) \cap B \neq \varnothing$ and, consequently, f is a transitive function.

4. Two examples

Now we show that, in general, the converse of Theorem 15 is not true.

Example 4.1 (Translations of the circle). If $\lambda \in \mathbb{R}$ is an irrational number and we define $T_\lambda : S^1 \to S^1$ by $T_\lambda\left(e^{i\theta}\right) = e^{i(\theta + 2\pi\lambda)}$, then it was shown by Devaney [1] that each orbit $\left\{T_\lambda^n\left(e^{i\theta}\right)/n \in \mathbb{N}\right\}$ is dense in S^1 and, due Proposition 2, T_λ is transitive. Nevertheless, T_λ has no periodic points and, because T_λ is isometric, it does not exhibit sensitive dependence on initial conditions either.

If $K \in \mathcal{K}\left(S^1\right)$, because $\overline{T_\lambda}$ preserves diameter, then $diam(K) = diam\left(\overline{T_\lambda}^n(K)\right)$, for all $n \in \mathbb{N}$.

Now, let $K \in \mathcal{K}\left(S^1\right)$ such that $diam(K) = 1$, and let $\epsilon > 0$ sufficiently small. Then

$$\begin{aligned} F \in U = B(K, \epsilon) \quad &\Rightarrow \quad diam(F) \approx 1 \\ G \in V = B(\{1\}, \epsilon) \quad &\Rightarrow \quad diam(G) \approx 0. \end{aligned}$$

Thus, $diam\left(\overline{T_\lambda}^n(F)\right) \approx 1 \quad \forall n \in \mathbb{N}$ and, consequently, $\overline{T_\lambda}^n(U) \cap V = \varnothing$ for all $n \in \mathbb{N}$, which implies that $\overline{T_\lambda}$ is not transitive on $\mathcal{K}\left(S^1\right)$.

Example 4.2 Define the "tent" function $f : [0, 1] \to [0, 1]$ as $f(x) = 2x \ \ if \ \ 0 \leq x \leq 1/2$ and $f(x) = 2(1 - x) \ \ if \ \ 1/2 \leq x \leq 1$.

It is not difficult to show that f is an exact function on [0,1]. In fact, intuitively we can see that, after each iteration, the number of tent in the graphics is increasing, whereas the base of each tent is decreasing and they are uniformly distributed over the interval $[0, 1]$.

Thus, if U is an arbitrary non-empty open subset of $[0, 1]$, then U contains an open interval J and, after certain number of iterations, there exists a tent, with height equal to one, whose base is contained in J, which implies that $f(U) = [0, 1]$ and, according to Remark 3, f is an exact mapping and, consequently, f is a mixing function.

The conclusions in Examples 4.1 and 4.2 come from the next result, Banks [17] in 2005.

Theorem 17 *If $f : X \to X$ is continuous, then the following conditions are equivalent:*

i) f is weakly mixing, ii) $\overline{f}$ is weakly mixing, iii) $\overline{f}$ is transitive.

Hitherto, we have used the strong topology induced by the H-metric on $\mathcal{K}(X)$. However, considering the w^e-topology on $\mathcal{K}(X)$ generated by the sets $e(A)$ with A an open set in X, we obtain the following complementary result, see [5]:

Theorem 18 *For a continuous map $f : X \to X$ the following conditions are equivalent:*

i) f is transitive in (X, d), ii) $\overline{f}$ is transitive in the w^e-topology.

5. Sensitivity and periodic density of $\overline{f}$

Let $f : X \to X$ be a continuous function and let $\overline{f}$ be its corresponding extension to the hyperspace $\mathcal{K}(X)$. Then, the study of sensitivity of f in the base space in relation to the sensitivity of $\overline{f}$ on $\mathcal{K}(X)$ has been very exhaustively analysed in the last years. Román and Chalco published the first result in this direction [18] in 2005, where the authors prove

Theorem 19 *$\overline{f}$ sensitively dependent implies f sensitively dependent.*

Proof: If $\overline{f}$ has sensitive dependence, then there exists a constant $\delta > 0$ such that for every $K \in \mathcal{K}(X)$ and every $\epsilon > 0$ there exists $G \in B(K, \epsilon)$ and $n \in \mathbb{N}$ such that $H(f^n(K), f^n(G)) \geq \delta$.

Now, let $x \in X$ be and $\epsilon > 0$. Then, taking $K = \{x\} \in \mathcal{K}(X)$, we have that there exists $G \in B(\{x\}, \epsilon)$ and $n \in \mathbb{N}$ such that $H(f^n(\{x\}), f^n(G)) = H(f^n(x), f^n(G)) \geq \delta$.

Thus, $H(f^n(x), f^n(G)) = \sup_{y \in G} d(f^n(x), f^n(y)) \geq \delta$ and, due to the compactness of G and the continuity of f, there exists $y_0 \in G$ such that $H(f^n(x), f^n(G)) = d\left(f^n(x), f^n\left(y_0\right)\right) \geq \delta$.

But, $G \in B(x, \epsilon)$ implies $G \subset B(x, \epsilon)$ and, consequently, $y_0 \in B(x, \epsilon)$. This proves that f is sensitively dependent (with constant δ).

The reverse of this theorem is not true. In fact, recently Sharma and Nagar [19] show an example where (X, d) is sensitive but $(\mathcal{K}(X), H)$ is not. Now, in order to overcome that shortcoming, the authors in [19] introduce the following notion of sensitivity:

Definition 20 *(Stronger sensitivity* [19]*). Let $f : X \to X$ be a continuous function. Then f is strongly sensitive if there exists $\delta > 0$ such that for each $x \in X$ and each $\epsilon > 0$, there exists $n_0 \in \mathbb{N}$ such that for every $n \geq n_0$, there is a $y \in X$ with $d(x, y) < \epsilon$ and $d(f^n(x), f^n(y)) > \delta$.*

Obviously, the notion of stronger sensitivity is more restrictive than sensitivity, and the authors in [19] obtain the following results:

Theorem 21 *If $f : X \to X$ is a continuous function and $\left(\mathcal{K}(X), H, \overline{f}\right)$ is strongly sensitive then (X, d, f) is strongly sensitive.*

In the compact case, it is possible to obtain a characterization as follows.

Theorem 22 *Let (X, d) be a compact metric space and $f : X \to X$ a continuous function. Then $\left(\mathcal{K}(X), H, \overline{f}\right)$ is strongly sensitive if and only if (X, d, f) is strongly sensitive.*

In connection with these results, recently Subrahmomian ([20], 2007) has been shown that most of the important sensitive dynamical systems are all strongly sensitive (the author here calls them cofinitely sensitive). Hence, we can say that for most cases, sensitivity is equivalent in both cases (X, d) and $(K(X), H)$. It turns out that, strongly sensitivity and sensitivity are equivalent on the class of interval functions, which implies that

Theorem 23 *If $f : I \to I$ is a continuous function, the following conditions are equivalent.*

a) (I, d, f) is sensitive, b) $\left(K(I), H, \overline{f}\right)$ is sensitive.

We finish this section assuming the existence of a dense set of periodic points for $\overline{f}$, we have

Theorem 24 *Let (X, d) be a compact metric space and $f : X \to X$ a continuous function. If $f : X \to X$ has a dense set of periodic points then $\overline{f} : \mathcal{K}(X) \to \mathcal{K}(X)$ has the same property.*

Proof: Let $K \in \mathcal{K}(X)$ and $\epsilon > 0$. Then there exists a $\epsilon/2$-net covering K, That is to say, there are $x_1, \ldots, x_p$ in K such that $K \subset B(x_1, \epsilon/2) \cup \ldots \cup B\left(x_p, \epsilon/2\right)$. Because f has periodic density, there are $y_i \in X$ and $n_i \in N$ such that:

$$y_i \in B(x_i, \epsilon/2) \ , \forall i = 1, \ldots, p \ \text{ and } \ f^{n_i}\left(y_i\right) = y_i \ , \forall i = 1, \ldots, p.$$

Now, take $G = \left\{y_1, \ldots, y_p\right\}$. By construction, we have $H(K, G) < \epsilon$ and, moreover, $f^{n_1 n_2 \ldots n_p}\left(y_i\right) = y_i$, for all $i = 1, \ldots, p$. Therefore, $f^{n_1 n_2 \ldots n_p}(G) = G$, which implies that $\overline{f}$ has periodic density.

The converse of this theorem is no longer true (for a counterexample, see Banks [17]). However, to find conditions on $\overline{f}$ warranting the existence of a dense set of periodic points for f is a very hard problem which still remains open.

6. The dynamics on the $(\mathcal{K}_c(I), H)$ extension

In the previous sections, we have studied the diagram

$$\begin{array}{ccc} (\mathcal{K}(X), H) & \overset{\overline{f}}{\rightarrow} & (\mathcal{K}(X), H) \\ \uparrow & & \uparrow \\ (X, d) & \overset{f(X,d)}{\rightarrow} & \end{array} \tag{4}$$

and the chaotic relationships between f and $\overline{f}$. However, in the setting of mathematical modelling of many real-world applications, it is necessary to take into account additional considerations such as vagueness or uncertainty on the variables. This implies the use of interval parameters and, consequently, to deal with interval systems. That is, it is necessary to consider an interval $X = I$ and to study the following new diagram:

$$\begin{array}{ccc} (\mathcal{K}_c(I), H) & \overset{\overline{f}_c}{\rightarrow} & (\mathcal{K}_c(I), H) \\ \uparrow & & \uparrow \\ (I, d) & \overset{f(I,d)}{\rightarrow} & \end{array} \tag{5}$$

along with the analysis of the connection between their respective dynamical relationships. Here $\overline{f}_c$ denotes the restriction of $\overline{f}$ to $\mathcal{K}_c(I)$, the class of all compact subintervals of I. For $A = [a, b], B = [c, d] \in \mathcal{K}_c(I)$, the Hausdorff metric can be explicitly computed as

$$H(A, B) = \max\{|a - c|, |b - d|\}. \tag{6}$$

The aim of this section is to show that the Devaney complexity of the extension $\overline{f}_c$ on $\mathcal{K}_c(I)$ is less or equal than the complexity of f on the base space I. More precisely, $\overline{f}_c$ is never transitive for any continuous function $f \in \mathcal{C}(I)$. Also, we will show that $\overline{f}_c$ has no dense set of periodic points for most functions $f \in \mathcal{C}(I)$. Finally, we prove that $\overline{f}_c$ has no sensitive dependence for most functions $f \in \mathcal{C}(I)$.

As a motivation, we present the following examples.

Example 6.1 Consider the "tent" function $f : [0, 1] \rightarrow [0, 1]$ defined by

$$f(x) = \begin{cases} 2x & \text{if } 0 \leq x \leq \dfrac{1}{2} \\ 2(1 - x) & \text{if } \dfrac{1}{2} \leq x \leq 1. \end{cases}$$

Then it is well known that f is D-chaotic on $[0, 1]$ (see [1]). Moreover, because f is a mixing function on $[0, 1]$, then $\overline{f}$ is transitive on $\mathcal{K}([0, 1])$ (see [17]). Also, we observe that $x = \frac{2}{3}$ is a fixed point of f. On the other hand, it is clear that if K is a compact and convex subset of $X = [0, 1]$, then $\overline{f}(K)$ is also a compact and convex subset of X. Consequently, if we let $\mathcal{K}_c([0, 1])$ denote the class of all closed subintervals of $[0, 1]$, then we can consider $\overline{f}_c$ as a mapping $\overline{f}_c : \mathcal{K}_c([0, 1]) \rightarrow \mathcal{K}_c([0, 1])$. We recall that $\mathcal{K}_c([0, 1])$ is a closed subspace of $\mathcal{K}([0, 1])$ (see [21]). Now, considering the open balls $B\left([0, 1], \frac{1}{10}\right)$ and $B\left(\{0\}, \frac{1}{10}\right)$ in $\mathcal{K}_c([0, 1])$, we have.

$K \in B\left([0, 1], \frac{1}{10}\right) \Rightarrow \frac{2}{3} \in K$ which implies $\frac{2}{3} \in \overline{f}_c^p(K)$, $\forall p \in \mathbb{N}$..

On the other hand, if $F \in B\left(\{0\}, \frac{1}{10}\right)$, then $F \subset [0, 1/10]$. Consequently, $H\left(\overline{f}_c^p(K), F\right) \geq \frac{17}{30}$ for every $K \in B\left([0, 1], \frac{1}{10}\right)$ and $F \in B\left(\{0\}, \frac{1}{10}\right)$.

Therefore,

$$\overline{f}_c^p\left(B\left([0,1],\frac{1}{10}\right)\right)\cap B\left(\{0\},\frac{1}{10}\right)=\varnothing,\ \ \forall p\in\mathbb{N}.$$

Thus, $\overline{f}_c$ is not transitive on $\mathcal{K}_c([0,1])$.

Example 6.1 shows a function f which is transitive on the base space $X=[0,1]$ and $\overline{f}$ is also transitive on the total extension $\mathcal{K}([0,1])$, but $\overline{f}_c$ is not transitive on the subextension $\mathcal{K}_c([0,1])$.

The following example shows a function $f:[0,1]\to 0,1]$ with a dense set of periodic points, and where the total extension of f to $\mathcal{K}([0,1])$ also has a dense set of periodic points, whereas $\overline{f}_c$ does not have a dense set of periodic points on $\mathcal{K}_c([0,1])$.

Example 6.2. Let $X=[0,1]$ and consider the "logistic" function $f:[0,1]\to[0,1]$ defined by $f(x)=4x(1-x)$. It is well known that f is D-chaotic on $[0,1]$ (see [1]). Moreover, f is a mixing function. Thus, in particular, f has a dense set of periodic points and, therefore, $\overline{f}$ also has a dense set of periodic points on the total extension $\mathcal{K}([0,1]))$ (see Theorem 24).

However, $\overline{f}_c$ has no a dense set of periodic points on $\mathcal{K}_c(X)$.

In order to see this, we claim that the open ball $B\left(\left[\frac{1}{8},\frac{3}{8}\right],\frac{1}{8}\right)$ in $(\mathcal{K}_c([0,1]),H)$ does not contain periodic points of $\overline{f}_c$.

In fact, if $K=[c,d]\in B\left(\left[\frac{1}{8},\frac{3}{8}\right],\frac{1}{8}\right)$, then $\left|c-\frac{1}{8}\right|<\frac{1}{8}$ and $\left|d-\frac{3}{8}\right|<\frac{1}{8}$, which implies that $0<c<\frac{1}{4}$ and $\frac{1}{4}<d<\frac{1}{2}$.

Thus, we obtain that $\frac{1}{4}\in K\Rightarrow\frac{3}{4}\in f(K)\Rightarrow f(K)\neq K$.

On the other hand,

$$\frac{3}{4}\in f(K)\Rightarrow\frac{3}{4}\in f^n(K),\forall n\geq 2\Rightarrow f^n(K)\neq K,\forall n\geq 1$$

and, consequently, $\overline{f}_c$ has no periodic points in the ball $B\left(\left[\frac{1}{8},\frac{3}{8}\right],\frac{1}{4}\right)\subseteq(\mathcal{K}_c([0,1]),H)$, which implies that $\overline{f}_c$ has no dense set of periodic points on $(\mathcal{K}_c([0,1]),H)$.

Lemma 25 $\overline{f}_c$ *transitive on* $\mathcal{K}_c([a,b])$ *implies* f *transitive on* $[a,b]$.

Proof. Let U,V non-empty open subsets of $X=[a,b]$. We can choose $x\in U$, $y\in V$ and $\epsilon>0$ such that $B(x,\epsilon)\subset U$ and $B(y,\epsilon)\subset V$. Now, in $\mathcal{K}_c([a,b])$ consider the open balls $B(\{x\},\epsilon)$ and $B(\{y\},\epsilon)$ with respect to the H-metric. Due to the transitivity of $\overline{f}_c$ on $\mathcal{K}_c([a,b])$, there exists $n\in\mathbb{N}$ such that $\overline{f}_c^n(B(\{x\},\epsilon))\cap B(\{y\},\epsilon)\neq\varnothing$.

Therefore, there exists an interval $J\in B(\{x\},\epsilon)$ such that $\overline{f}_c^n(J)=f^n(J)\in B(\{y\},\epsilon)$. However, $J\subset B(x,\epsilon)$ and, analogously, $f^n(J)\subset B(y,\epsilon)$, which implies that $f^n(B(x,\epsilon))\cap B(y,\epsilon)\neq\varnothing$ and, consequently, $f^n(U)\cap V\neq\varnothing$. And f is a transitive function on $[a,b]$.

It is well-known that if $X = I$ is an interval, then most functions $f \in \mathcal{C}(I)$ has no dense orbits, that is to say, there exists a residual set $D \subset \mathcal{C}(I)$ such that every function $f \in D$ has no point whose orbit is dense in I (see [22]) and, consequently, most functions $f \in \mathcal{C}(I)$ are not transitive. From Lemma 24, we can conclude that $\overline{f}_c$ is not transitive for most functions $f \in \mathcal{C}(I)$.

The next theorem provides a stronger result.

Theorem 26 *Let $f : [a, b] \to [a, b]$ be continuous. Then $\overline{f}_c$ is not transitive on $\mathcal{K}_c([a, b])$.*

Proof. By Schauder Theorem, f has at least one fixed point $p \in [a, b]$.

Case 1. Suppose that $p \in (a, b)$ and let $r = \max\{p - a, b - p\}$. Without loss of generality, we can suppose that $r = p - a$ and, because $a < b$, it is clear that $r > 0$.

Now, let $r' = b - p > 0$ and let $\epsilon = \frac{r'}{2}$. If we consider the open balls $B([a, b], \epsilon),\ B(\{a\}, \epsilon) \in \mathcal{K}_c([a, b])$, it follows that $K \in B([a, b], \epsilon) \Rightarrow p \in K \Rightarrow p \in \overline{f}^n(K)$ for any $n \in \mathbb{N}$.

On the other hand,

$$F \in B(\{a\}, \epsilon) \Rightarrow H(F, \{a\}) < \epsilon \Rightarrow F \subset a, a + \epsilon] \ .$$

Because $r' < r$ we get

$$H\left(\overline{f}^n(K), F\right) \geq p - a - \epsilon = r - \frac{r'}{2} > 0$$

for each $K \in B([a, b], \epsilon),\ F \in B(a, \epsilon)$ and for any $n \in \mathbf{N}$. Thus,

$$\overline{f}^n(B([a, b], \epsilon)) \cap B(a, \epsilon) = \varnothing \ , \quad \forall n \in \mathbb{N}.$$

Consequently, $\overline{f}$ is not transitive on $\mathcal{K}_c([a, b])$.

Case 2. Suppose that f has no fixed points in (a, b). From the continuity of f, we have that $f(x) > x$ for all $x \in (a, b)$ or $f(x) < x$ for all $x \in (a, b)$. This clearly implies that f is not a transitive function, and consequently, due to Lemma 24, $\overline{f}_c$ is not transitive on $\mathcal{K}_c([a, b])$.

An important question to answer is what about the size of the set of periodic points of $\overline{f}_c$. It is clear that there are some functions $f \in \mathcal{C}(I)$ with a dense set of periodic points on I, and such that their extensions $\overline{f}_c$ also has a dense set of periodic points on $\mathcal{K}_c(I)$ (for instance, $f(x) = x$). Therefore, an analogous result to Theorem 26, but for periodic density of $\overline{f}_c$, cannot be obtained. However, as we will see, most functions $f \in \mathcal{C}(I)$ do not have an extension $\overline{f}_c$ with a dense set of periodic points on $\mathcal{K}_c(I)$. To prove it, we need the following lemma.

Lemma 27 *Let I be a compact interval in $\mathbb{R}$, and $f : I \to I$ be a continuous function. If we suppose that $\overline{f}_c$ has periodic density on $\mathcal{K}_c(I)$, then f has periodic density on I.*

Proof. If $x_0 \in I$ and $\epsilon > 0$ then $\{x_0\} \in \mathcal{K}_c(I)$ and, consequently, there exists $K \in \mathcal{K}_c(I)$ and $n \in \mathbb{N}$ such that

a. $H(\{x_0\}, K) < \epsilon$

b. $\overline{f}_c^n(K) = K$.

Combining a. and b. we get

$$d(x_0, f^n(x)) < \epsilon, \quad for \ \ all \ \ x \in K. \tag{7}$$

Because $\overline{f}^n(K) = \overline{f^n}(K) = f^n(K) = K$ and f^n is continuous on K then, by the Schauder's Fixed Point Theorem, there exists $x_p \in K$ such that $f^n(x_p) = x_p$. Thus, x_p is a periodic point of f and, due to (7), we obtain $d(x_0, x_p) < \epsilon$. Hence, f has periodic density on I. □

Theorem 28 *Let $I = [a, b]$ be a compact interval in $\mathbb{R}$. Then $\overline{f}_c$ does not have a dense set of periodic points in $\mathcal{K}_c(I)$, for most functions $f \in C(I)$.*

Proof. The proof is based on an exhaustive analysis of the behaviour of the fixed points of f. We connect this analysis with an adequate residual set in $C(I)$. The analysis of each fixed point of f is fundamental to decide whether the function f allows or not an extension $\overline{f}_c$ that has a dense set of periodic points. More precisely, the behaviour of each fixed point will imply only two (mutually exclusive) options:

A. $\overline{f}_c$ does not have a dense set of periodic points, or.

B. $f \in [\mathcal{CNL}(I)]^c$, which is a set of first category in $C(I)$.

Towards this end, let $f : [a, b] \to [a, b]$ be a continuous function. By the Schauder's Fixed Point Theorem, f has at least one fixed point $p \in [a, b]$. The proof is divided in.

Case 1. f has no fixed points in (a, b).

In this case, we have the following three subcases:

1i) $p = a$ is the unique fixed point of f.

We have, either

$$f(x) > x \ , \forall \ x \in (a, b) \quad (\Rightarrow x < f(x) < f^2(x) < \ldots < f^n(x) < \ldots), \text{or}$$

$$f(x) < x \ , \forall \ x \in (a, b) \quad (\Rightarrow x > f(x) > f^2(x) > \ldots > f^n(x) > \ldots).$$

In both cases it follows that f has no periodic points in (a, b).

1ii) $p = b$ is the unique fixed point of f.

This case is analogous to the case 1i).

1iii) $p = a$ and $p = b$ are the unique fixed points of f.

This case is also analogous to the cases 1i) and 1ii).

Therefore, in case 1 the function f does not have a dense set of periodic points in $[a, b]$. Due to Lemma 24, $\overline{f}_c$ does not have a dense set of periodic points in $\mathcal{K}_c([a, b])$.

Case 2. f has at least one fixed point $p \in (a, b)$.

We have the following subcases:

2*i*) $\exists\ q \in (a, b)\ , q \neq p$ such that $f(q) = p$.

Without loss of generality, suppose that $q \in (a, p)$. Then, taking $0 < \epsilon < \min\{\frac{q-a}{2}, \frac{p-q}{2}\}$, we can consider the open ball $B([q-\epsilon, q+\epsilon], \epsilon)$ in the space $\mathcal{K}_c([a, b])$. If $J = [c, d] \in B([q-\epsilon, q+\epsilon], \epsilon)$, from (6) we have

$$|c-(q-\epsilon)| < \epsilon \quad and \quad |d-(q+\epsilon)| < \epsilon$$

which implies that $a < c < q$ and $q < d < p$ and, consequently, $q \in J$ whereas $p \notin J$. Thus,

$$q \in J \ \Rightarrow f(q) = p \in f(J) \ \Rightarrow f(J) \neq J\ . \tag{8}$$

On the other hand, $p \in f(J)$ implies that

$$p \in f^n(J), \forall n \geq 2 \Rightarrow f^n(J) \neq J, \forall n \geq 2\ , \tag{9}$$

and, consequently, $\overline{f}_c$ has no periodic points in the ball $B([q-\epsilon, q+\epsilon], \epsilon) \subseteq (\mathcal{K}_c([a, b]), H)$, which implies that $\overline{f}_c$ does not have a dense set of periodic points on $(\mathcal{K}_c([a, b]), H)$.

2*ii*) $q = a,\ \ q \neq p$, is the unique point such that $f(a) = p$.

Without loss of generality, we can suppose that $f(x) > p$, for all $x \in (a, p)$.

Now, in addition to hypothesis 2*ii*), we have two subcases:

2*iia*$_1$) f does not cross the line $y = p$ and $f(x) > p$ for all $x \in (a, p)$.

In this situation, $f(x) \geq p$ for all $x \in a, b]$. Thus, choosing $q \in (a, p)$ and $0 < \epsilon < \max\{\frac{q-a}{2}, \frac{p-q}{2}\}$, we can consider the open ball $B(\{q\}, \epsilon)$ to have

$$K = [c, d] \in B(\{q\}, \epsilon) \Rightarrow K \subset (a, p). \tag{10}$$

From our hypothesis, we obtain

$$f^n(z) > p\ ,\ \ \forall z \in K,\ \ \forall n \in \mathbb{N}, \tag{11}$$

which implies that $f^n(K) \neq K$, $\forall n \in \mathbb{N}$. Consequently, $\overline{f}_c$ has no periodic points in the ball $B(\{q\}, \epsilon)$. In other words, $\overline{f}_c$ does not have a dense set of periodic points in $\mathcal{K}_c(I)$.

2*iia*$_2$) f does not cross the line $y = p$ and $f(x) < p$ for all $x \in (a, p)$.

In this case, $f(x) \geq p$ for all $x \in [a, b]$. Thus, choosing $q \in (p, b)$ and $0 < \epsilon < \max\left\{\frac{q-p}{2}, \frac{b-q}{2}\right\}$, we can consider the open ball $B(\{q\}, \epsilon)$ to obtain

$$K = [c, d] \in B(\{q\}, \epsilon) \Rightarrow K \subset (p, b). \tag{12}$$

Again, from our hypothesis, we get

$$f^n(z) < p\ ,\ \ \forall z \in K,\ \ \forall n \in \mathbb{N}, \tag{13}$$

which implies that $f^n(K) \neq K$, $\forall n \in \mathbb{N}$ and, consequently, $\overline{f}_c$ has no periodic points in the ball $B(\{q\}, \epsilon)$. In other words, $\overline{f}_c$ does not have a dense set of periodic points in $\mathcal{K}_c(I)$.

$2iib)$ f crosses the line $y = p$.

It is clear that, in this case, $f \in [\mathcal{CNL}(I)]^c$ which, due to Theorem 8 and Remark 6, is a set of first category in $\mathcal{C}([a, b])$.

$2iii)$ $q = b,\ \ q \neq p$, is the unique point such that $f(b) = p$.

This case is analogous to case $2ii)$ and, consequently, if f does not cross the line $y = p$ then $\overline{f}_c$ does not have a dense set of periodic points in $\mathcal{K}_c(I)$, whereas if f crosses the line $y = p$, then $f \in [\mathcal{CNL}(I)]^c$.

$2iv)$ $q_1 = a$ and $q_2 = b,\ \ q_1, q_2 \neq p$, are the unique points such that $f(a) = f(b) = p$.

In this case, we have the following subcases:

$2iva_1)$ f does not cross the line $y = p$ and $f(x) > p$ and $f(x) > p$ for all $x \in (a, b)\ \{p\}$.

This case is analogous to the case $2iia_1)$ and the same is true for $2iva_2)$ when f does not cross the line $y = p$ and $f(x) < p$ for all $x \in (a, b)\ \{p\}$ which is analogous to the case $2iia_2)$ Finally, there only remains two subcases:

$2ivb_1)$ f crosses the line $y = p$ and $f(x) > p$ in (a, p) and $f(x) < p$ in (p, b), and.

$2ivb_2)$ f crosses the line $y = p$ and $f(x) < p$ in (a, p) and $f(x) > p$ in (p, b).

It is clear that in both cases $f \in [\mathcal{CNL}(I)]^c$.

Thus, as a direct consequence of the analysis of the behaviour of the set of fixed points of f, it turns out that the unique cases in which f could have an extension $\overline{f}_c$ with a dense set of periodic points on $\mathcal{K}_c(I)$ are when there exists a fixed point p of f such that f crosses the line $y = p$ at $x = p$. In other words, we obtain

$$\mathcal{HDS}(I) = \{f \in \mathcal{C}(I) /\ \overline{f}_c \text{ has a dense set of periodic points in } \mathcal{K}_c(I)\} \Rightarrow \mathcal{HDS}(I) \subseteq [\mathcal{CNL}(I)]^c,$$

But, $\mathcal{CNL}(I)$ is a residual set in $\mathcal{C}(I)$, therefore from Remark 6, we conclude that $\mathcal{HDS}(I)$ is of first category in $\mathcal{C}(I)$. Equivalently, $\overline{f}_c$ does not have a dense set of periodic points, for most functions $f \in \mathcal{C}(I)$, which ends the proof.

Finally based on the following result,

Theorem 29 ([23]) *For most functions $f \in \mathcal{C}(I)$, the set of all points where f is sensitive is dense in the set of all periodic points of f.*

we show an analogous result for the sensitivity property, as follows.

Theorem 30 *For most functions $f \in \mathcal{C}(I)$, the extension $\overline{f}_c \in \mathcal{C}(\mathcal{K}_c(I))$ is not sensitive.*

Proof. This is a direct consequence of Theorem 28 and Theorem 29.

7. Control sets of linear systems and chaotic dynamics

The aim of this section is twofold. First of all, to start to apply to the class of linear control systems on Lie groups, the existent relationship between control sets of an affine control system Σ on a Riemannian manifold M with chaotic sets of the shift flow induced by Σ on $M \times \mathcal{U}$, [6]. In particular, we are looking for the consequences of this relation on the controllability property The second part is intended to motivate the research on this topic to writing down some open problems relatives to this relationship.

7.1. Linear control systems on lie groups

Let G be a connected d dimensional Lie group with Lie algebra $\mathfrak{g}$. A linear control system Σ_L on G is an affine system determined by

$$\Sigma_L : \dot{x}(t) = \mathcal{X}(x(t)) + \sum_{j=1}^{m} u_j(t) Y^j(x(t)), \qquad u = (u_1, \dots, u_m) \in \mathcal{U} \tag{14}$$

where $\mathcal{X}$ is linear, that is, its flow $(\mathcal{X}_t)_{t \in \mathbb{R}}$ is a one-parameter group of G-automorphism, the control vectors Y^j, $j = 1, \dots, m$ are invariant vector fields, as elements of $\mathfrak{g}$. The restricted class of admissible control $\mathcal{U}$ is the same as before.

Certainly, the drift vector field $\mathcal{X}$ is complete and the same is true for every invariant vector field Y^j, $j = 1, \dots, m$. As usual, we assume that Σ_L satisfy the Lie algebra rank condition, i.e.

$$\text{for any } x \in M \Rightarrow Span_{\mathcal{LA}}\{\mathcal{X}, Y^1, \dots, Y^m\}(x) = d.$$

The system is said to be controllable if $\mathcal{A}(e) = \mathcal{A}$ is G.

The class of systems Σ_L is huge and contains many relevant algebraic systems as the classical linear and bilinear systems on Euclidean spaces [6], and the class of invariant systems on Lie groups, [24]. Furthermore, according to the Jouan Equivalence Theorem [25], Σ_L is also relevant in applications. It approaches globally any affine non-linear control system Σ on a Riemannian manifold when the Lie algebra of the dynamics of Σ is finite dimensional.

One can associate to $\mathcal{X}$ a derivation $\mathcal{D}$ of $\mathfrak{g}$ defined by $\mathcal{D}Y = -[\mathcal{X}, Y](e)$, $Y \in \mathfrak{g}$.Indeed, the Jacobi identity shows $\mathcal{D}[X, Y] = [\mathcal{D}X, Y] + [X, \mathcal{D}Y]$ is in fact a derivation. The relation between φ_t and $\mathcal{D}$ is given by the formula

$$\varphi_t(\exp Y) = \exp\left(e^{t\mathcal{D}}Y\right), \quad \text{for all } t \in \mathbb{R}, Y \in \mathfrak{g}.$$

Consider the generalised eigenspaces of $\mathcal{D}$ defined by

$$\mathfrak{g}_\alpha = \{X \in \mathfrak{g} : (\mathcal{D} - \alpha)^n X = 0 \text{ for some } n \geq 1\}$$

where $\alpha \in Spec(\mathcal{D})$. Then, $\left[\mathfrak{g}_\alpha, \mathfrak{g}_\beta\right] \subset \mathfrak{g}_{\alpha+\beta}$ when $\alpha + \beta$ is an eigenvalue of $\mathcal{D}$ and zero otherwise. Therefore, it is possible to decompose $\mathfrak{g}$ as $\mathfrak{g} = \mathfrak{g}^+ \oplus \mathfrak{g}^0 \oplus \mathfrak{g}^-$, where

http://dx.doi.org/10.5772/intechopen.72232

$$\mathfrak{g} = \mathfrak{g}^{+} \oplus \mathfrak{g}^{0} \oplus \mathfrak{g}^{-}, \text{ where}$$

$$\mathfrak{g}^{+} = \bigoplus_{\alpha:\mathrm{Re}(\alpha)>0} \mathfrak{g}_{\alpha}, \; \mathfrak{g}^{0} = \bigoplus_{\alpha:\mathrm{Re}(\alpha)=0} \mathfrak{g}_{\alpha} \text{ and } \mathfrak{g}^{-} = \bigoplus_{\alpha:\mathrm{Re}(\alpha)<0} \mathfrak{g}_{\alpha}.$$

Actually, $\mathfrak{g}^{+}, \mathfrak{g}^{0}, \mathfrak{g}^{-}$ are Lie algebras and $\mathfrak{g}^{+}$, $\mathfrak{g}^{-}$ are nilpotent. Denote by G^{+}, G^{-} and G^{0} the connected and closed Lie subgroups of G with Lie algebras $\mathfrak{g}^{+}$, $\mathfrak{g}^{-}$ and $\mathfrak{g}^{0}$ respectively.

Despite the fact that for an invariant system the global controllability property is local, this class has been studied for more than 50 years, see [24] and the references there in. The important point to note here is: for an invariant system the reachable set from the identity is a semigroup. However, in [26] the authors show that this is not the case for a linear system which turns the problem more complicated. Therefore, we would like to explore the mentioned connection between control sets and the Devaney and Colonius-Kliemann ideas. This section is the starting point for the Σ_L class. We begin with a fundamental result.

Theorem 31 *Assume the system Σ_L satisfy the Lie algebra rank condition. Therefore, there exists a control set*

$$\mathcal{C}_e = \mathrm{cl}(\mathcal{A}(e)) \cap \mathcal{A}^{*}(e)$$

which contains the identity element e in its interior. Here, $\mathcal{A}^{*}(e)$ is the set of states of G that can be sent by Σ_L to e in positive time.

For a proof in a more general set up, see [6].

Recently, we were able to establish some algebraic, topological, and dynamical conditions on Σ_L to study uniqueness and boundness of control sets and it consequences on controllability . But, the state of arts is really far from being complete. In order to approach this problem for Σ_L, as in [27] we assume here that G has finite semisimple centre, i.e. all semisimple Lie subgroups of G have finite center. We notice that any nilpotent and solvable Lie group, and any semisimple Lie group with finite centre has the finite semisimple centre property. But also, the product between groups with finite semisimple centre have the same property. We also assume that $\mathcal{A}$ is open. This is true if for example, the system satisfy the *ad* -rank condition. About the uniqueness and boundness of control sets of a linear systems, we know few things [27].

Theorem 32 *Let Σ_L a linear control system on the Lie group G.*

1. If $G = G^{-}G^{0}G^{+}$ is decomposable, $\mathcal{C}_e$ is the only control set with non-empty interior. In particular, this is true for any solvable Lie group.

2. Suppose that G is semisimple or nilpotent, it turns out that

$$\text{if } \mathrm{cl}(\mathcal{A}_{G^{-}}), \mathrm{cl}\left(\mathcal{A}^{*}_{G^{+}}\right) \text{ and } G^{0} \text{ are compact sets } \mathcal{C} \text{ is bounded.}$$

3. If G is a nilpotent simply connected Lie group, it follows that

$$\mathcal{C} \text{ is bounded} \Leftrightarrow cl(A_{G^{-}}) \text{ and } cl\left(A^{*}_{G^{+}}\right) \text{ are compact sets and } D \text{ is hyperbolic.}$$

Furthermore, it is possible to determine algebraic sufficient conditions to decide when $\mathcal{C}$ is bounded. Actually, in a forthcoming paper we show that

Theorem 33 *Let Σ_L be a linear control system on the Lie group G. Assume that G is decomposable and $G^{+,0}$ is a normal subgroup of G. Hence,* $\mathrm{cl}(G^- \cap \mathcal{A})$ *is compact.*

A analogous result is obtained for $G^+ \cap \mathcal{A}$ assuming that $G^{-,0}$ is normal. Of course, $G^{+,0}$ is a normal subgroup of G if and only if $\mathfrak{g}^+ \oplus \mathfrak{g}^0$ is an ideal of $\mathfrak{g}$. On the other hand,

$$\mathfrak{g}^+ \oplus \mathfrak{g}^0 \text{ and } \mathfrak{g}^+ \oplus \mathfrak{g}^0 \text{ are ideals of } \mathfrak{g} \Leftrightarrow [\mathfrak{g}^+, \mathfrak{g}^0] = 0 \text{ and } [\mathfrak{g}^+, \mathfrak{g}^-] \subset \mathfrak{g}^0.$$

7.2. Chaos and control sets

We start with an explicitly relationship between chaotic subsets of $M \times \mathcal{U}$ and the Σ-control sets.

Theorem 34 *Let $\mathfrak{C} \subset M \times \mathcal{U}$ and the canonical projection $\pi_M : M \times \mathcal{U} \to M$. Hence,*

$$\pi_M(\mathfrak{C}) = \{x \in M : \text{there exists } u \in \mathcal{U} \text{ with } (x,u) \in \mathfrak{C}\}$$

is compact and its non-void interior consists of locally accessible points. Then,

1. $\mathfrak{C}$ is a maximal topologically mixing set if and only if there exists a control C such that

$$\mathfrak{C} = cl\{(x,u) \in M \times \mathcal{U} : \varphi(t,x,u) \in \mathrm{int}(C) \text{ for every } t \in \mathbb{R}\}$$

   In this case, C is unique and $\mathrm{int}(C) = \mathrm{int}(\pi_M(\mathfrak{C}))$, $cl(C) = cl(\pi_M(\mathfrak{C}))$.

2. The periodic points of Φ are dense in $\mathfrak{C}$.

3. Φ restrict to $\mathfrak{C}$ is topologically mixing, topologically transitive and has sensitive dependence on initial conditions.

In order to apply this fundamental result for a non-controllable linear control system, the boundness property of its control set is crucial. Let us assume that C is a bounded control set with non-empty interior of Σ_L and define $\mathfrak{C} = \pi_M^{-1}(C) = cl(C \times \mathcal{U}_C)$ where

$$\mathcal{U}_C = \{u \in \mathcal{U} : \text{exist } x \in C \text{ with } \varphi(t,x,u) \in \mathrm{int}(C) \text{ for every } t \in \mathbb{R}\}.$$

The Lie group G is finite dimensional and $\mathcal{U}_C$ is a closed subset of the compact class of admissible control $\mathcal{U} \subset L^\infty(\mathbb{R}, \Omega \subset \mathbb{R}^m)$ with the weak* topology. Since the projection is a continuous map, it turns out that $\pi_M(\mathfrak{C})$ is compact and $\mathfrak{C}$, C are uniquely defined.

On the other hand, we are assuming that Σ_L satisfy the Lie algebra rank condition, hence the system is locally accessible at any point of the state space. Therefore, we are in a position to apply Theorem 32, first, for some classes of controllable linear systems, as follows.

Theorem 35 *Let Σ_L be a linear control system on a Lie group G. Any condition.*

1. G is compact, or

2. G is Abelian, or

3. G has the finite semisimple centre property and the Lyapunov spectrum of $\mathcal{D}$ is $\{0\}$ implies that the skew flow Φ is chaotic in $G \times \mathcal{U}$.

Proof. Under the hypothesis in (1), any control set is bounded. Furthermore, if G is compact, the Lie algebra rank condition assures that the linear control system Σ_L is controllable on G, see [15]. Hence, Φ is topologically mixing, topologically transitive and the periodic points of Φ are dense in $G \times \mathcal{U}$, which give us the desired conclusion.

It is well known that any Abelian Lie group is a product $G = \mathbb{R}^m \times T^n$ between the Euclidean space $\mathbb{R}^m$ and the torus $T^n = S^1 \times \ldots \times S^1$ (n times), for some $m, n \in \mathbb{N}$. In this case, Σ_L is also controllable [15]. Indeed, since the automorphism group of T^n is discrete, any linear vector field on the torus is trivial. But, we are assuming the Lie algebra condition on G which coincides with the Kalman rank condition in $\mathbb{R}^m$. And, on the compact part, we apply (1). Hence, the skew flow Φ is chaotic in $G \times \mathcal{U}$. In fact, $\pi_M^{-1}(\mathcal{C}) = G \times \mathcal{U}$ and the hypothesis of the compacity on the projection in Theorem 32 is not necessary for the lifting, see Proposition 4.3.3 in [6]. The same is true for (3). Actually, for this more general set up, we recently prove that the system is also controllable, [28, 29].

In the sequel, we use some topological properties of $\mathcal{C}_e$ to translate these properties to its associated chaotic set $\mathfrak{C}$, as follows.

Theorem 36 *Let Σ_L be a linear control system on a Lie group G. It holds.*

1. If $G = G^- G^0 G^+$ there exists one and only one chaotic set $\mathfrak{C} = \pi_M^{-1}(\mathcal{C}_e)$ in $G \times \mathcal{U}$ given by

$$\mathfrak{C} = cl\{(x,u) : \varphi(t,x,u) \in \text{int}(\mathcal{C}_e) \text{ for every } t \in \mathbb{R}\} \subset M \times \mathcal{U}$$

2. If G is nilpotent and $\mathcal{D}$ has only eigenvalues with non-positive real parts, then the only chaotic set $\mathfrak{C} = \pi_M^{-1}(\mathcal{C})$ in $G \times \mathcal{U}$ is closed

3. If G is nilpotent and $\mathcal{D}$ has only eigenvalues with non-negative real parts then the only chaotic set $\mathfrak{C} = \pi_M^{-1}(\mathcal{C})$ in $G \times \mathcal{U}$ is open

Proof. If G is decomposable, we know that there exists just one control set: the one which contains the identity element. Hence, $\mathfrak{C} = \pi_M^{-1}(\mathcal{C}_e)$ is the only chaotic set of Φ on $G \times \mathcal{U}$ which proves (1). To prove (2) and (3), we observe that the Lyapunov spectrum condition on the derivation $\mathcal{D}$ associated to the drift vector field $\mathcal{X}$ is equivalent to the control set $\mathcal{C}_e$ be closed or open, respectively. Since the projection $\pi_G : G \times \mathcal{U} \to G$ is a continuous map with the weak* topology on $\mathcal{U}$, the lifting $\pi_G^{-1}(\mathcal{C}_e)$ is both closed and open, respectively.

7.3. Challenge

In this very short section, we would like to invite the readers to work on the relationship between chaotic and control sets. We suggest to go further in this research through some specific examples on low-dimensional Lie groups. For that, we give some relevant information about two groups of dimension three: the simply connected nilpotent Heisenberg Lie group H and the special linear group $SL(2,\mathbb{R})$. We finish by computing an example on H.

1. The nilpotent Lie algebra $\mathfrak{h} = (\mathbb{R}^3, +, ,)$, has the basis $\{E_{12}, E_{23}, E_{13}\}$ with $[E_{12}, E_{23}] = E_{13}$. Here, E_{ij} denotes the real matrix of order 3 with zero everywhere except 1 in the position ij. The associated Heisenberg Lie group has the matrix representation

$$G = \left\{ g = \begin{pmatrix} 1 & x & z \\ 0 & 1 & y \\ 0 & 0 & 1 \end{pmatrix} : x, y, z \in \mathbb{R} \right\} \overset{\varphi: g \to (x,y,z)}{\longrightarrow} \mathbb{R}^3.$$

As invariant vector fields, the basis elements of $\mathfrak{g}$ has the following description

$$E_{12} = \frac{\partial}{\partial x}, E_{23} = \frac{\partial}{\partial y} + x\frac{\partial}{\partial z} \text{ and } E_{13} = \frac{\partial}{\partial z}.$$

The canonical form of any $\mathfrak{g}$-derivation is given by

$$\mathcal{D} = \begin{pmatrix} a & d & 0 \\ b & e & 0 \\ c & f & a+e \end{pmatrix} : a, b, c, d, e, \ f \in \mathbb{R}.$$

Any linear vector field $\mathcal{X}$ reads as

$$\mathcal{X}(x,y,z) = (ax+dy)\frac{\partial}{\partial x} + (bx+ey)\frac{\partial}{\partial y} + \left(\frac{b}{2}x^2 + \frac{d}{2}y^2 + cx + fy + (a+e)z\right)\frac{\partial}{\partial z}.$$

2. The vector space $\mathfrak{g} = \mathfrak{sl}(2,\mathbb{R})$ of all real matrices of order three and trace zero is the Lie algebra of the Lie group $G = SL(2,\mathbb{R}) = \det^{-1}(1)$. Let us consider the following generators of $\mathfrak{g}$: $Y^1 = \begin{pmatrix} 0 & 1 \\ -1 & 0 \end{pmatrix}$, $Y^2 = \begin{pmatrix} 0 & 1 \\ 0 & 0 \end{pmatrix}$ and $Y^3 = \begin{pmatrix} 1 & 0 \\ 0 & -1 \end{pmatrix}$. The Lie group G is semisimple, then any $\mathfrak{g}$ derivation is inner which means that there exists an invariant vector field Y such that $ad(Y)$ represents . Thus, a general form of a derivation reads as

$$\alpha \ ad(Y^1) + \beta \ ad(Y^2) + \gamma \ ad(Y^3).$$

Example 7.1 On the Heisenberg Lie group, consider the system

$$\Sigma_L : \dot{g}(t) = \mathcal{X}(g(t)) + u_1(t)E_{12}(g(t)) + u_2(t)E_{23}(g(t)), \qquad u = (u_1, u_2) \in \mathcal{U} \tag{15}$$

where $\mathcal{X}$ is determined by the derivation $\mathcal{D} = ad(E_{12}) = E_{32}$. Since the group is nilpotent, it has the semisimple finite centre property. The Lyapunov spectrum of $\mathcal{D}$ reduces to zero. Finally, the reachable set from the identity $\mathcal{A}$ is open. In fact, the ad-rank condition is obviously true because $\mathcal{D}(E_{12}) = E_{13}$. It turns out that the skew flow Φ is chaotic in $H \times \mathcal{U}$.

Author details

Heriberto Román-Flores and Víctor Ayala*

*Address all correspondence to: vayala@ucn.cl

Instituto de Alta Investigación, Universidad de Tarapacá, Sede Esmeralda, Iquique, Chile

References

[1] Devaney RL. An Introduction to Chaotic Dynamical Systems. Redwood City: Addison-Wesley; 1989

[2] Robinson C. Dynamical Systems: Stability, Symbolic Dynamics, and Chaos. New York: CRC Press; 1999

[3] Banks J, Brooks J, Cairns G, Stacey P. On the Devaney's definition of chaos. The American Mathematical Monthly. 1992;**99**:332-334

[4] Vellekoop M, Berglund R. On intervals, transitivity=chaos. The American Mathematical Monthly. 1994;**101**:353-355

[5] Román-Flores H. A note on transitivity in set-valued discrete systems. Chaos, Solitons & Fractals. 2003;**17**:99-104

[6] Colonius F, Kliemann C. The Dynamics of Control, Systems & Control: Foundations & Applications. Boston, MA: Birkäuser Boston, Inc.; 2000

[7] Román-Flores H, Barros LC, Bassanezi RCA. Note on the Zadeh's extensions. Fuzzy Sets and Systems. 2001;**17**:327-331

[8] Román-Flores H, Chalco-Cano Y. A note on dynamics of interval extensions of interval function. 2015 Annual Conference of the North American Fuzzy Information Processing Society (NAFIPS) held jointly with 2015 5th World Conference on Soft Computing (WConSC), 2015

[9] Dugundji J. Topology. Boston: Allyn and Bacon Inc.; 1966

[10] Thomson B, Bruckner J, Bruckner A. Elementary Real Analysis. Prentice Hall: Upper Saddle River; 2001

[11] Agronski S, Bruckner A, Laczkovich M. Dynamics of typical continuous functions. Journal of the London Mathematical Society. 1989;**40**:227-243

[12] Alikhani-Koopaei A. On the set of fixed points and periodic points of continuously differentiable functions. International Journal of Mathematics and Mathematical Sciences. 2013. Article ID: 929475

[13] Banach S. Über die Baire'sche Kategorie gewisser Funktionenmengen. Studia Math. 1931;**3**:174-179

[14] Mazurkiewicz S. Sur les fonctions non-dérivables. Studia Mathematica. 1932;**3**:92-94

[15] Ayala V, Tirao J. Linear control systems on lie groups and controllability. American Mathematical Society, Series: Symposia in Pure Mathematics. 1999;**64**:47-64

[16] Kliemann W. Analysis of nonlinear stochastic systems. Schiehlen W, Wedig W, eds. In: Analysis and Estimation of Stochastic Mechanical Systems: Springer-Verlag; 1988

[17] Banks J. Chaos for induced hyperspace maps. Chaos, Solitons & Fractals. 2005;**25**:681-685

[18] Román-Flores H, Chalco-Cano Y. Robinson's chaos in set-valued discrete systems. Chaos, Solitons & Fractals. 2005;**25**:33-42

[19] Sharma P, Nagar A. Inducing sensitivity on hyperspaces. Topology and its Applications. 2010;**157**:2052-2058

[20] Subramonian TK. Stronger forms of sensitivity for dynamical systems. Nonlinearity. 2007;**20**:2115-2126

[21] Klein E, Thompson A. Theory of Correspondences. New York: Wiley-Interscience; 1984

[22] Jones SH. Topical survey: Applications of the Baire category theorem. Real Analysis Exchange. 1997;**23**:363-394

[23] Bernardes N. On the predictability of discrete dynamical systems II. Proceedings of American Mathematical Society. 2005;**133**:3473-3483

[24] Sachkov Y. Survey on controllability of invariant control systems on solvable lie groups. AMS Proceedings of Symposia in Pure Mathematics. 1999;**64**:297-317

[25] Jouan P. Equivalence of control systems with linear systems on lie groups and homogeneous spaces. ESAIM: Control Optimization and Calculus of Variations. 2010;**16**:956-973

[26] Ayala V, San Martin L. Controllability properties of a class of control systems on lie groups. Lecture Notes in Control and Information Sciences. 2001;**258**:83-92

[27] Ayala V, Da Silva A, Zsigmond G. Control sets of linear systems on lie groups. Nonlinear Differential Equations and Applications. 2017;**24**:8, 99.1-99.15

[28] Ayala V, Da Silva A. Controllability of linear systems on Lie groups with finite semisimple center. SIAM Journal on Control and Optimization. 2017;**55**(2):1332-1343

[29] Ayala V, Da Silva A. Control systems on flag manifolds and their chain control sets. Discrete and Continuous Dynamical Systems. 2017;**37**(5):2301-2313

Chapter 7

Witnesses of Quantum Chaos and Nonlinear Kerr-Like Oscillator Model

Joanna K. Kalaga, Marcin W. Jarosik,
Wiesław Leoński and Radosław Szczęśniak

Additional information is available at the end of the chapter

http://dx.doi.org/10.5772/intechopen.70747

Abstract

Here, we present a brief insight into some current methods allowing for the detection of quantum chaos phenomena. In particular, we show examples of proposals of the parameters which could be applied as indicators of quantum-chaotic behavior and already were presented in the literature. We concentrate here on the quantum fidelity and the fidelity-like functions, defined for the wave functions describing system's evolution. The definition of the fidelity-like parameter also involves the operator of the mean number of photons/phonons. Discussing such parameter, we show here how it is possible to take into account in the discussion of quantum-chaotic systems simultaneously the behavior of the divergence of wave functions and the energy of the system represented by the mean number of photons/phonons. Next, we discuss entropy-type parameter which can also be a good candidate for the indicators of quantum chaos' phenomena. We show the ability of all considered here parameters to be witnesses of quantum-chaotic behavior for the systems of the quantum nonlinear Kerr-like oscillator—the classical counterpart of such system can exhibit chaotic evolution in its canonical form.

Keywords: quantum chaos, quantum nonlinear oscillator, Kerr-like oscillator, fidelity, entropy, photons, phonons

1. Introduction (some history)

The classical chaos phenomenon is related to the irregular and unpredictable evolution of nonlinear systems. What is important is that the behavior of such systems is determined, which means that time evolution of the system's state can be described by corresponding equations, usually in a form of nonlinear differential equations. The term "irregular evolution" is related to the nature of the dynamics of the system and is not related to the unpredictable influence of the environment. The chaotic behavior exhibits itself in high sensitivity of system's evolution to the initial conditions. In fact, it refers to the situation when we are not able to determine the final state of a system when we have limited information concerning its initial state. On the other hand, when the initial state of the system is well defined, according to the principle of determinism, its final state should be well determined. However, for real systems, such ideal situation cannot be observed, as the initial conditions are always determined with some accuracy.

One of first papers describing the chaotic behavior of the studied systems was published at the end of the nineteenth century. In the years 1892–1899, Henri Poincaré published the work of *Les Méthodes Nouvelles de la Mecanique Celeste* [1], which attempts to answer the question: whether the solar system is stable? Poincaré studied the behavior of the reduced Hill model. This model consists of three bodies, which interact with gravity forces. Additionally, the mass of one of the bodies is so small that does not affect on the behavior of the other two. On the other hand, the other two bodies influence the behavior of the first one. Henri Poincaré, in his research, has obtained very complex trajectories of motion for small body, which we now call chaotic.

The great importance in chaos theory plays studies initiated by Kolmogorov [2] and continued by Arnold [3] and Moser [4]. Their studies concerned the integrable Hamiltonian systems and the influence of small perturbations on such systems. They have shown that when small perturbations are present in a dynamical system, some fraction of orbits in the phase space remains indefinite in some region of the space. That result is now known as KAM theorem.

In 1963, Lorenz [5] numerically studied a simple model of cellular convection (called Rayleigh-Bénard convection model) and discovered that all equations of motion are unstable and almost all are nonperiodic. He also paid attention to the phenomenon of the sensitivity of the system's evolution to the initial conditions. The system which models cellular convection consists of two horizontal plates and a liquid medium placed between them. The temperature of the top plate is lower than that measured at the surface of the bottom plate. For some values of the temperature difference ΔT, although we observe the convection rolls in the fluid, the state of the system remains stationary. By increasing ΔT, the fluid flow rate changes, and the behavior of the system becomes chaotic. In the following years, Rayleigh-Bénard convection was also studied by Ahlers and Behringer [6], Gollub and Benson [7], Libchaber and Maurer [8], and Bergé et al. [9]. The model analyzed by Lorenz can be applied to describe the behavior of various physical systems. For example, in 1975 Haken applied Lorenz model to explain the irregular spiking behavior of laser system [10].

The same time when Lorenz was studying the model of cellular convection, Ueda analyzed Duffing's model [11, 12] which describes a periodically excited damping system. Ueda observed that for some values of the amplitude of excitation force and the damping parameter system's oscillations become accidental. Further studies showed that damped oscillators, which are excited by a periodic force, for certain values of the parameters describing excitation, are sensitive to initial conditions.

http://dx.doi.org/10.5772/intechopen.70747

In 1898, Hadamard studied the behavior of the geodesics on surfaces with constant negative curvature [13]. He proved that the motion along geodetic lines on negative curvature surfaces is unstable and this system exhibits sensitivity to initial conditions. That means that small change in initial direction of a geodesic entails large changes in predicted results after a long time. These studies were continued by Birkhoff [14]. In subsequent years successive systems were discussed in the context of chaotic behavior and their sensitivity to initial conditions. Nowadays, the chaos theory is applied to the discussions of a broad range, not necessarily physical problems, for instance, the motion of planets [15, 16], chemical reactions [17], medicine [18, 19], and others.

In the twentieth century, the new field of physics has been developed, including quantum mechanics. One of the main principles of quantum mechanics is proposed by Bohr, correspondence principle [20]. With accordance to it, when the value of the action associated with the energy of the system is much higher than the Planck constant, the quantum description of the system reduces to the classical one. In consequence, if for the classical counterpart of the quantum system we observe the transition to chaotic behavior, the similar effect should appear in the quantum system. However, such transitions appearing in quantum systems have the entirely different character from those originating in the classical ones. It can be explained as a result of the fact that the Schrödinger equation which describes the evolution of the quantum system is linear with respect to the wave function. In consequence, it gives periodic or quasi-periodic solutions which do not lead to the chaotic behavior in the classical sense. Additionally, as a result of the Heisenberg uncertainty principle, it is not possible to consider the trajectories in phase space, and the main feature of classical chaos cannot be observed. In quantum mechanics, all points in a $2n$-dimensional space which are located in the volume smaller than $\hbar^n$ are indistinguishable. Therefore, if the state of the system remains inside such region, when the system's dynamics is classically chaotic, in the quantum regime, such chaotic effects are not visible. Then, we cannot analyze the rate of separation of infinitesimally close trajectories known as the Lyapunov exponent. On the other hand, according to Bohr's correspondence principle when the Planck constant tends to zero, the results of quantum mechanics should correspond to the results of classical mechanics. According to that, the transition to the chaotic behavior of the classical system should lead to the appearance of the changes in dynamics of the quantum system. Therefore, when we study quantum chaos, we try to find some differences between the behavior of quantum systems for which classical counterpart exhibits regular evolution and quantum systems for which their classical counterparts are chaotic. Thus, one of the primary goals of the research in the field of quantum chaos is to find such parameters (witnesses) which allow for distinguishing between such two types of quantum behavior. For instance, the differences appearing in spectra of quantum-mechanical systems were predicted by Percival in 1973 [21] and then confirmed in 1979 by McDonald and Kaufman [22]. Those latter have studied the behavior of a particle which moves within the region confined inside rigid walls composed of two semicircles of radius r and two parallel segments of length d (see **Figure 1b**). Such system is called the *quantum billiard*, and its classical counterparts regularly behave when $d=0$ (**Figure 1a**). McDonald and Kaufman studied the distribution of distances $N(\Delta E)$ between two neighboring energy levels $\Delta E = E_{k+1} - E_k$. For a circular billiard ($d=0$), when E = 0 the distribution $N(\Delta E)$ reaches its greatest value (**Figure 2**).

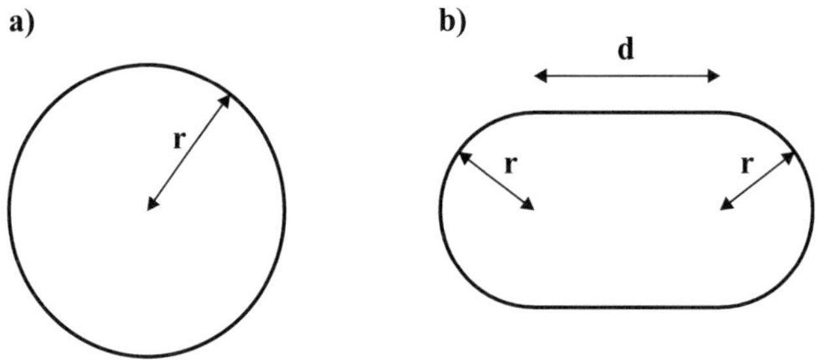

Figure 1. The billiard systems: (a) circular and (b) stadium.

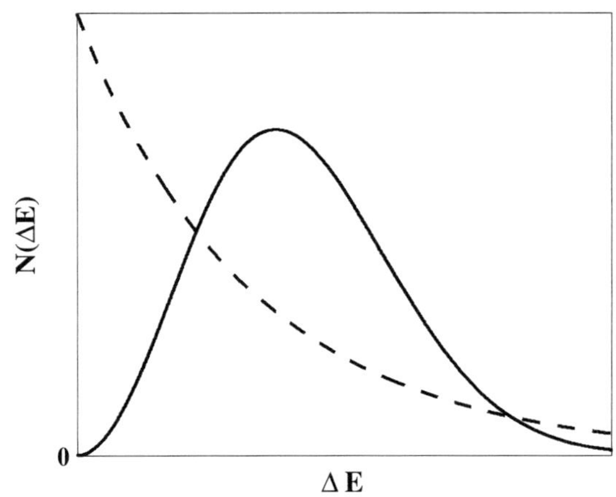

Figure 2. The distribution of distances between two neighboring energy levels $N(\Delta E)$ for circular billiard (dashed line) and stadium billiard (solid line).

When energy E increases, the value of $N(\Delta E)$ decreases. In consequence, we can observe the phenomenon called *attraction of energy levels* which can lead to their degeneracy. However, for stadium billiard ($d \neq 0$), the distribution $N(\Delta E)$ changes considerably. For $E = 0$ it does not take its maximum value as we observed for the earlier case—it reaches its maximum for another value of the energy $E \neq 0$. That means that for the stadium billiard systems the phenomenon called *repulsion of energy levels* appears. At this point, we should also mention that similar result for the quantum Sinai's billiard was obtained by Bohigas et al. [23].

In 1984 Peres proposed a new way of studying the dynamics of quantum systems [24]. His method was based on the comparison of the evolution of the unperturbed system to that corresponding to the same system for which small perturbations Δ were applied into the Hamiltonian H. The state of the unperturbed system is described by the wave function Ψ_u, whereas Ψ_p represents the state corresponding to the perturbed Hamiltonian. To determine the distance between such two states, we need to calculate the scalar product of two corresponding to them wave functions and then define parameter

$$F = |\Psi_u(t)|\Psi_p(t)|, \tag{1}$$

which is called *fidelity*. At this point, one should mention that in the literature the fidelity is sometimes defined as squared modulus, not modulus itself. Moreover, especially in the papers dealing with condensed matter physics, the fidelity is called *Loschmidt echo* (for instance, see ([25] *and the references quoted therein*). Such quantity was applied for investigation of quantum-chaotic phenomena for the first times by Peres [24] and then by Weinstein et al. and Emerson et al. [26, 28]. The fidelity was also discussed in Ref. [27], where anharmonic oscillator models excited by ultrashort pulses were considered. For a quantum system whose classical counterpart shows regular behavior, we observe regular oscillations of the fidelity. However, when the classical counterpart of a quantum system exhibits a chaotic behavior, the evolution of the fidelity changes its character. It was shown in [26, 28] that in such a case the value of F decreases. The way in which such fidelity decays depends on the value of perturbation Δ. The methods of investigation of quantum-chaotic systems based on the fidelity were applied in studies of the dynamics of various quantum systems such as the quantum kicked top [26, 29], quantum nonlinear oscillator [27], particle kicked by a Gaussian beam [30], Josephson junction [31], etc.

2. The quantum nonlinear Kerr-like oscillator system: its quantum and classical evolution

To show the ability of discussed here parameters to describe quantum-chaotic phenomena, we need to choose a physical model which can exhibit quantum chaos' effects. The model should be a nonlinear type and allows to compare its quantum dynamics with its classical counterpart. We decided to discuss nonlinear Kerr-like oscillator systems. The models which we will apply are general enough to be applied in various fields. For instance, they can be applied to description nanomechanical resonators and various optomechanical systems [32–38], boson trapped in lattices [39–41], Bose-Hubbard chains [41, 42], circuit QED models [43, 44], etc.

The Hamiltonian for the anharmonic oscillator excited by a series of ultrashort pulses can be written as

$$\hat{H} = \hat{H}_{NL} + \hat{H}_K, \tag{2}$$

where the first part $\hat{H}_{NL}$ describes "free" evolution of the oscillator during the time between two subsequent external pulses. $\hat{H}_{NL}$ can be written with the use of boson creation and annihilation operators as

$$\hat{H}_{NL} = \frac{\chi}{2}\left(\hat{a}^{\dagger}\right)^2 \hat{a}^2. \tag{3}$$

The parameter χ appearing here describes nonlinearity of the oscillator. Here, we will assume for the convenience that $\chi = 1$ and, then, other quantities will be expressed in units of χ. The second Hamiltonian $\hat{H}_K$ is related to the interaction of the system with the external coherent pulses. It can be expressed in the following form:

$$\hat{H}_K = \varepsilon\left(\hat{a}^{\dagger} + \hat{a}\right)\sum_{k=1}^{\infty}\delta(t - kT), \tag{4}$$

where ε describes the strength of external excitation, whereas T denotes the duration of the time between two subsequent pulses (for the cases discussed here, we will assume that $T = \pi$). Appearing here Dirac-delta function models a single, infinitely short external pulse. In fact, every single pulse is much shorter than the time interval between two successive pulses but is sufficiently long to allow nonlinear system interact with the field.

As we neglect here all damping effects, the system's evolution can be described by unitary operators defined with the use of two Hamiltonians. We can notice that the whole evolution can be divided into two types of subsequent stages. Thus, for the moments of time, when $t = kT$ ($k = 1, 2, \ldots$), the external pulses act on the oscillator. It is described by the Hamiltonian H_K. On the other hand, during the period between two subsequent pulses, the anharmonic oscillator evolves "freely," and such evolution is governed by H_{NL}. In consequence, we can define two unitary evolution operators $\hat{U}_K$ and $\hat{U}_{NL}$, respectively. They are.

$$\hat{U}_K = e^{-i\varepsilon\left(\hat{a}^{\dagger} + \hat{a}\right)} \tag{5}$$

and

$$\hat{U}_{NL} = e^{-i\chi T\hat{n}(\hat{n}-1)/2}, \tag{6}$$

where $\hat{n} = \hat{a}^{\dagger}\hat{a}$ is the photon number operator. Applying $\hat{U}_{NL}$ and $\hat{U}_K$, we can define the operator $\hat{U}_u$ transforming the wave function from that corresponding to the moment of time just after kth external pulses to that for the moment after $(k + 1)$th one. Such defined time evolution operator allows for a so-called quantum mapping of the system. For unperturbed system $\hat{U}_u$ has the following form:

$$\hat{U}_u = e^{-i\varepsilon\left(\hat{a}^{\dagger} + \hat{a}\right)}e^{-i\chi T\hat{n}(\hat{n}-1)/2}. \tag{7}$$

When we apply the perturbation Δ, corresponding to it evolution operator $\hat{U}_p$ is defined as

$$\hat{U}_p = e^{-i(\varepsilon+\Delta)\left(\hat{a}^{\dagger} + \hat{a}\right)}e^{-i\chi T\hat{n}(\hat{n}-1)/2}. \tag{8}$$

Next, to find solutions we need to choose initial state of the system. Here, we will assume that the system's evolution starts from the vacuum state $|\Psi(0)\rangle$. Thus, we are in the position to find two wave functions appearing in the definition of fidelity. After the k-fold operation of the evolution operators onto the initial state, we obtain the wave functions (perturbed and unperturbed ones) corresponding to the moments of time just after the kth pulse. They are

$$|\Psi_u(k)\rangle = \left(\hat{U}_u\right)^k|\Psi(0)\rangle \tag{9}$$

and

$$|\Psi_p(k)\rangle = \left(\hat{U}_p\right)^k |\Psi(0)\rangle, \tag{10}$$

respectively. Finally, the modulus of the scalar product of such calculated wave functions gives the fidelity defined in Eq. (1).

As we have mentioned earlier, it is necessary to determine the regions for which the classical counterpart of our model exhibits regular or chaotic dynamics. Therefore, we will follow the path shown in [45]. First, we will find the solution for the annihilation operator and, then, replace the operators appearing there by appropriate complex numbers. Such solution will allow drawing a bifurcation diagram for the classical system.

We remember that during the time between two subsequent pulses the energy is conserved and the total number of photons is constant. Therefore, we can write the equation describing the time evolution of $\hat{a}$ for such period of time:

$$\frac{d\hat{a}}{dt} = \frac{1}{i\hbar}\left[\hat{a}, \hat{H}_{NL}\right], \tag{11}$$

and it has the solution of the form

$$\hat{a}(\tau) = e^{-i\chi\hat{a}^\dagger\hat{a}\tau}\hat{a}. \tag{12}$$

To transform such determined annihilation operator from that corresponding to the moment of time just before a single pulse to that just after it, we can use $\hat{U}_K$ defined in Eq. (8). Due to the fact that $\hat{U}_K$ is the displacement operator, the recurrence formula transforming $\hat{a}$ from the moment of time just after kth pulse to that after (k+1)th one can be written as

$$\hat{a}_{k+1} = e^{-i\chi\left(\hat{a}_k^\dagger + i\varepsilon\right)(\hat{a}_k - i\varepsilon)T}\left(\hat{a}_k - i\varepsilon\right). \tag{13}$$

We can replace $\hat{a}$ ($\hat{a}^\dagger$) by complex numbers α (α^*), now. In consequence, we get the following equation allowing for finding classical maps:

$$\alpha_{k+1} = (\alpha_k - i\varepsilon)e^{-i\left(\chi|\alpha_k - i\varepsilon|^2\right)T}. \tag{14}$$

The classical energy of the system is determined by $|\alpha|^2$, and, now, we can draw a bifurcation diagram for the classical nonlinear system. Thus, **Figure 3** shows such diagram plot for various values of the strength of external pulses ε. We see that the character of our system's dynamic depends on the value of this parameter—the evolution of the classical system is regular for $\varepsilon < 0.344$ and $0.362 < \varepsilon < 0.47$ and when $0.344 < \varepsilon < 0.362$ and $0.47 < \varepsilon$, the classical system exhibits chaotic evolution.

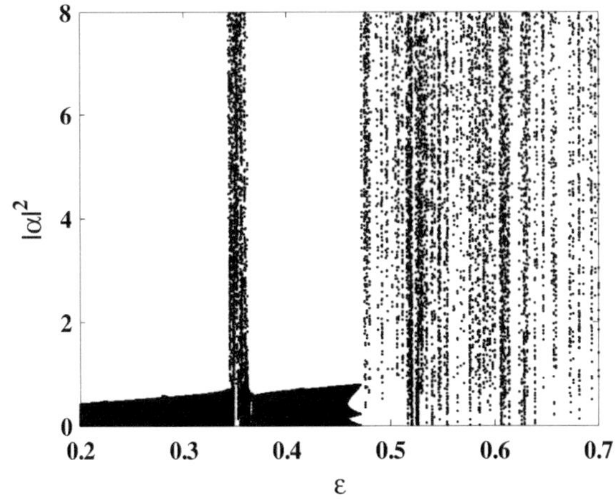

Figure 3. The bifurcation diagram showing the dependence of the average energy $|\alpha|^2$ on the excitation strength ε. The system is not damped, and the time between two subsequent pulses is assumed to be $T=\pi$.

3. Witnesses of quantum chaos

3.1. The fidelity

From the bifurcation diagram, we know for which values of external excitations ε the evolution of the classical counterpart of the quantum system is regular and for which it is chaotic. Choosing the appropriate values of ε, we can examine the time evolution of the fidelity:

$$F(k) = |\left\langle \Psi(0)|\hat{U}_u^{\dagger k}\hat{U}_p^k|\Psi(0)\right\rangle|, \tag{15}$$

where $\hat{U}_u$ and $\hat{U}_p$ are already defined in Eqs. (7) and (8). We concentrate here on the behavior of $F(k)$ in a long-time limit.

In **Figure 3** one can see that four regions of different characters of the system's dynamics appear there. There are regular area for $\varepsilon<0.344$, narrow chaotic band for $0.344<\varepsilon<0.362$, second regular area for $0.362<\varepsilon<0.47$, and area of deep chaos for $\varepsilon>0.47$. Therefore, we choose four values of ε to examine the behavior of $F(k)$ in all four areas. They are $\varepsilon=\{0.2; 0.35; 0.45; 0.65\}$, and for such values of ε, the time evolution of the fidelity is presented in **Figure 4**. In addition, we assumed here that the perturbation parameter $\Delta=0.001$.

Figure 4a shows the time evolution of fidelity for $\varepsilon=0.2$. For this value of ε, the dynamics of the classical counterpart of the quantum system is regular. We can observe here that the value of $F(k)$ changes in time periodically from zero to unity. We see that the both amplitude and period of oscillations remain constant even for the long-time limit. Here, the value of the period of oscillations is equal to 3178 pulses (after such number of pulses $F(k)$ reaches its initial value $F(0)=1$). The similar situation we observe for $\varepsilon=0.45$ (see **Figure 4c**). In bifurcation diagram, this value of the external excitation corresponds to the second regular region

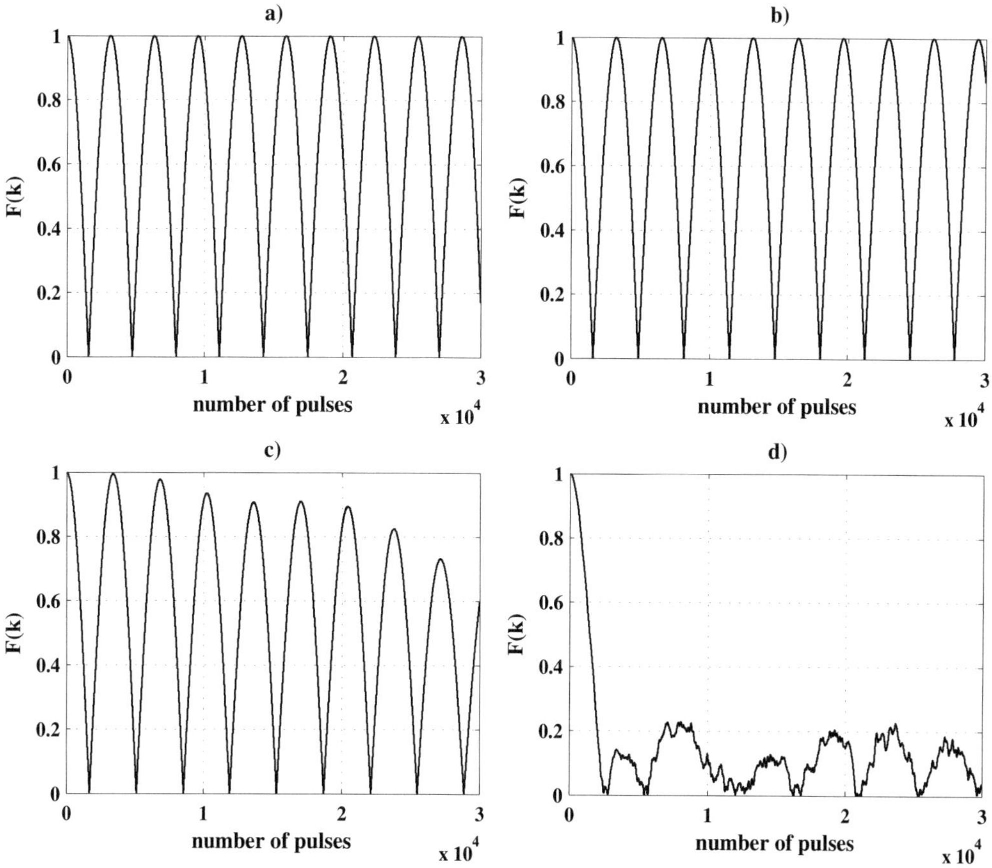

Figure 4. The fidelity versus the number of pulses for (a) $\varepsilon = 0.2$, (b) $\varepsilon = 0.35$, (c) $\varepsilon = 0.45$, and (d) $\varepsilon = 0.65$. The perturbation parameter $\Delta = 0.001$.

(band). The amplitude of oscillations is slowly modulated, so we observe beating effect. This effect appears as a result of the proximity of chaotic region which affects oscillations of F, and additional frequency appears in the evolution. Analogously to the case (a), the fundamental oscillations of the fidelity are regular, and its period is constant and equal to 3414 pulses (the period differs slightly from that of case (a)). Appearing of additional frequencies is related to the bifurcations which appear for the values of ε slightly smaller than that for that corresponding to the deep chaos border.

The case when $\varepsilon = 0.35$ seems to be more attractive. Such value of the external excitation corresponds to the chaotic band which is located between two regular areas. The same as for the case when $\varepsilon = 0.2$; the fidelity changes periodically from zero to unity. Thus, we could conclude that we are in the regular area, and the question arises: why the evolution of the fidelity for $\varepsilon = 0.35$ is practically the same, as that for $\varepsilon = 0.2$? Probably, such evolution is strongly influenced by the neighborhood of the two regular areas which we see in the bifurcation diagram. Moreover, such behavior of the system becomes more clear when we plot the map defined in a two-dimensional phase space for the classical case and, then, overlap it with

Husimi Q-function. Q-Function is one of the quasi-probabilities which gives the information concerning system's quantum state presented in a phase space (for the discussion of various quasi-probabilities usually applied in quantum optics, see, for instance, [46] *and the references quoted therein*). We should note at this point that the parameter of mutual information which was also proposed as a tool which can be applied in a finding of the quantum-chaotic behavior [47] is derived with the use of Husimi Q-function. Moreover, Q-function is not the only one quasi-probability function which can be applied in an investigation in that field. For instance, in [48] the parameter derived on the basis of the Wigner quasi-probability function was also considered in a context of finding quantum chaos witnesses.

Figure 5 shows the classical map (represented by dots) and contour plot of Q-function (dashed lines). We see that the main peak of Q-function (and the greatest probability) is placed in the region corresponding to the regular trajectories in the phase plane. This fact explains why the time evolution of F exhibits regular character.

For $\varepsilon = 0.65$ (this situation corresponds to the area of deep chaos in the bifurcation diagram) the behavior of F completely differs from the previous cases (a)–(c) in **Figure 4**. When the system starts its evolution, we observe decay of the fidelity. The character of such initial vanishing of F was discussed in [26], where it was shown that it changes at the border of chaotic region and, thus, it can be applied as the witness of quantum chaos. Let us concentrate on the time evolution of F for the longer times. So, apart from the initial decay, we can see that the fidelity evolves in an irregular way in the long-time regime. Such irregularity appears when the values of excitations correspond to the area of deep chaos in the bifurcation diagram.

For each case discussed here, the perturbation parameter Δ is small, according to the perturbation theory. Therefore, the initial decay of the fidelity is described by the Gaussian functions [26]. This means that the decay of F can be characterized by the function $\exp(-const \cdot t^2)$. The rate of decay changes with the value of the external excitations. **Figure 6** shows how many

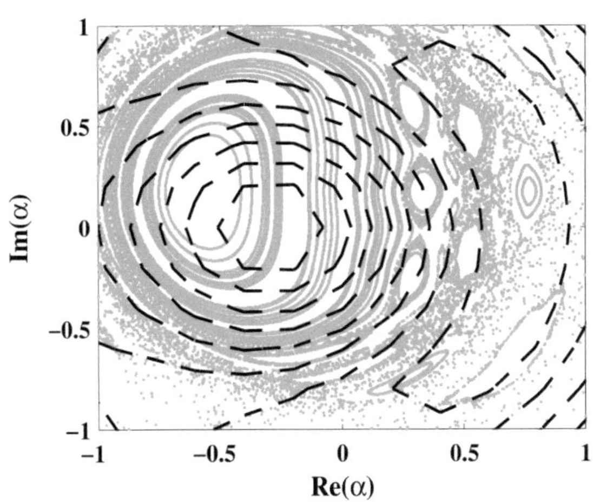

Figure 5. Classical map (dots) overlapping the contour plot of Q-function (dashed lines). We assume here that $\varepsilon = 0.35$. The remaining parameters are the same as those for **Figure 4**.

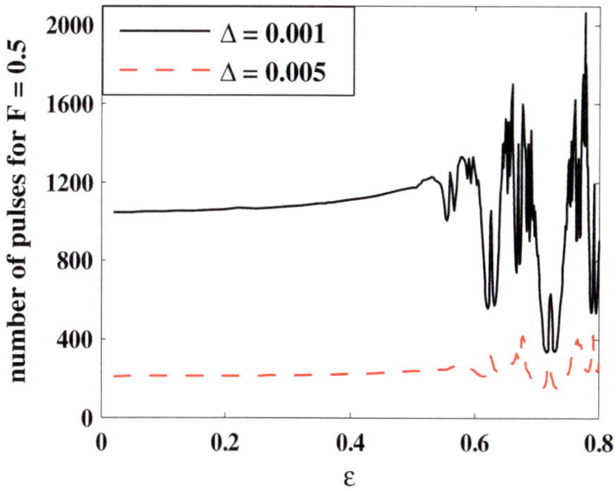

Figure 6. The number of pulses for which the fidelity reaches 0.5 for the first time, as a function of the strength of excitation for two values of the perturbation parameter Δ.

pulses are necessary for the fidelity to get the value 0.5 for the first time, for various values of the strength of the external excitation ε. We see that when ε increase, the time (in fact, the number of the pulses) for which F reaches 0.5 also increases, and, hence, the rate of initial decay of the fidelity decreases. We observe such relation between the decay rate and the strength of the external pulse for $\varepsilon < 0.47$ (it corresponds to both areas of regular motion and the narrow chaotic band in the bifurcation diagram). On the other hand, for the excitations corresponding to the region of deep chaos, the rate of fidelity decay changes irregularly. We observe similar behavior for various values of perturbation parameter Δ. However, when Δ increases, the time of decay becomes shorter, and the rate of fidelity decay is greater (see **Figure 6**). What is important is that when the values of the perturbation parameter become greater and greater, the transition to the phase of its irregular changes with ε is less pronounced, so it is harder to detect the edge of chaotic behavior from discussed dependence.

3.2. Entropic parameter ε

Entropic measures, especially the Kolmogorov entropy, are the most relevant parameters of characterizing chaotic dynamics [49]. Therefore, we will define here the entropy-like quantity ε to show how it could be applied in quantum chaos detection. What is important is that ε will be defined for the quantum, not a classical model.

Thus, first, we calculate the Fourier transform $F(k)$:

$$F(\omega) = \sum_{k} F(t) e^{-i\omega t} dt. \tag{16}$$

We applied here discrete transform due to the discrete character of the system's evolution which is influenced by the train of ultrashort external pulses. Then, we calculate the power spectrum $P(\omega) = |F(\omega)|^2$, and after its proper normalization, we define the entropy-like parameter ε in the form

$$E = -\sum_{\omega} P_N(\omega) \log \left(P_N(\omega)\right). \quad (17)$$

Thus, **Figure 7** shows how the value of ε depends on the strength of external excitation ε. We see that when the dynamics of the classical counterpart of our system is regular, the value of the parameter ε changes slightly with increasing ε. For strengths of the external excitation corresponding to the border of deep chaos, the value of ε increases rapidly. For even higher values of ε, when the classical system exhibits purely chaotic behavior, the value of the parameter ε increases, and, additionally, irregular oscillations appear with increasing ε. This result seems to be very promising. As for classical systems, the bifurcation diagram allows us to determine when it exhibits regular, or chaotic, evolution; the character of quantum system's dynamics could be confirmed by the application of the parameter defined in Eq. (17). The procedure discussed here to other parameters, for instance, Kullback–Leibler quantum divergence [50], is also a worth considering application.

3.3. The fidelity-like parameter

In the bifurcation diagram, we showed the values of $|\alpha|^2$ calculated for the long-time limit and corresponding to various values of ε. The classical value of $|\alpha|^2$ corresponds to the mean number of photons in the quantum picture. From another side, the fidelity $F(k)$ does not contain any information concerning the energy or, equivalently, numbers of photons for considered system. Thus, there is a need to define such parameter that would contain the information concerning both divergence of wave function and energy of the system. Therefore, we will discuss here the fidelity-like parameter $F_n(k)$ which could be not only a good witness of the divergence of two wave functions in Hilbert space but also contain the information concerning the mean number of photons. The definition of $F_n(k)$ should involve the operator $\hat{n} = \hat{a}^{\dagger}\hat{a}$ and two wave functions (one corresponding to the perturbed system and second for the unperturbed

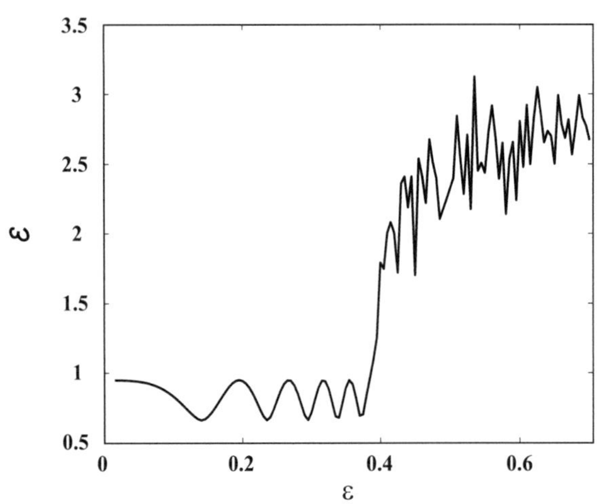

Figure 7. The entropic-like quantity $\mathscr{E}$ versus the strength of external excitation ε.

one). Here, we discuss one of the parameters which its definition fulfills such requirements. Its definition can be written as [51]

$$F_n(k) = |\left\langle \Psi(0)|\hat{U}_u^k\left(\hat{a}^+\hat{a}\right)\hat{U}_p^k|\Psi(0)\right\rangle|. \tag{18}$$

The parameter F_n gives us the possibility to directly compare the behavior of F_n with the information obtained from the bifurcation diagram. Analogously to the cases discussed earlier (see the discussion concerning the fidelity $F(k)$), we will analyze here four cases for which the external force takes the values $\varepsilon = \{0.2; 0.35; 0.45; 0.65\}$. They correspond to the four different areas in the bifurcation diagram shown in **Figure 3**. And thus, **Figure 8** depicts the time evolution of $F_n(k)$ (solid lines) and, additionally, for subfigures (a) and (b), previously defined fidelity $F(k)$ (dashed line).

When $\varepsilon = 0.2$, which corresponds to the regular evolution of the classical system, the value of F_n oscillates regularly (**Figure 8a**). Those oscillations are modulated, and we observe a beating

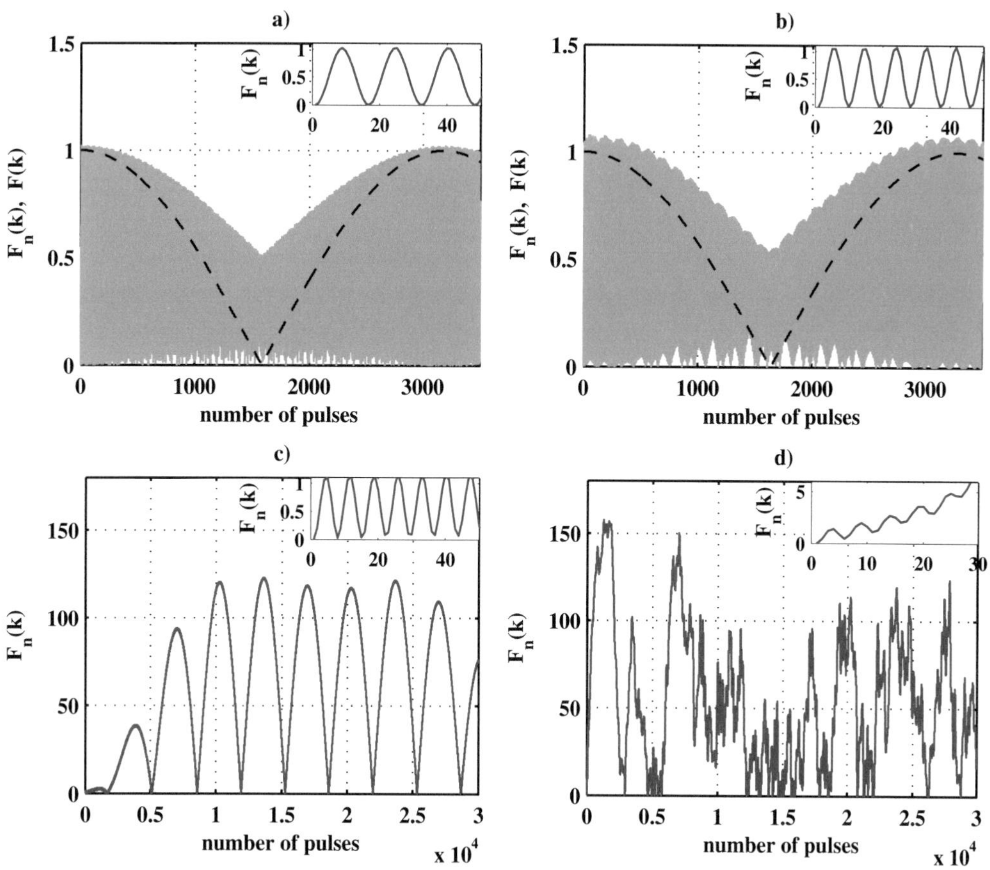

Figure 8. The fidelity-like parameter $F_n(k)$ (solid line) and fidelity $F(k)$ (dashed line) versus the number of pulses for (a) $\varepsilon = 0.2$, (b) $\varepsilon = 0.35$, (c) $\varepsilon = 0.45$, and (d) $\varepsilon = 0.65$. In the inset we have shown F_n in an extended timescale.

effect in the longer timescale. Such beating effect is related to the presence of two frequencies. The first of them corresponds to the low-frequency changes which we already observed for the fidelity (dashed line). The second frequency corresponds to the oscillations of the mean number of photons. As we see, the parameter $F_n(k)$ combines the features of the fidelity and the average number of photons.

For the case when $\varepsilon = 0.35$, the fidelity-like parameter $F_n(k)$ changes regularly (see **Figure 8b**). The same as for $\varepsilon = 0.2$, the time evolution of $F_n(k)$ is determined by two frequencies. The first frequency has the same value as the frequency of oscillation of fidelity. The second is related to oscillation of the mean number of photons. The same as for the case discussed previously and depicted in **Figure 4**, despite the presence of the chaotic band in the bifurcation diagram, all oscillations appearing in **Figure 8b** are of the regular character. Obviously, the regular changes in the time evolution of F_n are observed when $\varepsilon = 0.45$, as well (**Figure 8c**). However, for $\varepsilon = 0.45$ the time dependence of $F_n(k)$ is not clear like that discussed in the previous two cases. It is a result of the appearance of additional frequencies because, here, when $\varepsilon = 0.45$, we are in the vicinity of the chaotic region.

In contrast, when $\varepsilon = 0.65$ (chaotic area in the bifurcation diagram), the behavior of the $F_n(k)$ differs from all previous cases. In the beginning, we observe a characteristic increase of the value of F_n. Moreover, apart from the initial rise in the value of the fidelity-like parameter, we see its irregular variations. Contrary to the characteristic initial decay of the fidelity $F(k)$, which rate depends on the value of perturbation Δ, the fidelity-like parameter $F_n(k)$ exhibits initial rise. In **Figure 9** we present the first stages of time evolution of $F_n(k)$ for various values of Δ. For very early stages of the evolution, the growth of F_n is almost identical for all values of Δ. However, for the next moments of time, the rate of increase becomes damped for the cases of weak perturbation.

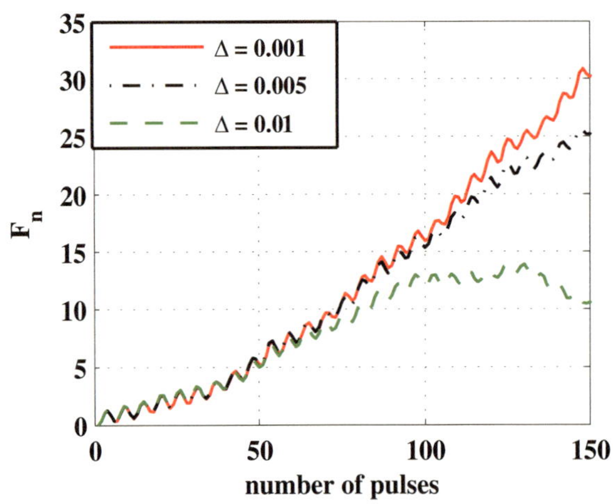

Figure 9. The initial rise of the fidelity-like parameter $F_n(k)$ for various values of the perturbation parameter Δ.

http://dx.doi.org/10.5772/intechopen.70747

4. Conclusion

We have discussed here some proposals for the witnesses of quantum-chaotic behavior. In particular, we considered such parameters as the quantum fidelity and the fidelity-like parameter which characterizes not only the divergence of the wave functions but also the energy of the system. Moreover, the entropic witness describing the chaotic evolution of the fidelity (in a classical sense) was presented here. We discussed all those parameters in a context of their ability of detection of quantum-chaotic behavior. Using the exemplary system of quantum Kerr-type oscillators excited by a train of ultrashort pulses, we have shown how all presented here witnesses could be applied in detection of quantum chaos phenomena. We have shown how they are sensitive to the chaotic behavior when we are dealing with narrow chaotic bands and regions of deep chaos. We believe that we succeed here to show that considered here parameters are not only good witnesses of quantum chaos but also seem to be (with applied here methods) a good starting point in defining other quantities allowing for investigation of quantum chaos.

Author details

Joanna K. Kalaga[1], Marcin W. Jarosik[2], Wiesław Leoński[1]* and Radosław Szczęśniak[2]

*Address all correspondence to: w.leonski@if.uz.zgora.pl

1 Quantum Optics and Engineering Division, Faculty of Physics and Astronomy, University of Zielona Góra, Zielona Góra, Poland

2 Institute of Physics, Częstochowa University of Technology, Częstochowa, Poland

References

[1] Poincaré H. Les Méthodes Nouvelles de la Méchanique Celeste. Paris: Gauthier-Villars; 1892-1899

[2] Kolmogorov AN. On conservation of conditionally periodic motions for a small change in Hamilton's function. Doklady Akademii Nauk SSSR. 1954;**98**:527-530

[3] Arnold VI. Proof of a theorem by A. N. Kolmogorov on the invariance of quasi-periodic motions under small perturbations of the Hamiltonian. Russian Mathematical Surveys. 1963;**18**(5):13-40

[4] Moser JK. Convergent series expansions for quasi-periodic motions. Mathematische Annalen. 1967;**169**:136-176

[5] Lorenz EN. Deterministic nonperiodic flow. Journal of the Atmospheric Sciences. 1963;**20**(2):130-141. DOI: 10.1175/1520-0469(1963)020<0130:DNF>2.0.CO;2

[6] Ahlers G, Behringer RP. Evolution of turbulence from the Rayleigh-Bénard instability. Physical Review Letters. 1978;**40**:712-716. DOI: 10.1103/PhysRevLett.40.712

[7] Gollub JP, Benson SV. Many routes to turbulent convection. Journal of Fluid Mechanics. 1980;**100**(3):449-470. DOI: 10.1017/S0022112080001243

[8] Libchaber A, Maurer J. Une Expérience de Rayleigh-Bénard en géométrie réduite: multiplication, accrochage et démultiplication de fréquences. Le Journal de Physique Colloques. 1980;**41**(C3):51-56. DOI: 10.1051/jphyscol:1980309

[9] Bergé P, Dubois M, Mannevillel P, Pomeau Y. Intermittency in Rayleigh-Bénard convection. Journal de Physique Lettres. 1980;**41**:341-345. DOI: 10.1051/jphyslet:019800041015034100

[10] Haken H. Analogy between higher instabilities in fluids and lasers. Physics Letters A. 1975;**53**(1):77-78. DOI: 10.1016/0375–9601(75)90353-9

[11] Ueda Y. Randomly transitional phenomena in the system governed by Duffing's equation. Journal of Statistical Physics. 1979;**20**(2):181-196. DOI: 10.1007/BF01011512

[12] Ueda Y. Steady Motions Exhibited by Duffing's Equation: A Picture Book of Regular and Chaotic Motions, New Approaches to Nonlinear Problems in Dynamics. Philadelphia: SIAM; 1980

[13] Hadamard J. Les surfaces á courbures opposées et leurs lignes géodésiques. Journal de Mathématiques Pures et Appliquées. 1898;**4**:27-74

[14] Birkhoff GD. On the periodic motions of dynamical systems. Acta Math. 1927;**50**:359-379. DOI: 10.1007/BF02421325

[15] Hartley K. Solar system chaos. Astronomy. 1990;**18**:34-39

[16] Thuan TX. Chaos in the Cosmic Machinery, and Uncertainty in Determinism, in Chaos and Harmony: Perspectives on Scientific Revolution of Twentieth Century. Oxford: Oxford University Press; 2001

[17] Field RJ, Györgyi L. Chaos in Chemistry and Biochemistry. Singapore: World Scientific Publishing Co. Pte. Ltd.; 1993

[18] Żebrowski JJ, Popławska W, Baranowski R. Entropy, pattern entropy, and related methods for the analysis of data on the time intervals between heartbeats from 24-h electrocardiograms. Physical Review E. 1994;**50**:4187-4205. DOI: 10.1103/PhysRevE.50.4187

[19] Amaral LAN, Goldberger AL, Ivanov PC, Stanley HE. Scale-independent measures and pathologic cardiac dynamics. Physical Review Letters. 1998;**81**:2388-2391. DOI: 10.1103/PhysRevLett.81.2388

[20] Bohr N. Niels Bohr—Collected Works, the Correspondence Principle (1918–1923). Vol. 3. In: Rosenfeld L, Rud Nielsen J, editors. North Holland; 1976. DOI: 10.1016/S1876-0503(08)70081-1

[21] Percival IC. Regular and irregular spectra. Journal of Physics B. 1973;**6**(9):L229

[22] McDonald SW, Kaufman AN. Spectrum and eigenfunctions for a hamiltonian with stochastic trajectories. Physical Review Letters. 1979;**42**:1189-1191. DOI: 10.1103/PhysRevLett.42.1189

[23] Bohigas O, Giannoni MJ, Schmit C. Characterization of chaotic quantum spectra and universality of level fluctuation laws. Physical Review Letters. 1984;**52**:1-4. DOI: 10.1103/PhysRevLett.52.1

[24] Peres A. Stability of quantum motion in chaotic and regular systems. Physical Review A. 1984 Oct;**30**:1610-1615. DOI: 10.1103/PhysRevA.30.1610

[25] Woźniak D, Drzewiński A, Kamieniarz G. Quantum chaos systems and fidelity. Acta Physica Polonica A. 2016;**130**(6):1395-1400. DOI: 10.12693/APhysPolA.130.1395

[26] Weinstein YS, Lloyd S, Tsallis C. Border between regular and chaotic quantum dynamics. Physical Review Letters. 2002;**89**:214101. DOI: 10.1103/PhysRevLett.89.214101

[27] Kowalewska-Kudłaszyk A, Kalaga JK, Leoński W. Long-time fidelity and chaos for a kicked nonlinear oscillator system. Physics Letters A. 2009;**373**(15):1334-1340. DOI: 10.1016/j.physleta.2009.02.022

[28] Weinstein YS, Emerson J, Lloyd S, Cory D. Fidelity decay saturation level for initial eigenstates. Quantum Information Processing. 2002;**1**(6):439-448. DOI: 10.1023/A:1024018431394

[29] Prosen T, Znidaric M. Stability of quantum motion and correlation decay. Journal of Physics A: Mathematical and General. 2002;**35**(6):1455

[30] Krivolapov Y, Fishman S, Ott E, Antonsen TM. Quantum chaos of a mixed open system of kicked cold atoms. Physical Review E. 2011;**83**:016204. DOI: 10.1103/PhysRevE.83.016204

[31] Pozzo EN, Domínguez D. Fidelity and quantum chaos in the mesoscopic device for the josephson flux qubit. Physical Review Letters. 2007;**98**:057006. DOI: 10.1103/PhysRevLett.98.057006

[32] Bose S, Jacobs K, Knight PL. Preparation of nonclassical states in cavities with a moving mirror. Physical Review A. 1997;**56**:4175-4186. DOI: 10.1103/PhysRevA.56.4175

[33] Jacobs K. Engineering quantum states of a Nanoresonator via a simple auxiliary system. Physical Review Letters. 2007;**99**:117203. DOI: 10.1103/PhysRevLett.99.117203

[34] Stobińska M, Milburn GJ, Wódkiewicz K. Wigner function evolution of quantum states in the presence of self-Kerr interaction. Physical Review A. 2008;**78**:013810. DOI: 10.1103/PhysRevA.78.013810

[35] Liu YX, Miranowicz A, Gao YB, Bajer J, Sun CP, Nori F. Qubit-induced phonon blockade as a signature of quantum behavior in nanomechanical resonators. Physical Review A. 2010;**82**:032101. DOI: 10.1103/PhysRevA.82.032101

[36] Rabl P. Photon blockade effect in optomechanical systems. Physical Review Letters. 2011;**107**:063601. DOI: 10.1103/PhysRevLett.107.063601

[37] Wang H, Gu X, Liu YX, Miranowicz A, Nori F. Tunable photon blockade in a hybrid system consisting of an optomechanical device coupled to a two-level system. Physical Review A. 2015;**92**:033806. DOI: 10.1103/PhysRevA.92.033806

[38] Kalaga JK, Kowalewska-Kudłaszyk A, Leoński W, Barasiński A. Quantum correlations and entanglement in a model comprised of a short chain of nonlinear oscillators. Physical Review A. 2016;**94**:032304. DOI: 10.1103/PhysRevA.94.032304

[39] Wu L, Miranowicz A, Wang X, Liu Y, Nori F. Perfect function transfer and interference effects in interacting boson lattices. Physical Review A. 2009;**80**:012332. DOI: 10.1103/PhysRevA.80.012332

[40] Barasiński A, Leoński W, Sowiński T. Ground-state entanglement of spin-1 bosons undergoing superexchange interactions in optical superlattices. Journal of the Optical Society of America B: Optical Physics. 2014;**31**(8):1845-1852. DOI: 10.1364/JOSAB.31.001845

[41] Islam R, Ma R, Preiss PM, Tai ME, Lukin A, Rispoli M, et al. Measuring entanglement entropy in a quantum many-body system. Nature. 2015;**528**:77. DOI: 10.1038/nature15750

[42] Preiss P, Ma R, Tai M, Lukin A, Rispoli M, Zupancic P, et al. Strongly correlated quantum walks in optical lattices. Science. 2015;**347**:1229-1233. DOI: 10.1126/science.1260364

[43] Boissonneault M, Gambetta JM, Blais A. Dispersive regime of circuit QED: Photon-dependent qubit dephasing and relaxation rates. Physical Review A. 2009;**79**:013819. DOI: 10.1103/PhysRevA.79.013819

[44] Rebić S, Twamley J, Milburn GJ. Giant kerr nonlinearities in circuit quantum electrodynamics. Physical Review Letters. 2009;**103**:150503. DOI: 10.1103/PhysRevLett.103.150503

[45] Leoński W. Quantum and classical dynamics for a pulsed nonlinear oscillator. Physica A: Statistical Mechanics and its Applications. 1996;**233**:365-378. DOI: 10.1016/S0378-4371(96)00250-6

[46] Gerry CC, Knight PL. Introductory Quantum Optics. Cambridge: Cambridge University Press; 2005

[47] Kalaga JK, Leoński W, Kowalewska-Kudłaszyk A. System of nonlinear quantum oscillator and quantum correlations—Proposal for quantum chaos indicator. Proceedings of SPIE. 2014;**9441**:94410W

[48] Kowalewska-Kudłaszyk A, Kalaga JK, Leoński W. Wigner-function nonclassicality as indicator of quantum chaos. Physical Review E. 2008;**78**:066219-066211

[49] Schuster HG, Just W. Deterministic Chaos—An Introduction. Weinheim: Wiley-VCH Verlag; 2005

[50] Kowalewska-Kudłaszyk A, Kalaga JK, Leoński W, Cao LV. Kullback-Leibler quantum divergence as an indicator of quantum chaos. Physics Letters A. 2012;**376**:128012-128086

[51] Kalaga JK, Leoński W. Two proposals of quantum chaos indicators related to the mean number of photons: Pulsed Kerr-like oscillator case. Proceedings of SPIE. 2016;**10142**: 101421L

Chapter 8

Different Approaches of Synchronization in Chaotic-Coupled QD Lasers

Hussein B. Al Husseini and Kais A.M. Al Naimee

Additional information is available at the end of the chapter

http://dx.doi.org/10.5772/intechopen.72500

Abstract

The investigation of synchronization phenomena on measured theoretical data such as time series has recently become an increasing focus of interest. In this chapter, the synchronized states (including steady state, periodic or chaotic) in coupled quantum dot lasers (dimensionless rate equations) are considered with both bidirectional and unidirectional synchronization. Different approaches for measuring synchronization have been proposed that rely on certain characteristic features of the dynamical system under investigation. Results show that the measure to be applied to a certain task can be chosen according to information in test applications, although certain dynamical features of a system under investigation (e.g., bifurcation and amplitude correlation) may render certain measures more suitable than others.

Keywords: quantum-dot (QD) laser, optical feedback, bifurcation, dimensionless rate equations, chaos synchronization

1. Introduction

Idea of "exploit quantum effects in heterostructure semiconductor lasers to produce wavelength tunability" and achieve a "lower lasing threshold "via" the change in the density of states, which outcome from reducing the number of translational degrees of freedom of the carriers", was firstly introduced by Dingle and Henry in 1976 [1]. This is performed by reducing the thickness of the smaller band gap material (the active region) in the heterostructure to the scale of the deBroglie wavelength of the carrier (~ few nanometers). This results in a quantum well (QW) structure. Reducing the size of another dimension results in a quantum wire (QWi) structure. Further reduction of the remaining dimension results in a quantum dot (QD) structure where all dimensions are quantized. However, for about a quarter of century, lasers using structures with carrier confinement in two ("quantum wire") or all in three ("quantum dot") directions appear to lack practical realization compared to so-called QW lasers, where quantum confinement of carriers occurs in one dimension.

The most important advantage of using size-quantized heterostructures in lasers originates from the increase in the density of states for charge carriers near band edges. When used as an active layer for the laser, this focuses most of the injected carriers in an increasingly narrow energy range near the bottom of the conduction band and/or the peak of the valence band. This enhances the maximum material gain (assuming the same homogeneous or inhomogeneous broadening as in bulk lasers) and reduces the influence of temperature on device performance making it less temperature dependent. This also makes further reduction in the threshold current. The electronic states in a QD are spatially localized and the energy is fully quantized, similar to a single atom [1]. So, the system is more stable against any thermal perturbation. In addition, due to the quantization, the probability becomes higher for optical transitions. Also, the electron localization may radically reduce the scattering of electrons by bulk defects and reduce the rate of non-radiative recombination. These properties, among the others, are directly related with the high thermal stability and the high quantum efficiency of QD lasers, and they are of great importance in terms of device applications.

From a dynamical behavior systems' point of view, semiconductor lasers are characterized by a time scale separation between the fast-slow systems, that is, fast photon and the slower carrier subsystem [2]. As a result, their turn-on dynamics shows damped nonlinear intensity oscillations, which are called relaxation oscillations. The damping of relaxation oscillations is a key point in order to understand the stability properties of the laser subject to external perturbations, for example, optical injection or optical feedback. QW laser shows obvious, weakly damped relaxation oscillations, while the relaxation oscillations of QD lasers are strongly damped [3]. As a result, QD lasers under optical injection display a higher dynamical stability [4] and optical feedback [5]. In QD devices, the carriers are first injected into a surrounding QW acting as a carrier reservoir, before they scatter into the discrete energy levels of the QDs, between which the optical transition takes place. The scattering rates of carrier strongly depend on the energy spacing between the band gap of the QW and the discrete QD levels, that is, on the band structure of the device. The scattering rates provide lifetimes of the nonlinear carriers in the QD levels, which yield additional time scales compared to QW lasers. The discrete energy levels determine how these time scales compare to the carrier lifetimes in the carrier reservoir and the photon lifetime. For a small energy spacing as example, short lifetimes (large scattering rates) are obtained, which are on the same time scale or shorter than the photon lifetime yielding over-damped, very stable system, which work similar to gas lasers, i.e., typical class A of lasers. For high level of energy, long carrier lifetimes are obtained, which guarantee an apparent time-scale separation between the carrier and the photon system (time-scale of femtoseconds) resulting in weakly damped, less stable lasers, whose dynamics is similar to conventional QW lasers, that is, typical class B lasers. QD lasers dynamics lie between these two limiting cases and show typical dynamical features of class B and class A lasers [3].

A characteristic of semiconductor lasers is its high sensitivity to external optical disturbances due to the relatively low reflection of its facets [4]. On the one hand, this may be a disadvantage, because in optical applications, expensive isolators are needed to ensure a stable constant wave (CW) emission of lasers. Conversely, the basic physics of the views, the laser semiconductor display, subject to optical injection or optical feedback, a wealth of different dynamic systems ranging from stable cw emissions, with period behavior intensity modulations, to chaotic behavior [5].

Numerous applications arise from optical injection ranging from noise reduction [6], over a reduction of relative intensity noise [7], the strengthening side-mode suppression [8], to a larger bandwidth under direct optical alteration [9], and the generation of microwave signals [10].

Furthermore, the semiconductor lasers subject to delayed optical feedback are the ideal candidates to study the stabilization of steady states and limit cyclical orbits due to the control of nongaseous delayed feedback [10].

Moreover, delay synchronization of coupled lasers, bubbling in coupled lasers, and networks of delay coupled lasers [11] are subject of current research.

2. Nonlinear dynamics of QD

Currently, nonlinear laser dynamics is a field that continues to grow from active research, and this chapter focuses and reviews recent developments in this area with the approach of a new dimensional model. In a multipronged approach, it will also focus on mathematical and physical aspects. By discussing problems such as exploiting the chaotic laser for secure communications, using the QD laser applications, it will introduce innovative foundations and hope to inspire future research on the subject. Nowadays, self-organized semiconductor quantum dot (QD) lasers are promising candidates for telecommunication applications [1]. For an introduction to QD-based devices, their growth process, and their optical properties see, for example, [2].

This chapter focuses on the modeling of these QD laser devices and on the discussion of their dynamic properties. Since QD semiconductor materials have a discrete energy sub-bands, one could expect symmetric emission lines, and then the subject of great current interest is a sensitivity of QD semiconductor lasers to optical feedback.

3. Synchronization in chaotic coupled QD lasers

Chaotic synchronization has attracted more interest because of its potential applications in the field of private communication and for the control of chaos in different dynamical systems [1]. Starting in 1990 and following the development of the theory of deterministic chaos synchronization, synchronization was extended to the case of interacting chaotic oscillators [2–5]. Since the definition of chaos involves a quick relationship to decorate the nearby orbits due to their high sensitivity in initial conditions, the synchronization of two associated chaos systems is a fairly intuitive antiretroviral phenomenon. An examination of synchronization phenomena in quantum dot (QD) laser chaotic has been a topic of increasing interest since the past few years [6] because of sensitive to external perturbation as optical feedback, and these materials have discrete transitions of energy, with expected symmetric emission lines and therefore a low linewidth enhancement factor. This has motivated many studies, with expected benefits including elimination of lasers.

Recently, various methods such as occasional coupling [2, 3], unidirectional coupling [7], and bidirectional coupling [8] with optical feedback [9] have been shown to induce chaos and achieve chaotic synchronization in laser systems. There are different methods for detecting different types of synchronization. Complete synchronization can be identified by drawing a driver component against the responder component while the stage synchronization can be defined by the average frequency [7].

Here, to check for a complete synchronization in both unidirectional and bidirectional, corresponding to this diversity of concepts and complete methods, all the synchronization detection has many different approaches suggested with the aim of quantifying the degree of synchronization between two systems on a continuous scale. These approaches consist of such linear, cross-correlation or time-series tracking as well as nonlinear measures mainly such as bifurcation diagrams.

The remaining chapter is organized as follows: Before we perform any numerical bifurcation studies, we introduce the QD laser model with external optical feedback in Section 2. Section 3 is devoted to the study of the full delay differential equation for the representative value of the frequency of the solitary laser w_o, basic bifurcations of coupling strength in bidirectional synchronization for $k_c \geq 0$ and unidirectional synchronization for $k_c > 0$. Section 4 is devoted to amplitude correlation for two chaotic systems. Finally, we summarize in Section 5.

3.1. Coupling QD laser model

In this section, we consider two semiconductor QD lasers that are delay-coupled to each other with a coupling delay and additionally receive self-feedback with the same delay time τ. The basic coupling scheme is depicted in **Figure 1** (one can see our model with principle translations in Appendix). The coupled system is described by dimensionless rate equations

$$x_1^{\bullet} = x_1(y_1 - 1) + k_{11}\sqrt{x_1 x_{1\tau}}\cos(\phi_1 - \phi_{1_\tau} + \Theta) + k_{21}\sqrt{x_2 x_{2\tau}}\cos(\phi_1 - \phi_{2_\tau} + \Theta) \tag{1a}$$

$$\Phi_1^{\bullet} = -\frac{\alpha}{2}y_1 - \frac{k_{11}}{2}\sqrt{x_{1\tau}/x_1}\sin(\phi_1 - \phi_{1_\tau} + \Theta) - \frac{k_{21}}{2}\sqrt{x_{2\tau}/x_2}\sin(\phi_1 - \phi_{2_\tau} + \Theta) \tag{1b}$$

$$x_2^{\bullet} = x_2(y_2 - 1) + k_{22}\sqrt{x_2 x_{2\tau}}\cos(\phi_2 - \phi_{2_\tau} + \Theta) + k_{12}\sqrt{x_1 x_{1\tau}}\cos(\phi_2 - \phi_{1_\tau} + \Theta) \tag{1c}$$

$$\Phi_2^{\bullet} = -\frac{\alpha}{2}y_2 - \frac{k_{22}}{2}\sqrt{x_{2\tau}/x_2}\sin(\phi_2 - \phi_{2_\tau} + \Theta) - \frac{k_{12}}{2}\sqrt{x_{1\tau}/x_1}\sin(\phi_2 - \phi_{1_\tau} + \Theta) \tag{1d}$$

where x_k and Φ_k are the normalized photon density and the phase of the kth QD laser, respectively, and α is the linewidth enhancement factor, the phase shift of the light during one round trip in the external cavity ($\tau = 2L/c$) is given by $\Theta = \omega_o\tau$, c is the speed of light. With w_o denoting the frequency of the solitary laser at the lasing threshold. The field labeled by the subscript τ, and k_{ii}, k_{ij} is the feedback and the coupling strength, respectively. The three

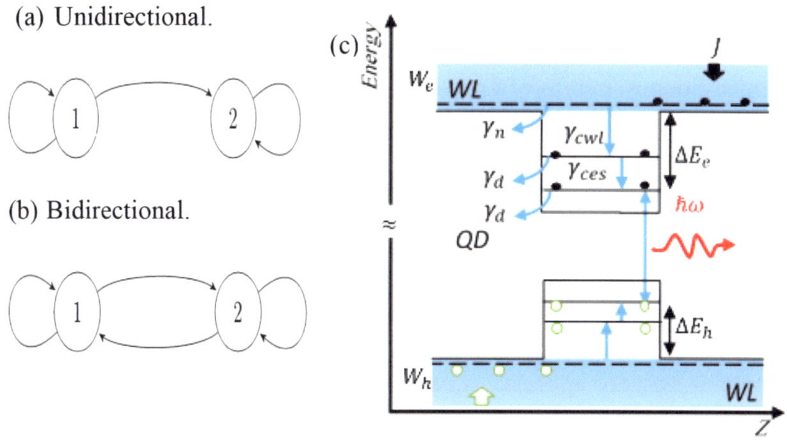

Figure 1. Schematic diagram of two chaotic systems of QD laser with optical feedback object. (a) Unidirectional coupling system. (b) Bidirectional coupling system: (1) transmitter QD laser and (2) receiver QD laser. (c) Schematic energy band diagram of QW and QD. ΔE_e and ΔE_h denote the energy spacing of the QW band edge and the QD ground state (GS) for electrons and holes. $\hbar\omega$ marks the GS lasing energy of the QD.

equations for the occupation probability of a ground and excited states in the QDs (ρ_{gs} and ρ_{es}) and carrier density in the WL (N_{wl}) read:

$$y_k^{\bullet} = \Gamma z_k(\Gamma_1 - y_k) - \Gamma_2 y_k(1 + 2x_k) - \Gamma_1\Gamma_2 \tag{1e}$$

$$z_k^{\bullet} = \Gamma_1 w_k(1 - z_k) - \Gamma_2 z_k - \Gamma z_k(1 - y_k/\Gamma_1)/2 \tag{1f}$$

$$w_k^{\bullet} = \Gamma_3\delta_o - \Gamma_4 w_k - 2\Gamma_3 w_k(1 - z_k) \tag{1g}$$

where the dot denotes derivation with respect to time, δ_o is the bias current (see Appendix for more details). The last terms in (1a)–(1d) are the effect of the chaotic signal. When the chaotic signal from the receiver is zero in the transmitter system, that is, $k_{21} = 0$, the model reduces to the unidirectional system in **Figure 1a**.

3.2. Coupling QD laser results

A QD semiconductor laser display is just one of many examples that interact between many nonlinear similar systems that can lead to a variety of rich emerging behaviors [10]. Neurons, chemical oscillations, or Josephson intersections are other representative cases of nonlinear dynamics that have attracted the attention of researchers from special fields. But, quite astonishingly, only lately has the effects of limited rapid use of signals in the interaction and coupling of several of these systems taken into account.

In this chapter, we accurately focus on the effect of these mismatching strength and delay times, which constitute a rich basis of instabilities, on the dynamics and synchronization of semiconductor QDs laser systems.

In the past work, we emphasized that the QD semiconductors are the ideal candidates for exploring the behavior of nonlinear systems when combined or susceptible to external disturbances [11]. In addition to nonlinear joints in this type of device, it can be well characterized and controlled in experiments, rather than most biologically oriented systems. Besides their inherent nonlinearity, these types of devices can be well characterized and controlled in experiments, as opposed to most of biologically oriented systems. Since then, different configurations of QD semiconductors have been theoretically investigated. The optical interaction of QD-LED has been mostly studied in a single device subject to feedback [12–14].

In a bidirectional optical coupling section, dynamical properties of two semiconductor QD lasers subject to a bidirectional optical coupling are studied. The organization of work in two parts is separated in order to approach separately the cases in which each laser (in addition to the reciprocal function) is subject to self-nourishment or not. First, we start by investigating the coupling of the two chaotic systems in the presence of self-feedback. Unless explicitly mentioned, a symmetric configuration is chosen for the feedback lines ($k_{11} = k_{22}$ and $\tau_1 = \tau_2 \equiv \tau_c$).

Figure 2 shows coupling without self-feedback case, here, we consider the situation in which the self-feedback is zero ($k_{ii} = 0$), and only the mutual coupling excites both lasers simultaneously ($k_{ij} > 0$). This result supports the understanding that threshold decrease in QD semiconductor lasers can just occur during coherent interactions where a superposition of the intra-cavity laser and some injected fields is achievable. In this case, because of the optical interaction is by naturally of phase insensitive, no threshold reduction is expected. Similar to the solitary case, as the strength of feedback is increased, the defeat of stability of the steady state is mediated by a collision in the phase space with the periodic state in a transcritical bifurcation scenario.

In **Figure 2(a)** and **(b)**, we plot a path and indicate the stability of coupling systems as a coupling strength function. **Figure 2** is generated by assuming a small time delay of the coupling so that we promise that no Hopf bifurcation can influence as we will show in the other case. The way to the previous virtual contradiction depends on appreciating that merely at the critical coupling for the system stationary conditions. Eqs. (1a)–(1e) allow for an additional solution consisting of a continuum of steady-states, it is found to connect the two systems at $[w = 0, w = \pi]$ involved in the stability.

Once the dynamics of our mutually coupled configuration have been characterized in coupling with self-feedback case, we can now approach the different effects and questions raised by the addition of self-feedback to each one of the QD lasers. Thus in the second part of this work, in **Figure 3(a)** and **(b)**, we are investigating the disturbances caused by the delayed reaction between two of the self-oscillation of QD laser. Given the inclusion of feedback loops, we can control the dynamics of the unescorted laser valve between the constant, oscillation, pulsating, and chaotic behavior so that we can investigate the impact of delays on different system synchronization properties. Other dynamic phenomena such as phase synchronization are reviewed.

We now examine the dynamical properties of two semiconductor QD lasers subject to a unidirectional optical coupling. The approach of this cases where two chaotic systems in the

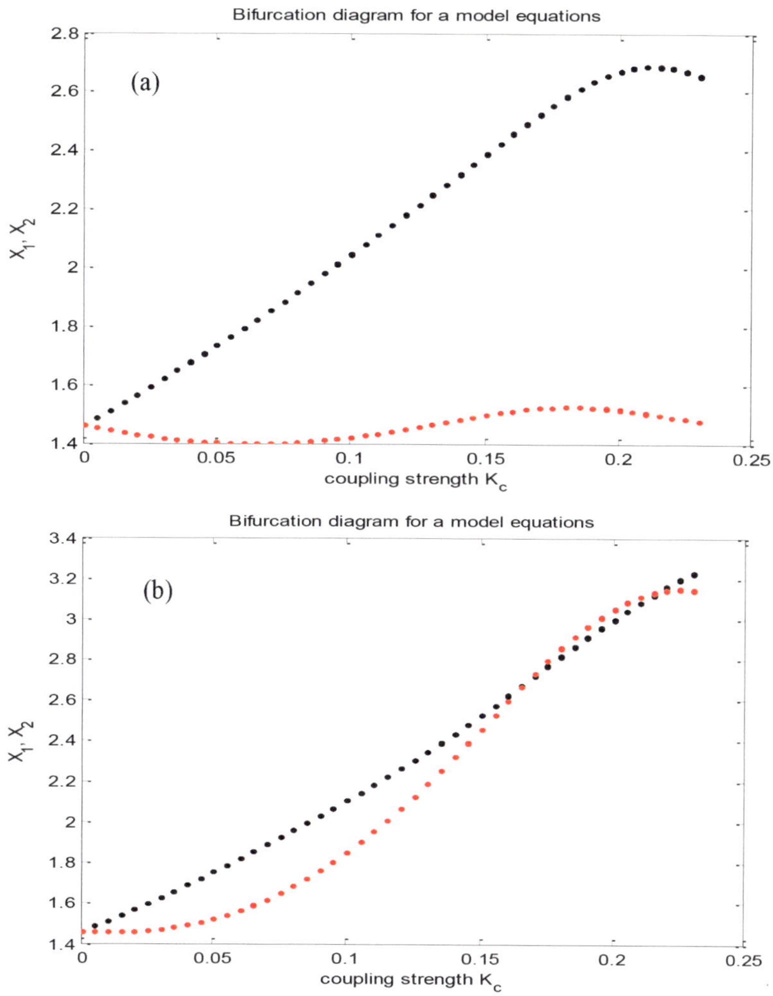

Figure 2. Bifurcation for bidirectional two coupling systems without self-feedback. (a) $w_o = 0$ and (b) $w_o = \pi$. At active delay optical feedback $\tau = 5.7802$, the other conditions are $\delta_o = 0.1$, $k_{ii} = 0$ and $\alpha = 0.9$.

presence of self-feedback ($k_{ii} \neq 0$) and coupling excite lasers ($k_{21} = 0$). **Figure 4(a)** and **(b)** shows the bifurcation diagram for unidirectional two coupling systems with self-feedback objected. In **Figure 4(a)** disynchronization mode appears after a certain value of feedback coupling strength, which suddenly turns into the state of the chaos while the other continues with the steady state. **Figure 4(b)** shows unexpected result when an array of synchronized oscillators becomes desynchronized through the changing of a parameter of the solitary laser. The other parameters are as follows: active delay optical feedback $\tau = 5.7802$, $\delta_o = 0.33$, $k_{ii} = 0.3054$ and $\alpha = 0.9$.

3.3. Different synchronization approaches

In what follows, we pay attention to the investigation on different approaches for achieving synchronization between coupling systems. The synchronization of both lasers is studied here

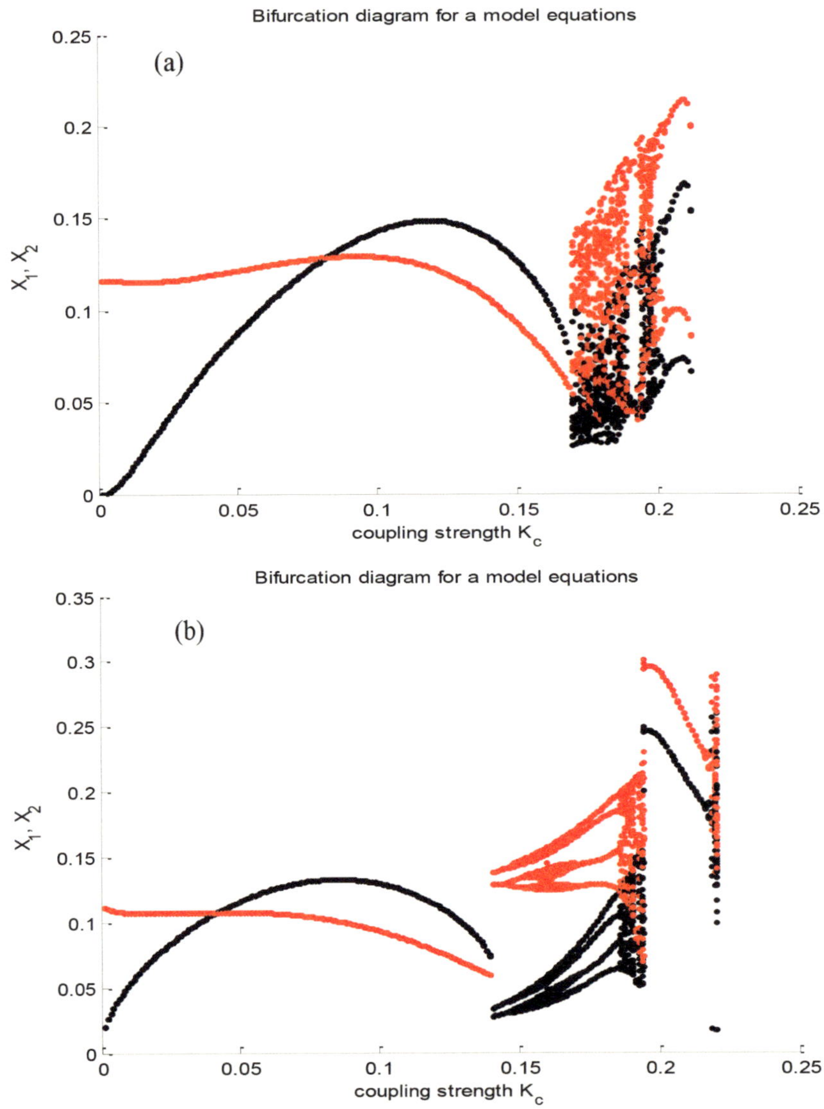

Figure 3. Bifurcation for bidirectional two coupling chaotic systems with self-feedback objected. (a) $w_o = 0$ (b) $w_o = \pi$. At active delay optical feedback $\tau = 5.7802$, the other conditions are $\delta_o = 0.06$, $k_{ii} = 0.258$ and $\alpha = 0.9$.

for three different situations. For identical QD lasers, we first consider the case of bidirectional coupled chaotic oscillators, and secondly, we address the synchronization of unidirectional chaotic oscillators. Finally, we study the unidirectional coupling systems without feedback operation of the receiver laser. The different types of synchronization are characterized by two figures of merit, namely, the correlation degree between amplitudes and the relative time series of the oscillations.

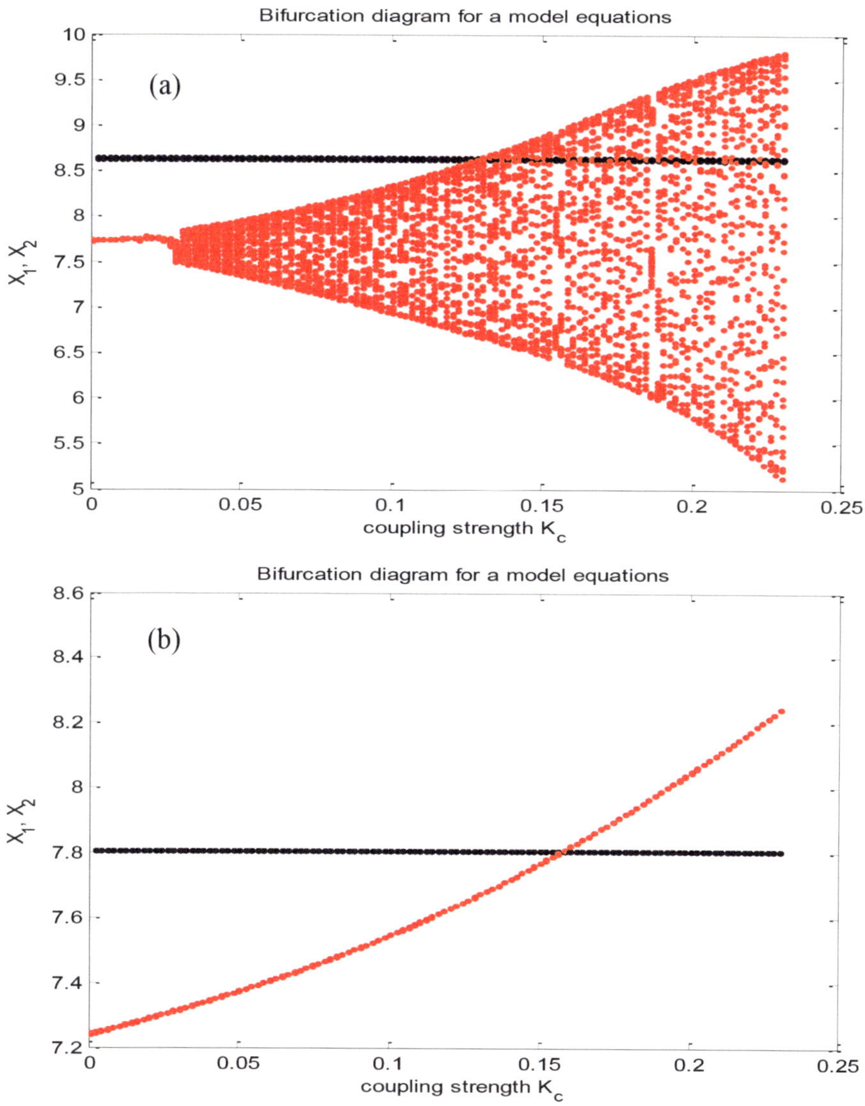

Figure 4. Bifurcation for unidirectional two coupling systems with self-feedback objected. (a) $w_o = 0$ and (b) $w_o = \pi$. At active delay optical feedback $\tau = 5.7802$, the other conditions are $\delta_o = 0.33$, $k_{ii} = 0.3054$, and $\alpha = 0.9$.

Figure 5 shows chaos synchronization in a bidirectional system at conditions $\delta_o = 0.13$, $k_{ii} = 0.25$, $\alpha = 0.9$ and $w = 0$. Output amplitude signal at active delay optical feedback $\tau = 5.7$ of two chaotic systems where output amplitude signal of transmitter (black point-line) and receiver, generalized chaos synchronization at coupling strength ($k_c \geq 0.038$) was shown in **Figure 5(a)**. **Figure 5(b–e)** shows chaotic time series corresponding with (a), which appeared generalized chaos synchronization in **Figure 5(b)**.

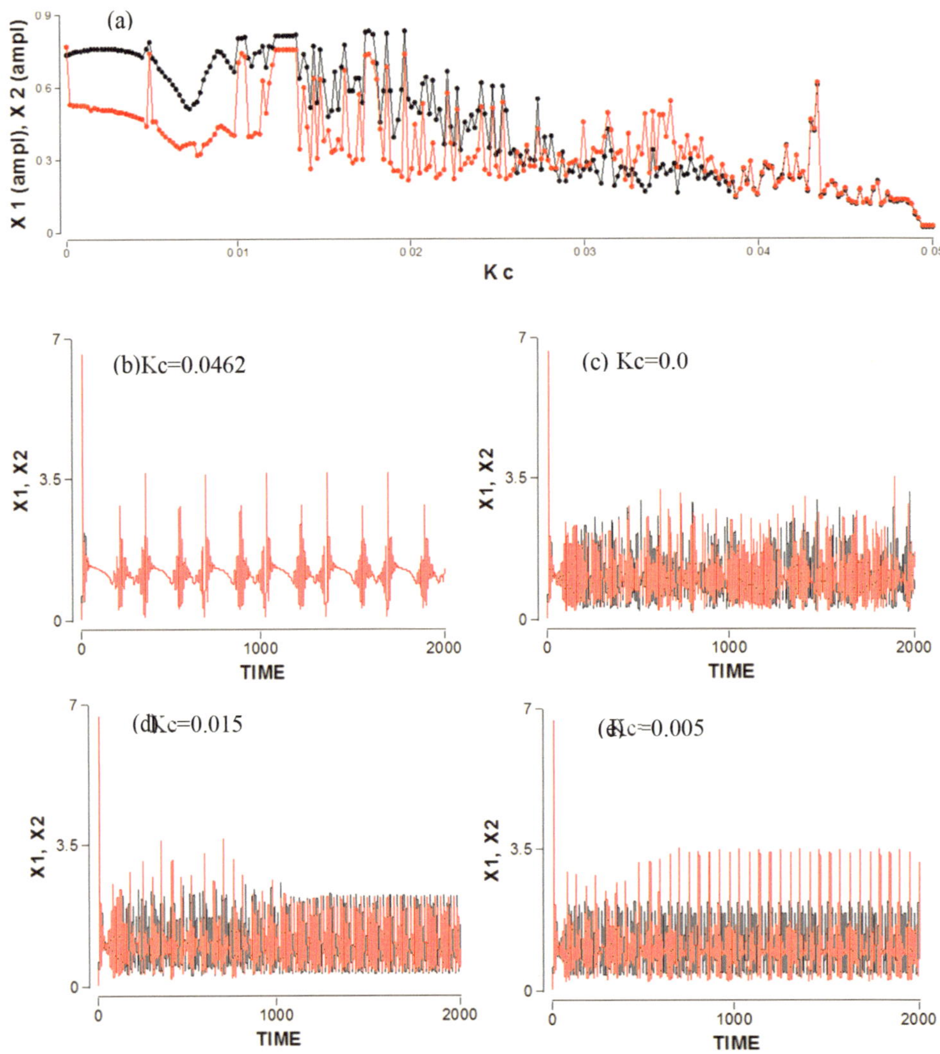

Figure 5. Chaos synchronization in a bidirectional system. (a) Two chaotic systems output amplitude signal, transmitter (black point-line) at active delay optical feedback $\tau = 5.7$ and receiver without feedback (red point-line). (b–e) Chaotic time series corresponding with (a).

Figure 6 shows chaos synchronization in a unidirectional system. **Figure 6(a)** shows generalized chaos synchronization at coupling strength (k_c = 0.01526). **Figure 6(b–e)** shows chaotic time series corresponding with (a), noted that the transmitter behavior is still without change compared with **Figure 6(a)**.

Figure 7 shows unidirectional coupling systems without feedback operation of the receiver laser. Chaos synchronization follows feedback strength of transmitter shown in **Figure 7(a–d)** when coupling strength is projected.

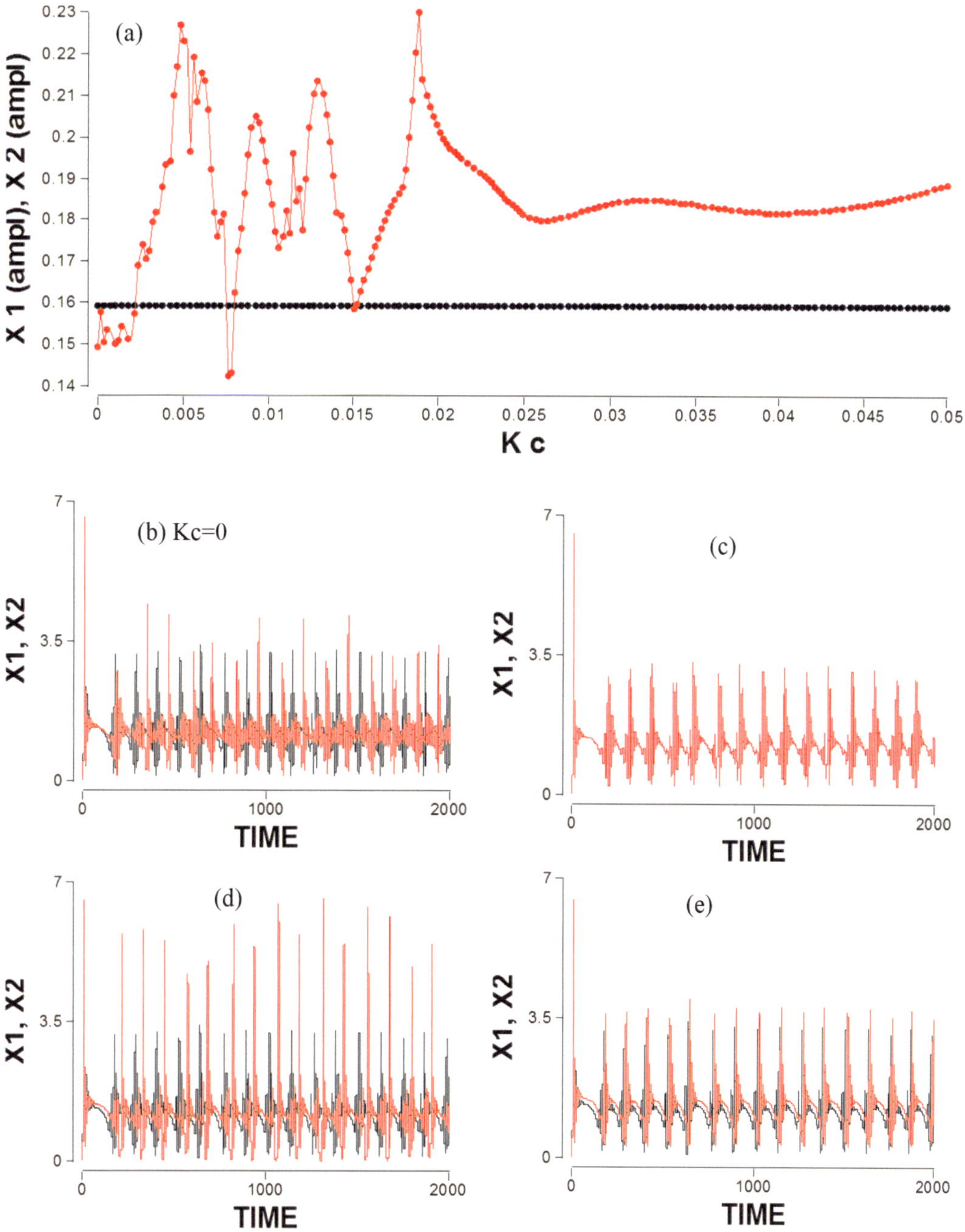

Figure 6. Chaos synchronization in a unidirectional system. (a) Two chaotic systems output amplitude signal, transmitter (black point-line) at active delay optical feedback $\tau = 5.7$ and receiver without feedback (red point-line), generalized chaos synchronization at coupling strength ($k_c = 0.01526$). (b–e) Chaotic time series corresponding with (a). The other conditions are $\delta_o = 0.13$, $k_{ii} = 0.35$, $\alpha = 0.9$, and $w = 0$.

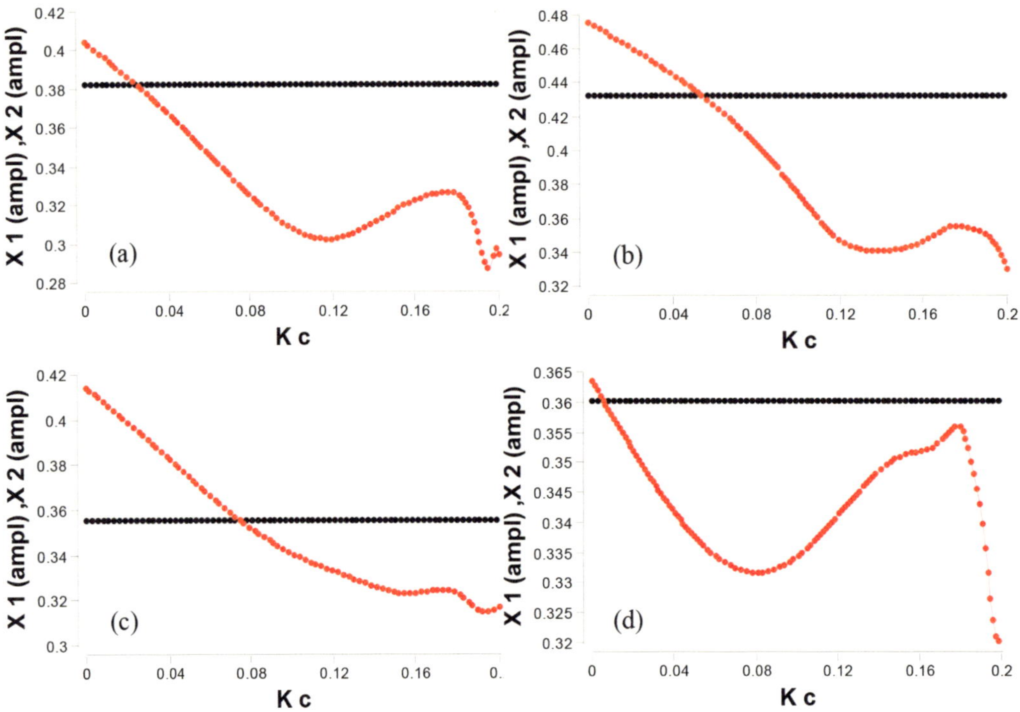

Figure 7. Chaos synchronization in a unidirectional system. Two chaotic systems output amplitude signal, transmitter (black point-line) at active delay optical feedback $\tau = 5.7$ and receiver without feedback (red point-line). Chaos synchronization follows feedback strength when coupling strength is projected. (a) $k_{11} = 0.299$, (b) $k_{11} = 0.3$, (c) $k_{11} = 0.304$, and (d) $k_{11} = 0.3054$. The other conditions are $\delta_o = 0.13$, $\alpha = 0.9$, and $w = 0$.

4. Conclusion

This chapter is concerned with the problem of chaos synchronization estimation in a new semiconductor quantum dot laser dimensionless model. The need to know effect of parameters in our model with coupling case at different approach of chaos synchronization occurs throughout the development of bifurcation diagrams, which reduced dynamics of model. The approach presented here builds on the existing work that uses synchronization as a tool for parameter estimation. Some important issues of chaos synchronization are addressed in this chapter. The central issue is the choice of coupling strength between the systems, which is considered through bifurcations depending on coupling kind.

A. Appendix

The field equation is defined as a complex stochastic differential equation. The aim is to transform the complex stochastic differential equation form field equation (E) into two real stochastic differential equations for the photon density $S = |E|^2$ and the phase Φ. This is just a transformation to polar coordinates without the stochastic term [14]. Averaging over the stochastic terms, the final rate equations for the photon density S, the phase of the electric field Φ, and the three equations for the occupation probability of a ground and exited states in the QDs (ρ_{gs} and ρ_{es}) and carrier density in the WL (N_{wl}) read:

$$S^{\bullet} = \left[v g_o \left(2\rho_{gs} - 1 \right) - \gamma_s \right] S + \gamma \sqrt{S S_\tau} \cos\left(\phi - \phi_\tau \right) \tag{2a}$$

$$\phi^{\bullet} = -\frac{\alpha}{2} v g_o \left(2\rho_{gs} - 1 \right) - \frac{\gamma}{2} \sqrt{S_\tau / S} \sin\left(\phi - \phi_\tau \right) \tag{2b}$$

$$\rho_{gs}^{\bullet} = \gamma_{c_{es}} \rho_{es} \left(1 - \rho_{gs} \right) - \gamma_d \rho_{gs} - g_o \left(2\rho_{gs} - 1 \right) S \tag{2c}$$

$$\rho_{es}^{\bullet} = \gamma_{c_{wl}} N_{wl} (1 - \rho_{es}) - \gamma_d \rho_{es} - \gamma_{c_{es}} \rho_{es} \left(1 - \rho_{gs} \right) \tag{2d}$$

$$N_{wl}^{\bullet} = \frac{J}{e} - \gamma_n N_{wl} - 2\gamma_{c_{wl}} N_{wl} (1 - \rho_{es}) \tag{2e}$$

In our approach, the carrier-light interaction is summarized in the photon density S, which includes all longitudinal modes. The factor 2 in Eq. (2e) accounts for the twofold spin degeneracy in the quantum dot energy levels. A similar factor 2 is included in the definition of the differential gain factor g in Eq. (2a) [11]. For numerical purposes, it is useful to rewrite Eqs. (2) in a dimensionless form. To this end, we introduce the new variables

$x = \frac{g_o}{\gamma_d} S$, $\Phi \equiv \Phi$, $y = \frac{g_o v}{\gamma_s} \left(2\rho_{gs} - 1 \right)$, $z \equiv \rho_{es}$, $w = \frac{\gamma_{c_{wl}}}{g_o v} N_{wl}$, $\Gamma = \frac{\gamma_{c_{es}}}{\gamma_s}$, $\Gamma_1 = \frac{g_o v}{\gamma_s}$, $\Gamma_2 = \frac{\gamma_d}{\gamma_s}$, .

$\Gamma_3 = \frac{\gamma_{c_{wl}}}{\gamma_s}$, $\Gamma_4 = \frac{\gamma_n}{\gamma_s}$, $\delta_o = \frac{J}{g_o v q}$ and the time scale $t' = \gamma_s t$. The rate

$$x^{\bullet} = x(y - 1) + \varepsilon \sqrt{x x_\tau} \cos\left(\phi - \phi_\tau \right) \tag{3a}$$

$$\Phi^{\bullet} = -\frac{\alpha}{2} y - \frac{\varepsilon}{2} \sqrt{x_\tau / x} \sin\left(\phi - \phi_\tau \right) \tag{3b}$$

$$y^{\bullet} = \Gamma z (\Gamma_1 - y) - \Gamma_2 y (1 + 2x) - \Gamma_1 \Gamma_2 \tag{3c}$$

$$z^{\bullet} = \Gamma_1 w (1 - z) - \Gamma_2 z - \Gamma z (1 - y/\Gamma_1)/2 \tag{3d}$$

$$w^{\bullet} = \Gamma_3 \delta_o - \Gamma_4 w - 2\Gamma_3 w (1 - z) \tag{3e}$$

where $\varepsilon = \gamma / \gamma_s$. The well-established assumptions here are that the delay time τ is larger than the laser roundtrip time inside the active region (**Figure 1**).

Author details

Hussein B. Al Husseini[1] and Kais A.M. Al Naimee[2,3]*

*Address all correspondence to: kais.al-naimee@ino.it

1 Nassiriya Nanotechnology Research Laboratory (NNRL), Science College, Thi-Qar University, Nassiriya, Iraq

2 Department of Physics, College of Science, University of Baghdad, Baghdad, Iraq

3 Istituto Nazionale di Ottica—CNR Firenze, Italy

References

[1] Ohtsubo J. Chaotic dynamics in semiconductor lasers with optical feedback. In: Wolf E. editor. Progress in Optics. Vol. 44. Amsterdam: North-Holland; 2002. p. 25. Chap. 1

[2] Usman M. Multi-million atom electronic structure calculations for quantum dots [PhD thesis]. Purdue University; 2011

[3] Al-Khursan AH. Intensity noise characteristics in quantum-dot lasers: Four-level rate equations analysis. Journal of Luminescence. 2005;**113**:129-136

[4] Sprott JC. Chaos and Time–Series Analysis. Oxford; 2003

[5] Al Khursan AH, Ghalib BA, Al Obaidi SJ. Numerical simulation of optical feedback on a quantum dot lasers. Physics of Semiconductor Devices. 2012;**46**(2):213-220. ISSN: 1063-7826

[6] Pikovsky AS, Rosenblum MG, Kurths J. Synchronization. A Universal Concept in Nonlinear Sciences. Cambridge, UK: Cambridge University Press; 2001

[7] Ghalib BA, Al-Obaidi SJ, Al-Khursan AH. Quantum dot semiconductor laser with opto-electronic feedback. Superlattices and Microstructures. 2012;**52**:977-986

[8] Ananthakrishna G, Bharathi MS. Dynamical approach to the spatiotemporal aspects of the portevin - le chatelier effect: Chaos, turbulence, and band propagation. Physical Review E. 2004;**70**:026111

[9] Al Naimee K, Al Husseini H, Abdalah SF, Al Khursan A, Khedir AH, Meucci R, Arecchi FT. Complex dynamics in quantum dot light emitting diodes. European Physical Journal D. 2015;**69**(257):1-5

[10] Voss HU, Timmer J, Kurths J. Nonlinear dynamical system identification from uncertain and indirect measurements. International Journal of Bifurcation and Chaos. 2004;**14**:1905-1933

[11] Al Husseini HB. Control of nonlinear dynamics of quantum dot laser with external optical feedback. Journal of Nanotechnology in Diagnosis and Treatment. 2016;**4**:5-14

[12] Al Husseini HB, Al Naimee KA, Al-Khursan AH, Khedir AH. External modes in quantum dot light emitting diode with filtered optical feedback. Journal of Applied Physics. 2016;**119**:224301. DOI: 10.1063/1.4953651

[13] Huyet G, O'Brien D, Hegarty SP, McInerney JG, Uskov AV, Bimberg D, Ribbat C, Ustinov VM, Zhukov AE, Mikhrin SS, Kovsh AR, White JK, Hinzer K, Spring Thorpe AJ. Quantum dot semiconductor lasers with optical feedback. Physica Status Solidi (b). 2004;**201**:345-352

[14] Fu Y, Jiang G. Chaos and chaos synchronization of semiconductor lasers with optoelectronic feedback and bidirectional couplings. Journal of Optoelectronics and Advanced Materials. 2010;**12**(6):1350-1355

Chapter 9

Coherence Resonance in Optical Feedback Chaos: Hiding Frequency in Chaos Communication

Ban M. Al Bayati, Ahmad K. Ahmad and
Sudad S. Ahmed

Additional information is available at the end of the chapter

http://dx.doi.org/10.5772/intechopen.71389

Abstract

In this chapter, an experimentally and numerically conducted investigation of the existence of high chaotic spiking in the dynamics of semiconductor lasers with AC-coupled optical feedback, the bifurcation diagram by feedback strength attenuation and the bias current as a control parameter was done. A semiconductor laser subjected to an external optical feedback can present a big change of dynamic behaviors, such as periodic and quasi-periodic oscillations, chaos, coherence collapse, and low-frequency fluctuations (LFF's) that degrade the laser characteristics. The chaotic instability is experimentally investigated on feedback strength as a control parameter, and the resulted dynamic is monostability. Finally, we indicated that the observed chaotic dynamic is a good candidate to hide information in order to investigate the resonance phenomena, which is important for chaos to encrypt data in optical communication, where data disappear when modulated in a chaos carrier. The aim of this chapter is to investigate the encryption area in the chaotic system when the applied frequency is 1–500 MHz, for satisfying the secure communication.

Keywords: chaos communication, chaotic instability, chaos modulation, hidden frequency, resonance phenomena

1. Introduction

In communication, one requests the data to be transferred efficiently. In another expression, the data must be transferred fast and with very low deformation. In classical communication sketches, the maximum limits for high efficiency is enjoined with the properties of the channel, while in chaos communication, this maximum limit is dependent on the characteristic of the dynamical system being utilized [1]. Chaos mathematically and physically was studied to describe an attitude of dynamical systems that are extremely sensitive to the initial state of the system, that is, a tiny disturbance in the initial condition produces significantly varying attitude, known as the butterfly effect [2]. It indicates that the long-term prognosis is hopeless even if the system is deterministic, which is defined as a deterministic chaos [2]. The state of a dynamical system develops with time that may exhibit dynamics [2]. Several systems dynamic display the chaotic behavior everywhere; however, in most states, the chaos exists only in a subset space, for a group of initial conditions may lead to the same chaotic area, for example, the chaotic attitude may take place on the attractor [3]. Methods for steadying changeful cases in a nonlinear dynamical system employing a tiny perturbation fall into two general groups: feedback and non-feedback sketches. A concept of chaos and instabilities can be controlled efficiently utilizing feedback (closed-loop) system to steady changeful cases, which was proposed by Ott et al. [4] in 1990 [5].

In this chapter, the chaos optical communication was generated. Then the chaos control with feedback attenuation as a control parameter was investigated experimentally. The bias current as a control parameter was investigated numerically, and also the chaotic instability of the semiconductor laser was demonstrated experimentally. Finally, we find the encryption range in the chaotic carrier by applying frequency of 1–500 MHz, and then we observed the low-frequency fluctuations (LFF) phenomena with high frequency.

2. Chaotic spiking generation

The dynamical chaos is an irregular oscillation for time evolutions in nonlinear dynamical systems, appearing clearly in their outputs as a deterministic manner and it is different from random processes [6]. Nonlinearity of a system is one of the important factors to observe chaos [7]. Semiconductor lasers have been shown to be relevant devices in the research of dynamical systems [8]. The intensity of the light emitted by a semiconductor laser is stable when there is no external perturbation, while the semiconductor lasers are easily destabilized by external perturbation, since they are the introduction of an extra degree of freedom to lasers. When the light of the laser is reflected and part of it re-enters into the laser, the laser intensity can become unstable, displaying a broad range of dynamical behaviors [9]. The semiconductor laser-based oscillators' operation in the chaotic regime can be achieved by applying optical feedback [10], optoelectronic feedback [11], or optical injection [12], and their chaotic behavior appears either in the amplitude or in the wavelength regime. A semiconductor laser subjected to external optical feedback can present a large variety of dynamic behaviors, such as periodic and quasi-periodic oscillations, chaos, coherence collapse, and LFF that degrade the laser characteristics [13]. One special unsteady attitude is known as LFF [14, 15], that occurring repeatedly when the laser operates near to the threshold and also submitted to moderate optical feedback from the external cavity in which the round-trip time that is much longer than the period of the solitary laser's relaxation oscillation frequency [5].

Theoretically, the LFF was demonstrated as an impact between the local chaotic attractor and the antimode [16] as a chaotic route by the drift [16] or as a contest between steady and unsteady external cavity modes. While it was experimentally explained that LFF is strongly dependent on the injection current. Initially, the LFF was known in the low-injection current close to the threshold, whereas lately it was also noticed in a high-current injection [16]. Therefore, LFF is a general event in semiconductor lasers by an optical feedback [16]. Several people studied in chaotic generation and control, theoretically and experimentally, and therefore, we show part of it. Al-Naimee et al. published several papers in semiconductor lasers with optoelectronic feedback, optical feedback, and optical injection. In 2009, they demonstrated experimentally and numerically the presence of slow chaotic spiking sequences in semiconductor laser dynamics with optoelectronic feedback, where the timescale of these dynamics was wholly determined by the high-pass filter which included in the feedback loop [17]. Then, they were presented in 2010; the experiment studied the analysis of chaos generation showing the generation of a mixed spectrum in the time series and the attractor is presented. They stated that the control of chaotic behavior can be achieved by applying a low level of perturbation signals [18]. They are also studied; the quantum dot light emitting diode (QD-LED) model was examined first under bias current without any external perturbation where it exhibits chaotic phenomena since the model has multi-degrees of freedom [19]. The nonlinear dynamics of a semiconductor quantum-dot (QD) laser subject to external optical feedback was examined by using a dimensionless model in [19, 20]. It is perturbed by both small signal and direct current modulations (DCM). Then, this system exhibits mixed-mode oscillations (MMOs) under DCM [19]. Quantum dot light emitting diode dimensionless model displays homoclinic chaos; it is also able to reproduce mixed mode oscillations and chaotic spiking regimes [21]. Then, in 2015, they presented an experiment of the existence of chaotic spiking in the dynamics of a semiconductor laser output with an optical feedback using nonlinear optical fiber loop mirror [22]. Also, they presented in 2016, experimentally, the efficient bandwidth of chaotic signals which has been measured and can be increased by injecting current which is an important parameter in chaos communication [23].

3. Chaos in optical communication

3.1. Generation of optical chaotic carrier

The excellent model for nonlinear optical system is the semiconductor laser with feedback for chaotic dynamics [24]. Semiconductor lasers are different from other lasers in the low reflectivity of the internal mirrors in the laser cavity. That domain usually is from 10 to 300% of an intensity in the Fabry-Perot semiconductor lasers. Therefore, the feedback effects are important in the semiconductor lasers. A large absolute value of a line width enhancement factor α is another difference, which is α = -2 to −6, convened in semiconductor lasers, while the value of line width in another laser is roughly 0. This information drives to interesting and an assortment of dynamics of several other lasers. The optical feedback reflectivity is from weak to moderate, the output power of the laser shows interesting dynamical attitudes like a steady state, periodic and quasi-periodic oscillations, and chaos for the variety of system variables. The external reflectivity scopes are not just interesting but also really significant in current implementations of semiconductor lasers like an optical information storage arrangement. A semiconductor laser dynamical behavior with optical feedback is mainly influenced by three parameters in the system, which include the reflectivity and the length of the external mirror and the bias injection current. The dynamic behaviors of a semiconductor laser with optical feedback are not simple and strongly dependent on the feedback reflectivity. According to the behaviors of the laser output, by an increase of the feedback, reflectivity can be characterized by the dynamics of the output power into five regions (I–V) [25, 26]; depending on the phase of the returned light into the laser cavity, the laser line width is increased or decreased for the very tiny feedback regime I. The laser shows mode hopping among several external cavity modes (regime II) by an increase of the feedback scale. At moderate levels of the feedback amplitude reflectivity around 1%, chaos can be observed, that corresponds to the regimes III and IV. The coherence collapse occurs in the laser output power, with further increase of the feedback level, in which the line width is drastically broadened and the coherence length of the laser is much reduced. These regions are very important in actual optical data storage systems. A very high-feedback level (regime V) corresponds to a stable laser operation. They are much interested in the regimes III and IV, which show chaotic dynamics [24]. These regions are shown in **Figure 1** [27].

Here we present the experimental configuration for a semiconductor laser with optical feedback in order to investigate the existence of fast, chaotic spiking in the dynamics of a laser; this is schematically shown in the **Figure 2**. A closed-loop optical system consists of a semiconductor laser (1310 NM) (NOYSE FIBER SYSTEM). The output laser is connected to the 2 by 2 direction coupler (DC); the two output DCs are connected together to a variable optical attenuator (VOA), while another branch of the DC is connected to a photodetector (NEW FOCUSE; Model 1811–125 MHz an InGaAs/PIN). The output signal from photodetector is observed with a four-channels digital storage oscilloscope (DSO) (TEKTRONIX-TDS2024B), used to analyze the time series with the possibility of direct fast Fourier transformation. Then the results are analyzed by a personal computer with origin program. The round-trip time of external cavity of the laser used is 50 ns, which is given by this formula:

$$\tau_{ext} = 2nL/c \qquad (1)$$

where L is the length of the fiber which is equal 5 m, n is a refractive index of the fiber core (silica glass), and c is the speed of light in vacuum.

The effect of the attenuation feedback strength is a control parameter for generating chaotic behavior in the semiconductor. In our experiment, a VOA is used to control the attenuation feedback strength (0–15) dB. **Figures 3–7a** represent the time series of the nonlinear dynamic, which are important to show the time evolution of photon density. **Figures 3–7b** shows the phase space (attractor) of the oscillator by using an embedded technique with appropriate delays; the trajectories are different in diameters and dense and its looks very strange (strange attractor). While the **Figures 3–7c** represent the power spectra of the chaotic signal, the FFT figures are exponentially decayed to distinguish chaotic signal from other signals like noise; this agrees with [28]. The spiking rate and amplitude of the chaotic signal decrease with increasing the attenuation feedback strength as shown in **Figure 8** which

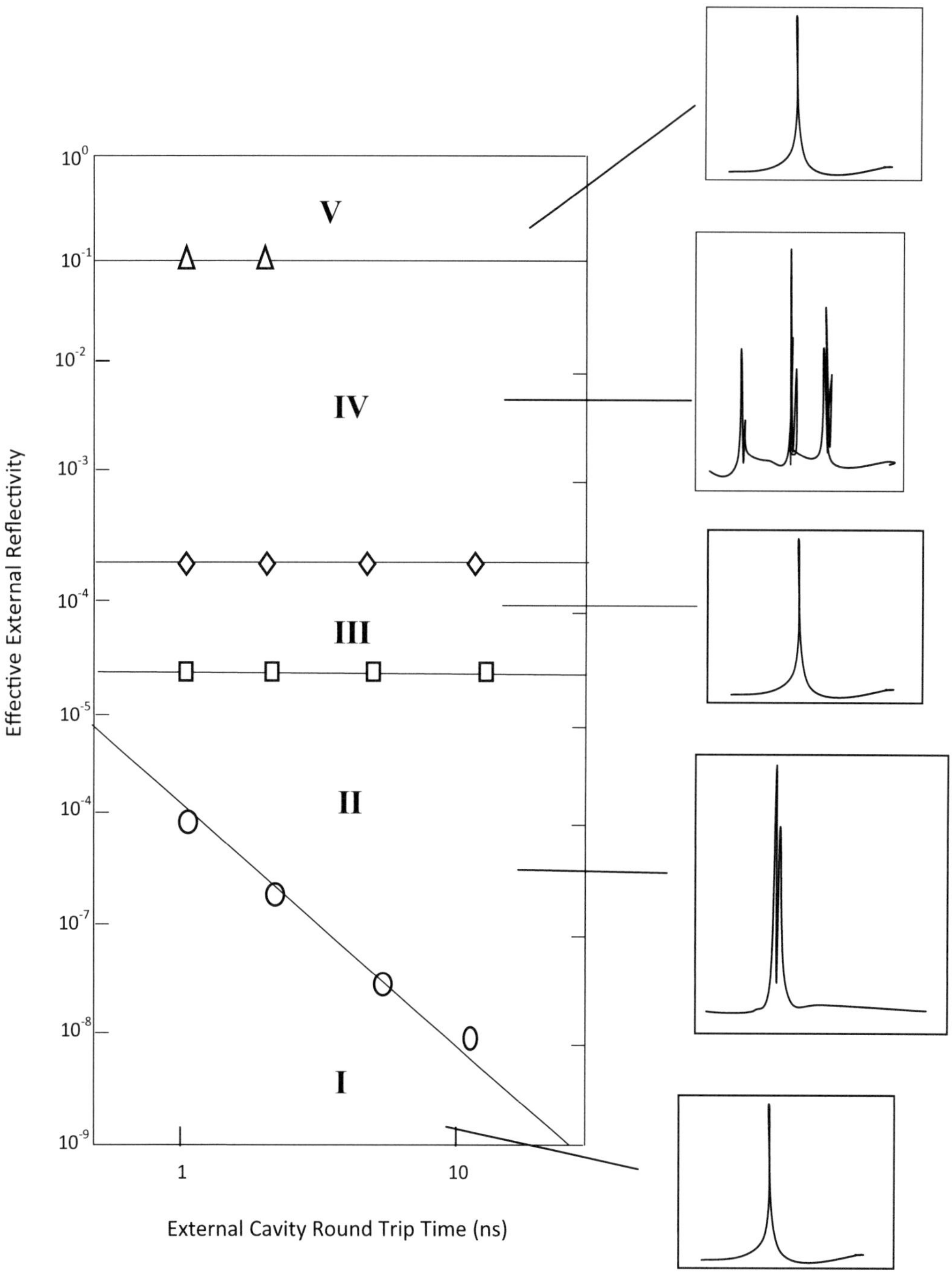

Figure 1. Regimes of optical feedback effects occurring for different values of the external reflectivity and the external cavity length [27].

is representing the bifurcation diagram. The bifurcation diagram represents the peak-to-peak laser output intensity versus the attenuation in feedback strength as a control parameter. In this plot the spiking rate and amplitude of the chaotic signal can be observed as

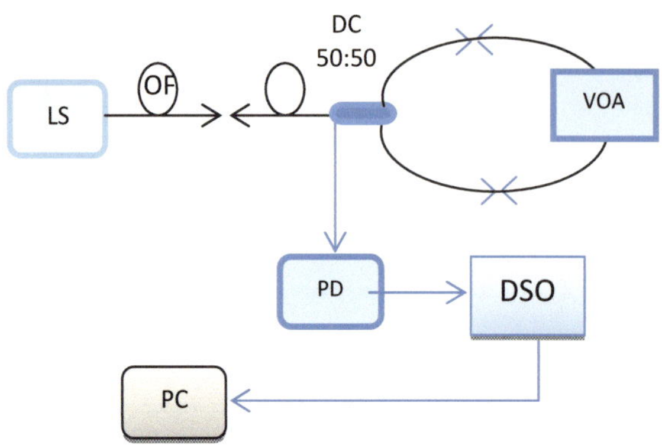

Figure 2. Experimental setup of semiconductor lasers with optical feedback systems. LS: semiconductor laser 1310 nm, OF: optical fiber, DC 50:50: directional coupler 2 by 2 single mode, VOA: variable optical attenuator, PD: photodetector, DSO: digital storage oscilloscope, and PC: personal computer.

decreasing gradually with increasing feedback strength; this result agrees with reference [22]; this type of feedback is called negative feedback. The bifurcation diagram for optical attenuation from 0 to 8.5 dB means high-feedback strength, the dynamics of the oscillator is chaotic with high intensity. When the optical attenuation increases from 9 to 12 Db, the dynamics of the oscillator becomes less because of the low ratio of the feedback strength and from 12.5 to 15 Db, the dynamics of the oscillator becomes constant because the chaos goes into saturation.

3.2. Chaotic instability of the semiconductor laser

By the chaotic evolution, the self-mixing outputs of the semiconductor lasers observed the bistability and multistability. In a periodic case, the output laser shows hysteresis in addition to simply periodic oscillation [25]. Based on these phenomena, proposed a novel application, for example, by counting the fringes obtained from bistable self-mixing interference between the internal field and an optical feedback light in the laser cavity, the displacement measured is performed. From asymmetric waveforms showing hysteresis, a direction of displacement is simultaneously determined [25]. In many different systems, by using intrinsic or hybrid optical circuits, the optical bistability was observed. If a system has two output states for the same value of input over some range of input values, the system is considered optically bistable. Under some operating conditions, the two optical cases originate from the stable-state and transient characteristics of the nonlinear optical system. That input and output relation is described by a multivalued function and has many stable and transient states in a nonlinear system which known as multistability [29]. In our experiment of chaotic instability, by using the configuration setup in **Figure 2**, the result appears that the chaotic instability of optical feedback by optical feedback attenuation as a control parameter is monostability, as shown in **Figure 9**. This figure is obtained by using a bifurcation diagram from 0 to 15 dBm and again plots the bifurcation diagram from 15 to 0 dBm in the same time to conserve the initial conditions of the chaotic system.

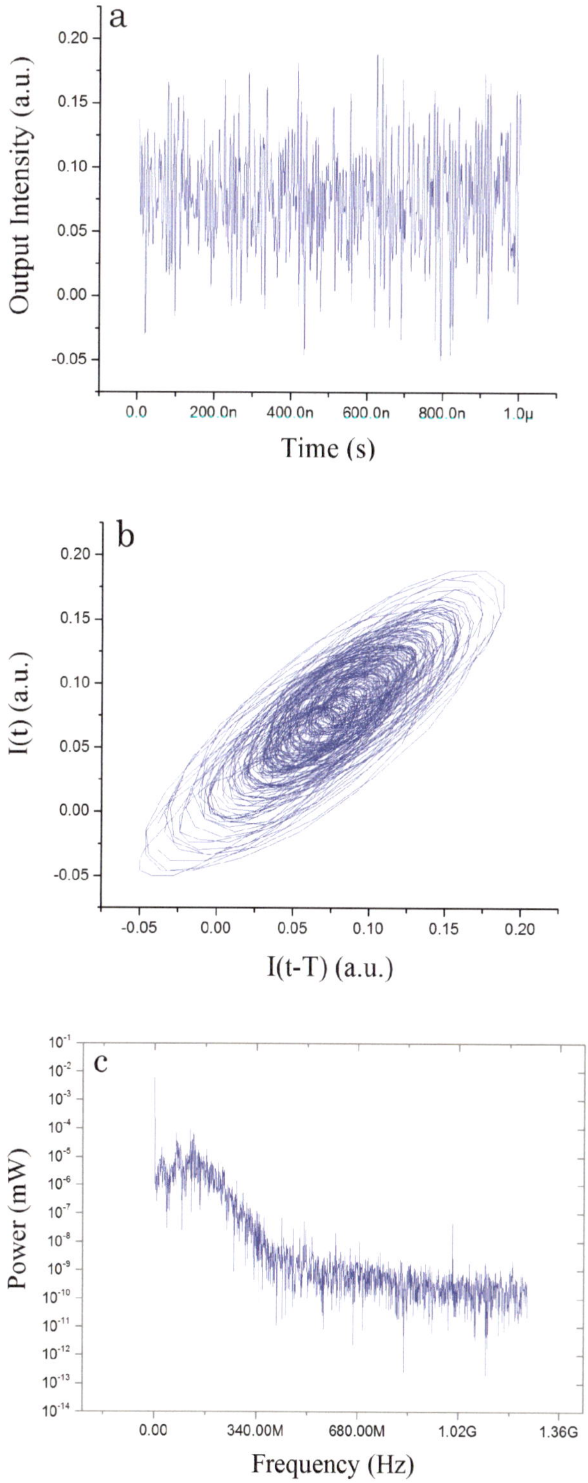

Figure 3. The effect of attenuation feedback strength of 0 dB (a) time series (b) attractor (c) FFT.

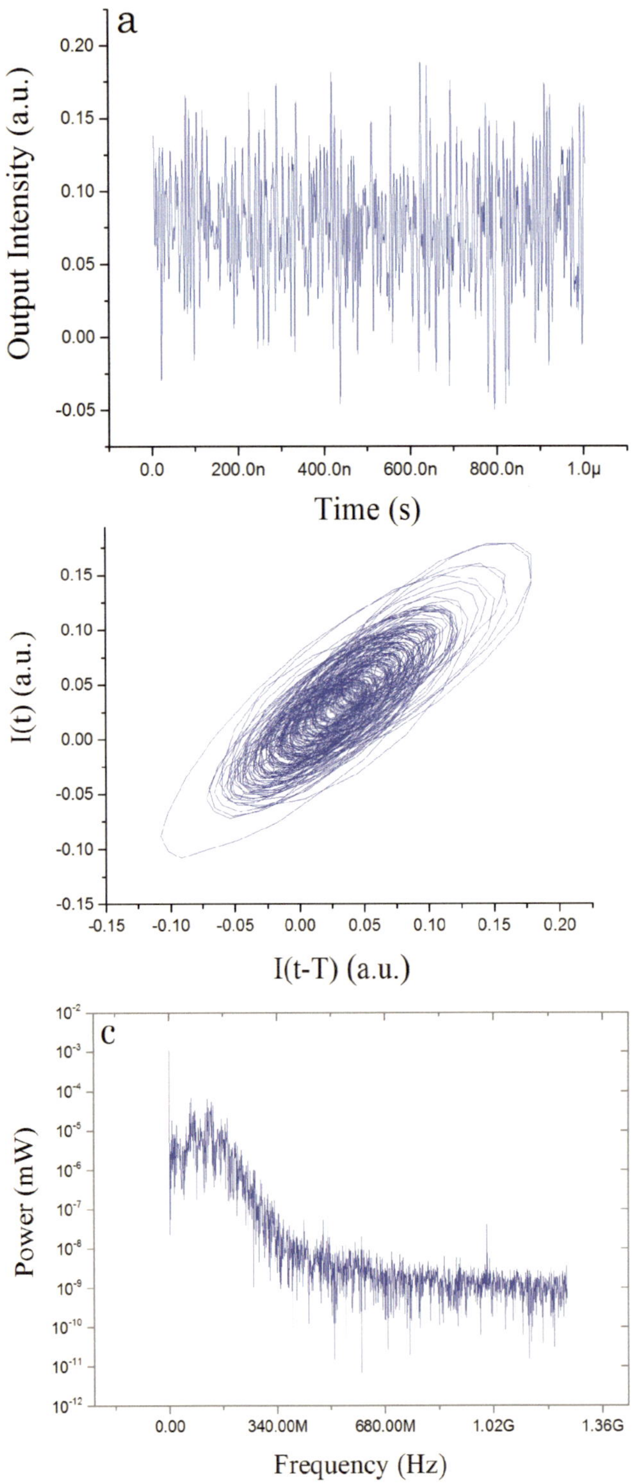

Figure 4. The effect of attenuation feedback strength of 2.5 dB (a) time series (b) attractor (c) FFT.

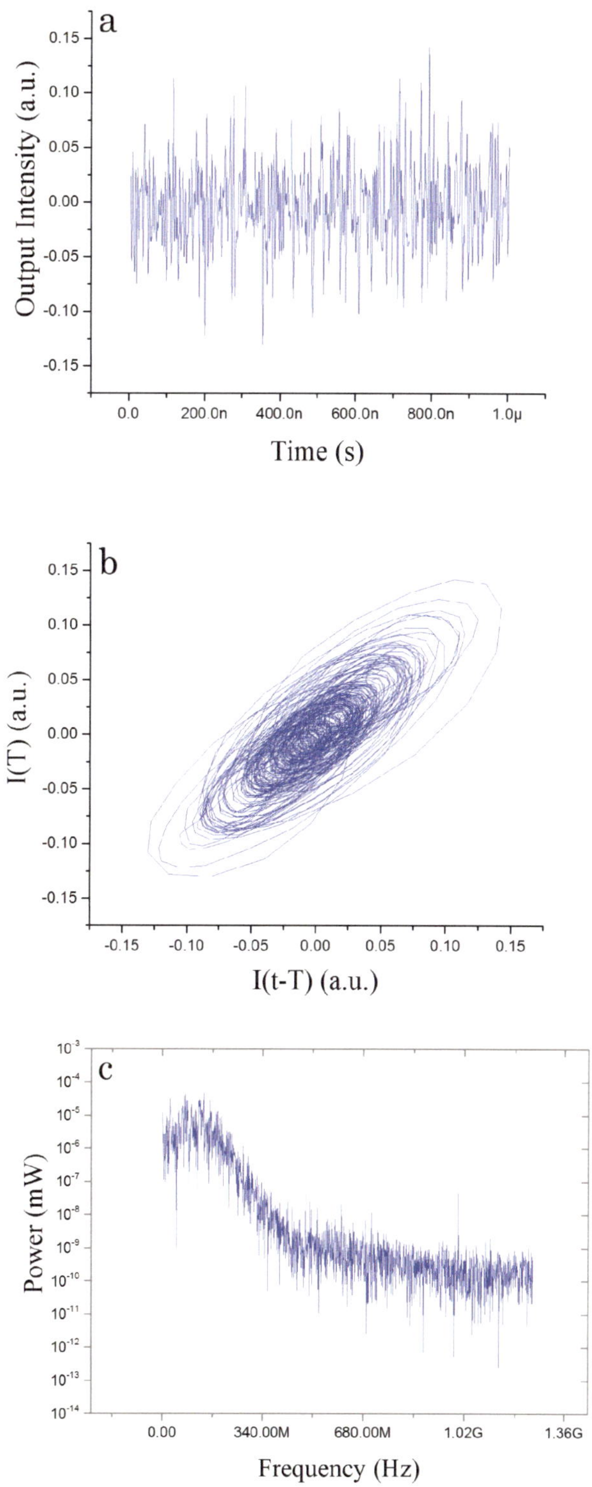

Figure 5. The effect of attenuation feedback strength of 6 dB (a) time series (b) attractor (c) FFT.

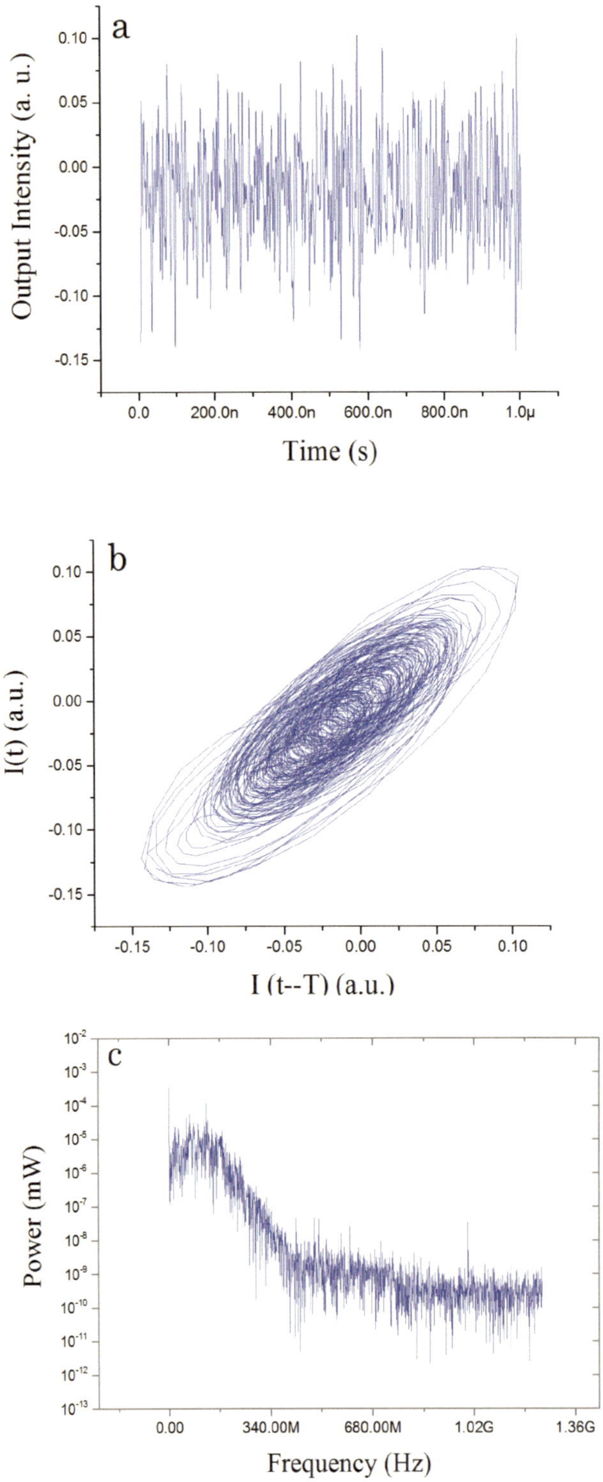

Figure 6. The effect of attenuation feedback strength of 10 dB (a) time series (b) attractor (c) FFT.

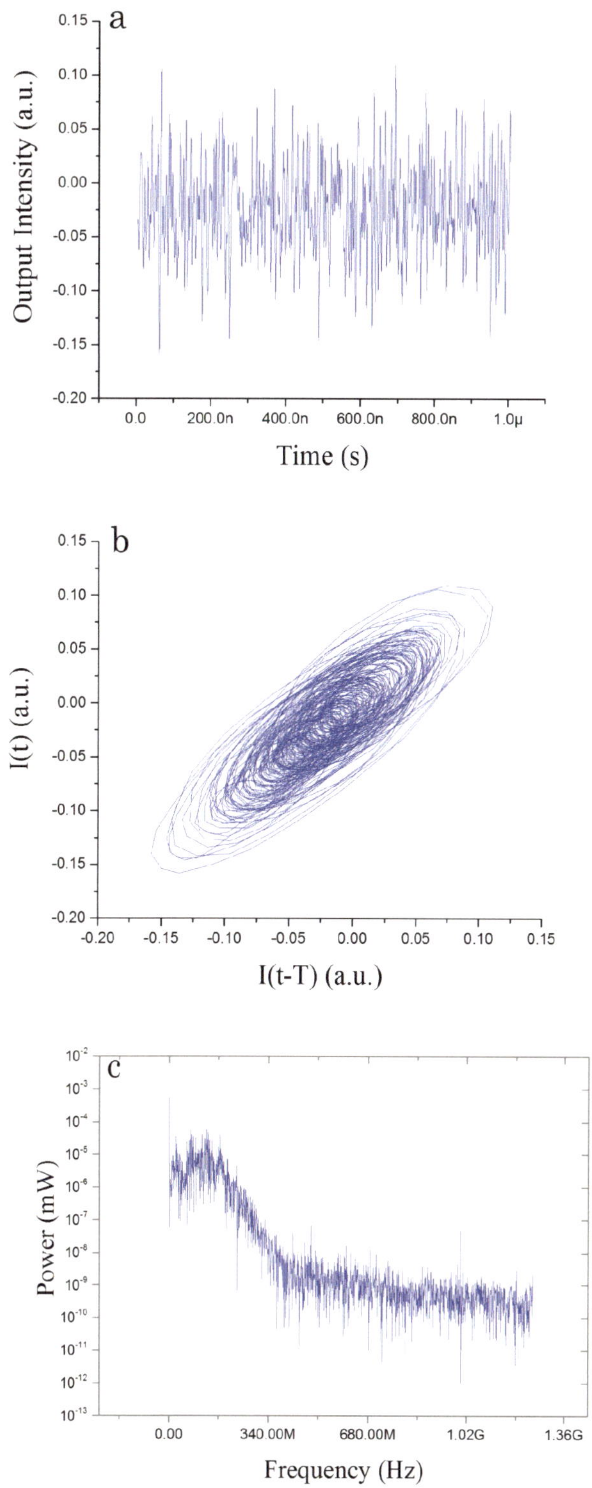

Figure 7. The effect of attenuation feedback strength of 15 dB (a) time series (b) attractor (c) FFT.

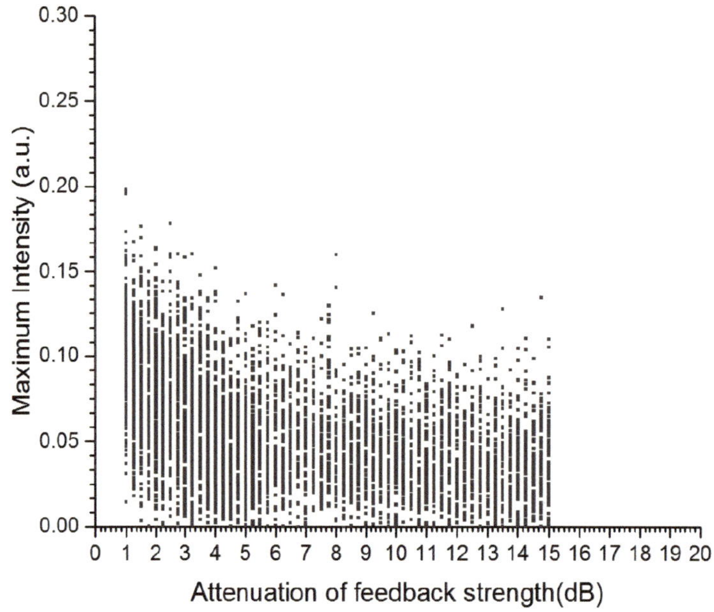

Figure 8. Bifurcation diagram of chaotic laser intensity as a function of the attenuation feedback strength (dB).

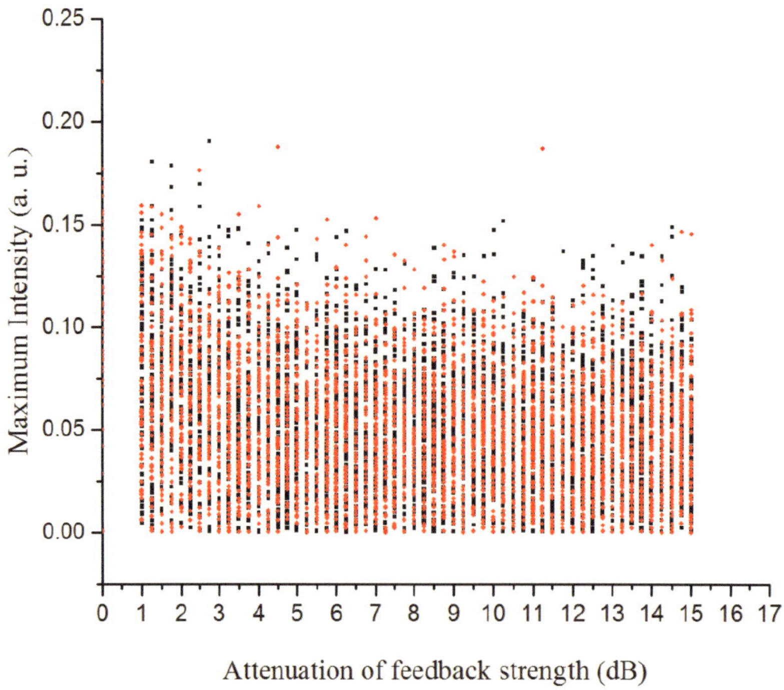

Figure 9. Chaotic instability of optical feedback as a function of the attenuation feedback strength (dB).

http://dx.doi.org/10.5772/intechopen.71389

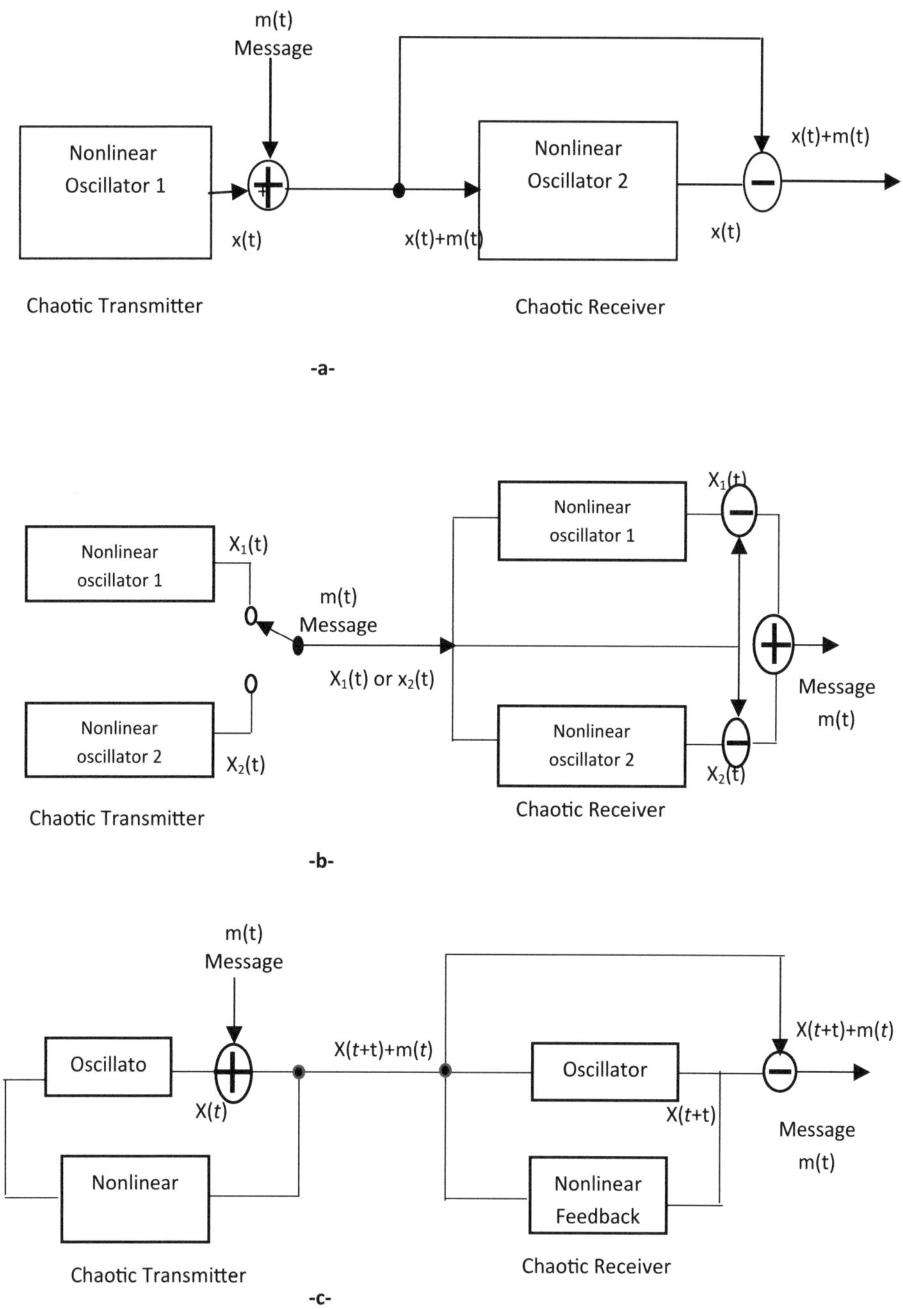

Figure 10. The schematic diagram of chaos encryption, (a) CMA, (b) CSK, and (c) CMO [31].

3.3. Encryption of message

There are three primary message encryption methods utilizing optical communications chaos [30], which will be explained in a next section.

- Chaotic masking (CMS): with a transmitter laser (TL), a chaotic carrier is generated. Then, the message is directly added to the chaotic carrier, see **Figure 10a**.
- Chaotic shift keying (CSK): the injection current of the transmitter laser is used to modulate the message directly. Therefore, the transmitter laser produces the chaotic carrier for a message concealed in it, as shown in **Figure 10b**.
- Chaotic modulation (CMO): it involves adding the output power of the transmitter laser to the message. Therefore, this mixer of the signal and message is sent back to the transmitter laser through a feedback loop as a modulation to produce a chaotic carrier as shown in **Figure 10c** [30].

There are two kinds of chaos modulation such as direct current modulation and external modulation of the semiconductor laser [32]; in our experiment, the external modulation was used. The external modulation in optical communication divides into two types. A first kind is dependent on the absorption modification of a semiconductor material when the external electric field is applied, which is known as an electro-absorption modulator, while the second kind relies on the refractive index variation observed in several crystals under an external electric field that is called an electro-optic modulator. Additionally, with the interferometry structure, like a Mach-Zehnder structure, there can be a modulation of the intensity of a light wave because a change in the refractive index itself does not allow modulation of the intensity of a light wave. A Mach-Zehnder structure enables to convert the induced phase modulation into the desired intensity modulation.

4. Electro-absorption modulation

The effective band gap Eg of a semiconductor material decreases when an external voltage is applied; hence, this fact is important in this kind of modulation. Then, if the frequency υ of an incoming light wave is chosen so that its energy $E = h\upsilon$ is smaller than the bandgap when no voltage is applied, the material will be transparent. In another word, the effective band gap will be reduced when an external voltage is applied, which means that the wave of light will be absorbed by a material when $E > Eg$, that is, a shift of a semiconductor absorption edge under the effect of the external voltage is delineated in **Figure 11**. Through duly selecting the wavelength signal so that it expertise a significant variation in the absorption when the voltage is applied, consequently it becomes possible to perfect optical modulation controlled via an electrical signal. An ideal absorption against the function of applied voltage transfer for an electro-absorption modulator is shown in **Figure 11**.

Since the refractive index of a semiconductor material and the absorption is linked by Kramers-Kronig relations of the kind

$$\Delta n(\omega) = \frac{c}{\pi}\int_{0}^{+\infty} \frac{\Delta\alpha(\omega')}{\omega'^2 - \omega^2} d\omega' \tag{2}$$

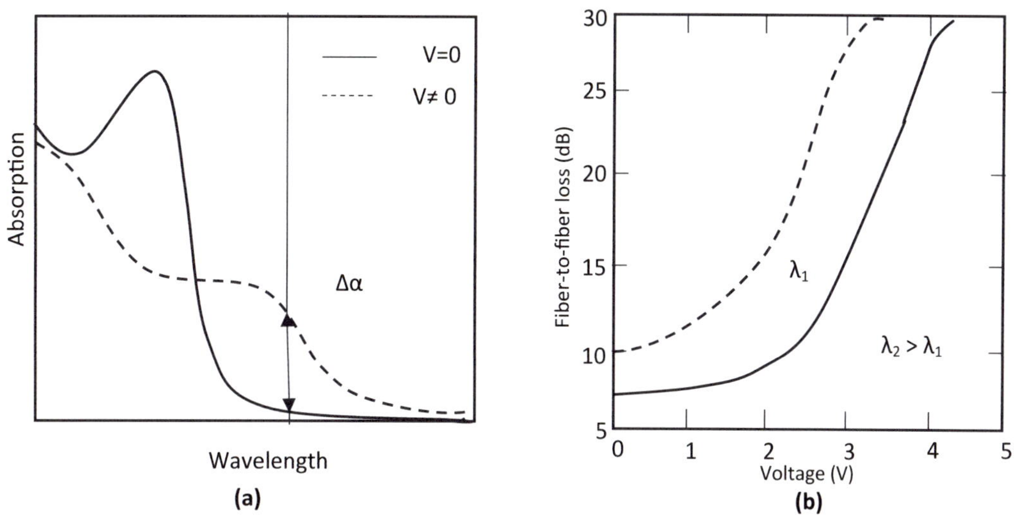

Figure 11. (a) Absorption of a semiconductor as a function of wavelength with and without an external an applied electric field. (b) Typical loss versus applied voltage curves for an electro-absorption modulator [32].

where Δn is change in the refractive index produced by a variation in the coefficient of absorption $\Delta\alpha$ and c is the speed of light in a vacuum, to achieve an optical modulation shifting by the absorption edge and also to make a change in the refractive index of the material; hence, the modulation occurred in the signal of a phase or instantaneous frequency. Hence, via an electro-absorption modulator, some amount of frequency chirping will be introduced. The produced frequency chirp will usually be lower than when a semiconductor laser direct current modulation is used, as shown **Figure 11** [32].

In this chapter, the experiment setup of semiconductor lasers and signal generators in order to satisfy chaos modulation and study the resonance phenomena is shown in **Figure 12**. This experimental setup consists of a fiber-coupled semiconductor laser source (HP/Agilent model 8150 A optical signal source) which is connected with a signal generator (Agilent N9310A

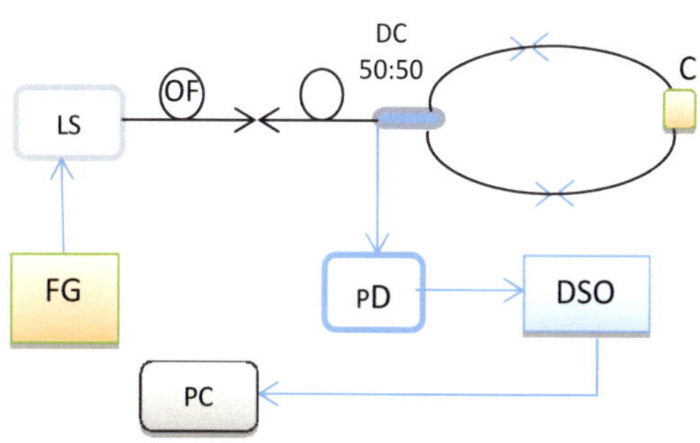

Figure 12. Experimental setup of chaos modulation [LS: semiconductor laser 850 nm, FG: function generator, DC 50:50: directional coupler 2 by 2 multi-mode optical fiber, C: adaptor FC: FC connector].

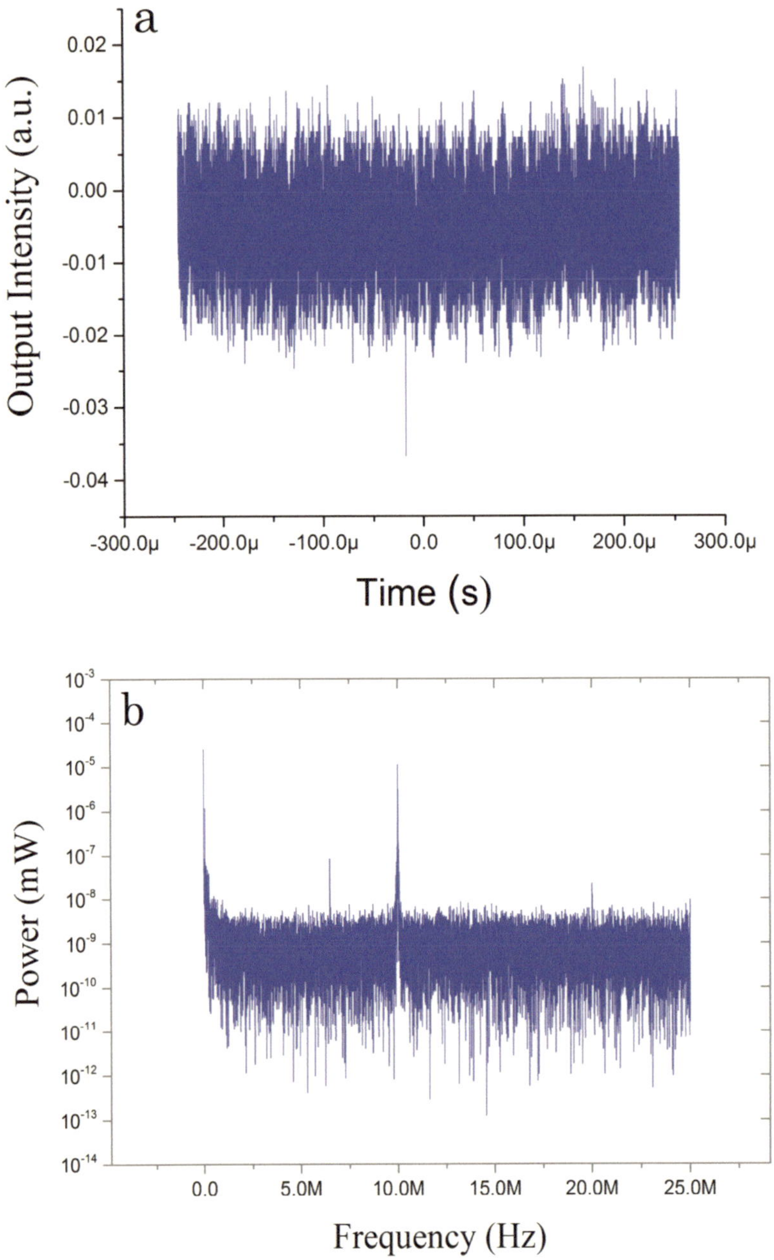

Figure 13. Experiment of chaos modulation 10 MHz (a) time series (b) FFT.

RF signal generator 9–3 GHz); the output power of the laser source is connected by a DC multimode fiber optics 2 by 2. Then, the two branch outputs are connected together by an FC adaptor to make a loop mirror, while the reflected light from coupler is split in two ways, one

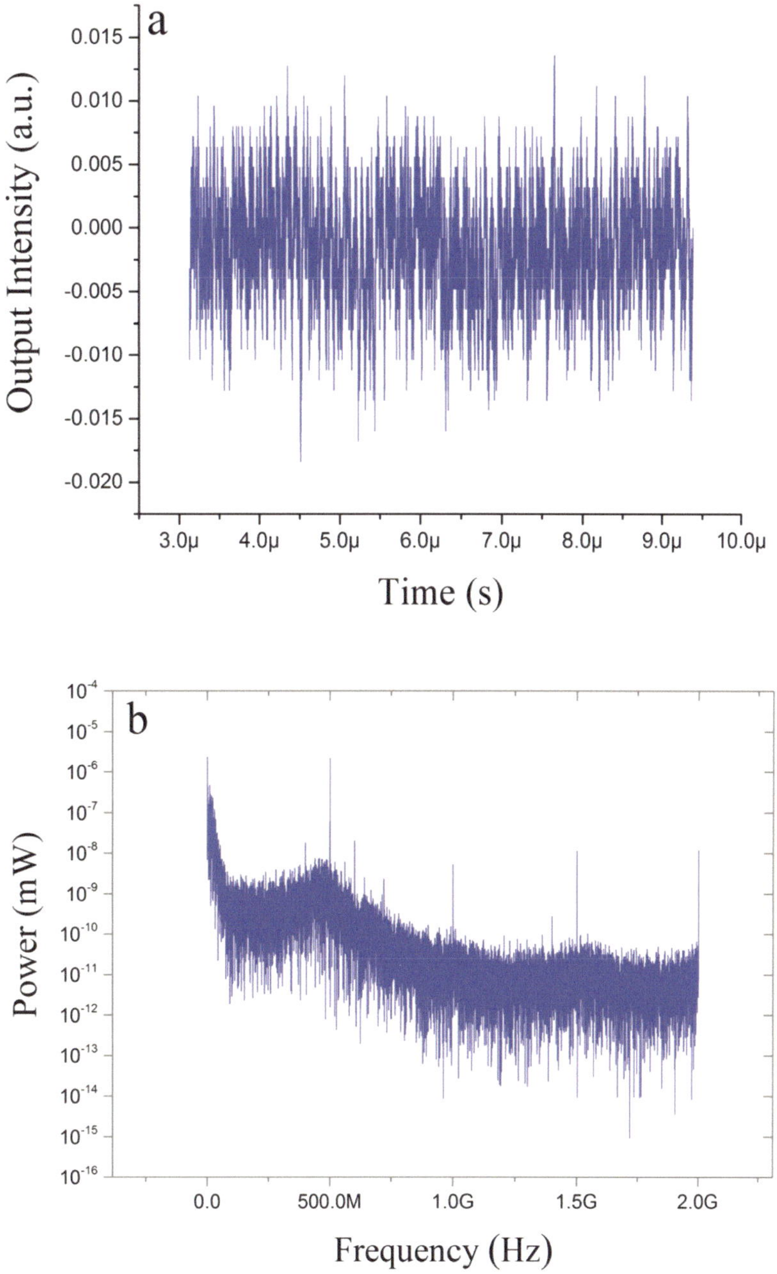

Figure 14. Experiment of chaos modulation 500 MHz (a) time series (b) FFT.

directed towards the cavity of semiconductor laser as feedback and the other detected by a fast InGaAs photodetector (rise/fall time < 1 ns, bandwidth 1.2 GHz, and the spectral response range is 800–1700 nm). Then the detected signal is amplified by an oscilloscope (GOS −652G

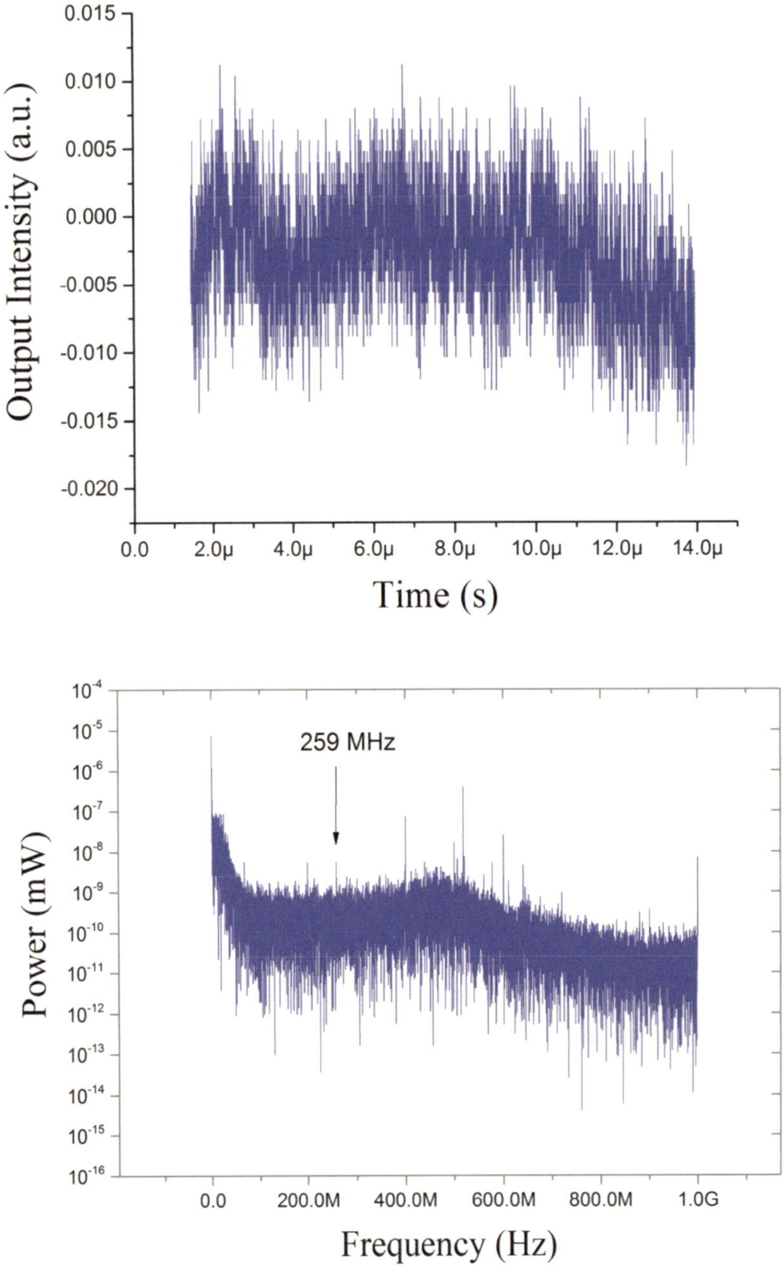

Figure 15. Experiment of chaos modulation 259 MHz (a) time series (b) FFT.

(20 MHz)); after that the output signal is observed by a four-channel oscilloscope DSO model GWinstek GDS-3504 (500 MHz –4GS/s) which is used to analyze the time series with the possibility of direct fast Fourier transformation. Then the results are analyzed by a personal computer with an origin program.

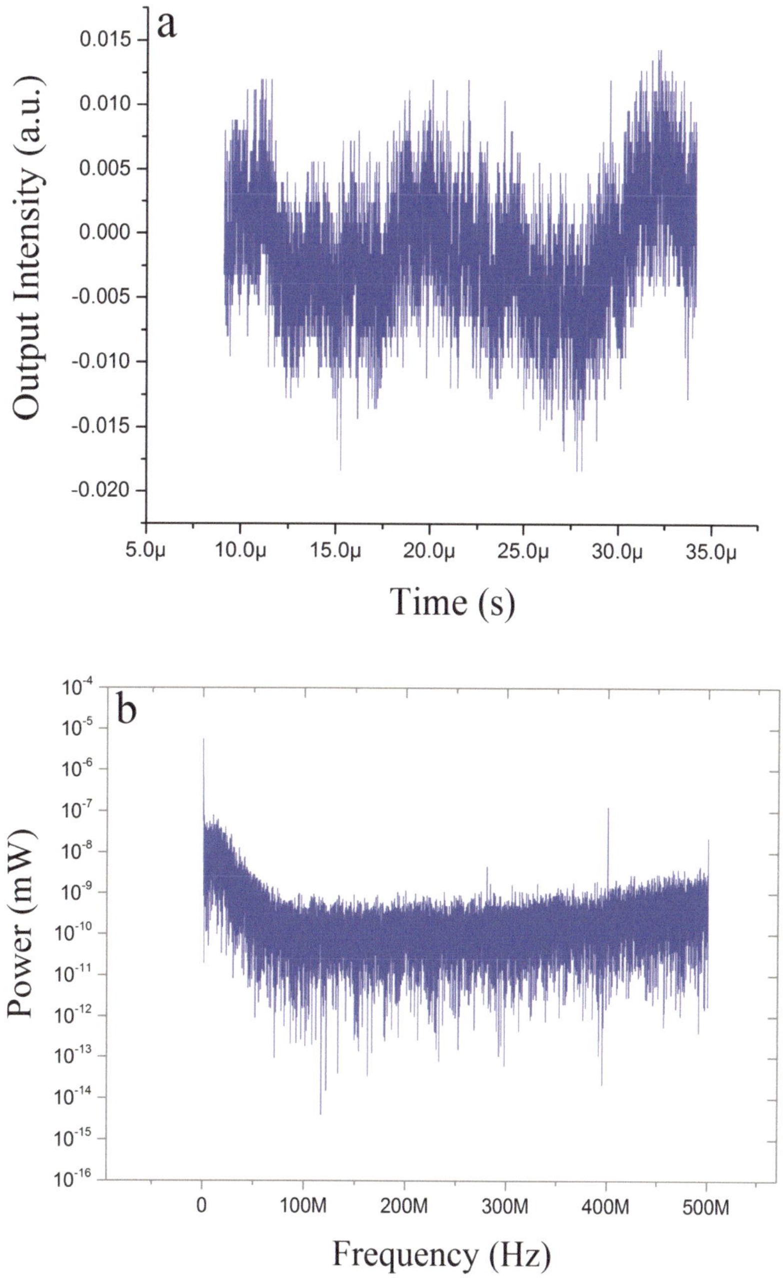

Figure 16. Experiment of chaos modulation 200 MHz (a) time series (b) FFT.

The intrinsic dynamic resonance in the photon-carrier interaction determines the modulation response of semiconductor lasers. To investigate the resonance phenomena for satisfying the encryption of secure optical communication, a frequency of 1–500 MHz is applied. We see that the external frequency in the pumping current is able to enhance the regularity of the drop-out

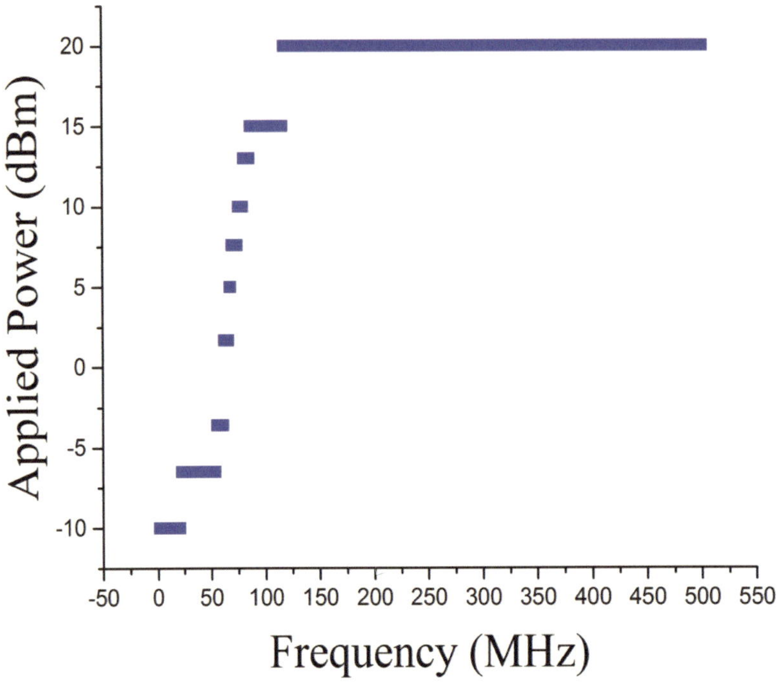

Figure 17. Distribution of change of applied power(dBm) as a function of applied frequency (MHz).

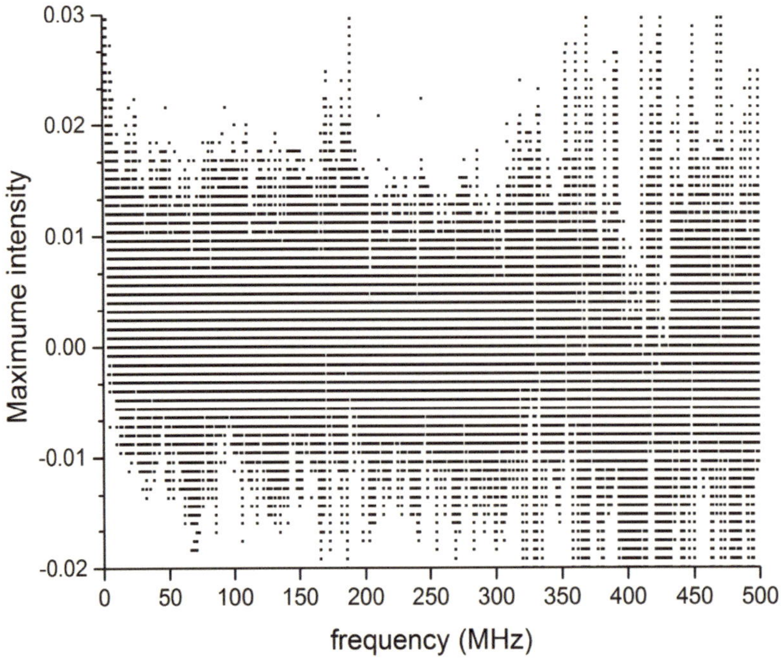

Figure 18. Bifurcation diagram of the laser intensity as a function of the external modulation frequency.

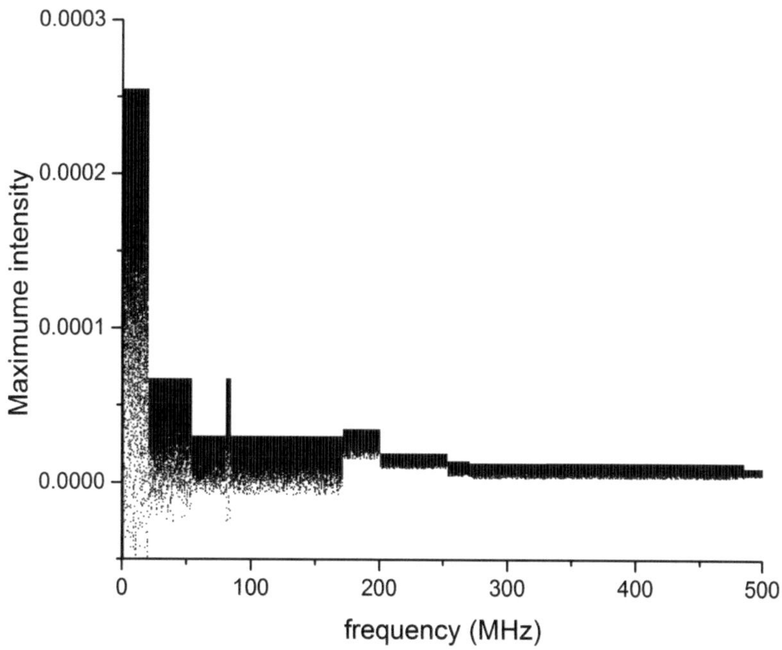

Figure 19. The distribution of the bifurcation diagram.

time series emitted by the laser. Frequency in this experimental setup can also enhance the response of the laser to an external periodic drive as shown in **Figures 13–16** which represent the chaos modulation. Coherence resonance is a manner in the chaotic dynamic, that is, regularity of the time between power dropouts for a given value of the feedback strength [33]. This phenomenon occurs by applying an external noise signal to the chaotic system [34], while the laser with optical feedback may display chaotic dynamics with fast pulses at the time scale of the time delay and much slower power drops [33]. In our experiment the coherence resonance phenomena appear when applied different frequencies. **Figures 13–16a** show the time series as a sinusoidal wave for different frequencies applied, the amplitude applied from the signal generator to modulate frequency is between −10 and 20 dBm, and the current density of the chaos signal is fixed at 595 μW/volt. The LFF was investigated for high-frequency injection-current modulation in a semiconductor laser with optical feedback. This result appears in **Figure 16a** at a frequency applied at 200 MHz; then, they observed resonant oscillation of the laser output power that was synchronized with the modulation, which is common in semiconductor lasers with optical feedback. However, LFF appeared for the detained modulation frequency from an external cavity mode. This result agrees with [16]. The power spectrum of different frequencies is analyzed, observing a sharp peak, low spiking peak, and hidden frequency peak. A sharp frequency peak in the modulation period for certain frequencies [(1–138), 140, (247–258), 260, (266–270), (272–278), 340, (344–346), 370 & 371, and (378–500 MHz)] corresponded to the amplitudes (-10,-6.5,-3.6, 1.7, 7.6, 10, 13, 15, and 20 dBm), while the low spiking frequencies appear at 144, 259, 271, 280, 300–304, 338, 339, 341–343, 347 & 348, 368 & 369, and 372 to 377 MHz corresponding to amplitude 20 dBm, as shown in **Figure 15b**. Then the area of hidden frequencies is in 139, 141–143, 145–239, 261–265, 279, 281–299, 305–337, and 349–367 MHz, which corresponds to amplitude 20 dBm, as shown in **Figure 16b**. **Figure 17** shows the changes in applied power with increased frequency. In this figure, one notices the increase in the applied power from the signal generator (−10 to 20 dBm) with an increase in the frequency modulation. **Figure 18** shows the bifurcation diagram of the laser intensity as a function of the external modulation frequency, in accordance with [35]. In this figure, one observed that the dynamic is chaotic behavior when applied to different frequencies. **Figure 19** shows the distribution of the bifurcation diagram. **Figure 19** shows different regions—instable regions (0– MHz and from 172 to 253 MHz) and then the stable regions (85–171 MHz and 255–500 MHz). These regions are important in satisfying an encryption message in the investigations of secure communication.

5. Theory of semiconductor lasers with optical feedback

A laser is described theoretically by three variables: the electric field in the laser, the polarization of the laser medium, and the population inversion to induce the laser oscillation [25]. Theoretically, the semiconductor lasers' static characteristics with optical feedback can be investigated by the relations among the reflectivity of internal cavity and external reflector, the gain in the medium, and other static laser parameters. However, the dynamic characteristics must be described with time-dependent equations of the systems. A laser is essentially a chaotic system; however, every laser does not show chaotic oscillations. According to the scales of the decay rates in the differential equations, lasers are classified into three categories. When we need all of three rate equations to describe a laser, the laser is a chaotic system and it is called a class C laser. Actually, infrared oscillating gas lasers like NH3 and Ne-Xe lasers exhibit chaotic oscillations in their output powers [25]. The second one is a class B laser, in which the time constant of the polarization is very fast and the polarization equation is adiabatically eliminated. Then, the laser is described by the two equations of field and population inversion, and it is a stable laser if there is no external perturbation. The third one is a class A laser, whose field equation is enough to describe the system, and it is the most stable class of lasers. The polarization term is adiabatically eliminated for class B semiconductor laser; this effect is replaced by a linear relation between polarization and the field. Semiconductor lasers population inversion is replaced by density carriers N produced by a recombination of the electron hole. The absolute square of the field amplitude (which is equivalent to the photon number) and the density carriers are frequently used as the variant of an equation rate for semiconductor lasers [25]. The dynamics of intensity fluctuation in a single-mode semiconductor laser is modeled by the Lang-Kobayashi model, which are historical milestone papers for semiconductor lasers' chaotic dynamics [36], which include the effect of optical feedback time delay [37]. The Lang-Kobayashi equations for the complex amplitude electric field E (t) and the carrier number N (t) are written as follows [38]:

$$\frac{dE(t)}{dt} = \frac{1}{2}(1 + ia)[G(t) - \gamma]E(t) + KE(t - \tau_f) \exp(-\omega\tau_f) + \sqrt{2\beta N(t)X} \quad (3)$$

$$\frac{dN(t)}{dt} = \frac{i}{q} - \gamma_d N(t) - G(t)\,|E(t)|^2 \tag{4}$$

where G(t) is the optical gain defined by this formula:

$$G(t) = \frac{g[N(t) - N_o]}{1 + s\,|E(t)|^2} \tag{5}$$

i: is the bias current and $|E(t)|^2$: the laser intensity or the number of photons inside the cavity which is calculated from the square of the electric-field amplitude, that is, $I = |E(t)|^2$. α is a line width enhancement factor, N_o is a transparency carrier number, g is a differential gain coefficient, s is again saturation coefficient, γ is a photon decay rate, γ_d is a carrier decay rate, β is a spontaneous emission rate, τ_f is a delay time, and K is the feedback strength. The spontaneous emission processes are considered by introducing independent Gaussian noise sources X with zero mean and unity variance into the rate equation. These equations represent the nonlinear dynamical system which produced chaos in the semiconductor laser with OFB.

6. Conclusions

The generated chaos in the semiconductor laser with optical feedback could be controlled by the feedback strength parameter. The chaotic instability was experimentally investigated with feedback attenuation as a control parameter and the resulting dynamics was monostability. Then, we indicated that the observed chaotic dynamic is a good candidate to hide information in order to investigate the resonance phenomena, which is an important part of chaos to encrypt data in optical communication, where data disappears when modulated in a chaos carrier. Therefore, the best regions for hiding frequency are 145–239 MHz, 281–299 MHz, 305–337 MHz, and 349–367 MHz. Finally, LFF appears with high frequency from 25 to 500 MHz.

Author details

Ban M. Al Bayati[1]*, Ahmad K. Ahmad[1] and Sudad S. Ahmed[2]

*Address all correspondence to: ban.muthafer@gmail.com

1 Department of Physics, College of Science, Al-Nahrain University, Baghdad, Iraq

2 Department of Physics, College of Science, University of Baghdad, Baghdad, Iraq

References

[1] Baptista MS, Macau EE, Grebogi C. Conditions for efficient chaos-based communication. CHAOS: An Interdisciplinary Journal of Nonlinear Science. 2003;**13**:145-150

[2] Stavroulakis P. Chaos Applications in Telecommunications. 1st ed. Boca Raton, London, NewYork: CRC Press Taylor & Francis Group; 2005. pp. 1-12

[3] Kamran R, Muhammad Y. Chaos based optical communication. International Journal Of Computer and Communication Engineering. 2013;**2**:97-100

[4] Ott E, Grebogi C, Yorke JA. Controlling chaos. Physical Review Letters. 1990;**64**:1196-1199

[5] Sukow DW, Gauthier DJ. Entraining power-dropout events in an external cavity semiconductor laser using weak modulation of the injection current. IEEE Journal of Quantum Electronics. 2000;**36**:175-183

[6] Sciamanna M, Shore KA. Physics and applications of laser diode chaos. Nature Photonics. 2015;**9**:151-162

[7] Uchida A. Optical Communication with Chaotic Lasers: Applications of Nonlinear Dynamics and Synchronization. Part one Basic Physics of Chaos and Synchronization in Lasers. 1st ed. Singapore: Wiley-VCH Verlag Gmbh & Co. Kgaa; 2012

[8] Fischer I, Vicente R, Buldu JM, Peil M, Mirasso CR, Torrent MC, Garcia-Ojalvo J. Zero-lag long-range synchronization via dynamical relaying. Physical Review Letters. 2006;**97**

[9] Aguado AA. Experimental Study of Feedback-Induced Dynamics in Semiconductor Lasers: From Symbolic Analysis to Subwavelength Position Sensing [Thesis]. Universitat Polit'Ecnica De Catalunya; 2014

[10] Annovazzi-Lodi V, Donati S, Scire A. Synchronization of chaotic lasers by optical feedback for cryptographic applications. IEEE Journal of Quantum Electronics. 1997;**33**:1449-1454

[11] Tang S, Liu JM. Message encoding/decoding at 2.5 Gb/S through synchronization of chaotic pulsing semiconductor lasers. Optics Letters. 2001;**26**:1843-1845

[12] Liu JM, Chen HF, Tang S. Optical communication systems based on chaos in semiconductor lasers. IEEE Transactions and Circuits Systems I. 2001;**48**:1475-1483

[13] Rogister F, Megret P, Deparis O, Blondel M, Erneux T. Suppression of low frequency fluctuations and stabilization of a semiconductor laser subjected to optical feedback from a double cavity: Theoretical Results.OSA. Optics Letters. 1999;**24**:1218-1220

[14] Risch C, Voumard C. Self-pulsation in the output intensity and Spectrum of Gaas-Algaas Cw diode lasers coupled to a frequency-selective external optical cavity. Journal of Applied Physics. 1977;**48**:2083-2085

[15] Tkach RW, Chraplyvy AR. Regimes of feedback effects in 1.5 μm distributed feedback lasers. IEEE. Journal of Lightwave Technology. 1987;**4**:1655-1661

[16] Takiguchi Y, Liu Y, Ohtsubo J. Low-frequency fluctuation induced by injection-current modulation in semiconductor lasers with optical feedback. Optics Letters. Optical Society of America. 1998;**23**:1369-1371

[17] Al-Naimee K, Marino F, Ciszak M, Meucci R, Arecchi FT. Chaotic spiking and incomplete Homoclinic scenarios in semiconductor lasers with optoelectronic feedback. New Journal of Physics. 2009;**11**:073022

[18] Abdalah SF, Al-Naimee A. K. And Meucci R.: Experimental evidence of slow spiking rate in a semiconductor laser by electro-optical feedback: Generation and control. Applied Physics Research. 2010;**2**:170-175

[19] Al Husseini HB, Al Naimee KA, Al Khursan AH, Abdalah SF, Khedir AH, Meucci R, Arecchi FT. Modulation response, mixed-mode oscillations and chaotic spiking in quantum dot light emitting diode. Chaos, Solitons and Fractals. 2015;**78**:229-237

[20] Al HH. Control of nonlinear dynamics of quantum dot laser with external optical feedback. Journal of Nanotechnology in Diagnosis and Treatment. 2016;**4**:5-14

[21] Al Naimee K, Al Husseini H, Abdalah SF, Al Khursan A, Khedir AH, Meucci R, Arecchi FT. Mixed mode oscillations and chaotic spiking in quantum dot light emitting diodes. IEEE, Complexity in Engineering (COMPENG). 2014:1-5

[22] Al-Hasani MH, Al Naimee KA. Experimental evidence of the influence of an optical feedback in semiconductor laser. International Journal on Numerical and Analytical Methods in Engineering (IRENA). 2015;**3**:53-56

[23] Younis YT, Musa SK, Abdalah SF, Ahmed AK, Meucci R, Al Naimee KA. The rule of bias current of semiconductor laser in chaos communications. Results in Physics. 2016;**6**:243-251

[24] Ohtsubo J. Feedback induced instability and chaos in Selniconductor lasers and their Applicatios. Optical Review. 1999;**6**:1-15

[25] Ohtsubo J. Semiconductor lasers stability, instability and chaos. In: Spring Series in Optical Sciences. 3rd ed. 2013. pp. 63-85

[26] Lawrence J. Diode Lasers with Optical-Feedback, Optical-Injection, and Phase-Conjugate Feedback. Phd. Thesis. Macquarie University; 2000

[27] Tkach RW, Chraplyvy AR. Regimes of feedback effects in 1.5 μm distributed feedback lasers. Journal of Lightwave Technology. 1986;**4**:1655-1661

[28] Ortego GJ. A new method to detect hidden frequencies in chaotic time series. Elsevier, Physics Letters A. 1995;**209**:351-355

[29] Ohtsubo J, Liu Y. Optical Bistability and multistability in an active interferometer. Optics Letters. 1990;**15**:731-733

[30] Liu JM, Chen HF, Tang S. Synchronized chaotic optical communications at high bit rates. IEEE Journal of Quantum Electronics. 2002;**38**:1184-1196

[31] Ohtsubo J. Semiconductor Lasers: Stability, Instability and Chaos. 1st ed. Springer-Verlag Berlin Heidelberg; 2006

[32] Peucheret C. Direct and external modulation of light. 34129 experimental course in optical. Communication. 2009

[33] Sciamanna M, Mousavi SHS, Bourouis A. Deterministic coherence resonance in chaotic lasers with time-delay. EOS, TOM 6 - Nonlinear Optics, Conference 29th September - 2nd October 2008; Paris, France

[34] Arecchi FT, Meucci R. Stochastic and coherence resonance in lasers: Homoclinic chaos and polarization Bistability. European Physics Journal B. 2009;**67**:93-100

[35] Rasheed BO, Aljaff PM, Al Naimee KA, Al Hasani MH, Meucci R. High chaotic spiking rate in a closed loop semiconductor laser with optical feedback. Results in Physics. 2016;**6**:401-406

[36] Mirasso C, Colet P, Garciafernandez P. Synchronization of chaotic semiconductor lasers: Application to encoded communications. IEEE Photonicstechnology Letters. 1996;**8**: 299-301

[37] Uchida A. Optical Communication with Chaotic Lasers: Applications of Nonlinear Dynamics and Synchronization. 1st ed. 2012

[38] Kanakidis D, Argyris A, Bogris A, Syvridis D. Influence of the decoding process on the performance of chaos encrypted optical communication systems. Journal of Lightwave Technology. 2006;**24**(1):335-340

Chapter 10

Metaheuristics and Chaos Theory

Rui Tang, Simon Fong and Nilanjan Dey

Additional information is available at the end of the chapter

http://dx.doi.org/10.5772/intechopen.72103

Abstract

Chaos theory is a novelty approach that has been widely used into various applications. One of the famous applications is the introduction of chaos theory into optimization. Note that chaos theory is highly sensitive to initial condition and has the feature of randomness. As chaos theory has the feature of randomness and dynamical properties, it is easy to accelerate the optimization algorithm convergence and enhance the capability of diversity. In this work, we integrated 10 chaotic maps into several metaheuristic algorithms in order to extensively investigate the effectiveness of chaos theory for improving the search capability. Extensive experiments have been carried out and the results have shown that chaotic optimization can be a very promising tool for solving optimization algorithms.

Keywords: chaos, optimization, metaheuristics algorithm

1. Introduction

Chaos theory is a novelty approach, which has been used into various applications widely [1]. One of the most famous applications is the introduction of chaos theory into optimization. Note that chaos theory is highly sensitive to initial condition and has the feature of randomness [2]. The most metaheuristic optimization algorithms belong to stochastic algorithms. The property of randomness is obtained by using probability distribution, such as uniform and Gaussian method. There is a randomness method in optimization filed called chaotic optimization (CO), which has the property of dynamical, nonrepetition, and ergodicity. The dynamical property ensures different solutions produced by algorithm and searches different modal objective search space, even on the complex multimodal landscape. Moreover, because of the ergodicity property of CO, it can perform searches at higher speeds compared to the stochastic algorithms with probability distribution. As chaos theory has the feature of randomness and dynamical properties, it is easy to accelerate the convergence of optimization algorithm and enhance the capability of diversity.

Since it has same properties of metaheuristic algorithms, it is natural that numerous metaheuristic algorithms have been combined with chaos theory. Generally, the most metaheuristic optimization algorithms are considered as stochastic approach. Compared to deterministic method, stochastic algorithm are much more flexible and universal. The simple idea of metaheuristic optimization algorithm is using greedy strategy for searching the promising solution areas to find out the optimum one. There are three categories of metaheuristic optimization algorithms: evolutionary algorithm, which mimics the evolution process, is the most popular algorithm in this kind. It contains genetic algorithm (GA) [3], different evolution (DE) [4], and the evolutionary strategy (ES) [5]. The second category is the swarm intelligence, the population-based algorithms. Particle swarm optimization algorithm (PSO) [6], wolf search algorithm (WSA) [7], and cuckoo search (CS) [8] are the well-known algorithms in this category. The third algorithm neither belongs to evolutionary algorithm nor SI, such as dynamic group optimization (DGO), [9, 10] which can be considered as the third category. In the most cases, metaheuristic algorithm has two phases: exploration and exploitation. Simply put, the exploration phase occurs when the algorithm discovers promising search area, and the exploitation phase refers to search the most promising solution obtained from the exploration phase as quickly as possible.

Although many metaheuristic algorithms can accelerate the search speed, they still have one major drawback, premature convergence. If the search space has many local optimums, it is very easy to stick into a local optimum. In order to deal with this problem, many researches proposed many methods, for example, using adaptive method adjusts parameters, using hybrid method enhances the search capability. However, balancing global exploration and local exploitation are still difficult, because better global exploration capability is usually accompanied by worse local exploitation, and vice versa. Introducing chaos is the most suitable approach to solve those problems. It has the property of the nonrepetition, ergodicity, and dynamic. The dynamic property ensures the solutions produced by algorithms variety, and searches different landscapes search space, and the ergodicity and nonrepetition enhance the speed of searching. Chaotic optimization not only accelerates the speed of algorithm but also enhances the variety of movement pattern. In this work, we integrated 10 chaotic maps into several metaheuristic algorithms to extensively investigate the effectiveness of chaos theory for improving the search capability. The performance of the approach is tested on 14 benchmark functions, which are the CEC2009 competition testing functions that contains unimodal functions and multimodal problems.

2. Methods

In reality, optimizations are very hard to solve, many of them belong to NP-hard problems. To solve such problems, optimization algorithms have to be used. According to the "No free lunch theorem," there is no such efficient algorithm for all problems. As a result, many optimization algorithms have been developed and tried to use various improving techniques to enhance the capability of searching to see that if they can cope with these challenging optimization problems. Chaos can be described as a bounded nonlinear system with ergodic and stochastic properties. It is very sensitive to the initial condition and the parameters.

Recently, numerous improvements, which rely on the chaos approach, have been proposed for metaheuristics algorithm.

2.1. Metaheuristics algorithms

In this section, we will introduce three most well-known chaotic optimizations which based metaheuristics optimization algorithms.

2.1.1. *Particle swarm optimization algorithms (PSO)*

Original particle swarm optimization is a population-based heuristic method which is discovered by mimicking social models of bird flocking and swarming to find the optimal solutions. It was proposed by Kennedy [6] in 1995.

The position of the *i*th particle can be described as $x_i = (x_{i1}, x_{i2}, \ldots, x_{iD})$, where D represents the number of dimensions. The velocity of the *i*th particle can be written as $v_i = (v_{i1}, v_{i2}, \ldots, v_{iD})$, each particle coexists and evolves simultaneously based on knowledge shared with neighboring particles; it makes use of its own memory and knowledge gained by the swarm as a whole to find the best solution. The best previously encountered position of the *i*th particle is denoted by its individual best position $p_i = (p_{i1}, p_{i2}, \ldots, p_{iD})$ and the global best $g_i = (g_{i1}, g_{i2}, \ldots, g_{iD})$. At each iteration/generation, the position and velocity of the *i*th particle are updated by p and g. The updated equations can be formulated as:

$$v_i^{t+1} = w * v_i^t + c_1 * r_1 * (p_i - x_i^t) + c_2 * r_2 * (g_i - x_i^t) \tag{1}$$

$$x_i^{t+1} = x_i^t + v_i^{t+1} \tag{2}$$

where r_1 and r_2 are random generator between (0, 1), and c_1 and c_2 are acceleration constants that control the speed of incensement. v_i^{t+1} means the velocity of ith particle at *t*th generation. w controls the impact of the previous velocity on its current one.

In chaotic particle swarm optimization algorithm [1], the random generator is replaced by sequence of chaotic maps. r_1 and r_2 are modified by the chaotic maps, and it can be described as follows:

$$C_{t+1} = k * C_t * (1 - C_t) \tag{3}$$

where C_t is the sequence generated by the chaotic map at each independent run, and k is the driving parameter which controls the behavior of C_t. When k increases, C_t goes through further bifurcations, eventually resulting in chaos. The mathematical updated formula is as follows:

$$v_i^{t+1} = w * v_i^t + c_1 * C * (p_i - x_i^t) + c_2 * (1 - C) * (g_i - x_i^t) \tag{4}$$

In Eq. (4), C is a function based on the chaotic maps with value between 0 and 1.

2.1.2. Krill herd algorithm (KH)

The krill herd algorithm mimics the behavior of krill individuals in krill herds (KH) [11]. This algorithm was proposed by Gandomi in 2012. There are three main actions in KH, which is shown as follows:

Motion induction: this activity refers to the density maintenance of the herd. It can be described as follows:

$$N_i(t+1) = N_{max}\alpha_i + \omega_n N_i(t) \tag{5}$$

where N_{max} is the maximum induced speed, $\alpha_i = \alpha_i^{local} + \alpha_i^{target}$, ω_n is the inertia weight. α_i^{local} and α_i^{target} are the local effect and target effect, respectively, and α_i^{target} is calculated as follows:

$$\alpha_i^{target} = C^{best} K_{i,\,best} X_{i,\,best} \tag{6}$$

where C^{best} is the coefficient and can be defined as follows:

$$C^{best} = 2\left(\frac{r+1}{Imax}\right) \tag{7}$$

where r is a random number located in (0,1).

The second activity is foraging, and the mathematic equation is shown as follows:

$$F_i(t+1) = v_f \beta_i + \omega_f F_i(t) \tag{8}$$

where $\beta_i = \beta_i^{food} + B_i^{best}$, v_f is the foraging speed, ω_f is the weight of foraging movement, β_i^{food} shows the attractive of food, and B_i^{best} is the best solution obtained so far.

The third activity is the diffusion, which is a random activity, and it can be defined as follows:

$$D_i(t+1) = D^{max}\left(\frac{1-I}{Imax}\right)\delta \tag{9}$$

where D^{max} is the maximum diffusion speed and δ is a random vector in $[-1, 1]$.

The position of krill i from t to $t+\Delta t$, which can be formulated as follows:

$$X_i(t+\Delta t) = X_i(t) + \Delta t\frac{dX_i}{dt} \tag{10}$$

Note: Δt can be regarded as a scale factor of the speed vector.

In the chaotic KH [12], researchers used chaotic maps in tuning the random vector; it improves the ability of KH to avoid local optimum. In the classical KH, the most important random value is calculated in Eq. (7); therefore, the parameter r is substituted by chaotic maps as follows:

$$C^{best} = 2\left(C(t) + \frac{I}{Imax}\right) \tag{11}$$

where $C(t)$ is the value of chaotic maps in the tth iteration.

2.1.3. Biogeography-based optimization algorithm (BBO)

The biogeography-based optimization algorithm (BBO) was inspired by biogeography [13]. It simulates relations between different species which are located in different habitats, such as immigration, mutation, and emigration. BBO can be summarized into three rules.

- Individuals living with high habitat suitability index (HSI) are more likely to immigrate to habitats with low HIS.
- Habitants living with low HSO are more likely to allow immigrations from high HSI.
- The HSI value may change randomly.

For each habitat, it has three rates: immigration λ, emigration μ, and mutation m. These three rates can be calculated in the following equations:

$$\mu = \frac{E * n}{N} \tag{12}$$

$$\lambda = I * \frac{1 - n}{N} \tag{13}$$

where n is the number of habitant, N is the maximum number of habitants, E is the maximum emigration rate, and I is the maximum immigration rate. The mutation rate is defined as follows:

$$m = M * \left(1 - \frac{p}{P}\right) \tag{14}$$

where M is defined by user, p is the mutation probability, and P equals to arg max(p).

In chaotic BBO [14], researchers used chaotic map to provide chaotic behaviors for selection operator, emigration, and mutation.

For selection operator, the rand value is substituted by the value from chaotic maps. The pseudo code is as follows:

if $C(t) < \lambda_i$ *then*

Emigrate from H_i *to* H_j *chosen with probability to* λ_i

End if

where $C(t)$ is the value from the chaotic map in the tth iteration.

For emigration, it can be calculated as follows:

if $C(t) < \mu_i$ *then*

select a random habitant in x_i *and replace it with* x_j

End if

The probability of mutation is defined by the chaotic map as follows:

for i = 1 to number of habitants at kth habitat

if $C(t) < mutation_{rate}(k)$ *then*

mutate the ith habitants

End if

End for

where mutation_rate(k) shows the mutation rate of kth habitat.

2.2. Phase in chaos embedded metaheuristics algorithms

From Section 2.1, we can find that the most chaos embedded metaheuristic algorithms have three key phases: initialization, operators, and random generator. In this section, we describe them as follows:

Initialization: the starting positions in metaheuristics algorithm are generated randomly. Diversity of initial population is very important for helping the population spread in search space. Therefore, the initial populations are generated by chaotic maps, which can produce a well distribution by the properties of random and ergodicity of chaos. The chaotic sequence can accelerate the convergence and enhance the global search capability. The pseudo code of initialization is as follows:

$$\begin{array}{l} \textit{for } i = 1 \textit{ to size of population} \\ x_i = \omega_i * C(t) * (U - L) \\ \textit{End for} \end{array} \tag{15}$$

where the ω_i is the weight of ith weight, and U and L are the boundaries of the upper and lower, respectively. $C(t)$ is the chaotic sequence generated by chaotic maps.

Operators: generally, metaheuristics algorithms have several operators, such as selection operator, crossover operator, and mutation operator. Most of them are controlled by probabilities. In order to improve the capability of searching optimum, the probabilities can be substituted by chaotic sequence. The mathematical formula can be described as follows:

For a crossover operator:

$$x_i(t+1) = \begin{cases} x_i(\mathrm{t}) + C(t) * \left(x_i(\mathrm{t}) - x_j(t)\right), & C(t) < 0 \\ x_i(t), & \textit{otherwise} \end{cases} \tag{16}$$

where $C(t)$ is the chaotic sequence produced by chaotic map.

For a mutation operator:

$$x_{i,k}(t+1) = \begin{cases} C(t) * (x_{i,k}(\mathrm{t})), & C(t) < 0 \\ x_{i,k}(t), & otherwise \end{cases} \tag{17}$$

Random generator: Random parameters in metaheuristics algorithms, for instance, polynomial variation, are replaced by chaotic sequences. For a solution xs, the polynomial mutation is described as

$$x_i(t+1) = x_i(\mathrm{t}) + C(t) * \left(x_i(\mathrm{t}) - x_j(t)\right) \tag{18}$$

The phase for random generator is that $C(t)$ is calculated by chaotic maps in iterations. For example, if the chaotic map is logistic map, then in the $(i+1)$th iteration, $C(t+1) = 4 \times C(t) * (1 - C(t))$.

2.3. Chaotic maps

In this section, we present the chaotic maps used, which generate chaotic sequences in the process of evolutionary algorithms. Ten chaotic maps are one-dimensional maps.

The first is the Chebyshev map, which is a common chaotic map and used in digital communication and neural network widely. It can be defined as follows:

$$x_{k+1} = \cos\left(k \cos^{-1}(x_k)\right), \tag{19}$$

where the range is $(-1,1)$. Note that x_k is the kth chaotic number, with k denoting the iteration number.

Circle map is a simplified model for both driven mechanical rotors. Furthermore, it is a one-dimensional map which maps a circle onto itself. Circle map is presented as follows:

$$x_{k+1} = x_k + b - \left(\frac{a}{2\pi}\right) sin\,(2\pi x_k) mod(1), \tag{20}$$

where $a = 0.5$ and $b = 0.2$, the range is (0,1), and the parameters b and a can be regarded as a strength to nonlinearity and externally applied frequency, separately. The circle map produces much unexpected behavior with the change of parameters.

Gauss/Mouse map can be described as follows:

$$x_{k+1} = \begin{cases} 0 & x_k \\ \dfrac{1}{x_k mod(1)} & otherwise, \end{cases} \tag{21}$$

This map also generates chaotic sequences in (0,1).

Iterative map with infinite collapses can be presented as follows:

$$x_{k+1} = sin\,(a\pi/x_k), \tag{22}$$

where $a = 0.7$ and the chaotic sequence in $(-1,1)$.

Logistic map can be written as follows:

$$x_{k+1} = ax_k(1 - x_k), \tag{23}$$

where $a = 4$ and the range is (0,1); it is the simplest map that appears in nonlinear dynamics of biological population, in which evidencing chaotic behavior belongs to a logistic map.

Piecewise map is governed by the following equation:

$$x_{k+1} = \begin{cases} \dfrac{x_k}{P} & 0 \leq x_k < P \\ \dfrac{x_k - P}{0.5 - P} & P \leq x_k < 1/2 \\ \dfrac{1 - P - x_k}{0.5 - P} & \dfrac{1}{2} \leq x_k < 1 - P \\ \dfrac{1 - x_k}{P} & 1 - P \leq x_k < 1 \end{cases}, \tag{24}$$

where $P = 0.4$ and the range is (0,1)

The sine map belongs to a unimodal map and is similar to the logistic map, which can be described as follows:

$$x_{k+1} = a/4\,sin\,(\pi x_k), \tag{25}$$

where $a = 4$ and the chaotic sequence in (0,1)

Singer map is a one-dimensional system like the following:

$$x_{k+1} = \mu(7.86x_k - 23.31x_k^2 + 28.75x_k^3 - 13.3x_k^4), \tag{26}$$

where $\mu = 1.07$ and the range is (0,1).

Sinusoidal map can be defined as follows:

$$x_{k+1} = ax_k^2\,sin\,(\pi x_k), \tag{27}$$

where $a = 2.3$ and the range is (0,1).

Tent chaotic map is very similar to the logistic map, which displays specific chaotic effects.

Tent map can be described as follows:

$$x_{k+1} = \begin{cases} \dfrac{x_k}{0.7} & x_k < 0.7 \\ \dfrac{10}{3}(1 - x_k) & otherwise. \end{cases} \tag{28}$$

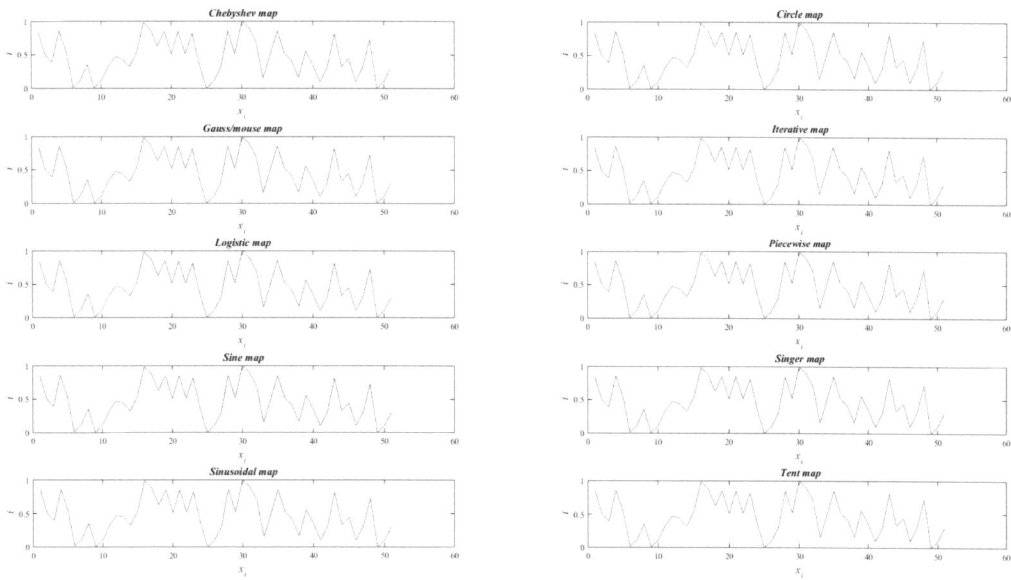

Figure 1. Visualization of employed 10 chaotic maps on one-dimensional space.

In order to get an unbiased result, we set the initial point as 0.7 for all chaotic maps in this work. Ten chaotic maps are shown in **Figure 1**.

3. Experiments

In this section, we evaluate the performance of the chaotic metaheuristics algorithms; several experiments were carried out to test the efficiency. Twenty-three benchmark functions were used in our experiment. In order to obtain an unbiased result, all experiments were performed in the same environment.

In our experiments, we used the average and StD of the function value to compare the performance of the algorithms. Our focus was to compare our proposed algorithm with the other algorithms using two evaluation criteria. We compared the performance of the chaotic algorithm with the other well-known algorithms. The maximum number of fitness evaluations (FEs) is 10,000 $\times$ D, where D is the dimension of the problem. Moreover, the Wilcoxon rank sum test was used in our experiment to test the significance of algorithms. The fitness evaluation criteria are as follows:

Objective function value: algorithms were run 50 times for each benchmark function, and the average and SD were calculated.

The number of function evaluations (FEs): FEs are also recorded in our study; they are required to be less than ε. ε is fixed at 10^{-6}, which is smaller and harder to reach than that used by Noman and Iba. The notation CNT indicates the number of runnings in which algorithms could reach ε. The maximum number of FEs is 10,000 $\times$ D.

Function	Result	PSO	CPSO	CKH	KH	BBO	CBBO
*f*1	Mean	2.54E−19	4.18E−77	3.84E−29	1.01E−05	2.40E−03	2.91E−117
	Std	1.44E−19	2.95E−77	8.06E−30	1.16E−06	5.47E−04	1.30E−116
	p-value	5.01E−11	5.01E−11	5.01E−11	5.01E−11	5.01E−11	N/A
	+/=/−	+	+	+	+	+	N/A
*f*2	Mean	1.07E−07	5.03E+02	5.20E−02	1.91E−01	5.25E−05	3.81E−67
	Std	6.31E−08	2.10E+03	3.68E−01	2.52E−01	1.44E−05	1.70E−66
	p-value	5.01E−11	5.01E−11	5.01E−11	5.01E−11	5.01E−11	N/A
	+/=/−	+	+	+	+	+	N/A
*f*3	Mean	8.83E−08	7.00E−04	7.84E−27	2.52E−05	1.96E−02	2.90E−21
	Std	6.56E−08	4.50E−03	1.86E−27	4.91E−06	8.50E−03	1.27E−20
	p-value	6.41E−04	5.01E−11	5.01E−11	5.01E−11	2.83E−10	N/A
	+/=/−	+	+	−	+	+	N/A
*f*4	Mean	7.41E−02	7.43E+00	2.71E−15	5.60E−03	1.02E+01	2.27E−02
	Std	2.22E−02	1.40E+01	3.55E−16	1.59E−02	5.87E+00	1.17E−02
	p-value	5.01E−11	5.01E−11	5.01E−11	7.41E−09	5.01E−11	N/A
	+/=/−	+	+	−	−	+	N/A
*f*5	Mean	1.80E+01	1.28E+03	1.60E−01	5.34E+00	1.92E+01	4.05E−01
	Std	9.88E+00	2.40E+03	7.97E−01	3.43E+00	5.15E+00	3.49E−01
	p-value	5.01E−11	5.01E−11	5.01E−11	5.01E−11	5.01E−11	N/A
	+/=/−	+	+	−	+	+	N/A
*f*6	Mean	7.74E−17	1.12E−30	4.50E−29	1.06E−05	2.40E−03	5.53E−19
	Std	2.04E−17	1.58E−30	1.25E−29	1.11E−06	4.97E−04	2.45E−18
	p-value	5.01E−11	5.01E−11	1.50E−09	5.01E−11	6.03E−01	N/A
	+/=/−	+	−	−	+	+	N/A
*f*7	Mean	3.47E−01	1.80E+00	9.21E−02	1.45E+00	6.30E−03	4.60E−03
	Std	9.30E−02	1.15E+00	4.53E−02	2.77E−01	1.80E−03	4.90E−03
	p-value	5.01E−11	1.06E−16	7.41E−09	5.01E−11	5.01E−11	N/A
	+/=/−	+	+	+	+	=	N/A
*f*8	Mean	−8.01E+02	−1.23e+03	−8.73E+03	−8.52E+09	−1.45E+02	−1.26E+04
	Std	1.72E+02	5.80e+03	1.70E+03	−4.57E+07	1.04E+01	5.47E−12
	p-value	5.01E−11	5.01E−11	5.01E−11	5.01E−11	5.01E−11	N/A
	+/=/−	+	+	+	+	+	N/A
*f*9	Mean	1.21E+01	2.59E+02	2.10E+02	3.86E+01	1.20E+02	1.32E−09
	Std	5.64E+00	1.40E+02	8.35E+01	1.39E+01	2.02E+01	4.85E−09
	p-value	5.01E−11	5.01E−11	5.01E−11	5.01E−11	5.01E−11	N/A
	+/=/−	+	+	+	+	+	N/A

Function	Result	PSO	CPSO	CKH	KH	BBO	CBBO
*f*10	Mean	4.67E−01	2.02E+01	1.95E+01	2.17E+00	5.35E+00	1.15E−11
	Std	7.59E−01	2.05E−01	1.05E−01	3.00E−01	1.04E+00	3.32E−11
	p-value	5.01E−11	5.01E−11	5.01E−11	5.01E−11	5.01E−11	N/A
	+/=/−	+	+	+	+	+	N/A
*f*11	Mean	2.70E−03	3.08E−02	2.96E−04	4.97E−07	1.84E−04	1.73E−15
	Std	8.20E−03	5.97E−02	1.50E−03	6.69E−08	4.18E−05	6.89E−15
	p-value	5.01E−11	5.01E−11	5.01E−11	5.01E−11	5.01E−11	N/A
	+/=/−	+	+	+	+	+	N/A
*f*12	Mean	3.32E−02	9.35E−01	1.16E−29	4.10E−03	7.64E−05	1.17E−16
	Std	4.94E−02	1.39E+00	2.65E−30	2.07E−02	3.18E−05	5.22E−16
	p-value	5.01E−11	5.01E−11	5.01E−11	5.01E−11	5.01E−11	N/A
	+/=/−	+	+	−	+	+	N/A
*f*13	Mean	7.90E−03	9.31E−01	1.80E−28	4.86E−01	2.88E+00	5.56E−17
	Std	5.90E−03	1.17E+00	3.65E−29	4.76E−01	5.90E−01	2.45E−16
	p-value	1.50E−09	1.82E−02	1.50E−09	2.83E−10	1.48E−07	N/A
	+/=/−	+	+	−	+	+	N/A
*f*14	Mean	1.13E+01	1.89E+00	1.09E+01	1.24E+01	1.27E+01	9.98E−01
	Std	6.50E−01	1.83E+00	3.86E+00	1.29E+00	2.34E−15	2.84E−16
	p-value	2.26E−06	2.64E−05	2.83E−10	7.41E−09	1.91E−01	N/A
	+/=/−	+	+	+	+	+	N/A
*f*15	Mean	8.96E−04	1.30E−03	1.13E−02	3.70E−03	3.52E−04	3.07E−04
	Std	2.56E−04	3.55E−04	2.75E−02	1.09E−02	8.14E−05	1.19E−05
	p-value	8.16E−05	2.64E−05	5.01E−11	1.50E−09	4.34E−01	N/A
	+/=/−	+	+	+	+	=	N/A
*f*16	Mean	−9.91E−01	−9.50E−01	−1.03E+00	−1.03E+00	−1.03E+00	−1.03E+00
	Std	1.83E−01	2.51E−01	2.10E−16	5.06E−11	2.58E−10	6.07E−15
	p-value	8.68E−03	1.63E−03	1.16E−01	6.03E−01	5.59E−01	N/A
	+/=/−	+	+	=	=	=	N/A
*f*17	Mean	3.98E−01	3.98E−01	3.98E−01	3.98E−01	3.98E−01	3.98E−01
	Std	0.00E+00	0.00E+00	2.56E−11	1.99E−11	1.47E−10	5.45E−12
	p-value	8.42E−02	6.42E−02	5.75E−02	8.80E−02	5.65E−02	N/A
	+/=/−	=	=	=	=	=	N/A
*f*18	Mean	3.00E+00	8.40E+00	3.00E+00	4.35E+00	3.00E+00	3.00E+00
	Std	5.39E−16	1.88E+01	2.10E−14	6.04E+00	1.14E−08	8.07E−13
	p-value	1.16E−01	6.41E−04	1.16E−01	1.91E−01	9.51E−02	N/A
	+/=/−	=	+	=	=	=	N/A

Function	Result	PSO	CPSO	CKH	KH	BBO	CBBO
*f*19	Mean	−3.86E+00	−3.86E+00	−3.86E+00	−3.79E+00	−3.86E+00	−3.86E+00
	Std	2.13E−15	5.23E−09	1.85E−15	2.38E−01	1.80E−07	1.85E−12
	p-value	8.68E−03	1.16E−01	2.96E−01	8.68E−03	1.82E−01	N/A
	+/=/−	+	=	=	+	=	N/A
*f*20	Mean	−3.24E+00	−3.28E+00	−3.32E+00	−3.27E+00	−3.32E+00	−3.32E+00
	Std	5.82E−02	7.81E−02	4.56E−16	5.98E−02	2.33E−04	6.07E−05
	p-value	8.68E−03	3.59E−02	2.96E−01	3.88E−03	1.16E−01	N/A
	+/=/−	+	+	=	+	=	N/A
*f*21	Mean	−5.46E+00	−5.13E+00	−4.79E+00	−5.31E+00	−7.35E+00	−1.02E+01
	Std	2.20E+00	2.80E+00	3.26E+00	1.14E+00	2.60E+00	6.80E−07
	p-value	5.01E−11	5.01E−11	5.01E−11	5.01E−11	2.26E−06	N/A
	+/=/−	+	+	+	+	+	N/A
*f*22	Mean	−3.96E+00	−6.67E+00	−8.80E+00	−5.02E+00	−9.87E+00	−1.04E+01
	Std	1.19E+00	3.23E+00	2.86E+00	3.05E−01	1.64E+00	2.88E−06
	p-value	5.01E−11	5.01E−11	5.97E−07	5.01E−11	3.59E−02	N/A
	+/=/−	+	+	+	+	+	N/A
*f*23	Mean	−4.49E+00	−5.77E+00	−9.36E+00	−5.26E+00	−1.03E+01	−1.05E+01
	Std	2.41E+00	3.71E+00	2.87E+00	1.38E+00	1.21E+00	2.12E−07
	p-value	5.01E−11	5.01E−11	6.41E−04	5.01E−11	1.63E−03	N/A
	+/=/−	+	+	+	+	+	N/A
	Sum(+/=/−)	21/2/0	20/2/1	12/6/5	19/3/1	16/7/0	N/A

Table 1. The average function values obtained by the average function values obtained by PSO, CPSO, KH, CKH, BBO, and CBBO at $D = 30$.

To obtain an unbiased result, we compared our algorithm with five well-known optimization algorithms of different types, such as evolutionary and warm-based algorithms. Several studies have shown that they have good performance on optimization problems. These algorithms include particle swarm optimization algorithm, Krill herd algorithm, and Biogeography-based optimization algorithm and their chaos-based algorithms. The experiments were carried out on a PC with a 3.60-Hz processor and 8.0 RAM in MatLab R2014b.

The global optimization toolbox used in our experiment includes PSO algorithms. We used the standard PSO algorithm; c_1 and c_2 used a default value of 1.49. For the CPSO, we used the same parameter settings. For the BBO and CBBO, the probability of modification is 1 and the initial mutation probability is 0.005. The max immigration and emigration rates for each island are 1. For the KH and CKH, the foraging speed is 0.02 and the maximum diffusion speed is 0.005.

This group contains twenty-three benchmark functions *f*1–*f*23, which have limited dimensions, many dimensions, and multiple modal cases. From **Tables 1** and **2**, we find that the chaotic

Function	Result	PSO	CPSO	CKH	KH	BBO	CBBO
*f*1	Mean	8.45E+03	2.23E+04	9.36E+03	8.55E+04	N/A	1.68E+04
	Std	7.83E+02	7.53E+02	1.45E+02	5.47E+03	N/A	7.21E+02
	CNT	50	50	50	31	N/A	50
*f*2	Mean	1.51E+05	6.05E+04	N/A	N/A	1.50E+05	8.56E+03
	Std	1.35E+04	5.64E+03	N/A	N/A	8.94E+03	9.66E+01
	CNT	5	3	N/A	N/A	29	50
*f*3	Mean	5.72E+05	2.18E+05	3.75E+04	2.65E+05	N/A	2.50E+03
	Std	3.67E+04	4.46E+04	1.17E+03	1.16E+05	N/A	1.25E+02
	CNT	50	8	50	45	N/A	50
*f*4	Mean	N/A	N/A	1.76E+04	N/A	N/A	6.95E+03
	Std	N/A	N/A	3.79E+02	N/A	N/A	4.96E+02
	CNT	N/A	N/A	50	N/A	N/A	50
*f*5	Mean	N/A	N/A	N/A	N/A	N/A	N/A
	Std	N/A	N/A	N/A	N/A	N/A	N/A
	CNT	N/A	N/A	N/A	N/A	N/A	N/A
*f*6	Mean	9.81E+04	3.45E+04	9.36E+03	4.54E+04	N/A	2.89E+04
	Std	7.35E+03	1.95E+03	1.30E+02	5.03E+03	N/A	2.51E+03
	CNT	50	50	50	9	N/A	50
*f*7	Mean	1.81E+05	3.58E+04	N/A	N/A	N/A	N/A
	Std	1.02E+05	4.20E+03	N/A	N/A	N/A	N/A
	CNT	11	2	N/A	N/A	N/A	N/A
*f*8	Mean	7.81E+00	N/A	N/A	N/A	N/A	5.43E+03
	Std	1.07E+04	N/A	N/A	N/A	N/A	1.32E+03
	CNT	1	N/A	N/A	N/A	N/A	50
*f*9	Mean	1.34E+05	N/A	N/A	N/A	N/A	3.77E+03
	Std	4.12E+03	N/A	N/A	N/A	N/A	7.38E+01
	CNT	2	N/A	N/A	N/A	N/A	50
*f*10	Mean	1.51E+05	4.27E+03	1.24E+04	N/A	N/A	6.89E+03
	Std	8.90E+03	1.56E+03	4.53E+03	N/A	N/A	8.73E+01
	CNT	50	13	44	N/A	N/A	50
*f*11	Mean	N/A	N/A	1.19E+04	2.91E+04	1.84E+05	1.54E+03
	Std	N/A	N/A	5.24E+03	4.92E+03	4.21E+03	7.03E+01
	CNT	N/A	N/A	48	49	19	50
*f*12	Mean	N/A	N/A	1.08E+04	4.18E+04	N/A	1.21E+04
	Std	N/A	N/A	4.08E+02	7.18E+03	N/A	4.78E+01
	CNT	N/A	N/A	50	45	N/A	50
*f*13	Mean	N/A	N/A	1.12E+04	2.23E+05	N/A	2.90E+05
	Std	N/A	N/A	2.80E+02	0.00E+00	N/A	4.08E+01
	CNT	N/A	N/A	50	1	N/A	50

Function	Result	PSO	CPSO	CKH	KH	BBO	CBBO
*f*14	Mean	N/A	N/A	N/A	N/A	N/A	1.55E+04
	Std	N/A	N/A	N/A	N/A	N/A	8.78E+03
	CNT	N/A	N/A	N/A	N/A	N/A	50
*f*15	Mean	1.02E+04	2.44E+03	3.72E+04	N/A	1.12E+05	2.55E+05
	Std	6.25E+03	1.09E+03	8.14E+03	N/A	5.55E+04	3.21E+04
	CNT	29	18	42	N/A	40	40
*f*16	Mean	3.60E+03	3.62E+04	5.70E+04	8.56E+04	9.31E+04	3.45E+04
	Std	2.80E+02	1.98E+02	2.36E+03	4.69E+03	2.90E+03	1.10E+03
	CNT	48	46	50	50	50	50
*f*17	Mean	3.65E+04	1.01E+04	8.63E+03	5.94E+04	1.09E+05	7.53E+02
	Std	4.75E+02	1.83E+02	1.47E+02	4.73E+03	8.85E+03	5.04E+02
	CNT	50	50	50	50	50	50
*f*18	Mean	4.00E+04	1.34E+04	3.52E+03	1.06E+04	2.04E+03	8.59E+02
	Std	3.64E+02	2.75E+02	2.11E+03	8.55E+03	4.01E+03	1.05E+03
	CNT	50	41	50	49	50	50
*f*19	Mean	4.58E+04	6.60E+03	1.12E+03	6.98E+03	1.08E+04	3.90E+03
	Std	4.48E+02	1.12E+03	8.49E+02	4.88E+02	8.05E+03	3.45E+02
	CNT	50	50	50	44	50	50
*f*20	Mean	2.48E+05	1.32E+04	3.75E+03	1.82E+05	5.13E+04	8.55E+04
	Std	3.45E+03	5.41E+03	7.78E+03	1.03E+05	3.66E+04	5.66E+04
	CNT	27	42	50	32	50	50
*f*21	Mean	4.89E+04	3.76E+04	1.85E+05	4.56E+04	8.50E+04	4.33E+03
	Std	3.93E+02	4.48E+02	8.80E+03	4.57E+02	1.29E+03	9.19E+02
	CNT	25	22	19	5	46	50
*f*22	Mean	4.91E+04	3.70E+04	5.79E+04	8.94E+04	1.84E+05	5.80E+04
	Std	5.22E+02	7.49E+02	5.46E+03	8.95E+03	8.79E+03	1.32E+03
	CNT	8	17	47	34	12	50
*f*23	Mean	4.91E+04	3.73E+04	1.52E+05	2.55E+05	2.13E+05	8.79E+04
	Std	4.67E+02	4.35E+02	2.35E+04	1.79E+04	5.65E+04	2.13E+03
	CNT	11	7	32	16	41	50

Table 2. The average FEs obtained by PSO, CPSO, KH, CKH, BBO and CBBO at $D = 30$.

Algorithm	PSO	CPSO	CKH	KH	BBO	CBBO
Average ranking	3.30	4.13	2.6	3.52	3.39	1.39
Final ranking	3	6	2	5	4	1

Table 3. The average rank of PSO, CPSO, KH, CKH, BBO and CBBO.

http://dx.doi.org/10.5772/intechopen.72103

algorithms easily reach the global best result on all benchmark functions. The other algorithms cannot obtain the results as good as those of the chaotic algorithms. For example, the KH and PSO algorithms both obtain very few global best results on this set of functions. **Table 2** shows that the convergence of the chaotic algorithms also outperforms those of the other algorithms and requires very few FEs to reach the ε level. For example, on function *f*18, the FE of the CBBO algorithm is 8.59E+02, which is significantly lower than the others. **Table 3** shows the rank of all functions.

From the results of the 23 benchmark functions, we can find that, in general, the chaotic algorithms outperform the other algorithms in terms of the average function value and the number of function evaluations. The results presented in this section confirm that the proposed chaotic algorithm exhibits a higher convergence velocity and greater robustness than the other algorithms.

4. Discussion and conclusion

The convergence properties of metaheuristics algorithms are strongly related to its stochastic nature and they use a random sequence for its parameters during running. Generating random sequences with a long period and a good uniformity are very important for easy simulating complex phenomena, sampling, numerical analysis, decision-making, and especially in heuristic optimization. Its quality determines the reduction of storage and computation time to achieve a desired accuracy. Chaos has properties of randomness, nonrepetition, and ergodicity; it matched the stochastic feature of metaheuristic optimization algorithms perfectly. Chaotic optimization not only accelerates the speed of algorithm, but can also enhance the variety of movement pattern.

Chaos has been observed in various applications widely. In this chapter, we used chaos theory combined with the latest algorithm to analyze the properties. The first advantage of chaotic algorithms is using fewer chaotic maps to enhance the searching capability. Secondly, chaotic optimization performs search at higher speed compared to the stochastic searches that rely on probability. Moreover, chaotic optimization is a simple structure and easy to implement. For future studies, it may be well worth employing chaotic algorithms for solving real-world engineering problems.

Author details

Rui Tang[1], Simon Fong[1]* and Nilanjan Dey[2]

*Address all correspondence to: ccfong@umac.mo

1 Department of Computer and Information Science, University of Macau, Taipa, Macau SAR, Macau

2 Department of Information Technology, Techno India College of Technology, India

References

[1] Assarzadeh Z, Naghsh-Nilchi AR. Chaotic particle swarm optimization with mutation for classification. Journal of Medical Signals and Sensors. 2015;**5**(1):12

[2] Saremi S, Mirjalili S, Lewis A. Biogeography-based optimisation with chaos. Neural Computing and Applications. 2015;**25**(**5**):1077-1097

[3] Goldberg DE, Holland JH. Genetic algorithms and machine learning. Machine Learning, 1988;**3**(2):95-99

[4] Storn R, Price K. Differential evolution–a simple and efficient heuristic for global optimization over continuous spaces. Journal of global optimization, 1997;**11**(4):341-359

[5] Hansen N, Ostermeier A. Completely derandomized self-adaptation in evolution strategies. Evolutionary computation, 2001;**9**(2):159-195

[6] Kennedy J. Particle swarm optimization. In Encyclopedia of machine learning. 2011;760-766. Springer US

[7] Tang R, Fong S, Yang XS, Deb S. Wolf search algorithm with ephemeral memory. In: InDigital Information Management (ICDIM); 2012 Aug 22; IEEE; 2012

[8] Gandomi AH, Yang XS, Alavi AH. Cuckoo search algorithm: A metaheuristic approach to solve structural optimization problems. Engineering with Computers. 2013;**29**(1):17-35

[9] Tang R, Fong S, Deb S, Raymond W. Dynamic group search algorithm. Computational and Business Intelligence (ISCBI). 2016

[10] Tang R, Fong S, Deb S, Wong R. Dynamic group search algorithm for solving an engineering problem. Operational Research

[11] Gandomi AH, Alavi AH. Krill herd: A new bio-inspired optimization algorithm. Communications in Nonlinear Science and Numerical Simulation. 2012

[12] Wang GG, Guo L, Gandomi AH, Hao GS, Wang H. Chaotic krill herd algorithm. Information Sciences. 2014

[13] Simon D. Biogeography-based optimization. IEEE transactions on evolutionary computation. 2008

[14] Guo W, Li W, Kang Q, Wang L, Wu Q. Chaotic biogeography-based optimisation. International Journal of Computing Science and Mathematics. 2014

Chapter 11

Bifurcation Theory of Dynamical Chaos

Nikolai A. Magnitskii

Additional information is available at the end of the chapter

http://dx.doi.org/10.5772/intechopen.70987

Abstract

The purpose of the present chapter is once again to show on concrete new examples that chaos in one-dimensional unimodal mappings, dynamical chaos in systems of ordinary differential equations, diffusion chaos in systems of the equations with partial derivatives and chaos in Hamiltonian and conservative systems are generated by cascades of bifurcations under universal bifurcation Feigenbaum-Sharkovsky-Magnitskii (FShM) scenario. And all irregular attractors of all such dissipative systems born during realization of such scenario are exclusively singular attractors that are the nonperiodic limited trajectories in finite dimensional or infinitely dimensional phase space any neighborhood of which contains the infinite number of unstable periodic trajectories.

Keywords: nonlinear systems, dynamical chaos, bifurcations, singular attractors FShM theory

1. Introduction

Well-known, that chaotic dynamics is inherent practically in all nonlinear mappings and systems of differential equations having irregular attractors, distinct from stable fixed and singular points, limit cycles and tori. However, many years there was no clear understanding of that from itself represent irregular attractors and how they are formed. In this connection it was possible to find in the literature more than 20 various definitions of irregular attractors: stochastic, chaotic, strange, hyperbolic, quasiattractors, attractors of Lorenz, Ressler, Chua, Shilnikov, Chen, Sprott, Magnitskii and many others. It was considered that there are differences between attractors of autonomous and nonautonomous nonlinear systems, systems of ordinary differential equations and the equations with partial derivatives, and that the chaos in dissipative systems essentially differs from chaos in conservative and Hamiltonian systems. There was also an opinion which many outstanding scientists adhered, including Nobel prize winner I.R. Prigogine, that irregular attractors of complex nonlinear systems cannot be described by trajectory approach, that are systems of differential equations. And only in twenty-first century it has been proved and on numerous examples it was convincingly shown, that there is one universal bifurcation scenario of transition to chaos in nonlinear systems of mappings and differential equations: autonomous and nonautonomous, dissipative and conservative, ordinary, with private derivatives and with delay argument (see, for example, [1–9]). It is bifurcation Feigenbaum-Sharkovsky-Magnitskii (FShM) scenario, beginning with the Feigenbaum cascade of period-doubling bifurcations of stable cycles or tori and continuing from the Sharkovskii subharmonic cascade of bifurcations of stable cycles or tori of an arbitrary period up to the cycle or torus of the period three, and then proceeding to the Magnitskii homoclinic or heteroclinic cascade of bifurcations of stable cycles or tori. All irregular attractors born during realization of such scenario are exclusively singular attractors that are the nonperiodic limited trajectories in finite dimensional or infinitely dimensional phase space any neighborhood of which contains the infinite number of unstable periodic trajectories.

However, in the scientific literature many papers continue to appear in which authors, not understanding an essence of occurring processes, write about opened by them new attractors in nonlinear systems of differential equations. Such papers are, for example, papers [10, 11] which authors with surprise ascertain an existence of chaotic dynamics in nonlinear system of ordinary differential equations with one stable singular point and try to explain this phenomenon by presence in the system of Smale's horseshoe. Numerous papers continue to be published also in which presence of chaotic attractor in the system of ordinary differential equations is connected with Lyapunov's positive exponent found numerically, diffusion chaos in nonlinear system of equations with partial derivatives is explained by the Ruelle-Takens (RT) theory and is connected with birth of mythical strange attractor at destruction of three-dimensional torus, and presence of chaotic dynamics in Hamiltonian or conservative system is explained by the Kolmogorov-Arnold-Mozer (KAM) theory and is connected with consecutive destruction in the system of rational and mostly irrational tori of nonperturbed system.

The purpose of the present paper is once again to show on concrete new, not entered in [1–9], examples, that chaos in the system considered in Refs. [10, 11], and also chaos in one-dimensional unimodal mappings, dynamical chaos in systems of ordinary differential equations, diffusion chaos in systems of the equations with partial derivatives and chaos in Hamiltonian and conservative systems are generated by cascades of bifurcations under the FShM scenario. Thus, in any nonlinear system there can be an infinite number of various singular attractors, becoming complicated at change of bifurcation parameter in a direction of the cascade of bifurcations. Presence or absence in system of stable or unstable singular points, presence or absence of saddle-nodes or saddle-focuses, homoclinic or heteroclinic separatrix contours and Smale's horseshoes and also positivity of the calculated senior Lyapunov's exponent are not criteria of occurrence in system of chaotic dynamics. And the birth in the system of three-dimensional and even multi-dimensional stable torus leads not only to its destruction with birth of mythical strange attractor, but also to cascade of its period-doubling bifurcations along one of its frequencies or several frequencies simultaneously. Chaotic dynamics in Hamiltonian and conservative systems also is consequence of cascades of bifurcations of birth of new tori, instead of consequence of destruction of some already ostensibly existing mythical tori of nonperturbed system. Thus, for the analysis of chaotic dynamics of any nonlinear system, attempts of calculation of a positive Lyapunov's exponent, application of KAM and RT theories and the proof of existence of Smale's horseshoes are absolutely senseless. Let us notice, that the results of Feigenbaum and Sharkovsky are received only for one-dimensional unimodal maps and then were transferred by Magnitskii at first on two-dimensional systems of differential equations with periodic coefficients, then on three-dimensional, multi-dimensional and infinitely dimensional dissipative and conservative autonomous systems of ordinary differential equations and then on systems of the equations with partial derivatives. Besides this, it is proved by Magnitskii, that the subharmonic cascade of Sharkovsky bifurcations can be continued by homoclinic or heteroclinic bifurcations cascade both in the differential equations, and in continuous one-dimensional unimodal mappings.

1.1. FShM-cascades of bifurcations of stable cycles and a birth of singular attractors in one-dimensional unimodal mappings

Let us give a summary of bifurcation FShM theory of chaos in one-dimensional continuous unimodal mappings. Detailed proof of statements of the present section can be found in Ref. [1].

1.1.1. FShM-cascade of bifurcations in logistic mapping

Studying the properties of logistic mapping

$$f(x,\mu) = \mu x(1-x), \quad x \in [0,1], \quad \mu \in [1,4] \tag{1}$$

Feigenbaum proved that in this equation there is a cascade of period-doubling bifurcations of its cycles and found a sequence of values of the parameter μ at which these bifurcations occur. Further studies have shown that the complex chaotic dynamics of the logistic mapping is also characteristic of any continuous difference equation of a kind $x_{n+1}=f(x_n, \mu)$ in which one-dimensional mapping $f: I \to I$ is unimodal at corresponding choice of scale, that is, it has the only extremum on an interval I. Return mapping f^{-1} has in this case two branches on I.

Considering the map (1) on an interval $x \in [0, 1]$, Feigenbaum has established, that there is the infinite sequence μ_n of parameter values μ converging with a speed of the geometrical progression with a denominator $1/\delta \approx 1/4.67$ to value $\mu_\infty \approx 3.57$ in which period-doubling bifurcations of the cycles of logistic map occur. That is at all parameter values $\mu_n < \mu < \mu_{n+1}$ Eq. (1) has unique regular attractor—a stable cycle of the period 2^n and a set of unstable cycles of all periods $2^k, k=0, \ldots, n-1$. Thus, the first most simple and low-power singular attractor, born in unimodal one-dimensional continuous mapping at the end of the Feigenbaum period-doubling bifurcation cascade, is a nonperiodic trajectory consisting of points, any neighborhood of each contains points belonging to some unstable cycles of the periods $2^n, n>0$. This attractor is called Feigenbaum attractor. It is, obviously, everywhere not dense set of points on an interval. In the case of logistic mapping (1), Feigenbaum attractor exists at the parameter value $\mu_\infty \approx 3.57$. However, logistic mapping is defined on the interval $x \in [0, 1]$ at all parameter values $\mu \leq 4$. The answer to a question, that occurs with trajectories of logistic mapping and with any other unimodal continuous mapping at parameter values $\mu > \mu_\infty$, gives Sharkovsky theorem. It follows from this theorem that complication of structure of cycles of iterations of one-dimensional unimodal mappings, as a rule, does not come to the end with the cascade of

Feigenbaum bifurcations and Feigenbaum attractor, and it is continued by more complex cascade of bifurcations according to the order established by Sharkovsky in his theorem.

Definition. Ordering in set of the natural numbers, looking like

$$1 \lhd 2 \lhd 2^2 \lhd \ldots 2^n \lhd \ldots \lhd 2^2 \cdot 7 \lhd 2^2 \cdot 5 \lhd 2^2 \cdot 3 \lhd \ldots 2 \cdot 7 \lhd 2 \cdot 5 \lhd 2 \cdot 3 \lhd \ldots \lhd 7 \lhd 5 \lhd 3. \qquad (2)$$

is called as Sharkovsky's order. Theorem of Sharkovsky approves, that if continuous unimodal map $f: I \to I$ has a cycle of the period n then it has also all cycles of each period k, such that $k \lhd n$ in the sense of the order (2). Consequence of the theorem is the statement, that if map f has a cycle of the period 3, then it has cycles of all periods.

It also follows from the Sharkovsky theorem, that at change of values of bifurcation parameter, stable cycles in one-dimensional unimodal continuous mappings are obliged to be born according to the order (2). And their births occur in pairs together with unstable cycles as a result of saddle-node (tangent) bifurcations. Each stable cycle of Sharkovsky cascade, which has born thus, undergoes then the cascade of period-doubling bifurcations, generating its own window of periodicity (**Figure 1**). A limit of such cascade is more complex singular attractor—nonperiodic almost stable trajectory any neighborhood of which contains the infinite number of unstable periodic trajectories. Hence, the cascade of Feigenbaum bifurcations is an initial stage of the full subharmonic cascade of bifurcations, described by Sharkovsky order. In the case of logistic mapping (1) cycle of the period three is born at value $\mu \approx 3.828$ (**Figure 1**). Hence, the subharmonic cascade of Sharkovsky bifurcations does not cover all area of change of values of bifurcation parameter $\mu \leq 4$.

Behind subharmonic Sharkovsky cascade, homoclinic (heteroclinic) cascade of bifurcations lays, opened by Magnitskii at first in nonlinear systems of ordinary differential equations, and then found out in logistic and other unimodal continuous mappings. Homoclinic (heteroclinic) cascade of bifurcations consists of a consecutive birth of stable homoclinic (heteroclinic) cycles of the period n converging to a homoclinic (heteroclinic) contour. As a rule, it is a separatrix loop of a saddle-focus (heteroclinic separatrix contour) in nonlinear system of ordinary differential equations and a separatrix loop of a fixed point (heteroclinic separatrix contour) in one-dimensional unimodal mapping. Born before, unstable cycles and

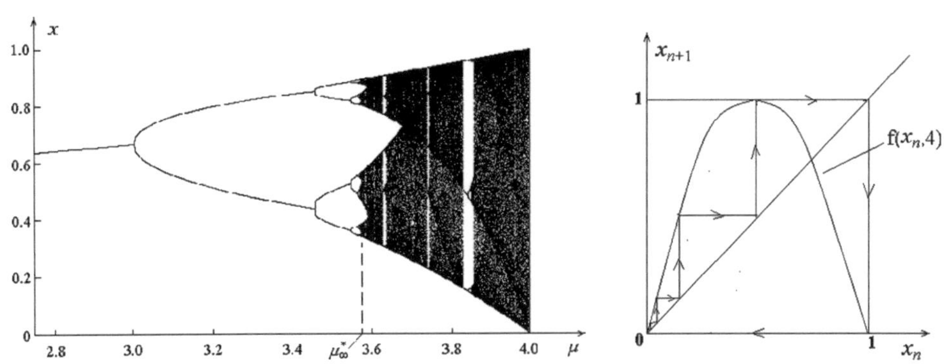

Figure 1. Full bifurcation diagram of logistic mapping at $\mu \leq 4$ and the separatrix loop of the zero fixed point at $\mu = 4$.

nonperiodic trajectories (singular attractors) remain in system, therefore dynamics of unimodal mapping in a neighborhood of a homoclinic (heteroclinic) contour is the most complex. The first cycles of homoclinic cascade are the most simple cycle of the period two of the Feigenbaum cascade and the most complex cycle of the period three of Sharkovsky cascade. In logistic mapping stable homoclinic cycle of the period four exists at $\mu = 3.9603$, and the separatrix loop of the fixed point $x = 0$ exists at $\mu = 4$, that completely covers all area of change of values of bifurcation parameter (**Figure 1**). So, in one-dimensional unimodal mappings at various parameter values stable periodic (regular) attractors and nonperiodic singular attractors can exist together with finite or infinite number of unstable periodic trajectories, and all such attractors are born as a result of cascades of soft bifurcations (saddle-node and period-doubling) in full accordance with the Feigenbaum-Sharkovsky-Magnitskii (FShM) theory.

2. Dynamical chaos in nonlinear dissipative systems of ordinary differential equations

Bases of the FShM theory with reference to nonlinear dissipative systems of ordinary differential equations are stated in Refs. [1–3, 7]. Thus in systems with strong dissipation it is realized both the full subharmonic cascade of Sharkovsky bifurcations, and full (or incomplete) homoclinic (or heteroclinic) cascade of Magnitskii bifurcations depending on, whether exists homoclinic (or heteroclinic) separatrix contour in the system. In systems with weak dissipation the FShM-order of bifurcations can be broken in its right part. Hence, attractors of such systems are regular attractors (stable singular points, stable cycles and stable tori of any dimension), or singular cyclic or toroidal attractors—limited nonperiodic almost stable trajectories or the toroidal manifolds, being limits of cascades of the period-doubling bifurcations of regular attractors (cycles, tori). In Refs. [1–3, 7] it is proved, that the FShM scenario of transition to chaos takes place in such classical two-dimensional dissipative systems with periodic coefficients, as systems of Duffing-Holmes, Mathieu, Croquette and Krasnoschekov; in three-dimensional autonomous dissipative systems, as systems of Lorenz, Ressler, Chua, Magnitskii, Vallis, Anishchenko-Astakhov, Rabinovich-Fabricant, Pikovskii-Rabinovich-Trakhtengertz, Sviregev, Volterra-Gause, Sprott, Chen, Rucklidge, Genezio-Tesi, Wiedlich-Trubetskov and many others; in multi-dimensional and infinitely dimensional autonomous dissipative systems, as systems of Rikitaki, Lorenz complex system, Mackey-Glass equation and many others. These systems describe processes and the phenomena in all areas of scientific researches. Lorenz system is a hydrodynamic system, Ressler system is a chemical system, Chua system describes the electro technical processes, Magnitskii system is a macroeconomic system, Widlich-Trubetskov system describes the social processes and phenomena, Mackey-Glass equation describes the processes of hematopoiesis.

2.1. Transition to chaos in the system with one stable singular point

In this chapter, let us consider the three-dimensional system of ordinary differential equations with one stable singular point which has been proposed in Ref. [10]

$$\dot{x} = yz + 0.006, \quad \dot{y} = x^2 - y, \quad \dot{z} = 1 - 4x \tag{3}$$

This system has the only stable singular point (0.25, 0.0625, −0.096) of stable focus type as Jacobian matrix in the singular point has eigenvalues (−0.96069, −0.01966 ± 0.50975 i), where $i^2 = -1$. The system (3) has no neither saddle-focuses, nor a saddle-nodes and, hence, it has no homoclinic or heteroclinic contours, but it has strongly expressed chaotic dynamics (see in Ref. [10] and below in **Figure 2**). In Ref. [11] attempt is undertaken to explain chaos in system (3) by presence in it of Smale's horseshoe. We shall show now, that transition to chaos in system (3) actually occurs in full accordance with universal bifurcation scenario of Feigenbaum-Sharkovsky-Magnitskii. For this purpose, it is necessary only to define correctly bifurcation parameter at which change the cascade of bifurcations under FShM scenario is realized in the system.

As bifurcation parameter we choose the parameter b and consider the system

$$\dot{x} = yz + 0.006, \quad \dot{y} = x^2 - by, \quad \dot{z} = 1 - 4x \tag{4}$$

At $b = 1$, the system (4) obviously passes into system (3). We shall search stable cycles of the system (4) by numerical modeling of the system by the Runge-Kutta method of the fourth order. The system (4) remains dissipative at all parameter values $b > 0$. At values $b < 0.39$ there are no attractors in the system, except for a singular point of a stable focus type. At value $b \approx 0.39$ there is a stable cycle in the system as a result a saddle-node bifurcation of births of stable and unstable cycles. This cycle exists up to the value $b \approx 0.8$, when the stable cycle of the double period is born in the system . Further the cascade of Feigenbaum period-doubling bifurcations follows: the cycle of period 2 is observed up to value $b \approx 0.9$, the cycle of the period 4—up to value $b \approx 0.926$, generating a stable cycle of the period 8, etc. At the further increase in parameter values b, the next cycles have been found: of the period 7 at $b \approx 0.956$, of the period 5 at $b \approx 0.965$ and of the period 3 at $b \approx 0.982$. This indicates the realization of full subharmonic cascade of Sharkovsky bifurcations in the system (4) (**Figure 2**). At $b = 1$ there exists a chaos in the system (4) and, hence, in the system (3), corresponding to an area of FShM scenario, which lies behind the Sharkovsky cascade. Homoclinic cascade in the system (4) is not found out, in view of absence in it of unstable singular points and homoclinic separatrix contours.

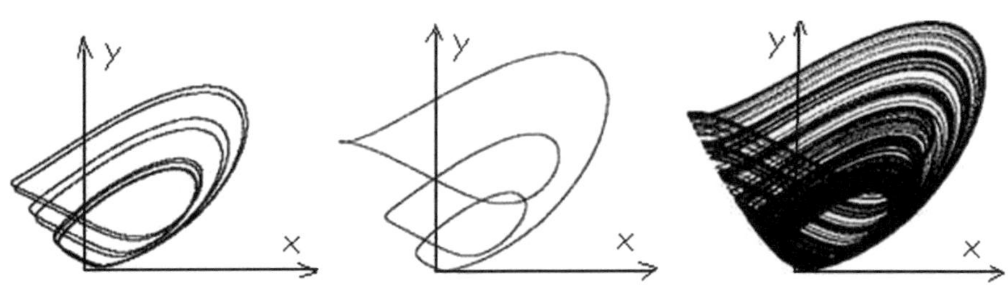

Figure 2. Projections to a plane (x, y) of cycles of periods 8 ($b = 0.927$), 3 ($b = 0.982$) and singular attractor ($b = 1$) of the system (4).

3. Dynamical chaos in Hamiltonian and conservative systems

Conservative system saves its volume at movement along the trajectories and, hence, cannot have attractors. Therefore studying of dynamical chaos in Hamiltonian and, especially, simply conservative systems is more a difficult task in comparison with the analysis of chaotic dynamics in dissipative systems which can be described by universal bifurcation FShM theory. The main problem solved by the modern classical theory of Hamiltonian systems (the Kolmogorov-Arnold-Moser theory) is the problem of integrability of such a system, that is, the problem of its reduction to the "action-angle" variables by constructing some canonical transformation. It is assumed that in such variables the motion in a Hamiltonian system is periodic or quasiperiodic and occurs on the surface of an n-dimensional torus. In this formulation, any non-integrable Hamiltonian system is considered as a perturbation of the integrable system, and the analysis of the dynamics of the perturbed system reduces to studying the problem of the destruction of the tori of an unperturbed system with increasing values of the perturbation parameter. But numerous examples of Hamiltonian and simply conservative systems, considered by the author in [4–7], deny existence such classical KAM-scenario of transition to chaos.

One of the most effective approaches to the decision of a problem of the analysis of chaotic dynamics in conservative systems is offered by the author in Ref. [4] (see also [5–7]). The approach assumes consideration of conservative system in the form of limiting transition from corresponding extended dissipative system (in which the dissipative member is added) to initial conservative system. This approach can be evidently shown by means of construction of two-parametrical bifurcation diagram which corresponds to transition from dissipative state to conservative state. Attractors (stable cycles, tori and singular attractors) of extended dissipative system can be found numerically with use of results of universal bifurcation FShM theory. Further transition to chaos in conservative (Hamiltonian) system is carried out through cascades of bifurcations of attractors of extended dissipative system when dissipation parameter tends to zero. Areas of stability of stable cycles of the extended system at zero dissipation turn into tori of conservative (Hamiltonian) system around of its elliptic cycles into which stable cycles transform. Thus tori of conservative (Hamiltonian) system touch through hyperbolic cycles into which saddle cycles of extended dissipative system transform. In [4–7] the considered above approach is described in detail with reference to Hamiltonian systems with one and a half, two, two and a half and three degrees of freedom, and also to simply conservative systems of differential equations, including the conservative Croquette equation, the equation of a pendulum with oscillating point of fixing, the conservative generalized Mathieu equation, well-known Hamiltonian system of Henon-Heiles equations. In Refs. [12, 13] the given approach has been applied and strictly proved by continuation along parameter of solutions from dissipative into conservative areas by means of the Magnitskii method of stabilization of unstable periodic orbits [1] at research bifurcations and chaos in the Duffing-Holmes equation

$$\ddot{x} + \mu \dot{x} - \delta x + x^3 - \varepsilon \cos(\omega t) = 0, \tag{5}$$

and in the model of a space pendulum

$$\ddot{x} + \mu\dot{x} + kx + \varepsilon \sin(2\pi x) = h\cos\omega t. \tag{6}$$

Corresponding bifurcation diagrams in a plane (ε, μ) of existence of cycles of various periods down to a conservative case at $\mu = 0$ are shown in [12–14]. Application of Magnitskii approach has revealed the essence of dynamical chaos in Hamiltonian and simply conservative systems. It became clear, that the chaos in such systems is not a result of destruction or non-destruction of some mythical tori of nonperturbed systems, as it follows from the KAM theory, but absolutely on the contrary, it is a consequence of limit transition of infinite number of cycles, tori and singular attractors, born according to the FShM theory as a result of cascades of bifurcations in extended dissipative system when dissipation parameter tends to zero.

3.1. Hamiltonian Yang-Mills-Higgs system with two degrees of freedom

In this chapter, let us illustrate Magnitskii approach by the example of Yang-Mills-Higgs system with two degrees of freedom and with Hamiltonian

$$H = \left(\dot{x}^2 + \dot{z}^2\right)/2 + x^2z^2/2 + \nu\left(x^2 + z^2\right)/2, \tag{7}$$

passing into classical system of the Yang-Mills equations at $\nu = 0$. We shall consider four-dimensional phase space of the system with coordinates $x, y = \dot{x},\ z, r = \dot{z}$:

$$\dot{x} = y,\ \ \dot{y} = -x\left(\nu + z^2\right),\ \ \dot{z} = r,\ \ \dot{r} = -z\left(\nu + x^2\right). \tag{8}$$

The system (8) has four sets of periodic solutions to which there correspond four basic cycles in phase space

$$C_x : z = r = 0,\ y^2 + \nu x^2 = 2;\ C_z : x = y = 0, r^2 + \nu z^2 = 2;\ C^{\pm} : z = \pm x, y^2 + \nu x^2 + x^4/2 = 1. \tag{9}$$

Assuming $H = 1$, we shall consider four-dimensional extended two-parametrical dissipative system of differential equations of a kind

$$\dot{x} = y,\ \ \dot{y} = -x\left(\nu + z^2\right) - \mu y,\ \ \dot{z} = r + (1 - H(x, y, z, r))z,\ \ \dot{r} = -z\left(\nu + x^2\right), \tag{10}$$

where $r = \dot{z}$. Complication of solutions of Hamiltonian system (8) of the Yang-Mills-Higgs equations down to full chaotic dynamics occurs at $\nu \to 0$. In turn for each value $\nu > 0$ the structure of solutions of Hamiltonian system (8) is completely determined by cascades of bifurcations of cycles of extended dissipative system (10) when dissipation parameter $\mu \to 0$. Stable cycles of dissipative system (10), born as a result of cascades of bifurcations, pass into elliptic cycles of Hamiltonian system (8), and their areas of stability—into tori around of these elliptic cycles. The contact of born tori of conservative system occurs on hyperbolic cycles in which corresponding unstable cycles of extended dissipative system transform. These unstable cycles are born in the dissipative system together with stable cycles as a result a saddle-node bifurcations, or at loss of stability of a cycle as a result of pitchfork

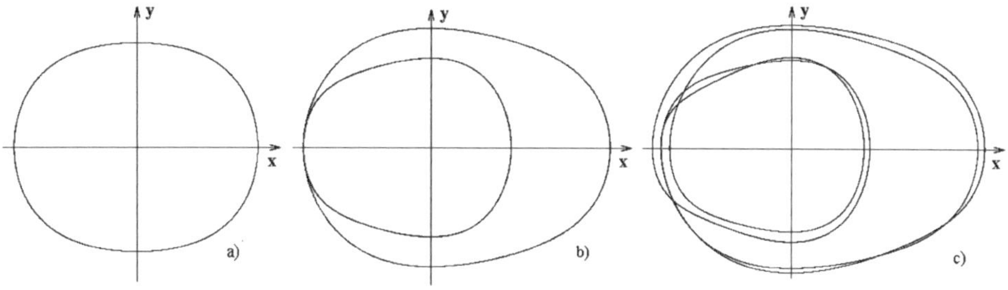

Figure 3. Projections of cycles of Hamiltonian system (8) on a plane (x, y): an initial cycle C^+ at $\nu = 0.73$ (a), cycles of the double and quadruple periods at $\nu = 0.65$ (b) and at $\nu = 0.534$ (c).

bifurcation or period-doubling bifurcation. In neighborhoods of separatrix surfaces of hyperbolic cycles there is a formation of new more complex hyperbolic and elliptic cycles according to nonlocal effect of multiplication of cycles and tori in conservative systems (see [4–7]). Last effect plays a key role in the system of Yang-Mills-Higgs equations at an initial stage of transition from regular dynamics to chaotic dynamics. At the same time, as numerical calculations show, the further complication of dynamics of solutions of system (10) at reduction of parameter value ν occurs not only by means of multiplication of elliptic and hyperbolic cycles and tori, but also by means of the cascade of period-doubling bifurcations of the basic cycles and by means of the subharmonic cascade of bifurcations. Initial cycles of the cascade of period-doubling bifurcations of the cycle C^+ are presented in **Figure 3**. In Ref. [14] stabilization of unstable cycles of system (8) by modified Magnitskii method [1] is carried out.

Further, the process continues with the birth of infinitely folded heteroclinic separatrix manifold, stretched over separatrix Feigenbaum tree, both in extended dissipative system (10), and in Hamiltonian system (8) close to it. Accordions of corresponding heteroclinic separatrix zigzag fill the whole phase space of the system, however the limited accuracy of numerical methods does not allow to track this process up to the value $\nu = 0$, corresponding to the initial system of the Yang-Mills equations.

4. Spatio-temporal chaos in nonlinear partial differential equations

Bases of FShM theory with reference to a wide class of nonlinear systems of partial differential equations are stated in Refs. [6–9]. This class includes systems of the equations of reaction-diffusion type, describing various autowave oscillatory processes in chemical, biological, social and economic systems, including the well-known brusselator equations; the equations of FitzHugh-Nagumo type, describing processes of chemical and biological turbulence in excitable media; the equations of Kuramoto-Tsuzuki (or Time Dependent Ginzburg-Landau) type, describing complex autooscillating processes after loss of stability of a thermodynamic branch in reaction-diffusion systems; the systems of Navier-Stokes equations, describing laminar-turbulent transitions in hydrodynamical and gazodynamical mediums.

4.1. Diffusion chaos in reaction-diffusion systems

Wide class of physical, chemical, biological, ecological and economic processes and phenomena is described by reaction-diffusion systems of partial differential equations

$$u_t = D_1 u_{xx} + f(u, v, \mu), \quad v_t = D_2 v_{xx} + \ g(u, v, \mu), \ 0 \leq x \leq l, \tag{11}$$

depending on the scalar or vector parameter μ. The dynamics of the solutions of such a complex system of equations depends on the boundary conditions, the length of the spatial region, and the values of the diffusion coefficients. In many cases, there is a value of the system parameter μ_0, such that for $\mu < \mu_0$ the system (11) has a stable spatial homogeneous stationary solution (U, V), called the thermodynamic branch. In the case of loss of stability of the thermodynamic branch, when $\mu > \mu_0$, solutions of the system (11) can be various homogeneous and inhomogeneous periodic solutions, spiral waves, running impulses, stationary dissipative structures, as well as nonstationary nonperiodic inhomogeneous solutions, called space-time or diffusion chaos.

The nonlinear processes occurring in so-called excitable media, are described by a special case of systems of the reaction-diffusion equations—FitzHugh-Nagumo type systems

$$u_t = D u_{xx} + f(u, v, \mu), \ \ v_t = g(u, v, \mu). \tag{12}$$

Solutions of the system (12) are: switching waves, traveling waves and running impulses, dissipative stationary spatially inhomogeneous structures, and diffusion chaos—nonstationary nonperiodic inhomogeneous structures, sometimes called biological or chemical turbulence. All such solutions can be analyze on a line by replacement $\xi = x - ct$ and transition to three-dimensional system of ordinary differential equations

$$\dot{u} = y, \ \dot{y} = -(cy + f(u, v, \mu))/D, \ \ \dot{v} = -g(u, v, \mu)/c, \tag{13}$$

where the derivative is taken over the variable ξ. Therefore, the separatrix of the heteroclinic contour of system (13) describes the switching wave of the system (12), the limit cycle and the separatrix loop of the singular point of system (13) describe the traveling wave and the running impulse of system (12). And diffusion chaos in system (12) is described by singular attractors of the system of ordinary differential Eq. (13) in full accordance with the universal bifurcation Feigenbaum-Sharkovsky-Magnitskii theory. The greatest interest represents a case when c is a bifurcation parameter, describing a speed of wave distribution along an axis x, which is not included obviously into initial system (12). This case means, that system of a kind (12) with the fixed parameters can have infinitely number of various autowave solutions of any period running along a spatial axis with various speeds, and infinite number of modes of diffusion chaos. One of such system, describing chemical turbulence in autocatalytic chemical reactions, is studied in [6, 7, 15].

In this chapter, let us consider the system of a kind (12) describing distribution of nervous impulses in a cardiac muscle [16]:

$$u_t = u_{xx} + \frac{1}{\varepsilon} u(1-u)\left(u - \frac{0.06+v}{0.75}\right), \quad v_t = u^3 - v. \tag{14}$$

where u is the activator, v—ingibitor, slowing down development of the activator, the parameter $1/\varepsilon$ defines time of restoration of the system after perturbation. Let us show, that transition to diffusion chaos in system (14), during complication of periodic fluctuations occurring in it, occurs according to universal bifurcation scenario of the FShM theory. We shall analyze solutions of system (14) by means of automodeling replacement of independent variables $\xi = x - ct$, having reduced the initial system of partial differential equations to three-dimensional system of ordinary differential equations

$$\dot{u} = w, \quad \dot{w} = -\left(cw + \frac{1}{\varepsilon} u(1-u)\left(u - \frac{0.06+v}{0.75}\right)\right), \quad \dot{v} = \left(v - u^3\right)/c, \tag{15}$$

where derivative is taken with respect to the variable ξ. If $(u(\xi), v(\xi), w(\xi))$ is the solution of system of ODE (15) then $(u(x-ct), v(x-ct), w(x-ct))$ will be the solution of system in private derivatives (14). Thus running waves in system (14) are described by limit cycles of system (15), and running impulses—by separatrix loops of saddle-focuses. Let us carry out numerical research of system (15) in the field of where one of singular points is a saddle-focus. The greatest interest represents a case when c is the bifurcation parameter which describes a speed of waves distribution along an axis x and which is not included obviously into initial system (14). This case means, that the system (14) with the fixed parameters can have infinitely number of various autowave solutions of any period running along a spatial axis with various speeds, and infinite number of modes of diffusion chaos. Let us fix a parameter value $\varepsilon : 1/\varepsilon = 17.4$, and take the parameter c as bifurcation parameter. At $c \in [1.6305, 1.6316]$ there is a stable cycle in the system (15). At $c \approx 1.6317$ the cascade of Feigenbaum period-doubling bifurcations of the initial cycle begins, and at $c \in [1.6317, 1.6331]$ the cycle of period 2 is observed, at $c \in [1.6332, 1.6335]$—the cycle of period 4, and at $c \approx 1.63375$ the first singular attractor—Feigenbaum attractor is found out (**Figure 4**).

At the further reduction of values of parameter c, cycles of period 5 and period 3 are found out at $c \approx 1.6344$ and at $c \approx 1.6347$ (**Figure 4**). Thus, it is established, that in system (15) at change of parameter c, Feigenbaum cascade of period-doubling bifurcations of stable limit cycles and the full subharmonic Sharkovsky cascade of bifurcations of stable cycles according to the Sharkovsky order are realized. To the found cycles of system (15) there correspond running waves of system (14), some of which are represented in **Figure 5**.

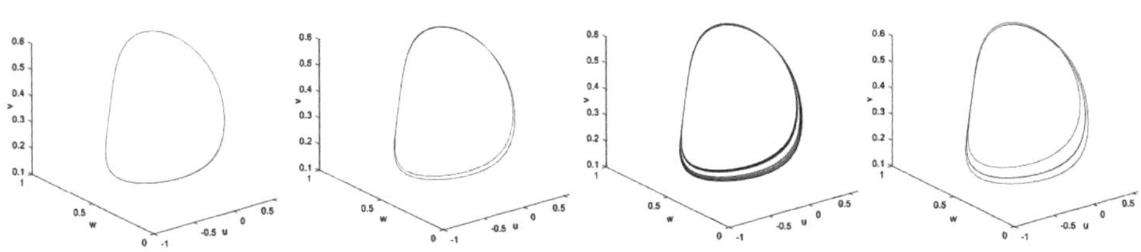

Figure 4. Cycles of periods 1, 2, 3 from Sharkovsky cascade and Feigenbaum attractor.

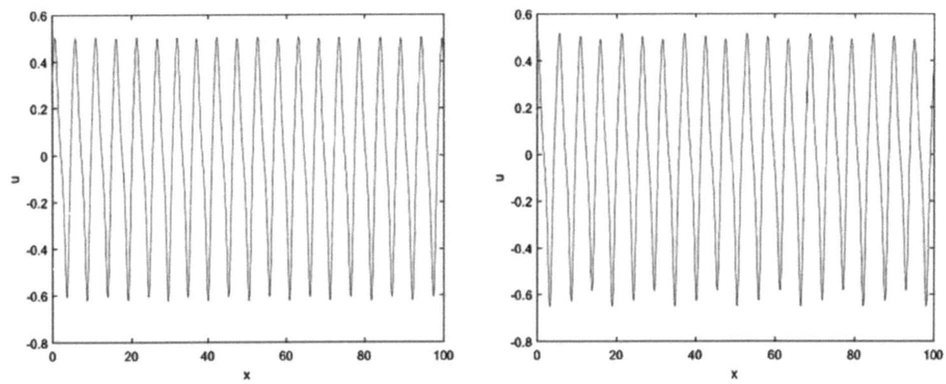

Figure 5. Running waves of system (14), corresponding to cycles of system (15) with periods 2, 3.

4.2. Spatio-temporal chaos in autooscillating mediums

It is well-known that any solution of the reaction-diffusion system (11) in a neighborhood $\mu > \mu_0$ of the thermodynamic branch can be approximated by some complex-valued solution $W(r,\tau) = u(r,\tau) + iv(r,\tau)$ of the Kuramoto-Tsuzuki (or Time Dependent Ginzburg-Landau) equation (see [1, 2, 6, 7]):

$$W_\tau = W + (1 + ic_1)W_{rr} - (1 + ic_2)|W|^2 W, \tag{16}$$

where $r = \varepsilon x, \tau = \varepsilon^2 t,\ \varepsilon = \sqrt{\mu - \mu_0}, 0 \le r \le R,\ c_1, c_2$—two real constants. Obviously, Eq. (16) has a spatial homogeneous solution $W(\tau) = \exp(-i(c_2\tau + \varphi))$ for an arbitrary phase φ. Consequently, each element of the medium (16) oscillates with a frequency c_2. This solution is stable in a certain area of parameters c_1 and c_2. So, such media are called as autooscillating media. Research of solutions of the Kuramoto-Tsuzuki (Ginzburg-Landau) Eq. (16) directly in its phase space has shown, that actually in this equation there is subharmonic cascade of bifurcations of stable two-dimensional tori of any period according to the Sharkovsky order over each of frequencies and over two frequencies simultaneously. In [1, 2, 6, 7] solutions of the second boundary-value problem for the Eq. (16) on an interval are analyzed in detail. It has been constructed four-dimensional subspace $(u(0), v(0), u(l/2), v(l/2))$ of infinitely dimensional phase space of solutions of the problem, and its Poincare section by the plane $u(l/2) = 0$ for various values of bifurcation parameters c_1 and c_2 has been considered. Poincare's method of the analysis of phase space of solutions of the Eq. (16) has allowed to find all cascades of bifurcations of two-dimensional tori in full accordance with the FShM theory.

In this chapter, we consider the problem of research of nonlinear effects in model of surface plasmon-polyariton. The passage of an electromagnetic wave through a configuration from three various environments dielectric-metal-dielectric can be described by following system of the equations in partial derivatives in the complex variables, turning out of Maxwell equations (see [17]):

$$i\frac{\partial\psi_p}{\partial z}+\frac{1}{2\beta}\frac{\partial^2\psi_p}{\partial y^2}+\left(il-\Delta\beta\right)\psi_p+\kappa\psi_a=0,$$
$$i\frac{\partial\psi_a}{\partial z}+\frac{1}{2\beta}\frac{\partial^2\psi_a}{\partial y^2}+\left(i(l-g)+\Delta\beta\right)\psi_a+f\Upsilon|\psi_a|^2\psi_a\kappa\psi_p=0, \tag{17}$$

The system (17) represents two connected Ginzburg-Landau equations, ψ_p and ψ_a—complex-valued functions, y and z—independent variables. The role of time in Ginzburg-Landau equation in this case is played with spatial coordinate z. The equation for ψ_p corresponds to a wave on border of metal and passive dielectric, and for ψ_a—on border of metal and active nonlinear dielectric. Parameters l g, κ—accordingly dimensionless factors of losses, strengthening and connection between two borders. In Ref. [17] the following fixed values of parameters were considered: $l=0.0026$, $\kappa=0.0028$, $\Delta\beta=0$, $\beta=1.43$, $f\Upsilon=f(\Upsilon'+i\Upsilon'')=3.5\cdot10^{-3}(1+0.1i)$. We shall research dynamics of system (17) at various values of parameter g, and as boundary conditions on spatial variable y we shall consider periodic boundary conditions. In analysis of dynamics of the system (17) we use the real functions: u_1, v_1, u_2, v_2 instead of complex-valued functions ψ_p and ψ_a where $\psi_p=u_1+iv_1$, $\psi_a=u_2+iv_2$. And vector of independent variables is denoted $\vec{x}=(u_1,v_1,u_2,v_2)^T$.

In the considered initial boundary-value problem it is possible to allocate a subclass of spatially homogeneous solutions, not dependent on a variable y. They can be found, solving the system of ordinary differential equations received from (17) by rejection of members, containing derivatives on y. The received system of ODE in coordinates $\vec{x}$ is

$$\frac{d\vec{x}}{dz}=\begin{pmatrix}-l & \Delta\beta & 0 & -\kappa\\ -\Delta\beta & -l & \kappa & 0\\ 0 & -\kappa & -(l-g) & -\Delta\beta\\ \kappa & 0 & \Delta\beta & g-l\end{pmatrix}\times\vec{x}+\left(u_2^2+v_2^2\right)f\begin{pmatrix}0\\ 0\\ \Upsilon''\cdot u_2+\Upsilon'\cdot v_2\\ \Upsilon''\cdot v_2-\Upsilon'\cdot u_2\end{pmatrix} \tag{18}$$

Critical value of parameter is $g=0.0052$. At smaller parameter values the zero solution is stable. At great values the solution loses stability, and the signs on the real parts are changed at once with four roots of the characteristic equation. Approximately at parameter value $g=0.00357$ a pair of periodic solutions appears in system (18) as a result of the saddle-node bifurcation At parameter value $g=0.0052$, when zero singular point loses its stability, the unstable periodic solution disappears as a result of subcritical Andronov-Hopf bifurcation. Thus, at $g>0.0052$ there is a stable limit cycle in the system. Let us consider the scenario of complication of dynamics of solutions in system (17) at value L = 10, where L is the size of physical area on a variable y. Phase portraits of system we build in a point y = L/3: $u_1(L/3,z)$, $v_1(L/3,z)$, $u_2(L/3,z)$, $v_2(L/3,z)$. In case of periodic boundary conditions, the first stages of complication go according to the Landau-Hopf scenario, that is, occurrence of periodic and quasiperiodic solutions of the increasing phase dimension have been found out. At parameter values $g<0.0095$ the homogeneous cycle described above saves the stability, and at a parameter value $g=0.0096$ he becomes non-homogeneous. The further complication of dynamics of system occurs at parameter value $g\approx0.0105$. At this value a quasiperiodic solution—torus of dimension two is born in the system as a result Andronov-Hopf bifurcation. A kind of this solution in phase space and its section by a plane $u_1=0$ are represented in **Figure 6**. It is visible, that the section represents the closed curve.

Following bifurcation in the system (17) occurs in a range of parameter values g from 0.01385 till 0.01390. As a result of one more Andronov-Hopf bifurcation more complex quasiperiodic solution is formed in the system—it is torus of dimension three. A phase portrait of this torus at $g=0.0139$ and its Poincare sections are represented in **Figure 7**. The first section $u_1=0$ represents two-dimensional torus which in turn in section $u_2=0$ gives two closed curves.

For the problem with Neumann's homogeneous boundary conditions also it was possible to observe a non-homogeneous stable cycle at $g=0.0060$. At $g=0.0095$ stable two-dimensional torus is born from this cycle, and at $g\approx 0.013$ stable three-dimensional torus is born from it as a result of the second Andronov-Hopf bifurcation. Thus, it is proved, that in complex nonlinear systems of partial differential equations stable three-dimensional tori can exist, that contradicts to the Ruelle-Takens theorem. The natural is not the decay of three-dimensional torus with forming uncertain mythical strange attractor, but further complication of dynamics of solutions as a result of following Andronov-Hopf bifurcation with forming four-dimensional torus, or as a result of period-doubling bifurcation of three-dimensional torus along one of its frequencies or along all frequencies simultaneously (that takes place in systems of Navier-Stokes equations).

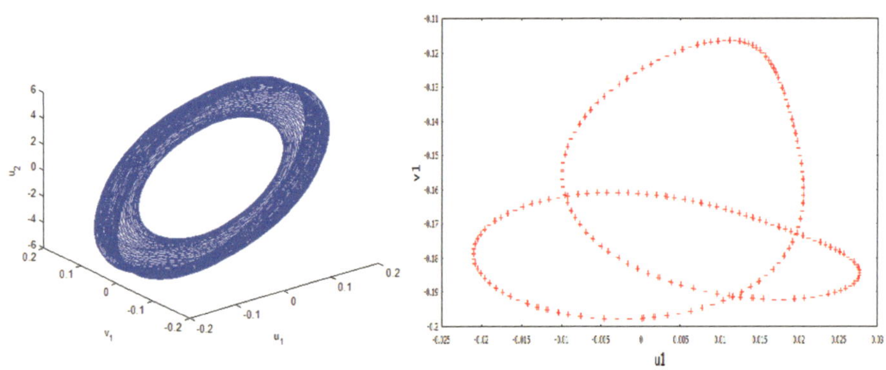

Figure 6. Phase portrait of system (17) and its section by the plane $u_1=0$, $g=0.0105$.

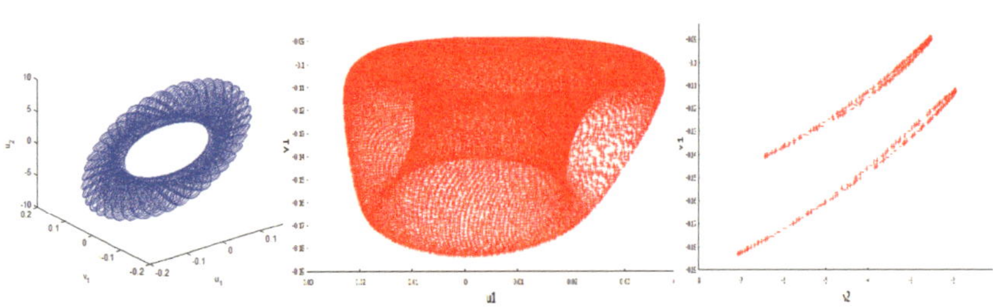

Figure 7. Phase portrait of system (17), its first section by the plane $u_1=0$ and second section by the plane $u_2=0$, $g=0.0139$.

4.3. Laminar-turbulent transition in Navier-Stokes equations

The problem of turbulence consists in explaining the nature of the disordered chaotic motion of a nonlinear continuous medium and in finding ways and methods of its adequate mathematical description. Originating more than a 100 years ago, the problem of turbulence is still one of the most complicated and most interesting problems in mathematical physics. It is in the list of seven mathematical millennium problems, named so by the Clay Institute of Mathematics [18]. In addition, the turbulence problem is formulated in the list of S.Smale's 18 most important mathematical problems of the twenty-first century [19]. The most important and interesting in the problem of turbulence is to elucidate the causes and mechanisms of chaos generation in a nonlinear continuous medium when passing from the laminar to the turbulent state. Currently, there are several mathematical models that claim to explain the mechanisms of generation of chaos and turbulence in nonlinear continuous media. The most famous among these models are: the Landau-Hopf model explaining turbulence by motion along an infinite-dimensional torus generated by an infinite cascade of Andronov-Hopf bifurcations; and the Ruelle-Takens model, which explains turbulence by moving along a strange attractor generated by the destruction of a three-dimensional torus. In recent years, the author and his pupils have proved (see [8, 9, 20–22]) that the universal bifurcation FShM mechanism for the transition to space-time chaos in nonlinear systems of partial differential equations through subharmonic cascades of bifurcations of stable cycles or two-dimensional and multi-dimensional tori also takes place in problems of laminar-turbulent transitions for Navier-Stokes equations

$$\begin{aligned} &\frac{\partial \vec{u}}{\partial t} + \left(\vec{u} \cdot \nabla\right) \vec{u} = -\nabla p + R^{-1} \Delta \vec{u} + \vec{f}, \\ &\nabla \vec{u} = 0, \end{aligned} \tag{19}$$

where R is the bifurcation parameter (Reynolds number). The existence of stable two-dimensional tori of doubled period and stable three-dimensional tori and their further bifurcations is established for the problem of fluid flow from the ledge [20]. The existence of subharmonic cascades of bifurcations of stable cycles and two-dimensional tori is established for Rayleigh-Benard convection in Ref. [21]. A numerically complete subharmonic cascade of bifurcations of stable two-dimensional tori is found up to a torus of period three in the famous Kolmogorov problem in two-dimensional and three-dimensional spatial cases [22]. The features of compressible flow and instabilities triggered by Kelvin-Helmholtz (KH) and Rayleigh-Taylor (RT) mechanisms are considered in Ref [9]. The Kelvin-Helmholtz instability is the instability of the shear layer, which is a tangential discontinuity for the inviscid liquid and which arises when there is a velocity difference at the interface of two liquids or when there is a velocity shift in one of the liquids. Rayleigh-Taylor instability is the instability of the boundary between two liquids, where a lighter liquid supports a heavier fluid in a gravitational or external potential field, the gradient vector of which is directed from the heavier liquid to the lighter one. Light fluid can also push heavier one. Those two instabilities are often considered together. Indeed, RT instability causes movement of adjusted fluids in different directions with the appearance of the shear layer that is subject to KH instability.

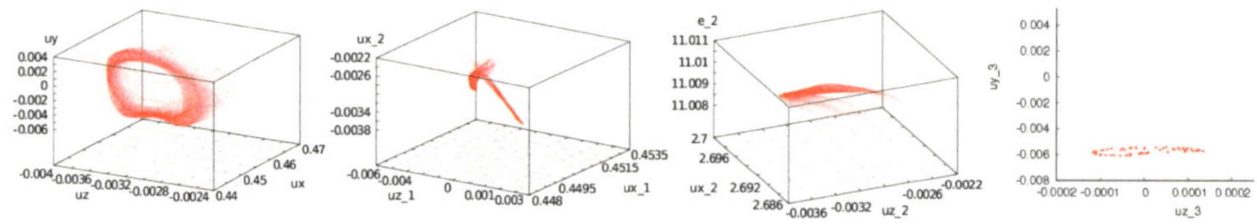

Figure 8. Projection of the invariant four-dimensional torus into three-dimensional phase subspace and sequential first, second and third sections in the phase space for $R = 520.5$ (left to right). Only parts of sections are shown.

In this chapter, we consider shortly the bifurcation scenario in coupled Kelvin-Helmholtz and Rayleigh-Taylor problem. This problem is solved in detail in Ref. [9]. We begin our consideration from the value of $R = 1$ for which the system has a stationary solution corresponding to a stable singular point in the phase space of solutions. Approximately for $R = 10.5$ the first bifurcation of the stationary solution occurs with the formation from the singular point of the stable limit cycle in the phase space of solutions. The next attractor that can be able to detect is the limited torus. Close resemblance to the cycle may indicate that this attractor was formed from the cycle as the result of Andronov-Hopf bifurcation. This indicates the existence of two irrational frequencies in the system. Further increase of the Reynolds number up to $R = 516$ resulted in the other Andronov-Hopf bifurcation with the formation of the three-dimensional invariant torus. This torus becomes singular (by period-doubling bifurcations along one of the frequencies). However this cascade of period-doubling bifurcations is reversed to the original 3D torus. The next bifurcation that could be traced at $R = 520.5$ is second Andronov-Hopf bifurcation leading to the formation of the four-dimensional invariant torus (**Figure 8**) . Further increase of the Reynolds number leads to the chaotic solution that corresponds to the dense field of points in phase subspace projections up to $R = 2100$. With the further increase of R, formation of inverse bifurcation cascades is observed. Thus, it seems reasonable, that there is no unified laminar-turbulent transition scenario in problems described by Navier-Stokes equations, it can be a cascade of stable limit cycles or cascade of stable two-dimensional or many dimensional tori, but all these scenarios lay in the frameworks of the FShM theory. However, the existence of computationally stable 4D invariant torus is a remarkable fact. It took $2.6 \cdot 10^9$ time samples to analyze and about 3.5 month to calculate this torus and its Poincare sections.

5. Conclusion

We make some general remarks on the chaotic dynamics of nonlinear systems of differential equations, since the very publication of papers [10, 11] and many similar papers, even in prestigious refereed journals, attests to a complete lack of understanding of the mechanism of transition to chaos in nonlinear systems of differential equations. In this chapter, on numerous examples, it is convincingly demonstrated that there exists one universal FShM bifurcation scenario of transition to chaos in all systems of nonlinear differential equations without exception: autonomous and nonautonomous, dissipative and conservative, ordinary, with partial derivatives and with delayed argument. All irregular attractors that arise during the implementation of this scenario are exclusively singular attractors. Each nonlinear system can have infinitely many different structurally unstable singular attractors for different values of the bifurcation parameter, which can enter implicitly into the equations of the system. Thus, neither the presence or absence of stable or unstable singular points in the system, nor the presence or absence of saddle-nodes or saddle-focuses, as well as homoclinic or heteroclinic separatrix contours, is not a criterion for the appearance of chaotic dynamics in the system. Also, neither the positivity of the senior Lyapunov exponent, nor the proof of existence of Smale's horseshoe, nor the KAM (Kolmogorov-Arnold-Moser) theory, nor the theory of RT (Ruelle-Takens), are such criteria either. The positivity of the Lyapunov exponent is purely a consequence of computational errors, because due to the presence of an everywhere dense set of nonperiodic trajectories, numerical motion is possible only over the whole region occupied by the trajectory of the singular attractor, and not along its trajectory itself. In addition, the Lyapunov exponent will also be positive when moving along a stable periodic trajectory of a large period in the vicinity of some singular attractor. The presence of Smale's horseshoe in the system testifies to the complex dynamics of the solutions, however, even in the neighborhood of the separatrix loop of saddle-focus, where by Shilnikov's theorem there exists an infinite number of Smale's horseshoes, the dynamics of solutions are determined not by horseshoes, but by a much more complex infinite set of unstable periodic solutions generated at all stages of all three cascades of bifurcations of the FShM scenario, whose homoclinic cascade of cycles ends in the limit precisely with the separatrix loop of saddle-focus. The only method that allows establishing reliably the presence of chaotic dynamics in the system is the numerical finding of stable cycles or tori of the FSM-cascades of bifurcations.

Acknowledgements

Paper is supported by Russian Foundation for Basic Research (grants 14-07-00116-a).

Author details

Nikolai A. Magnitskii

Address all correspondence to: nikmagn@gmail.com

Head of Laboratory, Federal Research Center "Informatics and Control", Institute for Systems Analysis of RAS, Moscow, Russia

References

[1] Magnitskii NA, Sidorov SV. New Methods for Chaotic Dynamics. Singapore: World Scientific; 2006

[2] Magnitskii NA, Sidorov SV. New Methods for Chaotic Dynamics. Moscow: URRS; 2004 (in Russian)

[3] Magnitskii NA. Universal theory of dynamical chaos in nonlinear dissipative systems of differential equations. Communications in Nonlinear Science and Numerical Simulation. 2008;**13**:416-433

[4] Magnitskii NA. New approach to analysis of Hamiltonian and conservative systems. Differential Equations. 2008;**44**(12):1682-1690

[5] Magnitskii NA. On topological structure of singular attractors. Differential Equations. 2010;**46**(11):1552-1560

[6] Magnitskii NA. Theory of Dynamical Chaos. Moscow: URSS; 2011 (in Russian)

[7] Magnitskii NA. Chapter 6: Universality of transition to chaos in all kinds of nonlinear differential equations. In: Nonlinearity, Bifurcation and Chaos - Theory and Applications. Intech; Croatia, 2012. p. 133-174

[8] Evstigneev NM, Magnitskii NA. Chapter 10: FSM scenarios of laminar-turbulent transition in incompressible fluids. In: Nonlinearity, Bifurcation and Chaos, Theory and Applications. Intech; Croatia, 2012. p. 251-280

[9] Evstigneev NM, Magnitskii NA. Chapter 2: Numerical analysis of laminar-turbulent bifurcation scenarios in Kelvin-Helmholtz and Rayleigh-Taylor instabilities for compressible flow. In: Turbulence Modelling Approaches - Current State, Development Prospects, Applications. Intech; 2017. p. 29-59

[10] Wang X, Chen GR. A chaotic system with only one stable equilibrium. Communications in Nonlinear Science and Numerical Simulation. 2012;**17**:1264-1272

[11] Huan S, Li Q, Yang X-S. Horseshoes in a chaotic system with only one stable equilibrium. International Journal of Bifurcation and Chaos. 2013;**23**(1):1350002

[12] Dubrovsky AD. Nature of chaos in conservative and dissipative systems of Duffing-Holmes oscillator. Differential Equations. 2010;**46**(11):1652-1656

[13] Burov DA, Golitsyn DL, Рябков OI. Research of transition from dissipative to conservative state in the two-dimentional nonlinear system of ordinary differential equations. Differential Equations. 2012;**48**(3):430-434

[14] Рябков OI. Structure of bifurcation diagram of two-dimensional nonautonomous nonlinear systems of differential equations with periodic right parts. In: Proceedings of 3 Int. Conf. "Systems analysis and Information Technologies", Zvenigorod, Russia, 2009. p. 106-115

[15] Karamisheva TV, Magnitskii NA (2014) Traveling waves, impulses and diffusion chaos in excitable media. Communications in Nonlinear Science and Numerical Simulation, v.19 (6), pp. 1742-1745

[16] Zaitseva MF, Magnitskii NA, Poburinnaya NB. Differential Equations. 2016;**52**(12):1585-1593

[17] Burov DA, Evstigneev NM, Magnitskii NA. On the chaotic dynamics in two coupled partial differential equations for evolution of surface plasmon polaritons. Communications in Nonlinear Science and Numerical Simulation. 2017;**46**:26-36

[18] Carlson A, Jaffe A, Wiles A, editors. The Millennium Prize Problems. Cambridge: Clay Mathematics Institute; 2006

[19] Sadovnichii VA, Simo S, editors. Modern Problems of Chaos and Nonlinearity. Moscow-Igevsk: Institute for Computational Studies; 2002

[20] Evstigneev NM, Magnitskii NA, Sidorov SV. On nature of laminar-turbulent flow in backward facing step problem. Differential Equations. 2009;**45**(1):69-73

[21] Evstigneev NM, Magnitskii NA, Sidorov SV. Nonlinear dynamics of laminar-turbulent transition in three dimensional Rayleigh-Benard convection. Communications in Nonlinear Science and Numerical Simulation. 2010;**15**:2851-2859

[22] Evstigneev NM, Magnitskii NA, Silaev DA. Qualitative analysis of dynamics in Kolmogorov problem on a flow of a viscous incompressible fluid. Differential Equations. 2015;**51**(10): 1292-1305

Chapter 12

Structural Analysis of Deterministic Mass Fractals Using Small-Angle Scattering and Lacunarity Techniques

Azat Mukhiddinuly Slyamov and
Eugen Mircea Anitas

Additional information is available at the end of the chapter

http://dx.doi.org/10.5772/intechopen.70885

Abstract

The structural characterization of deterministic mass fractals at nano- and microscales is presented in this chapter using two complementary techniques in both reciprocal and real spaces. In the former case, fractal and geometrical features are obtained from the small-angle scattering (SAS) (neutrons, X-rays, light) spectrum in the reciprocal space. The lacunarity technique is considered to extract structural properties and differentiate textures of fractals in real space. We present and discuss various types of mass fractals, such as thin and fat fractals, as well as fractals generated with the Chaos game representation (CGR). We show how the main structural properties of the fractals, such as the fractal dimension, the iteration number, the scaling factor, the overall size of the fractal, and the size of the basic units of the fractal, can be extracted by using SAS and lacunarity techniques.

Keywords: small-angle scattering (neutrons, X-ray, light), lacunarity, fractals, iterated function systems, chaos game

1. Introduction

Historically, the mathematical characterization of geometrical properties of objects has its roots in describing regular forms, such as circles, rectangles, spheres, or cuboids. However, most of the natural formations across the scales present fairly complex structures. The fractal geometry, in its turn, describes complex systems that completely or partially preserve their structure under a scale transformation. This property is often called self-similarity and is exhibited in many systems from macro to micro scales [1]. The development of fractal theory to describe natural systems was due to B. Mandelbrot, who was the first to introduce the term fractal from Latin "fractus" meaning "broken" [2]. However, naturally occurring fractals does not preserve self-similarity on all scales. For example, nano- and microfractals, at the bottom, are limited by the size of atoms and molecules and, at the top, by the size of the cluster/aggregate, etc.

Thus, fractals can be divided into two main classes: showing self-similarity at all scales (also known simply as fractals), and respectively showing self-similarity only on a finite range of scales. The latter ones are also known as pre-fractals but we refer to them as fractals to keep track with the common terminology in literature.

It is considered that one of the main properties that characterize the fractals is the fractal dimension [2, 3]. The fractal dimension D of any object can be defined by the minimal number $N(r)$ of the spheres of the radius r that are needed to cover the object, with the condition, that the spheres can penetrate each other and all points within the object are covered at least by one of the spheres. If the object is a fractal, then $N(r)$ has to satisfy the relation

$$N(r) = N_0 r^{-D}, \tag{1}$$

where N_0 is the constant. Applying that definition to the straight line or smooth surface shows that $D=1$ for the line and $D=2$ for the surface, because the number of spheres needed to cover a line is proportional to r^{-1} and to cover the surface, the number is proportional to r^{-2}. However, in the case of the fractals, D can take a noninteger value.

Several algorithms have been developed to generate various types of fractals, and roughly they can be divided into two types. Depending on the exact or statistical process involved in the construction algorithms, the obtained fractals may be deterministic (exact self-similar) or stochastic/random (statistically self-similar). Stochastically generated fractals have been proved as effective models for describing disordered systems, such as biological molecules, percolation clusters, diffusion-limited aggregates, etc. [4]. However, rapid progress in the field of materials science [5] allows creating exact deterministic fractal structures [6–9]. Since the influence of the fractal structure on the physical properties of the system is of significant research interest [11], investigations concerning structural properties of deterministic fractals have been recently suggested [14, 30, 31].

One of the most effective and representative methods for analyzing the structure of both mass [13] and surface [23] fractals, that provides information about the geometric and fractal properties of the sample in the reciprocal space is the small-angle scattering (SAS) (neutron, X-ray, light) [10, 11]. The main feature of the scattering from the mass fractals is the power-law behavior of exponent of the scattering intensity $I(q)$ and which gives the fractal dimension of the sample [12, 13]

$$I(q) \sim q^{D_m}, \tag{2}$$

where q is the momentum transfer and D_m is the mass fractal dimension of the sample. For surface fractals, the scattering exponent is $6 - D_s$, where D_s is the surface fractal dimension with $2 < D_s < 3$. Thus, in practice, if the absolute value of the measured scattering exponent is smaller than 3, the sample is a mass fractal with fractal dimension D_m, and if the exponent is between 3 and 4, the sample is a surface fractal with fractal dimension $6 - D_s$.

Although most of the modern fractal research techniques are aimed to analyze fractals according to their fractal dimensions [15, 16], such analysis does not directly provide complete information about the spatial arrangement of the mass inside the fractal. The ambiguity may

http://dx.doi.org/10.5772/intechopen.70885

arise from the fact that the particular value of the fractal dimension does not correspond to the unique fractal structure [2]. To deal with this issue, B. Mandelbrot introduced the notion of lacunarity (from Latin "lacuna" meaning "gap") that shows the inhomogeneity of the fractal structure by describing the spatial distribution of mass inside the fractal. This complementary method can be used to analyze real images obtained from SEM, MRI, CT, and other techniques [17, 18].

In this chapter, we present and discuss small-angle scattering and the lacunarity techniques for structural analysis of deterministic mass fractals. Discussion of structural properties of surface fractals [31] involves a separate analysis, which is beyond the scope of this chapter. These techniques are implemented to the deterministic mass fractals generated using iterated function systems (IFS) [19]. We also present the structural characterization of various types of mass fractals, such as fat fractals [20] and Chaos game representation (CGR) fractals [21]. We show how to extract from both methods the structural properties, such as the fractal dimension, the iteration number, the scaling factor, the sizes of units of the particular iteration, the sizes of the basic units, and the number of units composing the fractal.

2. Theoretical background

Structural characterization of the nano- and microscale systems is a rapidly developing field that has influenced many fundamental and applied research areas. The structure of nano- and microscale fractals are mainly obtained by using real space images or by scattering techniques operating in reciprocal space. In the following sections, we discuss the theoretical basics of both approaches.

2.1. Small-angle scattering

In a small-angle scattering experiment, beams of neutrons, X-rays, or light are generally used. A typical SAS experimental set-up is presented in **Figure 1** and consists of a source of monochromatic beam of particles with incident wave vector $\boldsymbol{k}_i$ that irradiates the sample. The particles with the wave vector $\boldsymbol{k}_f$ are scattered at the angle 2θ and are registered by the detector. The quantity measured is the differential cross-section per unit volume (for 3D samples) as a function of the momentum transfer or scattering vector $\boldsymbol{q} = \boldsymbol{k}_i - \boldsymbol{k}_f$ [11].

Let us suppose that the sample consists of identical units with the scattering length b_j. If $\boldsymbol{r}_j$ is the position vector of the fractal units, then the corresponding scattering length density (SLD) is

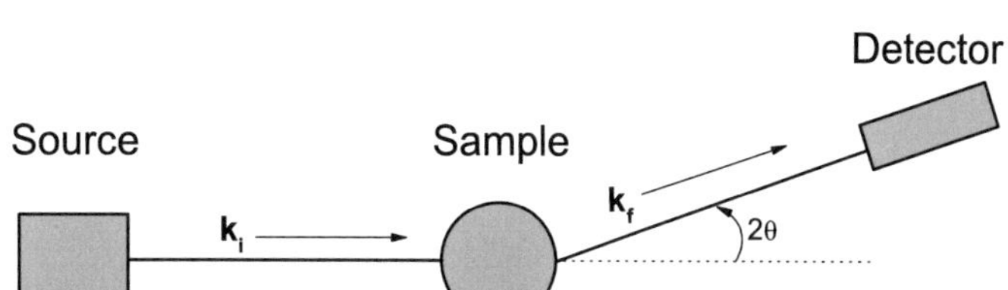

Figure 1. Schematic representation of the experimental small-angle scattering set-up.

$\rho_s(\mathbf{r}) = \sum_j b_j \delta(\mathbf{r} - \mathbf{r}_j)$, where δ is Dirac's delta function. If the particles have uniform SLD ρ_f and are placed in a matrix of SLD ρ_0, then the contrast will be given as $\Delta\rho = \rho - \rho_0$. The total scattering intensity in the case of two-dimensional fractal will be given by [11, 22]

$$I(q) \equiv \frac{1}{A'} \frac{d\sigma}{d\Omega} = n|\Delta\rho|^2 A^2 \left\langle |F(\boldsymbol{q})|^2 \right\rangle, \tag{3}$$

where n is the concentration of fractal, A and A' are the surface area of each fractal, and respectively of the irradiated area, $F(\boldsymbol{q}) \equiv (1/A)\int_A \exp(-i\boldsymbol{q} \cdot \boldsymbol{r})d\mathbf{r}$ is the normalized form factor, with $F(0) = 1$, $|F(\boldsymbol{q})|^2 = (1/4\pi) \int_0^\pi d\theta \sin\theta \int_0^{2\pi} d\phi |F(q, \theta, \phi)|^2$ is the averaging that takes into account the rotation of the fractals in a three-dimensional space, with equal probability.

Since for the construction of our models, we will use the IFS algorithm, defined in the next section, we shall compute the intensity spectrum starting from Debye formula [24]

$$I(q) = NI_s(q) + 2F_s(q)^2 \sum_{i=1}^{N-1} \sum_{j=i+1}^{N} \frac{\sin qr_{ij}}{qr_{ij}}, \tag{4}$$

where $I_s(q)$ and $F_s(q)$ are the scattered intensity and the form factor of each fractal unit, and r_{ij} is the distance between units i and j. However, the time consumption of the term $\sin(qr_{ij})/(qr_{ij})$ is increasing proportional to number of units, and even for modern computers the calculation of the scattering from few thousands of particles may take several hours. The problem can be resolved by introducing a pair-distance histogram $g(r)$ with a bin-width commensurate with the experimental resolution [25] and thus Eq. (4) can be rewritten as

$$I(q) = NI_s(q) + 2F_s^2(q) \sum_{i=1}^{N_{\text{bins}}} g(r_i) \frac{\sin qr_i}{qr_i}, \tag{5}$$

where $g(r_i)$ is the pair-distance histogram. We can consider $I_s(q) = F_s^2(q) = 1$ and then using normalization $I_0(q) = I(q)/N$, we obtain the following expression for the scattering intensity

$$I_0(q) = S(q) = 1 + \frac{2}{N} \sum_{i=1}^{N_{\text{bins}}} g(r_i) \frac{\sin qr_i}{qr_i}, \tag{6}$$

where $S(q)$ is called the structure factor, and it carries information about the structural properties of the samples. By using the last expression, we can easily implement it as a computational algorithm and to perform calculations few orders of magnitude faster.

2.2. Lacunarity

Lacunarity, as opposed to SAS, analyzes the objects in the real space. Nowadays, the technique is widely used in image analysis [26, 27]. The concept was introduced by Mandelbrot [2] in the context of characterizing the texture of the fractals. In this chapter, we present results obtained using probabilistic algorithm for estimating lacunarity based on differential box counting (DBC) due to its speed and simplicity in computational implementation. The algorithm was introduced by Voss in [28] and defines lacunarity as the entropy of the discreet pixels on the digital image of the fractal.

The algorithm begins by the consecutive covering of an image with the grid of nonoverlapping square boxes of the size r, as shown in **Figure 2**. The total number of boxes in the grid that cover the image is denoted as N. Then, the number of occupied boxes with M number of pixels (mass) inside, is determined as $n(M, r)$. The probability function that a box of size r contains M number of pixels is then defined by

$$P(M, r) = \frac{n(M, r)}{N}. \tag{7}$$

Statistical moments of $P(M, r)$ are defined as

$$Z^{(q)}(r) = \sum_{M=1}^{N} M^q P(M, r), \tag{8}$$

so $Z^{(1)}(r)$ and $Z^{(2)}(r)$ represent the mean of the occupied pixels and respectively, the variance. Thus, the lacunarity can be interpreted as the fluctuations of mass distribution over its mean

$$\Lambda(r) = \frac{Z^{(2)}(r) - \left(Z^{(1)}(r)\right)^2}{\left(Z^{(1)}(r)\right)^2}. \tag{9}$$

As it seen from the equation, Λ is increasing when the mean $Z(1)$ tends to 0, meaning that more clustered and inhomogeneous sets will have higher lacunarity. The lacunarity of the deterministic fractals shows periodicity in the spectrum [1]. As it will be shown in the next section, some structural properties of deterministic mass fractals can be extracted from such behavior.

Although, there are few definitions of lacunarity and several algorithms for its computation exist, we will use here an intuitive and elegant probabilistic approach, which is easily performed computationally ([28]). In spite of this simplicity, it has slight disadvantages in comparison with the gliding-box (GB) algorithm, which provides more precise and hence more time-consuming evaluations [29]. The GB algorithm calculates the lacunarity by placing

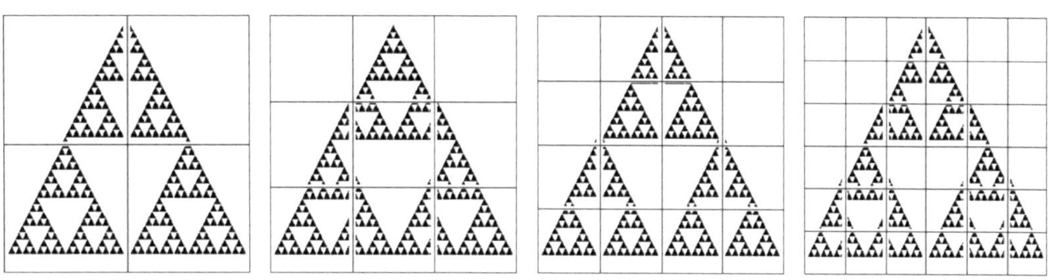

Figure 2. The process of covering the image with a grid of nonoverlaping boxes.

the square box of the size r in the corner of the image of the size L, and then glides the box pixel by pixel along horizontal and vertical directions, note that the box should not slide beyond the image. The number of boxes generated by GB algorithm in this case is $n_{GB}(r) = (L - r + 1)^2$. The DBC algorithm covers the image by a grid of boxes, and the number of such boxes is $n_{DBC}(r) = (L/r)^2$. When L and r are of the same order of magnitude, the difference in number of boxes for both algorithms is negligible, but when L is at least one order larger than r, the number of boxes will differ in two orders. Both algorithms calculate the number of pixels within the box, thus the computational time directly depends on the number of boxes.

3. Structural properties of mass fractals

In this section, we present the mathematical description of a very well-known fractal generating algorithm and discuss various types of fractals constructed using deterministic and random approaches.

3.1. Iterated function systems

There is no universal method to construct a fractal, but one of the most common algorithms to generate a large class of fractals is iterated function systems (IFS) [19]. The IFS image is defined as being the union of geometric transforms of itself. Rigorously, an IFS is a complete metric space $(\mathbf{X}, d)$ with a finite set of contraction mappings $w_n : \mathbf{X} \to \mathbf{X}$, and respective contractive factors s_n, $n = 1, 2, \cdots, N$.

By considering an IFS with contractive factor s, and $(\mathcal{H}(\mathbf{X}), h(d))$ as the space of nonempty compact subsets with the Hausdorff metric $h(d)$, the transformation $W : \mathcal{H}(\mathbf{X}) \to \mathcal{H}(\mathbf{X})$ are defined as

$$W(B) = \cup_{n=1}^{N} w_n(B), \forall B \in \mathcal{H}(\mathbf{X}). \tag{10}$$

The unique fixed point $A = \cup_{n=1}^{N} w_n(A), A \in \mathcal{H}(\mathbf{X})$ is given by $A = \lim_{m \to \infty} W^{\circ m}(B)$ for any$B \in \mathcal{H}(\mathbf{X})$, and the set A is called the *attractor* of the IFS [19].

The deterministic algorithm, which allows to find the attractor of an IFS, begins by choosing a compact set $A_0 \subset \mathbb{R}^2$, and then recursively A_m according to

$$A_m = \cup_{n=1}^{N} w_n(A_{m-1}), form = 1, 2, \cdots. \tag{11}$$

This process generates the sequence $\{A_m : m = 0, 1, \cdots\} \subset \mathcal{H}(\mathbf{X})$ that converges to the attractor of the IFS.

The random iteration algorithm begins by assigning the probability $p_n > 0$ to w_n for $n = 1, 2, \cdots, N$, where $\sum_{n=1}^{N} p_n = 1$.Then choosing a point $x_0 \in \mathbf{X}$ and then recursively,

$$x_k \in \{w_1(x_{k-1}), w_2(x_{k-1}) \cdots, w_N(x_{k-1})\}, \tag{12}$$

where the probability of the event $x_k = w_n(x_{k-1})$ is p_n, and $k = 1, 2, \cdots$. This process generates the sequence $\{x_k : k = 0, 1, \cdots\} \subset \mathbf{X}$ that converges to the attractor of the IFS.

For a two-dimensional fractal, an IFS can be represented in the matrix form as

$$w_i \begin{bmatrix} x \\ y \end{bmatrix} = \begin{bmatrix} \mathrm{a}_i & \mathrm{b}_i \\ \mathrm{c}_i & \mathrm{d}_i \end{bmatrix} \begin{bmatrix} x \\ y \end{bmatrix} + \begin{bmatrix} \mathrm{e}_i \\ \mathrm{f}_i \end{bmatrix} \tag{13}$$

where a_i, b_i, c_i, d_i, and e_i, f_i with $i=1, 2, \ldots, n$ are the transformation and translation coefficients of the contraction mapping.

3.2. Deterministically generated fractals

Let us consider a model that at the iteration number $m=0$ starts with the disk inscribed in the square of the side length a_0, situated at the origin (initiator). Then, in order to obtain the fractal structure, we establish the rule of evolution (generator) [30, 31], shown in **Figure 3**. The rule is the following: scale the initial disk by the factor of $\beta_s=1/3$ and make four copies of it, so the length size of the squares in which the disks at $m=1$ are inscribed as $a_1=a_0\beta_s$. Then, translate the obtained circles so that they are situated in the vertices of a square. To generate the structure of the fractal repeat the same rule for each new circle.

The size of the units at m – th iteration is $a_m = \beta_s^m a_0$ and the number of the units is $N_m = 4^m$. The fractal that we obtain is a Cantor fractal.The corresponding IFS coefficients of the contraction mappings that generate this fractal are presented in **Table 1**.

The fractal dimension of Cantor-like fractal is determined by [2]

$$D = \lim_{m\to\infty} \frac{\log N_m}{\log\left(a/a_m\right)} \approx 1.26, \tag{14}$$

where N_m and a_m are the number of units and their side length at m-th iteration. As it can be seen, the value of the fractal dimension depends on how many copies are created at each iteration, (in the terms of IFS, the number of the contraction mappings) and on the scaling factor. However, the fractal dimension is completely independent on the translations of the copies, and its value can be the same for different textures, as for the models shown in **Figure 4** for which the translation coefficients of one of the contraction mappings have different values, presented in **Table 2**. Note that the transformation coefficients of the fractals presented in **Figure 5** are not modified.

In order to differentiate textures of the above mass-fractal models, we consider them as the square digital images with the side length $L=300$ pixels. We calculate the lacunarity spectra according to Eq. (9). The results are shown in the left part of **Figure 6**. At first, one can find that

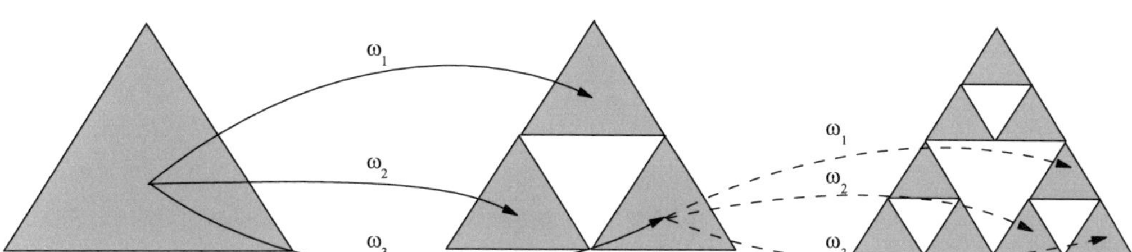

Figure 3. Graphical representation of the contraction mappings of IFS.

the fractal-d has the highest value of the lacunarity along all ranges, which is due to the most inhomogeneous and clustered distribution of the mass among all four models. On the contrary, the texture of the fractal-a has uniformly distributed mass and thus, the lowest lacunarity.

In addition to differentiating the texture, the lacunarity analysis also may reveal some geometrical and fractal properties. For example, when one covers the fractal by the boxes of the exact size as the size of its elements at the particular iteration *m*, the number of empty boxes takes maximum value. This leads to the highest variation in the mass distribution over the mean and the lacunarity at this scale will increase. The number of such maxima (denoted by vertical lines in **Figure 6**, left part) shows the iteration number of the fractal. The positions of these maxima reveal the size of the units at particular iteration, and from the periodicity of such maxima, one can obtain the scaling factor.

w	a	b	c	d	e	f
1	1/3	0	0	1/3	1/3	1/3
2	1/3	0	0	1/3	−1/3	1/3
3	1/3	0	0	1/3	1/3	−1/3
4	1/3	0	0	1/3	−1/3	−1/3

Table 1. IFS parameters of the Cantor-like fractal construction

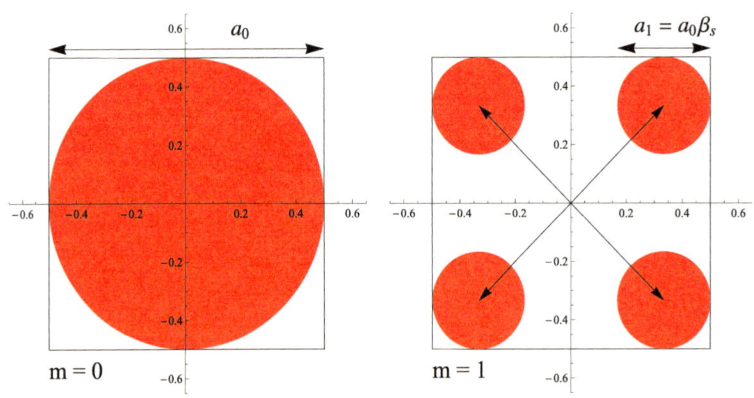

Figure 4. The rule of the deterministic mass-fractal construction.

	e	f
Fractal-a	1/3	1/3
Fractal-b	−1/3	0
Fractal-c	0	0
Fractal-d	−1/3	0

Table 2. Translation coefficients of one of the contraction mappings of the Cantor-like fractals construction

http://dx.doi.org/10.5772/intechopen.70885

The SAS data, on the other hand, gives information about structure in the reciprocal space. The typical SAS spectrum consists of the region with a constant intensity at small values of q which is called Guinier region. The rightmost part of the region shows the overall size of the fractal as $q = 2\pi/a$, where a is the side length of the fractal. A main feature of the SAS from fractals is that

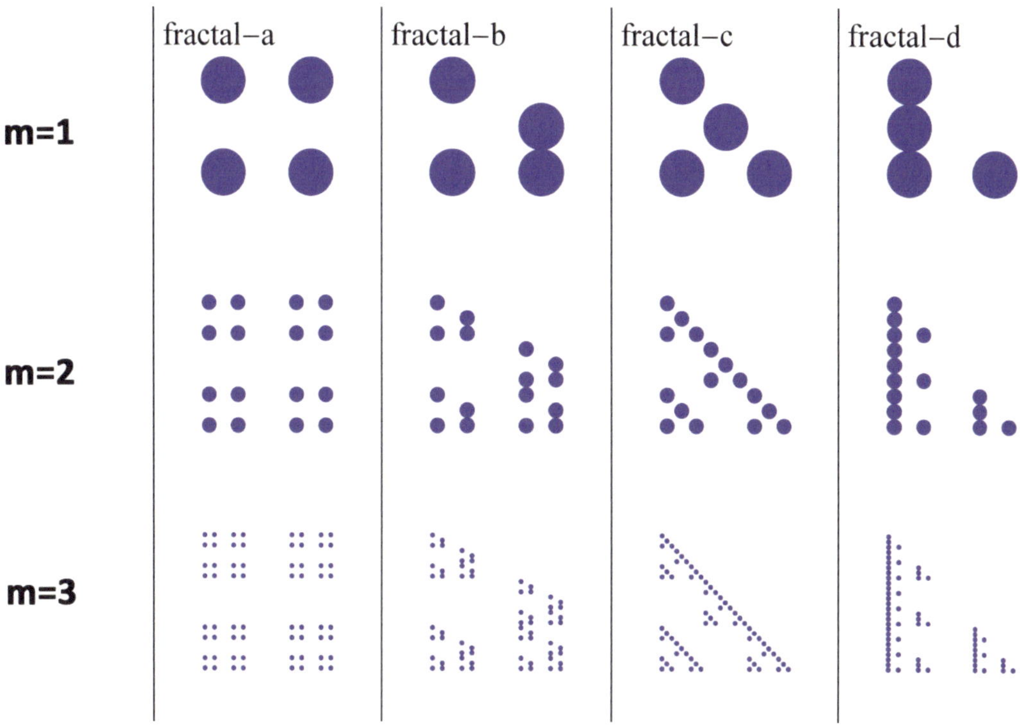

Figure 5. Construction of the deterministic Cantor-like mass fractals up to third iteration m = 3.

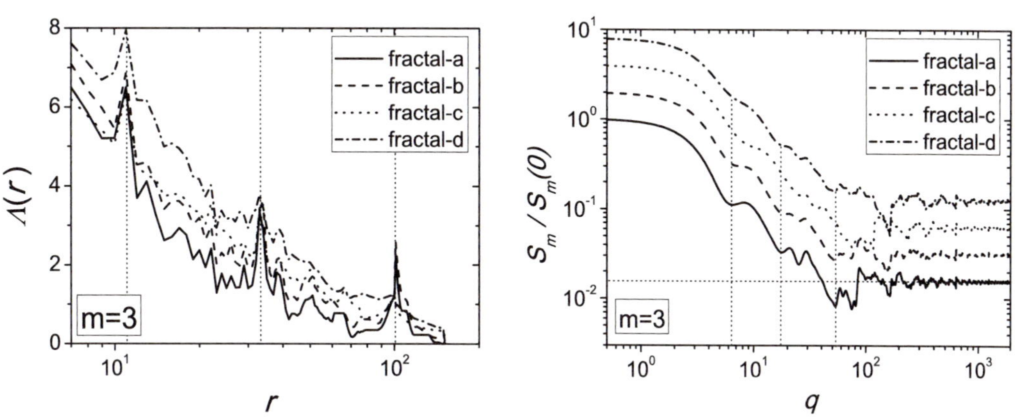

Figure 6. Left part: lacunarity spectra for the iteration number m = 3 of the deterministic mass-fractal models; right part: Scattering intensities for the iteration number m = 3 of the deterministic mass-fractal models. The values of the scattering intensities for the fractals -b, -c and -d are scaled up for clarity by the factor 2, 4, and 8, respectively.

the slope in the region that immediately follows the Guinier regime, so-called fractal region, gives the fractal dimension of the fractal, as discussed in the Introduction section. The number of the most pronounced minima in this region (denoted by vertical lines in **Figure 6**, right part) indicates the iteration number and the last minimum indicates the size of basic units as $q = 2\pi/\beta_s^m a$. The scaling factor of the fractal can be obtained from the periodicity of the minima [14]. Additionally, the asymptotic behavior of SAS spectrum at high values of q provides the information about number of basic units N_m at particular iteration [14].

A more general way to construct fractals may be thought in a framework of fat fractals, when the scaling factor is not constant but it depends on the iteration number [20, 32]. Here, we present a simple model of the fat fractal, represented by a two-dimensional deterministic Cantor-like mass fractal, as shown in **Figure 7**. In the presented model, the first two iterations $m=0$ and $m=1$ of construction of the Cantor-like fat fractal coincide with the structure of ordinary (thin) Cantor-like fractal, which obeys the rule from the **Figure 4**. To obtain the fat fractal, a modification of the algorithm used at iteration $m=1$ with the scaling factor $\beta_s^{(1)}$ must be done, by choosing another scaling factor $\beta_s^{(2)}$ at $m=2$. The superscript index (…) denotes to which iteration number the scaling factor belongs. In the suggested model shown in **Figure 7**, $\beta_s^{(1)} = 1/3$ and $\beta_s^{(2)} = 2/5$. It is clear from the construction that the regular version of the fractal is recovered when the scaling factors, at each iteration, are chosen to be equal $\beta_s^{(1)} = \beta_s^{(2)}$. The fat fractal does not have a unique value of the fractal dimension at every scale, since the scaling factor is not constant. The comparison of the SAS and the lacunarity spectra between thin and fat fractal models is demonstrated in **Figure 8**.

Here, we consider the square image from **Figure 7** with the side length $L=360$ pixels and the size of the fractal on the image coincides with the size of the image $a_0=L$. The rightmost maxima on the lacunarity spectrum from **Figure 8** left part, show the sizes of units $a_1 = \beta_s^{(1)} a_0$ at $m=1$, that coincide for both fat and thin fractals. The difference begins to be observed on the scale of the size of the fat fractal units (black disks) $a_2^{fat} = \beta_s^{(2)} a_1$; the left highest maximum shows the sizes of the units of thin fractal $a_2 = \beta_s^{(1)} a_1$ at $m=2$. As expected, the lacunarity of fat fractal, which occupies more space than thin has lower values in the range $r \le a_2^{fat}$. In the lacunarity obtained

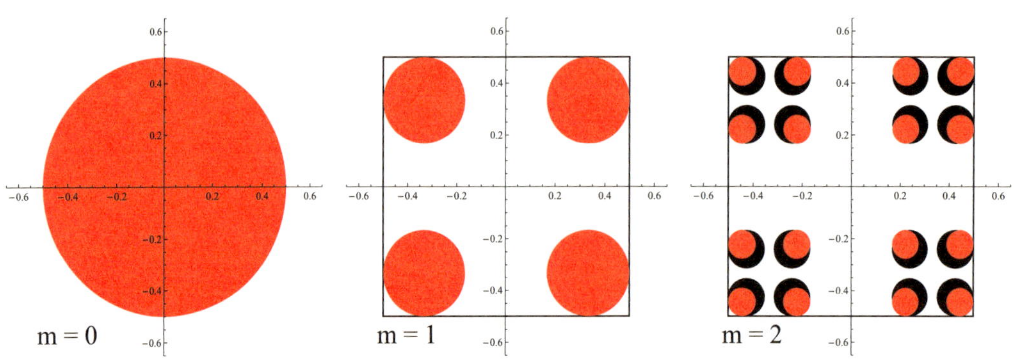

Figure 7. Construction of the Cantor-like fat fractal.

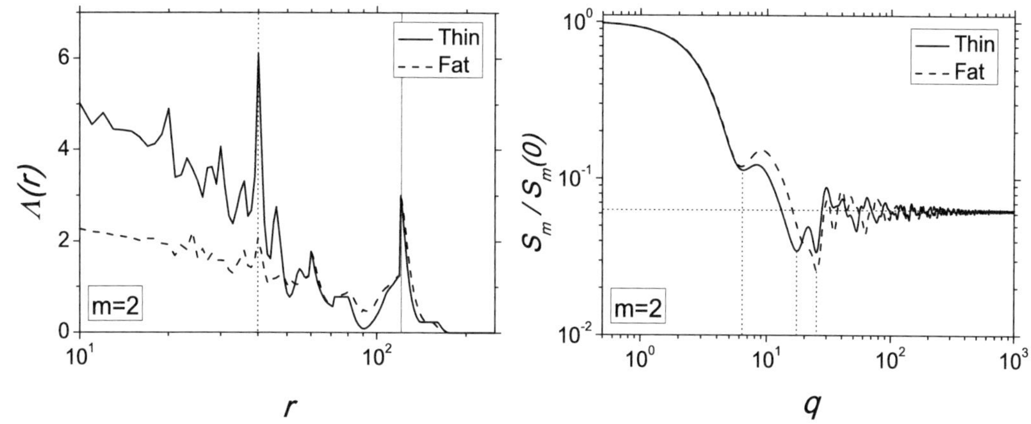

Figure 8. Left part: lacunarity spectra of thin and fat Cantor-like fractals at iteration number m = 2; right part: structure factor of thin and fat Cantor-like fractals at iteration number m = 2.

using DBC, we may not observe the maximum which corresponds to the size of fat fractal units $a_2^{fat} = \beta_s^{(2)} a_1^{fat}$ at iteration $m = 2$. However, such problem may be addressed using the gliding-box approach [29].

In the SAS spectrum, the difference between fat and thin fractals may be determined in the fractal region, from the different position of the minima, which correspond to the most common distance between units of the fractal. In the case of the fat fractal the most common distance is shorter than in the case of thin one, thus in the reciprocal space we observe a minimum corresponding to fat fractal, which is shifted to higher value of q. The behavior of scattering curves of both fat and thin fractals is similar at Guinier and asymptotic regions due to the same overall size and equals the number of units.

3.3. Stochastically generated fractals

One of the most known stochastic algorithms for the construction of the fractals is the Chaos game representation (CGR) [19], which is based on the random IFS. The CGR approach allows one to visually reconstruct a great number of the different types of fractals, from well-known deterministic fractals to various classes of disordered systems. Technically, CGR is an iterative map that generates the position of units, which cover the attractor of IFS, the image of the fractal. CGR algorithm is very convenient for structural investigations using SAS, because it generates directly the coordinates of the scatters, which can be used in the optimized Debye formula [25].

Here we are interested, how the set of the points generated using the CGR approach will recover the structure of the deterministic fractal. In order to quantitatively analyze the similarities and the differences in the structure of the fractals obtained by both algorithms, we calculate corresponding SAS and lacunarity spectra. In **Figure 9** are presented the deterministic and the CGR Cantor fractals. The well-known Cantor fractal is constructed by dividing the square of the side length a_0 into nine smaller squares with side $a_1 = \beta_s a_0$, and removing

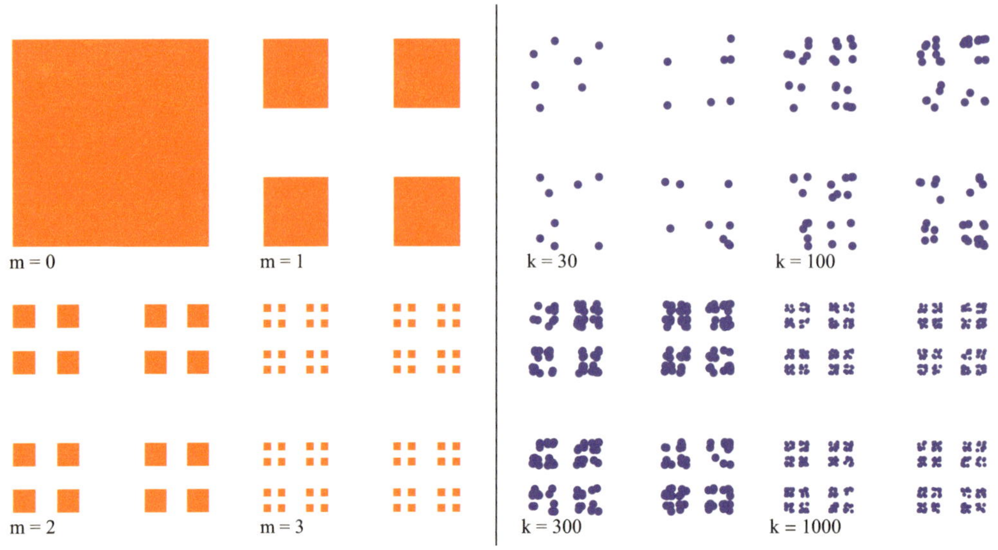

Figure 9. Right part: CGR of Cantor fractal at number of generated points k = 30,100,300, and 1000; left part; deterministic Cantor fractal at iterations m = 0, 1, 2, and 3.

consecutive five noncorner squares. The CGR Cantor fractal is generated using random IFS, with equal probability of choosing one of the contraction mappings presented in **Table 1**.

It is seen from **Figure 9** that the CGR Cantor fractal approaches the structure of the deterministic Cantor fractal with increasing the number of generated points (scattering units) k. To determine the number of generated points in the CGR algorithm needed to obtain the approximation of the deterministic Cantor fractal, we compare the particular iteration, the structure factor, and the lacunarity of the deterministic fractal, and the structure generated from CGR, respectively. Numerically, we calculate the small-angle scattering and the lacunarity spectra for the CGR algorithm at $k = 1000$ and the deterministic Cantor fractal at $m = 3$. The results are shown in **Figure 10**. The left part of the figure shows almost perfect agreement of the spectra of lacunarity. The number of the maxima in the spectrum of the CGR Cantor fractal shows that $k = 1000$ is enough to reconstruct the deterministic fractal at $m = 3$. The positions of the maxima show the sizes of the points in CGR and the sizes of the units at m-th iteration for deterministic fractal. Note that the size of the points of CGR algorithm is kept constant for any k. In general, the lacunarity has dependence on the sizes of the points, the larger points leading to smaller gaps and to lower lacunarity.

The SAS spectrum shows the approximation of the structure factors of CGR to deterministic algorithms. The Guinier regions coincide, showing that the overall sizes of the CGR and deterministic fractal are the same. The scattering curves almost completely overlap each other in the intermediate region, except the last minimum. The values of the slopes of the curves, which reveal the fractal dimension is approximately the same. The positions of the minima also coincide for both algorithms. Moreover, the SAS data shows that generating a number of $k = 1000$ points can reconstruct more than three iterations of the deterministic structure [21].

http://dx.doi.org/10.5772/intechopen.70885

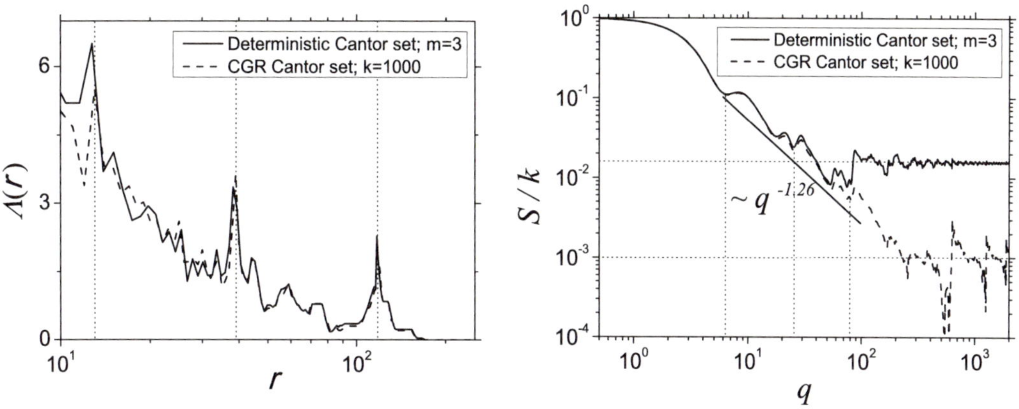

Figure 10. Left part: lacunarity spectra of deterministic and CGR Cantor fractal; right part: structure factor of deterministic and CGR Cantor fractal.

Different behavior of the curves in the asymptotic region indicates that the number of elements is not the same, $1/N_m$ for the deterministic and $1/k$ for the CGR algorithms.

In the last part of this section, we present a structural analysis of two well-known fractals generated using CGR. As a first example, we consider the pentaflake fractal, which is a single scale fractal, as shown in **Figure 11**. The pentaflake is generated using CGR, with the IFS parameters presented in **Table 3** for $k = 4000$ with the scaling factor $\beta_s = 0.38$. Thus, the fractal dimension is

$$D \approx -\log 5/\log 0.38 \simeq 1.67. \tag{15}$$

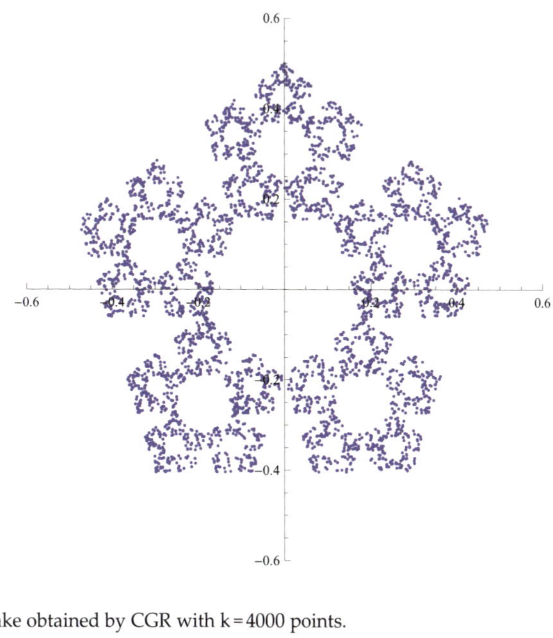

Figure 11. Fractal pentaflake obtained by CGR with k = 4000 points.

w	a	b	c	d	e	f
1	0.38	0	0	0.38	0	0.3
2	0.38	0	0	0.38	0.3	0.1
3	0.38	0	0	0.38	−0.3	0.1
4	0.38	0	0	0.38	−0.185	−0.25
5	0.38	0	0	0.38	0.185	−0.25

Table 3. IFS parameters of the pentaflake fractal construction

The corresponding structure factor of the pentaflake fractal is calculated using Eq. (6) and the lacunarity spectrum using Eq. (9). The results are shown in **Figure 12**. As in the case of the CGR Cantor fractal, all the main features of SAS from CGR pentaflake are presented in the spectrum and the numerical value of the fractal dimension coincides with the theoretical one given by Eq. (15). The periodicity of the positions of minima in the fractal region shows the value of the scaling factor $\beta_s = 0.38$, and this is a specific feature of scattering from fractals with a single scale [14, 32]. As expected, the lacunarity spectrum of the image of the pentaflake fractal gives the information about the scaling factor from the periodicity of the most pronounced maxima, the iteration number, and corresponding sizes of the units.

The CGR approach is often used to represent the structural properties of the DNA sequence, which exhibits the multi-scale fractal structure [21, 33]. As a second example, we consider that the four bases *"A"*, *"C"*, *"G"*, and*"T"* (or*"U"*) of DNA sequences may be expressed by the four contraction mappings of the random IFS, presented in the **Table 4**. Generating the CGR with a few thousand points, one can obtain the graphical representation of the DNA sequence clearly showing fractal patterns (**Figure 13**).

The number of genetic sequences is found with the missing subsequences, and the CGR approach can provide the visual representation of such patterns. The CGR algorithm can

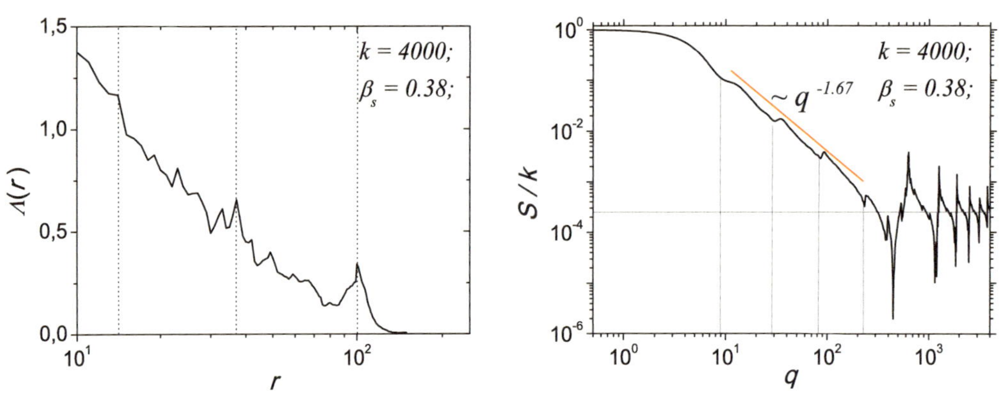

Figure 12. Left part: the lacunarity of pentaflake fractal; right part: the structure factor of pentaflake fractal.

http://dx.doi.org/10.5772/intechopen.70885

w	a	b	c	d	e	f
A	0.5	0	0	0.5	−0.5	−0.5
C	0.5	0	0	0.5	−0.5	0.5
G	0.5	0	0	0.5	0.5	0.5
T	0.5	0	0	0.5	0.5	−0.5

Table 4. IFS parameters of the DNA sequence

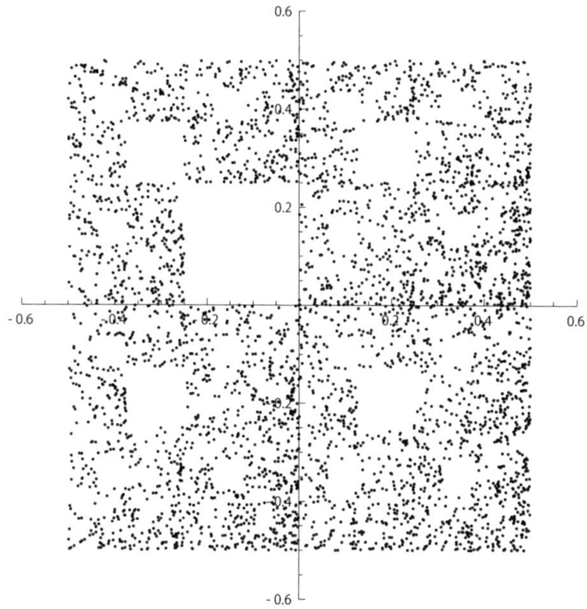

Figure 13. A CGR of the DNA with k = 4000 moves in the ACGT square when the sequence GC is eliminated.

restrict some of the moves of chaos game [33]. **Figure 13** shows the CGR in the square $ACGT$ of $k = 4000$ bases, with the eliminated sequence GC.

By considering the positions of the bases in the **Figure 13** as the coordinates that are used in Eq. (6), we can compute the corresponding SAS spectrum. The structural properties, such as the overall size of the fractal, the fractal dimension, and the number of units are obtained from the Guinier, the fractal, and from the asymptotic regions, respectively. Although in the scattering from the CGR fractals, we can observe a succession in the minima in the fractal region, as it was the case for the Cantor and the pentaflake fractals, for the DNA these minima are smeared out. Thus, for DNA fractals, the iteration and the scaling factor can hardly be recovered.

This feature may indicate the existence of the multi-fractal structure in the CGR of DNA sequence [3]. Multi-scale fractals are characterized by the presence of different (multiple) scaling factors for some of the fractal units and they cannot be obtained directly from the SAS spectrum. However, as we can see from the left part of **Figure 14**, the lacunarity spectrum of

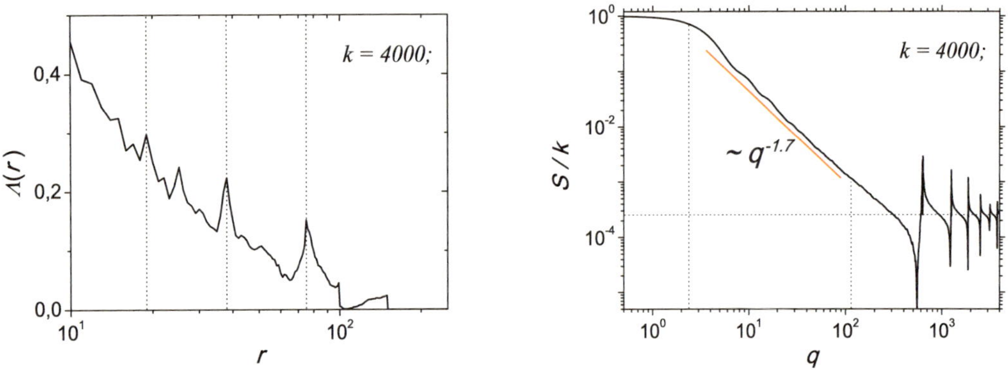

Figure 14. Left part: the lacunarity of the CGR DNA with 4000 moves; right part: the structure factor of the CGR DNA with 4000 moves.

the image of the CGR of the DNA sequence can reveal at least one of the scaling factors that belong to the major part of units. The size of the image of the CGR of the DNA is considered to have the length $L=320$ pixels. The maxima on the lacunarity spectrum correspond to the sizes of the gaps inside the image, and the maxima that show the periodicity in their behavior can reveal the scaling factors of the multi-fractal. Thus, the lacunarity technique can be used as the complementary analysis of the structural properties of multi-fractals.

4. Conclusions

In this chapter, we presented the structural characterization of deterministic mass fractals. The small-angle scattering and the lacunarity techniques are considered as complementary methods to analyze the structure of the nano- and microscale fractals. We present the theoretical foundations of both techniques, and show how they can be implemented in the investigating morphology of the fractals. The analysis is performed using an intuitive and an efficient implementation of Pantos and box-counting algorithms for calculating the spectra of the small-angle scattering and, the lacunarity, respectively.

The mathematical description of the general algorithm for the construction of the fractals, the iterated function systems (IFS) is explained. We show how to generate various types of the fractals, such as thin and fat fractals using deterministic IFS algorithm. We explain the difference in the construction of both models. Also the stochastic (random) IFS algorithm, the Chaos game representation (CGR) is used to reconstruct the structure of the deterministic fractal. The comparison of the structural characteristics of the CGR fractal with the deterministic one is presented.

For each introduced model, we calculate the scattering and the lacunarity spectrum, and we explain how to extract the main fractal and geometrical properties such as the fractal dimension, the iteration number, the scaling factor, the overall size, the sizes of the basic units, and the number of units in the system.

Author details

Azat Mukhiddinuly Slyamov[1,2] and Eugen Mircea Anitas[1,3]*

*Address all correspondence to: eanitasro@yahoo.com

1 Joint Institute for Nuclear Research, Dubna, Russian Federation

2 Institute of Nuclear Physics, Almaty, Kazakhstan

3 Horia Hulubei National Institute of Physics and Nuclear Engineering, Bucharest, Romania

References

[1] Gouyet J-F, Mandelbrot B. Physics and Fractal Structures. Paris: Masson; 1996

[2] Mandelbrot BB, Pignoni R. The Fractal Geometry of Nature. Vol. 173. New York: WH Freeman; 1983

[3] Falconer K. Fractal Geometry: Mathematical Foundations and Applications. Chichester: Wiley; 2004

[4] Vicsek T, Gould H. Fractal growth phenomena. Computers in Physics. 1989;**3**(5):108-108. DOI: 10.1063/1.4822864

[5] Shang J, Wang Y, Chen M, Dai J, Zhou X, Kuttner J, Hilt G, Shao X, Wu K. Assembling molecular Sierpiński triangle fractals. Nature Chemistry. 2015;**7**(5):389-393

[6] Newkome GR, Wang P, Moorefield CN, Cho TJ, Mohapatra PP, Li S, Hwang SH, Lukoyanova O, Echegoyen L, Palagallo JA, Iancu V, Hla SW. Nanoassembly of a fractal polymer: A molecular "Sierpinski Hexagonal Gasket". Science. 2006;**312**:1782-1785. DOI: 10.1126/science.1125894

[7] Cerofolini GF, Narducci D, Amato P, Romano E. Fractal Nanotechnology. Nanoscale Research Letters. 2008;**3**:381-385. DOI: 10.1007/s11671-008-9170-0

[8] Mayama H, Tsuji K. Menger sponge-like fractal body created by a novel template method. The Journal of Chemical Physics. 2006;**125**:124706. DOI: 10.1063/1.2336200

[9] Berenschot EJW, Jansen HV, Tas NR. Fabrication of 3D fractal structures using nanoscale anisotropic etching of single crystalline silicon. Journal of Micromechanics and Microengineering. 2013;**23**:055024. DOI: 10.1088/0960-1317/23/5/055024

[10] Feigin LA, Svergun DI. Structure Analysis by Small-Angle X-Ray and Neutron Scattering. New York: Plenum Press; 1987

[11] Brumberger H, editor. Modern Aspects of Small-Angle Scattering. Vol. 451. New York: Springer; 2013

[12] Martin JE. Scattering exponents for polydisperse surface and mass fractals. Journal of Applied Crystallography. 1988;**19**(1):25-27. DOI: 10.1107/S0021889886090052

[13] Teixeira J. Small-angle scattering by fractal systems. Journal of Applied Crystallography. 1988;**21**(6):781-785. DOI: 10.1107/S0021889888000263

[14] Cherny AY, Anitas EM, Osipov VA, Kuklin AI. Deterministic fractals: Extracting additional information from small-angle scattering data. Physical Review E. 2011;**83**:036203

[15] Sarkar N, Chaudhuri BB. An efficient differential box-counting approach to compute fractal dimension of image. IEEE Transactions on Systems, Man, and Cybernetics. 1994; **24**(1):115-120. DOI: 10.1109/21.259692

[16] Tolle C, McJunkin T, Gorsich D. Suboptimal minimum cluster volume cover-based method for measuring fractal dimension. IEEE Transactions on Pattern Analysis and Machine Intelligence. 2003;**25**:32-41

[17] Dougherty G, Henebry G. Fractal signature and lacunarity in the measurement of the texture of trabecular bone in clinical CT images. Medical Engineering & Physics. 2001;**23**: 369-380

[18] Utrilla-Coello RG et al. Microstructure of retrograded starch: Quantification from lacunarity analysis of SEM micrographs. Journal of Food Engineering. 2013;**116**:775-781

[19] Barnsley MF. Fractals Everywhere. London: Academic Press; 2014

[20] Anitas EM, Slyamov A, Todoran R, Szakacs Z. Small-angle scattering from nanoscale fat fractals. Nanoscale Research Letters. 2017;**12**:389

[21] Anitas EM, Slyamov A. Structural characterization of chaos game fractals using small-angle scattering analysis. PLoS One. 2017;**12**(7):e0181385

[22] Schmidt PW. Small-angle scattering studies of disordered, porous and fractal systems. Journal of Applied Crystallography. 1991;**24**:414-435. DOI: 10.1107/S0021889891003400

[23] Bale HD, Schmidt PW. Small-angle X-ray-scattering investigation of submicroscopic porosity with fractal properties. Physical Review Letters. 1984;**53**:596

[24] Debye P. Zerstreuung von röntgenstrahlen. Annalen der Physik. 1915;**351**(6):809-823

[25] Pantos E, Garderen HF v, Hilbers PAJ, Beelen TPM, Santen RA v. Simulation of small-angle scattering from large assemblies of multi-type scatterer particles. Journal of Molecular Structure. 1996;**383**:303-308

[26] Tolle C, McJunkin T, Rohrbough D, LaViolette R. Lacunarity definition for ramified data sets based on optimal cover. Physica D: Nonlinear Phenomena. 2003;**179**:129-152

[27] Plotnick R, Gardner R, Hargrove W, Preestegaard K, Perlmutter M. Lacunarity analysis: A general technique for the analysis of spatial patterns. Physical Review E. 1996;**53**:5461-5468

[28] Voss R. Characterization and measurement of random fractals. Physica Scripta. 1986;**13**: 27-32

[29] Allain C, Cloitre M. Characterizing the lacunarity of random and deterministic fractal sets. Physical Review A. 1991;**44**:3552-3558

[30] Cherny AY, Anitas EM, Osipov VA, Kuklin AI. Small-angle scattering from multiphase fractals. Journal of Applied Crystallography. 2014;**47**:198-206. DOI: 10.1107/S1600576713029956

[31] Cherny AY, Anitas EM, Osipov VA, Kuklin AI. Small-angle scattering from the Cantor surface fractal on the plane and the Koch snowflake. Physical Chemistry Chemical Physics. 2017;**19**:2261-2268

[32] Anitas EM. Small-angle scattering from fat fractals. The European Physical Journal B. 2014;**87**:139

[33] Jeffrey HJ. Chaos game representation of gene structure. Nucleic Acids Research. 1990;**18**(8): 2163-2170. DOI: 10.1093/nar/18.8.2163

Chapter 13

Private Communications Using Optical Chaos

Valerio Annovazzi-Lodi, Giuseppe Aromataris and
Mauro Benedetti

Additional information is available at the end of the chapter

http://dx.doi.org/10.5772/intechopen.70896

Abstract

After a brief summary of the basic methods for secure transmission using optical chaos, we report on most recent achievements, namely, on the comparison between the standard two-laser and the three-laser schemes and on the network architecture for multiuser secure transmission. From our investigations, we found that while both the basic two-laser and the three-laser schemes are suitable to secure data exchange, the three-laser scheme offers a better level of privacy due to its symmetrical topology. Moreover, while transmission based on optical chaos is usually restricted to point-to-point interconnections, a more advanced solution, derived from the well-known public key cryptography, allows for private message transmission between any couple of subscribers in a network.

Keywords: chaos, cryptography, steganography, laser, telecommunications, synchronization

1. Introduction

Chaos [1] is a widely studied regime of many nonlinear systems, which exhibit pseudorandom oscillations, strongly depending on starting conditions and parameter values. Several chaotic systems have been investigated and implemented in optics [2, 3]. For example, a semiconductor laser may be routed to chaos by injection from another source or simply by reflection or diffusion from an external optical element. In the last years, several chaos applications have been proposed in the telecommunication field. Among them, private communication using chaotic waveforms fully exploits the characteristic of chaos of being deterministic, exhibiting, however, a strong dependence on even minimal variations of the system parameters.

The basic approach to chaos secured data transmission consists in hiding or coding a message into the very complex noise-like waveform generated by a chaotic laser [4, 5].

In most schemes, chaos generation is based on delayed optical feedback, that is, on reflection of a fraction of the laser emission back into its cavity by an external mirror or even from the tip of the output fiber [4–7]. With this approach, we can select different chaos characteristics, such as amplitude and bandwidth, by acting on the mirror or fiber position. Using standard distributed feedback laser (DFB) telecommunication lasers, complex and robust chaotic waveforms can be generated, which modulate the laser on a large bandwidth, well in excess of its relaxation frequency.

A suitable method of chaotic transmission consists of simply superposing chaos to the message at the transmitter (Tx), in order to strongly reduce its signal-to-noise ratio (SNR). The composite signal is transmitted through the fiber link, and if the message is small enough, it is efficiently hidden both in the time and in the frequency domain. In well-designed systems, it cannot be extracted, neither by filtering nor by using a correlator.

In most cases, message recovery is performed by master/slave synchronization; at the receiver (Rx), another laser (the slave, SL) is used, having parameters very well matched with those of the transmitter laser (the master, MS). The waveform from the optical link (chaos + message) is injected into the slave. Under proper operating conditions, the slave laser is forced to synchronize to the chaos of the MS (i.e., the two devices generate almost exactly the same chaotic waveform), without, however, synchronizing the message. In other words, the SL behaves as a nonlinear "chaos-pass," "message-stop," filter. Thus, the message can be extracted by making the difference between the received composite signal and the recovered chaotic waveform.

The degree of matching required between master and slave for efficient synchronization is significantly high. A suitable pair of devices ("twins") must be selected in close proximity from the same wafer. This laser pair represents the (hardware) cryptographic key. Chaos cryptography is compatible, and can be superposed, to standard algorithmic cryptography.

2. Chaos-protected transmission schemes

In **Figure 1**, we show a typical implementation of the chaos transmission scheme, which is usually referred to as chaos masking (CM), since the message is added to the chaotic waveform, usually by an external amplitude modulator. Other schemes are possible [4, 5], which are broadly referred to as "chaotic cryptography" in the literature, even though in most cases, such as in **Figure 1**, the term "chaotic steganography" would better describe these methods. For example, in chaos shift keying (CSK), the message directly modulates the pump current of the transmitter laser, and in additive chaos masking (ACM), the message is applied by using a third laser modulated in amplitude by the analog or digital message, whose output is then combined with the chaotic waveform.

A large experimental and numerical work has been performed on such topic by different authors. Numerical analysis is usually based on the Lang-Kobayashi (L-K) model [8], which is generally accepted and has proven to correctly describe reflection-induced and injection phenomena for different applications, including feedback interferometry [9, 10].

http://dx.doi.org/10.5772/intechopen.70896

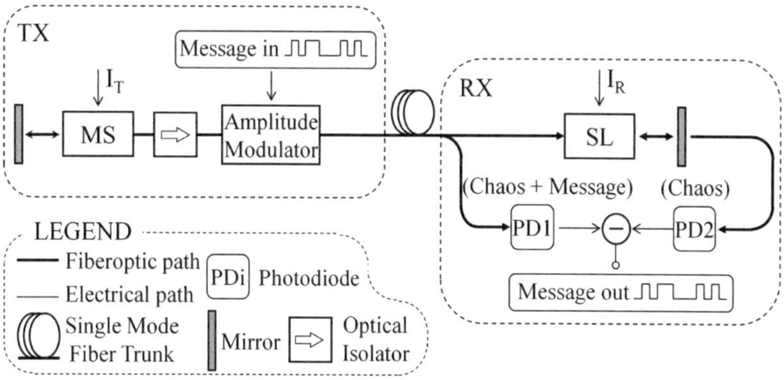

Figure 1. Two-laser scheme of chaos secured transmission (from Annovazzi-Lodi et al. [27]).

Other methods are suitable for chaos generation and synchronization, for example, a two-laser injection system [11, 12]. However, delayed optical feedback is used in virtually all schemes of chaos generation, while direct injection of the master into the slave is preferred for synchronization, since they are by far much easier to implement than other solutions proposed in the literature.

Improved schemes have been also proposed, which use specific methods to better reject eavesdropper attacks [13] or to improve SNR [14], also combining complete and generalized synchronization [15].

Based on this method, data transmission on a metropolitan network [7] has been performed. Several basic functional blocks have been already studied and experimentally demonstrated, such as chaotic signal repeaters [16], subsystems for wavelength multiplexing [17] and for wavelength conversion [18]. Moreover, integrated optics modules for chaotic transmitters and receivers [19, 20] have been designed. A system, specifically designed for transmission on free-space optics links (FSOL), has been presented [21]. Finally, methods to improve masking efficiency [22, 23] and the statistical properties of chaos residual after synchronization, as well as its impact on SNR, have been investigated [24].

Alternatives to the standard approach, still based on delayed optical feedback, have been also studied, and a remarkably different one, using three lasers [25, 26], is shown in **Figure 2**. Here, a common chaotic master laser (driver, DRV) injects two slave lasers (SL1, SL2), one at the transmitter (Tx) and the other at the receiver (Rx). If the two slaves are "twins," and both synchronized to the driver, they produce the same chaos and the message can be hidden at the transmitter and extracted at the receiver much as in the two-laser scheme.

The most important difference between the three-laser and the two-laser secure transmission schemes is that in the three-laser scheme, both SLs are symmetrically injected by the third laser and by their external mirrors, whereas in the two-laser scheme, the master is injected by its own external mirror only, and the slave by its mirror and by the master. Thus, in this second case, the twin devices work in different injection conditions.

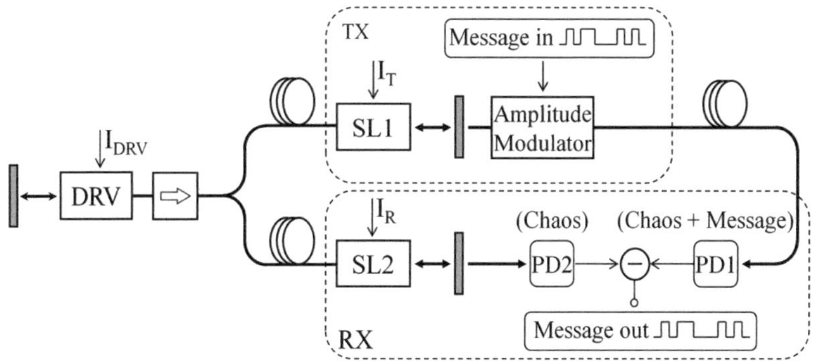

Figure 2. Three-laser scheme of chaos secured transmission (from Annovazzi-Lodi et al. [27]).

3. Comparison of two- and three-laser schemes

Since both the two- and the three-laser schemes have been proposed for secure transmission, it is important to compare their performances [27]. To this end, the bit error rate (BER) and a Q-factor of the optical link have been computed, in back-to-back conditions, as a function of parameter mismatch between Rx and Tx lasers, with the aim of evaluating the quality of the message retrieved by an eavesdropper, after the performance for the authorized sender and recipient has been optimized. This analysis has been carried out by numerical simulations, since selecting many laser pairs, with different combinations of parameters, would result in a very hard experimental effort.

The two-laser scheme (**Figure 1**) and the three-laser scheme (**Figure 2**) have been modeled as detailed in Ref. [27], and the L-K equations are shown below:

$$\frac{dE(t)}{dt} = \frac{1}{2}(1 + i\alpha)\left[G(t) - \frac{1}{\tau_p}\right]E(t) + \frac{K}{\tau_{in}}E(t - \tau)\exp(-i\omega\tau) + \frac{K'}{\tau_{in}}E'^{(t-T)}\,exp(-i\omega T) \quad (1)$$

$$\frac{dN(t)}{dt} = \frac{\eta}{eV}I - \frac{N(t)}{\tau_s} - G(t)\,|\,E(t)\,|^2 \quad (2)$$

$$G(t) = \frac{\xi[N(t) - N_o]}{1 - \varepsilon\Gamma\,|\,E(t)\,|^2} \quad (3)$$

In Eqs. (1)–(3), $E(t)$ is the slowly varying, complex electric field of the laser, $N(t)$ the carrier density, $G(t)$ the linear gain, I the pump current, e the electron charge, K is the feedback parameter from MS and SL external mirrors. Other parameters are listed in **Table 1**.

The first term on the right hand side of Eq. (1) together with Eqs. (2) and (3) describes the solitary laser. By adding the second term of Eq. (1), we describe a laser with reflection from an external mirror, that is, all lasers in **Figures 2** and **3**. By also adding the third term in Eq. (1), we describe a laser subject to both reflection and injection from another source, such as the SL

Parameters	Driver	Twin Rx/Tx	Unit
Linewidth enhancement factor	$\alpha = 2.8$	$\alpha = 3$	
Photon lifetime	$\tau_p = 1.9$	$\tau_p = 1.9$	ps
Carrier lifetime	$\tau_s = 1.9$	$\tau_s = 2$	ns
Gain coefficient	$\xi = 7.7\ 10^{-13}$	$\xi = 8\ 10^{-13}$	$m^3\ s^{-1}$
Carrier density at transparency	$N_o = 1.16\ 10^{-24}$	$N_o = 1.10\ 10^{-24}$	m^{-3}
Threshold current	$I_{th} = 12.4$	$I_{th} = 11$	mA
Laser cavity roundtrip time	$\tau_{in} = 8$	$\tau_{in} = 8$	ps
Solitary laser pulsation	$\omega = 1.2177\ 10^{15}$	$\omega = 1.2177\ 10^{15}$	s^{-1}
External cavity roundtrip time	$\tau = 0.3$	$\tau = 0.3$	ns
Active region efficiency	$\eta = 1$	$\eta = 1$	
Active region volume	$V = 8.0\ 10^{-17}$	$V = 8.0\ 10^{-17}$	m^3
Nonlinear gain coefficient	$\varepsilon = 2.5\ 10^{-23}$	$\varepsilon = 2.5\ 10^{-23}$	m^3
Confinement factor	$\Gamma = 0.36$	$\Gamma = 0.36$	
Active medium refractive index	$n = 3$	$n = 3$	
Stimulated emission cross-section	$\zeta = 1.0\ 10^{-20}$	$\zeta = 1.0\ 10^{-20}$	m^2

Table 1. Parameters used for numerical simulations.

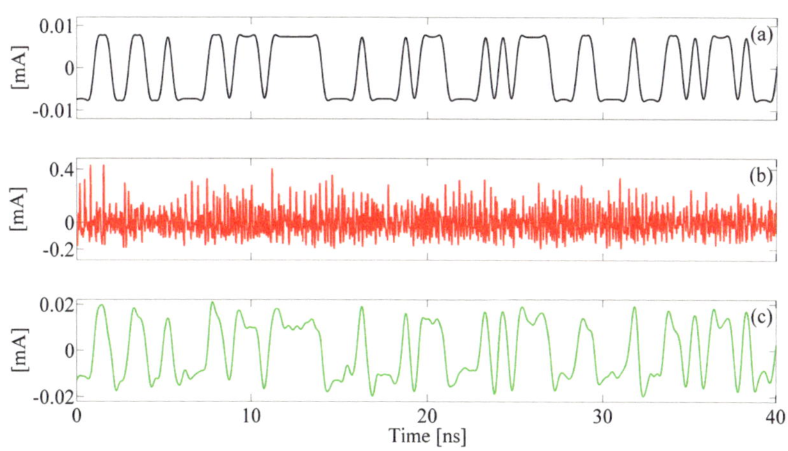

Figure 3. Message in clear (a), message hidden in chaos (b) and recovered message (c) (from Annovazzi-Lodi et al. [28]).

in **Figure 1** and the two SLs in **Figure 2**. The injecting source is described by E′(t), whereas T and K′ are the propagation delay time and the injection parameter between MS and SL, respectively.

In the previous equations, the electric fields are normalized in [$m^{-3/2}$] as usual, and the true value of each electric field (in [V/m]) is given by:

$$E_{true}(t) = \left(\xi\hbar\omega\frac{Z_0}{n\varsigma}\right)^{\frac{1}{2}} \tag{4}$$

where $Z_0 = 1/(\varepsilon_0\, c)$ is the vacuum impedance, ε_o is the vacuum permittivity, ħ is the Planck's constant, and c is the speed of light.

In our simulations, we used the typical parameter values [27] shown in **Table 1**. For simplicity, we have taken no propagation delay, T = 0. Langevin noise and photodetector noise (shot noise and Johnson noise of a 50 Ω load resistance) have been taken into account.

We started by assuming perfectly matched pairs for both schemes (i.e., twin MS and SL in the two-laser scheme and twin SL1, SL2 in the three-laser scheme). After selecting a suitable working point, the same for the lasers of both schemes, the message amplitude has been determined in order to get a BER = 10^{-9} for a non-return to zero (NRZ) 2 Gb/s digital signal. This data rate has been selected for the best message protection since the chaos had a broad amplitude maximum at 2 GHz for our devices.

Then, the laser parameters of the L-K model, that is, linewidth enhancement factor α, photon lifetime τ_p, carrier lifetime τ_s, gain coefficient ξ and carrier density at transparency N_0, have been varied by 1% steps, and BER and Q were computed again for all cases. In order to more closely simulate a real experiment for each parameter set, synchronization has been optimized by acting on the pump current of the Rx and on its injection from the MS or DRV laser. This is what the authorized recipient can do to optimize the message quality. This is also what an eavesdropper can do to try to force the cryptosystem.

For example, in **Figure 3**, a simulation of a digital message transmission is shown, assuming a small mismatch (1%) between the parameters of the twin lasers.

In **Figure 3**, the first trace (a) is without both MS and SL external reflectors and represents a measure of the channel transmission quality, which takes into account noise and bandwidth limitations, for reference; the second trace (b) shows message + chaos, whereas trace (c) visualizes the message extracted from chaos after synchronization. Some disturbances, mainly due to residual chaos, are visible on the recovered digital message; however, the message quality can be improved by suitable electronic processing, including filters and an amplitude discriminator, possibly after integration over the bit time.

From numerical simulations, it has been found that the best pair for the three-laser scheme is indeed the twin pair, as usually assumed in the literature, and that the BER rapidly drops with parameter mismatch.

This can be appreciated from **Figure 4**, where we plot the BER and Q values obtained for different parameter mismatch.

In this figure, points are shown, each representing one of all different combinations of parameters. Some points represent laser pairs where all parameters have been changed as shown on the abscissa; other points, pairs where only some parameters have been changed, while other parameters keep their nominal values. The different curves connect BER (and Q) values obtained for the same parameter combinations, with different mismatch amounts. It can be

http://dx.doi.org/10.5772/intechopen.70896

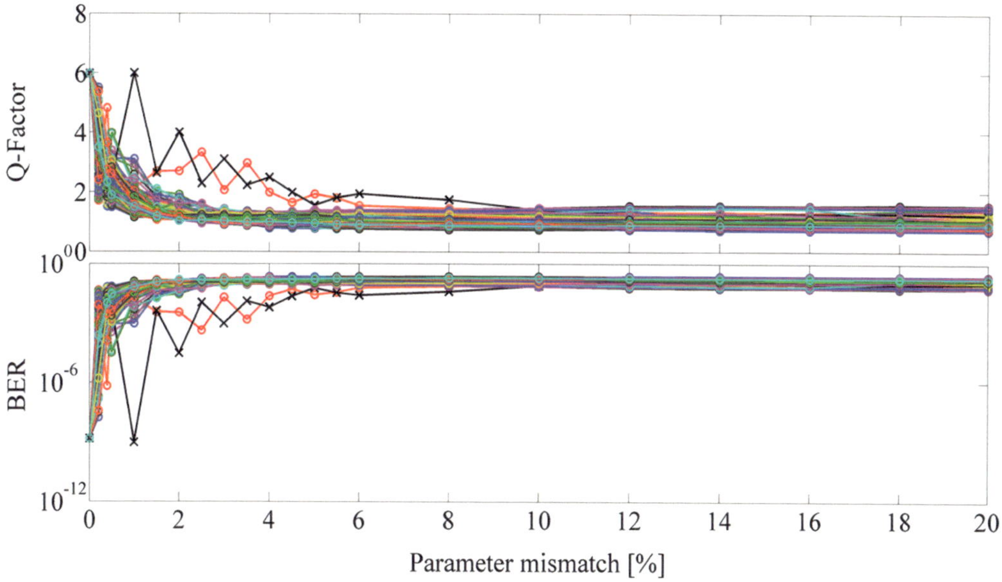

Figure 4. BER and Q as a function of laser parameter mismatch for the three-laser scheme (from Annovazzi-Lodi et al. [28]).

concluded that a mismatch of about 3–4% is enough to strongly reduce the BER, which demonstrates the high level of privacy of the three-laser scheme.

In practice, since it is virtually impossible to find a perfectly matched pair, even for the authorized users, the signal must be somewhat increased to still get low BER even in the presence of a small amount (≈1%) of mismatch. Alternatively, a somewhat higher transmission BER may be accepted by the authorized sender and recipient, who can then improve the BER by a forward error correction (FEC) algorithm. Since such algorithms usually have a threshold in terms of BER, which is difficult to match by the eavesdropper, this results in better transmission privacy.

Different results have been found for the two-laser scheme. In this case, the optimal performance was not obtained using the twin-pair, but, rather, with a pair where all parameters are matched but one, that is, the photon lifetime (curve with the arrow in **Figure 5**), that must be reduced in the SL with respect to the MS. We believe that the reason for this finding is the asymmetry of the two-laser scheme, where the double injection of the slave (by its mirror and by the master), must be compensated by larger cavity losses (i.e., shorter photon lifetime) with respect to the master (being injected by its mirror only).

With our simulated lasers, a reduction of 7% (or 12%) offered the best performances. Thus, we selected this laser pair (with 7% mismatch on photon lifetime) as the new reference and scaled the message amplitude to have BER = 10^{-9} for this optimal pair. The results shown in **Figure 5** for the BER as a function of parameter mismatch were finally obtained.

Figures 4 and **5** allow us to compare the two schemes in terms of privacy and of ease of implementation.

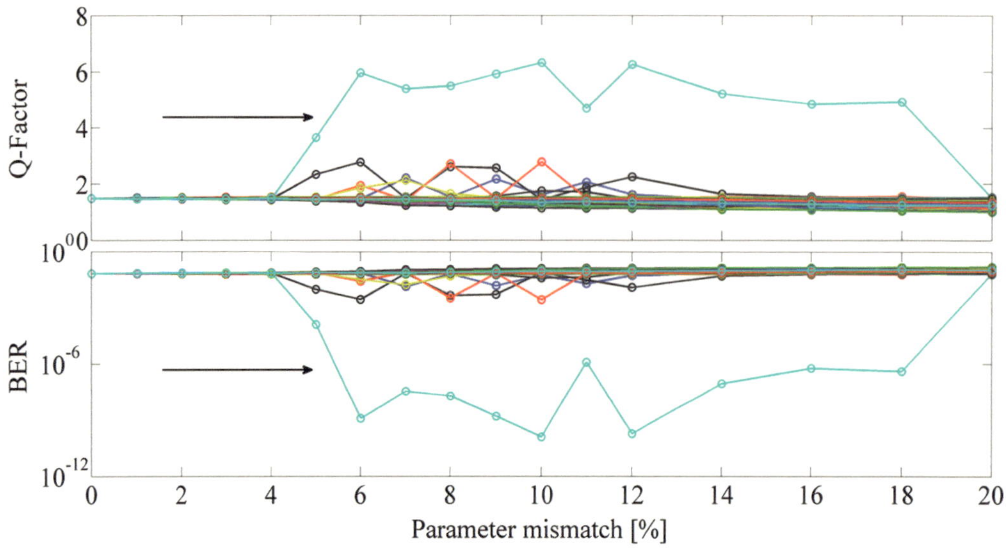

Figure 5. BER and Q as a function of parameter mismatch for the two-laser scheme (from Annovazzi-Lodi et al. [28]).

Since for the two-laser scheme, the authorized sender and recipient have to select a laser with a proper mismatch, they have a more difficult task than with the three-laser scheme, for which the twin pair can be usually found as close-proximity devices on the same wafer. On the other hand, such parameter does not need to be accurately met, which partially simplifies the job.

Once the optimal pair has been selected, the eavesdropper is in a slightly better situation than with the three-laser scheme: s/he has to find a laser similar to another one, without knowledge of its parameters; however, one of these parameters does not need to be accurately matched.

If the authorized sender and recipient prefer to use a twin pair to avoid the problem of selecting the optimal pair, the eavesdropper has the opportunity to extract the message with the same BER as the authorized users, or even better, in principle, if he gets the proper pair. This is not an easy job, however, since an accurate matching of all parameters, but one, is required, without the knowledge of their values. In practice, as it is usually assumed that the eavesdropper cannot match the laser parameters by better than 5%, it is virtually impossible for him/her to extract the message in any case.

4. Chaos-protected network

A common feature of all methods for chaos-protected message transmission is that only point-to-point interconnections between couples of users can be implemented, since a twin pair of lasers is required, one device being used by the transmitter (Tx) and the other by the receiver (Rx). Thus, to exchange data with other subscribers, every user must hold one pair of twin lasers for each possible correspondent. This is clearly unpractical, especially if the number of users is large.

A more convenient approach [28], similar to public key cryptography, has been proposed recently. By this method, we can build a network of subscribers, where all users can freely exchange data. This configuration is shown in **Figure 6**. The network consists of number of user nodes (US1, US2,…) and also includes a special provider node (PV), whose role is similar to the certifying authority of public-key cryptography.

For each user node US, the network requires a pair of twin lasers. A device of such pair is used by PV, whereas the other by US. The lasers are driven to chaos by a suitable method, such as delayed optical feedback, as in **Figures 1** and **2**.

In **Figure 6**, US1 and US2 are two subscribers at specific network nodes. Each user and the provider share a laser of a twin pair, L1 for US1 and L2 for US2.

If a user (e.g., US1) would like to send a message to another user (US2), s/he starts by sending a message in clear to PV to ask him to create a chaos-protected link.

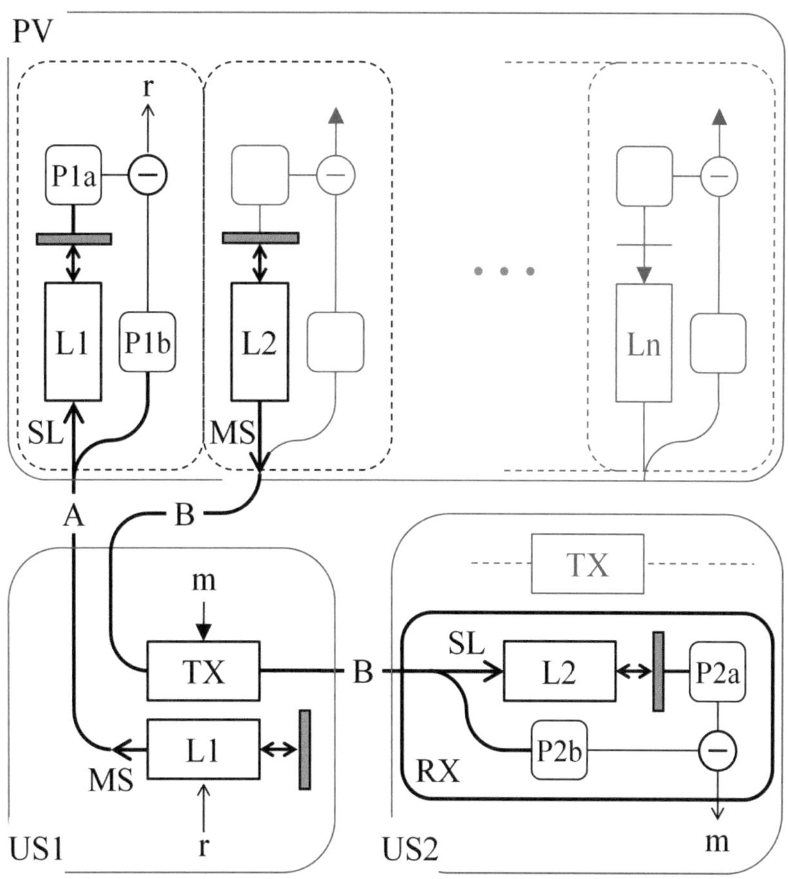

Figure 6. Chaos-protected network. Tx and Rx are the transmitter and receiver blocks and Pij are photodetectors. PV holds one laser for each user, but only L1 and L2 are shown (from Annovazzi-Lodi et al. [28]).

A secure connection from US1 to PV (A in **Figure 6**) is thus established by employing the twin pair held by PV and US1 (L1 in **Figure 6**). This is done by using the standard two-laser scheme, as exemplified in **Figure 6**, or by the three-laser or another suitable scheme.

Then, using the secure link A, US1 sends a message r to PV, asking to create a chaos-secured connection between himself and US2.

After receiving the request of US1, PV sends the chaotic waveform produced by laser L2 to user US1. US1 will use this chaotic carrier to transmit a message m to US2. S/he may use, for example, CM modulation, as in **Figure 6** path B, or another chaos-based transmission method. Exchanged data are protected, since only US2 can extract this message from chaos, because s/he is the only one to hold the required twin laser L2. Other subscribers, or an eavesdropper, cannot retrieve the message.

The same procedure applies, for example, when US2 wants to send a message to US1. US2 first contacts PV in clear; then, using her/his laser L2, s/he asks the provider to route the suitable chaotic waveform (laser L1) to her/him. PV decodes the message by his laser L2 and sends the required chaotic waveform to US2. Using this chaotic waveform, US2 can now send the message, which US1 can decode using her/his laser L1. In the same way, chaos-secured connections can be established between all pairs of users.

Lasers at the provider node are employed either to create a secure connection with a user or to produce a chaotic waveform to be routed to a user to enable her/him to create a secure connection with another user. Lasers at US nodes are used to create a secure connection with the provider or to decode a message of another user. In the proposed network architecture, the traffic between users does not pass by PV node. This is important to improve security and avoid congestion.

The transmission link between two users is usually implemented by simply modulating the chaotic waveform received by the provider, and in such case, only an amplitude modulator is required in block Tx of **Figure 6**. However, if the distance between users, and/or users and PV, is large, amplification of the chaotic waveform is required to adequately hide the message. In such case, an optical amplifier will also be included in block Tx.

Transmission of data between two users following the scheme of **Figure 6** is similar to a standard point-to-point connection. Thus, all the results obtained by the L-K model and by experimental investigations apply here, including our previous comparison of the two basic schemes.

5. Conclusions

In conclusion, after a brief introduction on chaotic cryptography, we have presented recent achievements, by comparing the two most widely used schemes for chaos-secured data transmission, showing that the three-laser scheme has some specific advantage over the two-laser scheme in terms of privacy.

Moreover, we have shown that private transmission based on optical chaos is suitable for multiuser networking, using a proper architecture. This approach is based on the usual, widely investigated and well-developed chaotic transmission schemes, but makes use of a provider to allow for data exchange between several users and requires only one twin laser pair for each subscriber.

Acknowledgements

The authors like to thank Sabina Merlo for fruitful discussions and Andrea Fanzio for technical assistance.

Author details

Valerio Annovazzi-Lodi*, Giuseppe Aromataris and Mauro Benedetti

*Address all correspondence to: valerio.annovazzi@unipv.it

Department of Electrical, Computer and Biomedical Engineering, University of Pavia, Pavia, Italy

References

[1] Schuster HG. Deterministic Chaos. Weinheim: VCH; 1989. 312 p. ISBN 10:35272668626

[2] Ohtsubo K. Semiconductor Lasers: Stability, Instability and Chaos. New York: Springer; 2009. 535 p. DOI: 10.1007/987-3-642-30147-6

[3] Arecchi FT, Puccioni GL, Tredicce JR. Deterministic chaos in laser with injected signal. Optics Communications. 1984;**51**(4):308-314. DOI: 10.1016/0030-4018(84)90016-6

[4] Donati S, Mirasso C. Feature section on optical chaos and applications to cryptography. IEEE Journal of Quantum Electronics. 2002;**38**(9):1137-1196. DOI: 10.1109/JQE.2002801951

[5] Larger L, Goedgebuer JP. Special number on "Criptography using optical chaos". Comptes Rendus de l'Academie des Sciences-Dossier de Physique. 2004;**6**(5):609-681 ISSN: 16310705

[6] Annovazzi-Lodi V, Benedetti M, Merlo S, Norgia M. Fiberoptics setup for chaotic cryptographic communications. Comptes Rendus de l'Academie des Sciences-Dossier de Physique. 2004;**6**(5):623-631. DOI: 10.1016/j.crhy.2004.03.005

[7] Argyris A et al. Chaos-based communications at high bit rates using commercial fiber-optic links. Nature. 2005;**438**:343-346. DOI: 10.1038/nature04275

[8] Lang R, Kobayashi K. External optical feedback effects on semiconductor injection laser properties. IEEE Journal of Quantum Electronics. 1980;**16**(3):347-355. DOI: 10.1109/JQE.1980.1070479

[9] Donati S, Giuliani G, Merlo S. Laser diode interferometer for measurements of displacements without ambiguity. IEEE Journal of Quantum Electronics. 1995;**31**(1):113-119. DOI: 10.1109/3.341714

[10] Annovazzi-Lodi V et al. Optical detection of the Coriolis force on a silicon micromachined gyroscope. Journal of Microelectromechanical Systems. 2003;**12**(5):540-549. DOI: 10.1109/JMEMS.2003.817893

[11] Annovazzi-Lodi V, Donati S. Injection modulation in coupled laser oscillators. IEEE Journal of Quantum Electronics. 1980;**16**(8):859-864. DOI: 10.1109/JQE.1980.1070582

[12] Annovazzi-Lodi V, Donati S, Scirè A. Synchronization of chaotic injected-laser systems and its application to optical cryptography. IEEE Journal of Quantum Electronics. 1966;**32**(6):953-959. DOI: 10.1109/3.502371

[13] Pisarchik AN, Jimenez-Rodriguez M, Jaimes-Reategui R. How to resist synchronization attacks. Discontinuity, Nonlinearity, Complexity. 2015;**4**(1):1-9. DOI: 10.5890/DNC.2015.03.001

[14] Pisarchik AN, Jaimes-Reátegui R, Sevilla-Escoboza JR, Ruiz-Oliveras FR, García-López JH. Two-channel optoelectronic chaotic communication system. Journal of Franklin Institute. 2012;**349**(10):3194-3202. DOI: 10.1016/j.jfranklin.2012.10.005

[15] Pisarchik AN, Ruiz-Oliveras FR. Optical chaotic communication using generalized and complete synchronization. IEEE Journal of Quantum Electronics. 2010;**46**(3):279-284. DOI: 10.1109/JQE.2009.2032429

[16] Lee W, Shore KA. Demonstration of a chaotic optical message relay using DFB laser diode. IEEE Photonics Technology Letters. 2006;**18**(1):169-171. DOI: 10.1109/LPT.2005.860039

[17] Matsuura T, Uchida A, Yoshimori S. Chaotic wavelength division multiplexing for optical communication. Optics Letters. 2004;**29**:2731-2733. DOI: 10.1364/OL.29.002731

[18] Annovazzi-Lodi V, Aromataris G, Benedetti M, Cristiani I, Merlo S, Minzioni P. All-optical wavelength conversion of a chaos masked signal. IEEE Photonics Technology Letters. 2007;**19**(22):1783-1785. DOI: 10.1109/LPT.2007.906847

[19] Syvridis D, Argiris A, Bogris A, Hamacher M, Giles I. Integrated devices for optical chaos generation and communications applications. IEEE Journal of Quantum Electronics. 2009;**45**(11):1421-1428. DOI: 10.1109/JQE.2009.2027336

[20] Tronciu VZ, Mirasso C, Colet P, Hamacher M, Benedetti M, Vercesi V, Annovazzi-Lodi V. Chaos generation and synchronization using an integrated source with an air gap. IEEE Journal of Quantum Electronics. 2010;**46**(12):1840-1846. DOI: 10.1109/JQE.2010.2049642

[21] Annovazzi-Lodi V, Aromataris G, Benedetti M, Merlo S. Secure chaotic transmission on a free-space optics data link. IEEE Journal of Quantum Electronics. 2008;**44**(11):1089-1095. DOI: 10.1109/JQE.2008.2001929

[22] Ursini L, Santagiustina M, Annovazzi-Lodi V. Enhancing chaotic communication performances by Manchester coding. IEEE Photonics Technology Letters. 2008;**20**(6):401-403. DOI: 10.1109/LPT.2008.916918

[23] Aromataris G, Annovazzi-Lodi V. Enhancing privacy of chaotic communications by double masking. IEEE Journal of Quantum Electronics. 2013;**49**(11):955-959. DOI: 10.1109/JQE.2013.2283584

[24] Aromataris G, Annovazzi-Lodi V. Error analysis of a digital message impaired by optical chaos. IEEE Photonics Technology Letters. 2012;**24**(11):903-905. DOI: 10.1109/LPT.2012.2190395

[25] Ohtsubo J. Chaos synchronization and chaotic signal masking in semiconductor lasers with optical feedback. IEEE Journal of Quantum Electronics. 2002;**38**(9):1141-1154. DOI: 10.1109/JQE.2002.801883

[26] Annovazzi-Lodi V, Aromataris G, Benedetti M, Merlo S. Private message transmission by common driving of two chaotic lasers. IEEE Journal of Quantum Electronics. 2010;**46**(2):258-264. DOI: 10.1109/JQE.2009.2030895

[27] Annovazzi-Lodi V, Aromataris G. Privacy in two-laser and three-laser chaos communications. IEEE Journal of Quantum Electronics, DOI. Jul 2015;**51**(7):7109819. DOI: 10.1109/JQE.2015.2434274

[28] Annovazzi-Lodi V, Aromataris G, Benedetti M. Multi-user private transmission with chaotic lasers. IEEE Journal of Quantum Electronics. 2012;**48**(8):1095-1101. DOI: 10.1109/JQE.2012.2202373